Between Elite and Mass Education

MAX PLANCK INSTITUTE FOR

HUMAN DEVELOPMENT AND EDUCATION

Berlin, Federal Republic of Germany

Between Elite and Mass Education
EDUCATION IN THE FEDERAL REPUBLIC OF GERMANY

With a Foreword by JAMES S. COLEMAN
Translated by RAYMOND MEYER
and ADRIANE HEINRICHS-GOODWIN

State University of New York Press

ALBANY

Published by State University of New York Press, Albany

All rights reserved

Printed in the United States of America

No part of this book may be used or reproduced in any manner whatsoever without written permission except in the case of brief quotations embodied in critical articles and reviews.

For information, address State University of New York Press, State University Plaza, Albany, N.Y., 12246

Originally published under the title DAS BILDUNGSWESEN IN DER BUNDES-REPUBLIK DEUTSCHLAND. Copyright © 1979 by Rowohlt Taschenbuch Verlag GmbH, Reinbek bei Hamburg

Library of Congress Cataloging in Publication Data

Bildungswesen in der Bundesrepublik Deutschland.
  English.
  Between elite and mass education.

  Translation of: Das Bildungswesen in der Bundesrepublik
Deutschland.
  1. Education and state—Germany (West) 2. Education
and state—United States. 3. Comparative education.
4. Education—United States. 5. Education—Germany
(West) I. Max-Planck-Institut fur Bildungsforschung.
II. Title.
LC93.G4B55313   1983   370'.943   83-18314

ISBN 0-87395-709-1
ISBN 0-87395-708-3 (pbk.)

10 9 8 7 6 5 4 3 2 1

Contents

CONTENTS

vi

Figures

FIGURES

Tables

TABLES

Acknowledgements

The history of this book goes back to the late nineteen-seventies, when a group of researchers at the Max Planck Institute for Human Development and Education prepared a set of popular lectures on education in Germany to be used by the Goethe Institutes for their informational activities in various countries. Out of these lectures grew a pocket-sized book for the German public summarizing and surveying the often confusing and, at the time, politically very controversial state of education in the Federal Republic.[1] The members of the working group collectively sharing the responsibility for that book were Jürgen Baumert, Reinhard Franzke, Diether Hopf, Beate Krais, Lothar Krappmann, Achim Leschinsky, Jens Naumann, Knut Nevermann, Gottfried Pfeffer, Jürgen Raschert, Ingo Richter, Peter Siewert, and Luitgard Trommer. Since that book was quite successful in Germany, we thought that an updated English-language edition might meet with some interest in the international community, especially in the United States. The efforts to revise, update and rewrite the original text for the non-German reader resulted, in fact, in a new book. One of the features it shares with its predecessor, however, is the renewed close cooperation of the project team in writing it.

We hope that our new work bears witness not only to the shortcomings but also to the strengths of such a cooperative venture. In

[1]. Arbeitsgruppe am Max-Planck-Institut für Bildungsforschung. Das Bildungswesen in der Bundesrepublik Deutschland: Ein Überblick für Eltern, Lehrer, Schüler. Reinbek bei Hamburg: Rowohlt, 1979, 280 pp.

spite of the many discussions and exchanges, the editing and the rewriting, the main responsibilities for the different chapters of this new edition were divided among the following members of the group: Jürgen Baumert (Chapters 9 and 10), with Jürgen Raschert (Chapter 4); Reinhard Franzke with Peter Siewert (Chapter 11); Dietrich Goldschmidt (Chapter 1); Diether Hopf (Chapter 5), with Lothar Krappmann (Chapter 6); Beate Krais (Chapter 13); Achim Leschinsky (Chapters 7 and 8); Jens Naumann (Chapter 12), with Gottfried Pfeffer (Chapter 2); Knut Nevermann with Ingo Richter (Chapter 3). Helmut Köhler and Luitgard Trommer were responsible for the statistical data and their presentation. General editorial functions were performed by Jürgen Baumert, Dietrich Goldschmidt, Achim Leschinsky, and Jens Naumann. Raymond Meyer was technical editor.

We thank Dagmar Freiberger and Roswitha Schütt for their careful preparation and critical scrutiny of the manuscript. We very much appreciate the collaboration of Metadesign, Berlin, which produced the more complicated—and nicer looking—figures. Our thanks go to the Rowohlt Verlag, Hamburg, for their generous cooperation in getting this project started.

All members of the team are associated with the Max Planck Institute, most of them belonging to its regular staff. We would like to acknowledge the general intellectual and institutional support of the Institute, which made this project possible.

Finally, we want to express our gratitude to Inter Nationes, Bonn, and Atlantik Brücke, Hamburg, without whose financial support for the translation and the editing we could not have completed this book.

The Project Team

Berlin, May 1982

Translators' Comments

A translation into American English of a work about the educational system of the Federal Republic of Germany runs the risk of making the latter seem more like that of the United States than in fact it is. The use of American terminology can all too easily filter out the particularities of this educational system and conceal the history of its evolution. Thus, one of the general principles that guided us in translating this work was to avoid terms that improperly suggest similarities between the two systems. The other was that the translation should be as clear and understandable as possible.

In keeping with the first principle, we chose, for example, to render 'Schulrat' into English as "school inspector" rather than "school superintendent." The same holds true for some features of West German society. 'Beamter' was translated as "state official," or sometimes simply as "official," and not as "civil servant," often used to render the German term. The description of the status of the 'Beamter' given in Chapter 3 will make clear why. Although in common American usage, the terms "pupils" and "students" are often used interchangeably to refer to young people in high schools and in the more advanced grades of primary schools, we have chosen to use these terms with rigorously distinct meanings to translate the rigorously distinct German terms 'Schüler' and 'Studenten'. As they are used in this translation, "pupils" refers only to young people attending primary or secondary school and vocational schools, "students" only to the young adults attending institutions of higher education. Likewise, according to German usage, the institutions of "tertiary," i.e. post-secondary, education are not referred to as "schools" in this book.

In the case of the three types of secondary school, we chose to use the German names: Hauptschule, Realschule, and Gymnasium, and the German plural forms of these names. This we did, first, because there are only three types of secondary school; second, because there has been inconsistency in the use of English terms to refer to these school types; and last, because the English designations sometimes used would not have been more informative than the German names. In the case of the vocational schools, however, we thought that the English designations we have used do tell something about these schools and their relations to one another, and that, in any case, it was too much to expect of readers that they not confuse seven German names, some of which are very similar.

As a result of its long and complex history, the term 'Bildung' connotes so much that it is impossible to find a simple but adequate English equivalent for it. The alternative, namely, explaining the history of the word 'Bildung' and its many connotations, and then using the German word, would have required a long excursus that would have been out of place in this book. Thus, when the word 'Bildung' appeared in the text, it was translated as "education."

Since the authors frequently speak of *the* state, and often use "state" in this sense as part of an adjectival phrase, we have referred to the constituent political units of the Federal Republic using their German names, 'Land' in the singular, and 'Länder' in the plural.

Finally, when the authors speak of the individual pupil, student, or teacher we have used the masculine pronoun for the sake of expository and stylistic convenience.

Raymond Meyer
Adriane Heinrichs-Goodwin

Foreword

In 1967, the results of the first of a series of international educational achievement studies was published, covering achievement in mathematics of 13- and 18-year-olds (Husén, 1967). Americans who examined the results of this research were astonished to learn that 13-year-olds in the United States averaged lower than those in all of the other countries studied. They were interested also to learn that the mathematics performance of pupils in the Federal Republic of Germany was near the top among the 12 sample countries studied.

As the authors of the International Educational Achievement studies pointed out, the American educational system was at the extreme of what could be called "mass education," while that of the Federal Republic was more nearly "class education," i.e., more structurally differentiated and keeping a much smaller proportion of pupils in school until age 18. In fact, as the authors showed, if certain assumptions about the mathematics skills of 18-year-olds who had left school were valid, much of the difference in performance had been overcome by American students between ages 13 and 18 in their more ponderous but more extended educational system.

Clearly the educational systems in the Federal Republic and the United States operate in quite different ways in performing their educational tasks, despite the fact that the two countries are at about the same level of economic development, have very similar occupational structures, and provide very similar life chances for their children. Thus, the considerable differences, both in the structure of the educational systems and in the profiles of cognitive achievement that they produce in their pupils and students, present puzzles to anyone concerned with educational policy.

How can two countries with quite similar economic and social structures have such different educational systems? Are the differences stable, or will they converge toward a common form with common content? If, as social research indicates, variations in schools are of so much less importance for achievement than variations in family background, then what accounts for the sharp differences in levels of achievement and in age profiles of achievement in the Federal Republic and the United States? If education is as important for personal and economic development as the human capital economists assert, then how can two countries with such different educational systems be so similar in level of economic development—while other countries with educational systems like those of either America or Germany are at considerable lower levels of economic development than these?

These questions, of extraordinary interest to those who make policy in education and to social scientists, cannot be easily answered. The basic information necessary even to begin to compare the structures of education, the curriculum, and the goals of educational policy in the Federal Republic and the United States are not easily found. Elementary and secondary education in most countries has been extremely inward-looking, seldom inquiring beyond national boundaries, and the Federal Republic and the United States have not been exceptions.

The chapters of this book are a great stride forward in facilitating comparisons between American and German education. Within the covers of a single book, they present a comprehensive view both of the current structures and policy issues in West German education, and of the changes that have occurred since the Second World War. I know of no comparable book on education in the United States, and with few exceptions, such panoramic views of a nation's educational system cannot be found. One exception is a broadly comparable book on Israeli education that will appear in both Hebrew and in German (the German edition is titled *Erziehung in Israel*, Stuttgart: Klett-Cotta, 1982). That book, it is interesting to note, was stimulated by Hellmut Becker, past director of the Max Planck Institute for Human Development and Education, Berlin, where the present book originated.

The first chapter of this book, by Dietrich Goldschmidt, draws together, from various unsuspected and sometimes obscure niches, the history of the interchanges that have taken place between American and German education. These have occurred from the early period of modern educational systems to the present, despite the general national insularity of educational systems. The history of such exchanges shown in this chapter makes even more striking the sharp differences in educational structure that continue to exist between the United States and the Federal Republic.

The remaining twelve chapters deal with the West German educational system since World War II. With the exception of the last two chapters, which treat university and adult education, respectively, and some general considerations in chapters 2 and 3, they focus on elementary and secondary education. The principal concentration is, in fact, on later elementary and secondary education—that is, on education after the Volksschule, which often ends after grade 4.

As in all Western European countries, there have been major changes in West German education in the past three decades. The experience of the Federal Republic, however, has been conditioned by special circumstances, in particular by the postwar efforts of the occupying powers to impose a different model of education—especially the American comprehensive secondary school model—than that which existed prior to the war. Despite these efforts, however, the Federal Republic has moved less toward a structure of mass education in comprehensive schools than have most Western European countries. Chapters 2, 3, and 4 show the developments which have taken place and the kind of structure that has emerged.

As in every developed country, there has been an increased consumer demand from an expanding middle class for more extended secondary education which does not foreclose post-secondary options. In the Federal Republic, this demand has not obliterated the differentiated structure. Rather, it has led to the growth and modification of the formerly elite level of that structure, the Gymnasium, and even more to growth of the intermediate level, the Realschule. This growth has been at the expense of the lower level, the Hauptschule, which developed as an extension of the early elementary grades, the Volksschule. The comprehensive school is not totally lacking. In some Länder, though, it exists only as an experimental form, and comprehensive secondary schools today comprise only a tiny fraction of the overall secondary school structure.

The character and growth or decline of these four secondary routes is described in Chapters 7–10, an entire chapter being devoted to each school type. This part of the book gives an extraordinarily rich view of the functioning of post-elementary education in the Federal Republic. In addition, these chapters show the great variation that has arisen among the 11 Länder of the Federal Republic both as a result of their official policies and of cultural differences among them.

Another component of West German education is the vocational system (which for many students follows attendance at the Hauptschule or the Realschule), a component that is far more developed than in other Western countries. Chapter 11 describes the structure and functioning of this vocational system, providing a further view of the considerable structural divergence between West German education of youth and that in the United States.

One chapter of this book, Chapter 6, focuses on problems that have occupied the center of attention in American education for some years, namely, education of ethnic minorities, educationally disadvantaged, and handicapped children. As the authors of several chapters point out, the problems of educating and integrating ethnic minorities will receive greater attention in the future in the Federal Republic as the extended stay of the "guest workers" becomes permanent residence and as their children multiply, while the birthrate of the native German population dwindles.

The panoramic and yet detailed view that this book gives of German education goes a long way toward providing the base—on the German side—upon which comparison of education in the United States and the Federal Republic can begin. Perhaps this book can be the first step in the attempts to answer the puzzling questions about the existence and effects of sharply different educational systems in two countries with very similar levels and directions of economic and social development.

James S. Coleman

Berlin
May, 1982

CHAPTER 1

Transatlantic Influences: History of Mutual Interactions between American and German Education*

1.0. Introduction

The influences of the educational systems of the Federal Republic of Germany and of the United States of America on one another are part of a two-hundred-year-old historical process. This process has consisted, on the one hand, in the gradual emancipation of the United States from Europe, accompanied up to the First World War by a continuing reception and appropriate integration into American pedagogical thought and practice of various impulses from Europe

* The chapter on the history of the relations between Germany and the United States in the sphere of education was occasioned by the revision of the text on the Federal Republic's educational system mentioned in the preface. Its purpose is to place this educational system in its historical context and in particular in the context of German-American relations. This chapter is, in the literal sense of the word, an essay—an attempt to give an overview of the complex and highly ramified reciprocal relations between the two countries with regard to education, and to do so against the background of general political history, while citing striking particular examples. Even the account given here of the actual relations cannot help but be sketchy, given the wealth of literature on the subject. Should the occasion present itself to treat this topic more thoroughly, then the American side of the relationship in particular would have to be treated more extensively.

The author wishes to give sincere thanks to all his German and American friends and colleagues, both at the Max Planck Institute for Human Development and Education and elsewhere, for their many helpful suggestions regarding the source material and also for generously sharing their knowledge.

in educational matters. These impulses came not least of all from Germany during and especially after Germany's national unification and rapid development. Both of the World Wars, however, served to break down the traditionally favorable American attitudes toward German education, German-speaking schools, the German concept of academic education, and the organization of German graduate studies. After the two World Wars German education and scholarship lost the widespread prestige they had once enjoyed. Yet in another sense German influence was re-established by the thousands of intellectuals fleeing Nazi rule, in Germany after 1933 and later in the countries it occupied. The growing positive response to their arrival created an atmosphere that, in the long run, proved advantageous even to the sons and daughters of German-speaking Jews who had earlier emigrated to the United States from Central and Eastern Europe. The imprint all these men and women left on science and scholarship in the United States has done much to earn for American higher education the high esteem it has come to enjoy internationally since the end of the Second World War.

On the other hand, in 19th century Germany, within the framework of a semifeudal political structure, there occurred a pronounced intellectual and cultural development that brought the German educational system a high degree of international respect until the outbreak of the First World War. Thereafter followed political and cultural catastrophes: the First World War, Nazi dictatorship, and the Second World War. In the western parts of the country—the present-day Federal Republic of Germany—the United States played a major role in recovery.

Today we are at the point where the one party to this ongoing exchange of ideas and experience—the United States—has risen to world power and enjoys a preeminence in cultural and intellectual affairs to match this status, whereas the other party, the Federal Republic of Germany, is in a manner of speaking still feeling its way after a period of assimilating ideas and considering educational models "Made in USA." Far from serving as an example as it did in the 19th century, German education today is still striving to strike a balance between worthy traditions and the need to adapt the system to modern requirements.

The influences of the United States and Germany on each other have been both general, and specific.

Cultural, intellectual, and scientific experiences, insights, and stimuli have been carried personally in both directions by visitors, especially to the United States by immigrants. But they are also

2

propagated through the printed word and the mass media. They are as general and comprehensive in their scope as they are diffuse, and they are so extensive that they can hardly be grasped in their entirety. Only the World Wars have interrupted this transfer, which is absolutely fundamental for the development of the individual academic disciplines.

More specific, and hence more easily grasped, are the impulses that go beyond stimulating or influencing the work of individuals and have an effect on the structuring of educational institutions. Each such impulse has its "historical moment," examples of which are the guiding influence of German models when American liberal arts colleges were expanded to universities in the second half of the 19th century, and American influences on reeducation efforts in Germany after the Second World War.

In discussing the reciprocal influences of the United States and Germany, one must keep in mind certain general developments. At the beginning of the 19th century, the German states as well as the United States were in the process of consolidating themselves into nation-states. Travel between the two countries during this time was on the whole by individuals and free from political considerations. As far as this travel concerned educational matters, an overview is relatively easy to obtain. Thanks to the progress in transportation technology (steamships began to cross the Atlantic in 1837) and the growth of international and intercontinental commerce, the connections between the two emerging nations increased in number and in strength from the middle of the century on, but especially after each nation was united, the one in 1865 with the defeat of the South, and the other in 1871 with the founding of the German Reich.[1] These points are the historical starting points of the following essay.

Towards the end of the nineteenth century, the United States and Imperial Germany encountered one another as great powers in competition for cultural prestige, economic power and political dominance—a competition which was sharpened by German imperialist strivings and American aggressiveness in the international economy. Since the Second World War, the concentration of world political power around the Soviet Union in the East and the United States in the West has drawn the latter country and the Federal Republic closely together. Inexpensive mass travel has done its share to broaden the base of this bond. Despite periodic ups and downs, the two countries' mutual knowledge and interest have been intense in education, science, and scholarship, as well as in other areas. It should be clear, then, that as we come to the present, the more our remarks must be confined to indicating general trends, rather than showing specific ways in which the United States and the Federal Republic have influenced each other. Indeed, in view of the increasing specialization that has taken place in education and science, it is all the more necessary to treat progress in these fields of human endeavor on a global scale.

1.1. Relations in higher education, science, and scholarship up to 1914

The first American to visit a German university was Benjamin Franklin, who came to Göttingen in 1766. Twenty-three years after the American colonies declared their independence, in 1799, that university was the first to confer a doctoral degree on an American. Beginning in 1815, a steady stream of American students travelled to Germany to pursue their studies, first to Göttingen, later to other universities as well. Among the first were four young men (Edward Everett, George Ticknor, George Bancroft, and Joseph Green Cogswell) who were later to become prominent scholars and diplomats and to whom we can trace the eventual establishment of the "American Colony of Göttingen".[2] Up to around 1870, Göttingen headed the list of German universities visited by young Americans. Later, Berlin exerted a stronger pull. These early visiting students came for the most part from Harvard, Yale, and other Eastern colleges.

From the outset, American visitors were, among other things, interested in the systems of education in various German states. However, German interest in and knowledge of the American education system remained very limited until close to the end of the century. In the 1830's and 1840's, the prominent educational philosophers Horace Mann (one of the first advocates of a "common school" for children from all walks of life) and Calvin P. Stowe published reports on the Prussian Volksschule which aroused considerable interest. They advocated a primary school of eight grades with pupils normally advancing one grade a year.[3]

Looking back on his years as a student at Harvard College (1854–1858), Henry Adams recalled:

> The literary world then agreed that truth survived in Germany alone, and Carlyle, Matthew Arnold, Renan, Emerson, with scores of popular followers, taught the German faith . . . . The middle class had the power, and held its coal and iron well in hand, but the satirists and

idealists seized the press, and as they were agreed that the Second Empire was a disgrace to France and a danger to England, they turned to Germany because at that moment Germany was neither economical nor military, and a hundred years behind western Europe in the simplicity of its standard. German thought, method, honesty, and even taste, became the standards of scholarship. Goethe was raised to the rank of Shakespeare—Kant ranked as a law-giver above Plato. All serious scholars were obliged to become German, for German thought was revolutionizing criticism.[4]

Laurence R. Veysey, in his history of the American university, emphasizes "the lure of the German university" at the middle of the 19th century (Veysey, 1965, pp. 125 ff.). The German university exercised its influence in various ways through its orientation toward idealist philosophy and its emphasis on the development of theory. Its greatest strength was seen in its use of the seminar in teaching and in the great importance it attached to research, i.e., to the rigorous and exact investigation of any given object of study. The work of men such as the historian Leopold von Ranke, the physicist Hermann von Helmholtz, and the psychologist Wilhelm Wundt set standards for modern research. It was probably at this time that the foundation was laid for modern empirical research, not only in the natural sciences but also in the humanities and social sciences. Such empirical research was subsequently developed further in the United States from where German psychological and social research picked up the thread after 1945.

On the basis of what he had learned while visiting German universities, Charles W. Eliot, who became president of Harvard College in 1869, developed this school into Harvard University. In 1874 there appeared the first reliable study of the German universities; written by J. M. Hart, it was well received.[5] Johns Hopkins University in Baltimore was founded in 1876; following the German model, the chief focus of its activities was research. Daniel C. Gilman, who had visited European universities and published his findings, decisively influenced the orientation of this university. Johns Hopkins University served as the model for other institutions of higher learning in the United States, among them Clark University in Worcester, Massachusetts (founded 1889) and the University of Chicago (founded 1890). By combining liberal arts colleges (the locus of education for a growing portion of secondary-school graduates) with graduate schools (the locus of research and of training of researchers), American universities acquired a unique character.

Many professors in the American universities, including the many of German origin, had studied in Germany, and many had obtained the doctoral degree there.[6] At the same time, the number of American students visiting Germany markedly increased. The total number of students formally enrolled in the period from 1815 to 1870 has been estimated at around 640.[7] Enrollments continued to grow, until by 1895–1896 about 450 Americans were registered in German universities and other institutions of higher education.[8] Studying and passing an examination at a German university enhanced the visitor's prestige in his home country. Thereafter, the flow of American students to Germany diminished somewhat up to the First World War. In the winter semester of 1911–1912, there were 255 American students, including 32 women, at German universities.[9] A stay in Germany had become more costly for Americans, while opportunities for graduate study in the United States had improved. At the same time, owing to the rising standards of science and scholarship in the United States, Americans were noting ever more critically that German universities also had their drawbacks. Not all of them were centers of excellence; not all German professors were exemplary, meticulous researchers.

Taking the available statistics and estimates together, one can assume that from 1815 to 1916, a total of 6,000 to 9,000 Americans studied at German universities. On the number of German students in the United States during this time there is only one item of statistical information. In the academic year 1911–1912, 143 Germans were studying at American universities.[10]

Toward the end of the nineteenth century, for the first time in Germany a specific interest in American universities developed (von Brocke, 1981).[11] Friedrich Althoff, the ministerial official responsible for Prussia's universities, and the dominant figure in Prussian higher education at the time, commissioned the economist and statistician Johannes Conrad to visit universities while on a trip to the United States in 1896. Upon the report's completion, he gave it wide publicity. It was also in this period that individual professors of German origin obtained respected positions in the United States. Hugo Münsterberg, a psychologist of German origin who had come to Harvard in 1892, saw to it that almost forty German scholars and scientists participated in the International Congress of Arts and Sciences held during the 1904 Universal Exposition in St. Louis. These men represented a broad spectrum of German learning, both in the variety of their fields and the number of universities they represented. Among these scholars were the theologians Adolf von

Harnack (Berlin) and Ernst Troeltsch (Heidelberg), the educational theorist Wilhelm Rein (Jena), the historian Karl Lamprecht (Leipzig), the economists Johannes Conrad (Halle) and Werner Sombart (Breslau), the sociologists Ernst Tönnies (Kiel) and Max Weber (Heidelberg), and the chemist Wilhelm Ostwald (Leipzig) (Münsterberg, 1909, p. 204).

During this congress, proposals for a regular exchange of prominent professors between Harvard and the University of Berlin as well as between the latter (in association with other German universities) and Columbia University were developed. The discussion of these proposals led to two formal agreements in 1905, on the basis of which the exchange was carried on until the outbreak of the First World War and then again from 1931 to 1933. Other American universities, including the University of Michigan, the University of California at Berkeley, and Cornell University, established guest professorships shortly before the First World War.

Even though the uncritical enthusiasm for German higher education and the direct institutional interest in German universities subsided in the United States from the turn of century on, fundamental interest in the German philosophy of education and in the history of German education remained strong. The persisting interest in these topics is shown by, among other things, the intense discussion of the works of the educational theorist Friedrich Paulsen (1846–1908) and by the research of American scholars on the history of the German university in the 19th century (which still continues). Furthermore, in many disciplines an ever-closer connection was sought with European, and specifically German, science and scholarship. When the latter was regarded as preeminent in a particular field, the exchange of individual scholars and scientists was intensified.

The growing German commitment to this exchange was certainly furthered by encounters among individual scholars and scientists on both sides of the Atlantic. There was a decisive difference between the two academic systems: whereas in the United States the scientific impulse was combined with specific ideas and organizational concepts through far-sighted university presidents, in the German context the decisive influence was wielded less by the university 'Rektor' and Senate than by the Prussian educational administration, most notably by Friedrich Althoff, its director from 1882 to 1907. Althoff, who in 1906 was awarded a honorary doctorate by Harvard, had an influence that cannot be underestimated: He recognized the importance of international academic exchanges as an instrument of 'Kulturpolitik'. The substance of Kulturpolitik was that German science and scholarship were to provide criteria for making rational decisions and to point the way to new scientific advances. The intention was to enhance Germany's prestige throughout the world, although it was also recognized that the study of other countries would enrich the cultural life, politics, and economics of one's own country, Germany. Thus in 1907, with the help of the Koppel Foundation, the *Internationale Wochenschrift für Wissenschaft, Kunst und Technik* (International Weekly for Science, Scholarship, Art and Technology) was founded, and in 1910, the Amerika-Institut was established in association with the University of Berlin.[12] Those involved in the planning of the universities of Frankfort and Hamburg studied how the American residential liberal arts colleges and universities were organized and financed. All these enterprises found patrons in wealthy businessmen and bankers, chiefly German Jews and American Jews of German origin.[13]

Some schools of German universities, however, only reluctantly joined in the exchange of faculty members with the "newcomer" American universities. The proposal that it should accept American guest professors was discussed by the School of Philosophy at the University of Berlin in 1905. Friedrich Paulsen reports that

. . . the idea met with a very hostile reception: some arrogant hotspurs deprecated the suggestion of thus placing the American universities on a par with the German universities as being in the nature of an affront to the dignity of the latter . . . . (Paulsen, 1938, p. 438)

The resistance was overcome, however, and in the following years the vast majority of the university professors of both countries came to regard professional exchanges as, on the whole, a success. The experience and the conclusions that individual professors drew from such exchanges are documented in scores of publications.

Although during the first years of this century German professors of the humanities continued to be somewhat reluctant to cooperate with their American counterparts, in other areas of learning there had long been a greater degree of interest in one another on both sides of the Atlantic. One could even say that increasing international competition had been creating political pressure on the universities to intensify contact with scientists abroad. This was especially true of the natural and engineering sciences. From 1840 on, the development of agricultural chemistry in the United States received its primary impulse from Justus Liebig (1803–1873), professor at the University of Giessen, who exerted this influence through his writings

8

and his American students. Agricultural chemistry subsequently became a central discipline at the land-grant colleges that were founded following the passage of the Morrill Land Grant Act in 1862 (Rossiter, 1975).

In 1869, Charles W. Eliot drew attention to the superiority of the German 'Realschule', a practically oriented secondary school, and urged teaching foreign languages at polytechnical schools. He wrote:

> If he [i.e., the student] learns French and German, it is chiefly because he would not have the best technical literature of his generation sealed for him.[14]

Turning to the German perspective, Professor Franz Reuleaux of Berlin's Industrial Academy (after 1879, the Technical University in Berlin-Charlottenburg) visited the Philadelphia World's Fair of 1876. In his reports he underlined the more advanced development of important areas of technology and the technical sciences in the United States in comparison with Germany. He told of hearing sharp criticism of Germany's industrial products, which the Americans considered shoddy, and which were felt to lack quality in design. Moreover, German products were said to smack of jingoism.[15] To increase exchange between the two countries in these fields, the American-German Association of Technical Engineers was founded in 1884.

Althoff promoted further trips to the United States for the purpose of gathering information about institutes and colleges prominent in the natural and engineering sciences, in particular Cornell, Yale, and the Massachusetts Institute of Technology. Close connections developed between MIT and the Technical Universities in Berlin and Aachen, and as German scientists became better acquainted with the accomplishments of their American colleagues, they found that the rationalization of technical production was more advanced in the United States. As a consequence, a chair was established at the Technical University of Berlin for the design of machine tools and for instruction in the factory system of production; in 1904 Georg Schlesinger was the first professor to be appointed to it.[16] In 1912 Professor A. Wallichs of the Technical University of Aachen published a German translation of Frederick W. Taylor's book, *Shop Management*, with his own supplementary notes, thereby making generally known in Germany the system of "Taylorism," the technique of modern industrial production based on the scientific analysis of the work process into its smallest constituent elements.

9

Concern about the state of the natural sciences in Germany relative to the rest of the world played a central role in the establishment of the Kaiser Wilhelm Society, which was supposed to take responsibility for furthering research in chemistry and in other natural sciences.

Prior to the First World War the prominent theologian Adolf von Harnack (1851–1930), who developed a close relationship with the imperial court, shaped official policy regarding science and scholarship in Germany. After his sojourn in the United States in 1904, von Harnack wrote to a colleague:

> Your assumption is entirely correct that my trip brought me powerful stimulating impressions, not available in Europe. It was a magnificent time; no dissonance or unpleasant experience troubled it. Germany—and especially its universities—still enjoys a tremendous capital of respect, love, veneration, and admiration in America! May it always justify this trust and remain worthy of it . . . .[17]

In these remarks one can hear an undertone of concern about Germany's future, about whether Germany, as a 'Kulturnation' (a term used by von Harnack), would be able in the future to lay claim to moral and intellectual leadership among the countries of the world. Only few men of learning attempted to lead the discussion in another direction, and raised their voices to call attention to the supranational character of science and scholarship in Germany.

International politics and international commerce had become—to borrow an expression from Ralph Waldo Emerson—a great battle for world supremacy.[18] In a 1909 memorandum on the "necessity of a new organization for the advancement of science in Germany"—a memorandum intended to prepare the way for the establishment of the Kaiser Wilhelm Society—von Harnack described in detail the ways in which research in medicine and the natural sciences was being furthered in other countries. In the United States, for example, he cited the efforts of Andrew Carnegie, John D. Rockefeller, Henry Phipps, and the federal government.[19] Von Harnack therefore called for the founding of research institutes for the natural sciences, and stressed the necessity of preventing the emigration of capable scientists by offering them well-equipped research facilities.[20] As far as possible provisions were also to be made for international cooperation in scientific matters. In spite of Germany's unfavorable financial situation, von Harnack argued, it had to be possible

> to procure the means to keep science in the Fatherland on its present high level. Military might and science are the two strong pillars of

Germany's greatness, and the Prussian state, in keeping with its glorious tradition, has the duty to insure the preservation of both.[21]

On the whole, until 1914 it was primarily in the United States that the exchanges with German professors and universities bore fruit, although indications of a significant impact in the other direction were already becoming evident. The First World War did not merely interrupt this exchange for a number of years; when it was resumed after the war, there was a changed political situation, and the two partners faced one another with new eyes.

1.2. Relations in school education and educational philosophy up to 1914

Prior to the First World War American interest in German education was concentrated on the universities. Nevertheless, the interest that had been shown by Horace Mann and others in Germany's system of primary and secondary education, and particularly in the German philosophy of education, did not by any means disappear. The growing influx of German immigrants, among them young teachers, scholars, and scientists, was of itself sufficient to maintain this interest.[22] In general, however, American educationists paid little attention to the institutional solutions to educational problems which had been established in Germany.

The exceptions were the admirers of German universities, who pointed out again and again the valuable contribution to the excellence of the German university made by the 'Gymnasium', a selective secondary school with emphasis on classical education. They argued for the establishment of selective schools modeled on the Gymnasium which would prepare for college entrance. But on the whole Americans charted their own democratic path. They built their systems of primary and secondary education up from 'below'; that is, from the communities. The schools in the United States were not supposed to be divided into different types according to different educational goals. Rather, they were, from the outset, designed to educate children from all social strata together. Thus, soon after the Civil War, American secondary schools were expanded into comprehensive programs of study with less emphasis on preparation for college entrance. At the turn of the century, 15 percent of the 14- to 17-year-olds in the United States attended high school,[23] a percentage much higher than that in the admittedly more demanding selective secondary schools in Germany.

In contrast, the influence of the German philosophy of education was strong in the United States. Primary education in Europe was markedly influenced by Swiss and German educational philosophers of the end of the 18th and the beginning of the 19th centuries. Under the influences of Jean-Jacques Rousseau, who called for "the immediate experience of nature," of Johann Heinrich Pestalozzi, who proclaimed the principle, "Primary education provides direct, sensory experience," of Friedrich Wilhelm Froebel, who established the first kindergarten in 1837, and of Johann Friedrich Herbart, who elaborated a "science of education," military discipline and rote learning were made to give way to the understanding that it is necessary to enable the child to learn from his own experience and to develop through sensory experience of his environment. Instruction and the imparting of moral discipline became objects of scientific observation and study, which then offered guidance for education.

These ideas and practices, however, were taken up in the United States only after noteworthy, and often considerable, delay. Mrs. Carl Schurz, a disciple of Froebel, whose husband immigrated to the United States in 1852 after participating in the unsuccessful German Revolution of 1848, founded the first private kindergarten in the United States. She did so during a period, lasting from 1851 to 1859, when kindergartens were forbidden in Prussia because they were considered "part of Froebel's socialist system, that is calculated to educate youth to be atheist."[24] In 1873, the first kindergarten which was part of a public school system was opened in St. Louis. In the following years many other cities followed St. Louis's example. Kindergartens were especially popular among German-Americans because they contributed significantly to the preservation of their mother tongue.

In 1869, the Pädagogischer Verein in Berlin conducted a survey of the environmental perceptions of children at the time they enter primary school. The psychologist G. Stanley Hall, a student of Wilhelm Wundt (and in 1887 to become the first president of Clark University), conducted a similar study in Boston schools in 1882, referring explicitly to the Berlin investigation in the report of his findings.[25] Hall praises the latter study as being "in some degree the first opening of a new field." Its results supported the beliefs motivating the movement for "object teaching," which had been spreading since the 1860's, owing particularly to the efforts of Edward A. Sheldon of the Oswego Normal School in New York. Invoking the Berlin and Boston studies, Hall stressed that the important role of the kindergarten was "to make the children acquainted with natural objects."[26]

Between 1890 and 1914, translations and expositions of the works of Froebel, Herbart, and Pestalozzi finally found a wide audience in the United States. In 1892 the National Herbart Society was founded; it acquired great importance as a professional association for educational research. In 1902 its name was changed to National Society for the Scientific Study of Education.

Until the First World War, there were some schools in the United States in which German was the primary language of instruction, especially in those regions heavily settled by immigrants from Germany. Close connections between these schools and Germany were maintained as a matter of course, principally by teachers' associations, which organized conferences and trips to Germany. Most important, however, these associations published their own journals in which appeared articles by German educators about primary and secondary education in Germany. In 1912, the National German-American League of School Teachers, the membership of which was entirely American, celebrated its 40th conference by holding it in Berlin. The members of the League numbered at that time about 550. The 1912 issues of its monthly journal, *Monatshefte für deutsche Sprache und Pädagogik*, then in its 13th year of publication, contain enthusiastic reports about the conference. In the letters by American and German specialists on language instruction and similar topics, and in the accounts of the conference, one is struck by the Americans' intense feeling of being strongly tied to Germany as their true homeland. When the group was received by the Empress, its members spontaneously sang the German national anthem.

These teachers functioned as a bridge between two cultures, a role that forced them to come to grips with teaching problems which only very much later were to be dealt with seriously in German schools. One example is the extensive discussion, in the *Monatshefte* of 1913, of the direct method of foreign language instruction, a method which did not become accepted in German schools until after the Second World War.

The American "common school" provided welcome support to the proponents in Germany of the 'Einheitsschule', a single form of the primary and secondary school. This movement, which had been in existence for a long time, strove to replace the socially differentiated schools with schools that would bring together pupils from all social strata, i.e., comprehensive schools. From the nineties on there also appeared in German journals reports on education in the United

13

States, in which details of American education, such as school libraries, self-government by pupils, independent learning, and co-education were noted with interest. They usually were criticized and almost all the authors of these reports remained convinced of the superiority of German schools. In spite of visits to the United States by German educators and the relatively numerous reports in journals, American primary and secondary education was not, on the whole, given much attention in Germany.[27] Even instruction in the English language was oriented exclusively to Great Britain. Speaking of the traditional Gymnasium, V. D. Rust thought that it was not an exaggeration to say that they "attempted to exhibit the superiority of German culture and German education by a deliberate disregard or degradation of that which was foreign." (Rust, 1965, p. 52).

The "dual system" of German technical and commercial training, combining study and practical work, was early the object of special interest in the United States. Industry and commerce continued to be driving forces in the international competition with Germany long after Emerson had taken note of this in 1856. In his book, *The Empire of Business*, published in 1902, Andrew Carnegie underlined the importance of a system of technical and commercial education for the success of American business in international competition. At the Carnegie Institute, a four-year technical college which he established in Pittsburgh, German was made a compulsory subject. As Franz Reuleaux had looked to American technical progress during his visit in 1876, Carnegie focused on the importance of German technical education!

Of importance in this context was the visit to the United States by Georg Kerschensteiner (1854–1932), the prominent school administrator and educationist. Kerschensteiner studied the American system of primary and secondary education in 1910 and in his reports compared it with that of Germany. In Chicago, Kerschensteiner gave lectures on his concept of the vocational school, the 'Arbeitsschule'. In his view, training a young person for a vocation— i.e., training him to take pride in doing a good piece of work— involved, and indeed depended upon, practical experience. This training was in his eyes at the same time moral education in a specific attitude toward the state. He saw the striving for satisfaction in one's work as but part of civic education to serve one's community, to do one's duty, to voluntarily adapt and subordinate oneself, to willingly make personal sacrifices in the interest of the ethical communal whole (sittliches Gemeinwesen).

14

From 1907 on, Kerschensteiner read intensively the writings of John Dewey (1859–1952), never, however, becoming personally acquainted with the American educational philosopher.[28] He took over the plan of basic education, and of the corresponding school organization which Dewey had sketched out, and made use of them in his own works, although not for the specifically democratic goals which Dewey had formulated on the basis of an action-oriented pragmatism.[29]

The influence of Dewey's concept of a basic education, the central element of which is the child's learning from experience and through discovery, extended beyond Kerschensteiner, however. Put into practice in the project method of education described by W. H. Kilpatrick, this kind of education became, and remains to the present time, an essential component of progressive American and German theories of primary and secondary education. On the other hand, the ideas of Kerschensteiner live on in the in-school part of the German dual system of vocational education for 15- to 18-year-olds, which has again and again been the object of studies by American researchers.

Dewey's writings had a great influence on the development of Kerschensteiner's theories of vocational education, and particularly on his endeavors to advance the development of vocational training in modern society, in which the foundation of production is occupational specialization.[30] By 1914, the one-sided German–American educational influence of the 19th century had begun to give way to a genuine exchange not only in higher education but also in primary and secondary education.

1.3. The Impact of the First World War, 1914–1918

During the First World War, the thinking of German professors, university students, and school teachers was guided almost exclusively by chauvinistic nationalism. At first the main targets of this nationalism were the other European powers. At that time there was still hope that the United States could be kept benevolently neutral, under the influence, in part, of the large population of German origin and of the professors who had participated in the educational exchange between the two countries, such as the German scholars Francke, Kühnemann, and Münsterberg, and American professors. One of them, John W. Burgess, made a noteworthy attempt to influence American opinion in favor of Germany. This illusion was shattered, however, when the United States entered the war in 1917.

The recently published compilation of speeches and appeals by German professors in the First World War (*Aufrufe und Reden deutscher Professoren im Ersten Weltkrieg*) (Böhme, 1975) offers only a small selection from the flood of pronouncements made by German academics during that period. But the book provides a clear outline for their belief in the superiority of the German nation and culture, and for the intention of the Germans, founded upon their belief in this superiority, to annex territory and to become a dominant power in the world. Only in 1917 did the voices of moderation in Germany begin to increase in number. Nevertheless, German university professors on the whole continued to reject, indeed to despise, Western democracy until—and even after—the end of the war. For example, the philosopher Max Wundt wrote a the beginning of 1918:

> In reality, democracy is the triumph of dead numbers over living forms . . . . Therefore it is the strong-willed individual who knows his own mind who should rule, not the multitude. (Böhme, 1975, p. 155)

In the United States the influence of those friendly to Germany diminished, while at the same time hostility to Germany intensified in many areas to the point where German-Americans were ostracized and even persecuted. The German language all but disappeared from school curricula. The umbrella organization of German-Americans, the National German-American Alliance, which had had approximately two million members prior to the war, dissolved itself in 1918.[31]

With regard to education, the essential impact of the First World War was the cultural withdrawal of the United States from Europe, and especially from Germany. Until 1914 Americans had always measured the excellence of their own educational system against those of Europe, while the fundamental attitude of Americans in their dealings with German culture, science, and scholarship had been the esteem of a junior for the senior member of a partnership. But the war not only engendered strong emotions; it also strengthened American self-confidence and opened the eyes of American educationists to deficiencies of the German educational system.

This criticism of German education was led by John Dewey, who had written his doctoral dissertation on Immanuel Kant. In February 1915, he gave a series of three lectures, which were published in the same year under the title, *German Philosophy and Politics* (Dewey, 1942). In these talks he contrasted the German idealist philosophy, elaborated by Immanuel Kant, Johann Gottlieb Fichte, and Georg

Wilhelm Friedrich Hegel, to his own American pragmatism as an ideological basis for social life. In his treatment of German idealism, Dewey above all laid bare the subjectivist root of this philosophy in the division of the world into the realms of inner freedom and external necessity.

Dewey saw the effect of this philosophy in the organizational structure of German universities and in the idea of the Gymnasium. Dewey comments on patriotic speeches given by German professors and generals, who enlarged upon conclusions drawn from this philosophy, asserting the Germans' claim to have always been the leading representatives of freedom of thought. Dewey summarizes these claims as follows:

> The main thing is that Germany, more than any other nation, in a sense alone of all nations, embodies the essential principle of humanity: freedom of spirit, combined with thorough and detailed work in the outer sphere where reigns causal law, where obiedence, discipline and subordination are the necessities of successful organizations. (Dewey, 1942, p. 75)

And about the Germans as a nation, Dewey wrote:

> In Germany there is a self which is self-wrought and self-owned. The very fact that Germany for centuries had had no external unity proves that its selfhood is metaphysical, not a gift of circumstance. This conception of the German mission has been combined with a kind of anthropological metaphysics which has become the rage in Germany. The Germans alone of all existing European nations are a pure race. They alone have preserved unalloyed the original divine deposit . . . . A purely artificial cult of race has so flourished in Germany that many social movements—like anti-Semitism—and some of Germany's political ambitions cannot be understood apart from the mystic identification of Race, Culture, and the State. (Dewey, 1942, p. 121)[32]

As this short resumé shows, Dewey exposed with great penetration darker sides of the German philosophical tradition and its vulgarization to the point of perversion. Later, his analysis of the intellectual and emotional currents that dominated Germany during the First World War was confirmed by the success of National Socialism. In 1942, he republished his lectures with an introduction in which he discussed the connection between National Socialism and German philosophy, stressing the following points:

> Facts which lie on the surface certainly forbid the attempt to trace direct influence of the established philosophical tradition of Germany upon

17

Adolf Hitler's creed. Absence of direct channels of transmission does not, however, do away with the all but incredible one-to-one correspondence that has been proved by events to exist between the terms of the appeal of Hitler and the response aroused in the German people— a correspondence without which Hitler would have remained an obscure agitator with at most a nuisance value. [There was] a kind of pre-established harmony between the attitudes of belief in which Germans had been indoctrinated and the terms of the Hitlerian appeal: terms whose adaptation to the state of German mentality must be judged by the triumph they speedily achieved. . . .
It is upon the side of infiltration of the teachings of the philosophic representatives of Germany into popular attitudes and habits that we find underlying continuity between them and the powerful components of Hitler's appeals. (Dewey, 1942, pp. 14 and 17)[33]

It must be added that in the conclusion of his lectures in 1915, and even more emphatically at the end of his 1942 introduction to the reprint of the lectures, he pointed out that "our own country is not free from the guilt of swollen nationalism" (p. 47). He went on to call for "free communication . . . in all the phases and aspects of social life, domestic and transnational," and to argue that

the democratic way of life commits us to unceasing effort to break down the walls of class, of unequal opportunity, of color, race, sect, and nationality, which estrange human beings from one another. (Dewey, 1942, p. 49)

1.4. The political situation of the Weimar Republic from 1919 to 1933

The defeat of Imperial Germany in the fall of 1918 was sealed by the Versailles Peace Treaty signed on June 18, 1919. Under the conditions of the treaty, the Germans had to accept considerable loss of territory, to suffer the military occupation, first, of the parts of their country west of the Rhine, and later also of the Ruhr region, and to accept the obligation to pay costly reparations. Entry into the newly founded League of Nations was denied Germany up to September 1926. Considering Germany's situation in its entirety, one can say that the country was rendered militarily and politically powerless and weakened economically; only gradually was it allowed to take part once again in international political and cultural exchanges.

The relationship of Germany to the United States was especially troubled by the fact that the hope of a liberal peace in accordance with the Fourteen Points proposed by President Wilson on January

8, 1918, was disappointed. For that reason, leaving aside a few exceptions, contacts and exchanges between the two countries, including those in education, science, and scholarship, recommenced only slowly. In general, the international boycott of German academics and their organizations began to ease off only in 1922. Germany's admission to the League of Nations was an important step toward normalizing its relations with the rest of the world, which was not attained completely before about 1930. However, before considering the effect on science, scholarship, and education more closely, let us turn our attention briefly to the consequences of Germany's military defeat for its domestic politics.

Following the capitulation of Imperial Germany in November 1918, the revolt of soldiers and workers forced the Kaiser to abdicate and brought the proclamation of the German Republic. In spite of the opposition of radical socialists further to the left, the majority of the Social Democrats managed to secure for themselves first the leadership of the revolution and then the government of the new republic. The new constitution of the German Reich, creating a parliamentary democracy, was approved in Weimar on August 11, 1919, by a National Assembly elected for this purpose. In order to achieve the adoption of the new constitution, the Social Democrats had to ally themselves with the liberal bourgeoisie and particularly with the "Zentrum Party" of the period, which at the time was still willing to cooperate with the left. This was the Catholic party, which had been established in protest against Bismarck's anti-papal policy, and which, like the Social Democratic Party, had been in the opposition in Imperial Germany.

The Weimar Republic which was brought into being by this alliance was plagued throughout its existence—ended by Hitler's seizure of power on January 30, 1933—by continuous tensions between, on the one hand, the left and the liberal forces, whose votes had secured the adoption of the constitution, and, on the other hand, the rightist Conservatives and the nationalist forces, which were reactionary in the literal sense of the term. Depending on their location in the rightist spectrum, the latter groups collaborated only reluctantly or not at all in the refashioning of the German people into a democratic republic. They interpreted the cause of "Germany's misfortune" not in its military defeat, but in the "stab in the back" given to the troops fighting at the front by the revolt of the proletariat at home. In their view, the Treaty of Versailles had been forced on Germany and, being based upon "the lie that Germany alone was guilty of

19

starting the war" had to be revised. Fundamental opposition to the Republic also came from the radical socialists and the Communists.

Defeat and revolution gave the democratic forces in Germany an opportunity to construct a truly democratic society following the Western model. However, neither the new constitution nor the blossoming of intellectual and artistic forces in Germany's cultural life during the so-called "Golden Twenties" were sufficient to accomplish this task. Moreover, the political leadership of the country was confronted with the necessity of solving, or at least alleviating, the economic problems that were made manifest in the massive inflation of 1923. They had also to defend Germany's national interests against its former adversaries by obtaining from them the easing of financial and political burdens imposed at Versailles, as well as to end its isolation in the sphere of international politics. These burdens and the isolation of Germany hindered all efforts to effect fundamental reforms within the country, while in the bastions of conservatism—the army, the bureaucracy, the management of industry, the churches, and in the universities and the Gymnasium—the signs of the times were simply not understood.

The overwhelming majority of German academics and, with them, the Gymnasium teachers, rejected the republic. Instead of celebrating the anniversary of the proclamation of the Weimar constitution on August 11, the universities celebrated the anniversary of the foundation of the German Empire in Versailles on January 18, 1871. Rather than quote from anti-democratic, nationalist speeches which were common on these occasions,[34] we will show how a prominent witness assessed the situation.

The Swiss theologian Karl Barth, spokesman for later resistance to the Hitler regime by members of the Protestant Church, taught at German universities from 1921 to 1933. In 1947, he wrote about his experiences during these years in the Göttingen University newspaper:

I found that the professors, as I came to know them socially, in their offices, in meetings of academic senates, and elsewhere, were, with a few exceptions, completely occupied with the struggle against "Versailles" that was common at that time, while their stance toward the poor Weimar Republic—far from giving it a fair chance—was one that even today I can only call sabotage. Not only did they offer no resistance to the political nonsense to which great numbers of students were assenting; on the contrary, they showed a paternal benevolence toward it, and some of them gave it their explicit support. They scornfully dismissed the idea that the year 1918 might have meant a liberation of Germany.[35]

20

1.5. Relations in higher education, science, and scholarship from 1919 to 1933

The First World War had made the nations of the world aware of how closely the age of technology was drawing them together. After a hesitant recommencement, German-American relations in education, scholarship, and science attained a level of intensity during the Weimar Republic not known before the war. The accent of these relations had partially shifted, however. On the German side, interest was particularly strong in becoming acquainted with the other country and in conveying a favorable image of Germany to its citizens. In the United States, interest in German educational and scientific institutions as models had diminished, but a new interest had emerged, an interest in observing the latest developments in the relations between left radicalism and nationalist reaction in the young democracy. The concern was directed much more to the danger of Communism than to that of rightist extremism. The humanitarian aid that began soon after the war, and especially the projects of philanthropic foundations, were supposed to help quell this danger. In addition, professors, students, school teachers, and shapers of Kulturpolitik from both sides of the Atlantic were soon striving to establish connections with their counterparts in the other country or to attend a university there, in order to broaden their own knowledge and exchange of information with other specialists in their fields.

The German national government as well as the Prussian Ministry of Culture, which led the way for the other 'Länder' in educational matters, was greatly interested in resuming international relations in the spheres of science and of education. During the war the Prussian Ministry of Culture and the national Ministry of Foreign Affairs had already urged that a systematic cultural policy be actively pursued. Following the war such a policy was doubly necessary to regain respect for Germany and to reintegrate the country into international cultural and scientific life. This policy was implemented by the Cultural Section of the Ministry of Foreign Affairs and by the Prussian Ministry of Culture, which from 1916 to 1930 was first decisively influenced, then headed by Carl Heinrich Becker (1876–1933). The fundamental positions of these two governmental bodies differed in one important nuance. Becker stood for a policy of modern, liberal-democratic reform, while the Ministry of Foreign Affairs tended to be nationalist and conservative in its orientation. Advocates of these two positions were to be found everywhere in

German schools and universities. The potential conflict continually threatened to surface, and created a situation which was hardly conducive to the creation of democracy in the Weimar Republic.[36]

Despite all efforts on the part of the German government, the first concrete steps to reestablish official relations between the two countries' educational institutions and associations came from the United States and were made by private individuals rather than by the government. In the fall of 1922, at the invitation of an American student group seeking to make contact with the German youth movement, Carl Joachim Friedrich, a student of sociology and political science at the University of Heidelberg, came to the United States to make a tour of the country. With his help, an invitation to German students to study at American universities was issued for the first time by Dr. Stephen Duggan, Director of the Institute of International Education and professor at the City College of New York. The invitation was extended to 13 German students.

There soon followed the founding of several German organizations, the purpose of which was to foster academic relations with other countries. The Ministry of Foreign Affairs and the Prussian Ministry of Culture actively participated in the establishment of these organizations, the most important of which were the Academic Exchange Service, which arose out of the Heidelberg Initiative, and the Alexander von Humboldt Foundation, which awarded scholarships to foreigners for study in Germany, using funds from the Ministry of Foreign Affairs. In 1931 these two organizations were merged to create the German Academic Exchange Service. This body functioned as a public institution well into the Second World War. (After the founding of the Federal Republic of Germany, the German Academic Exchange Service and the Alexander von Humboldt Foundation were reestablished as separate institutions.) The partner in the United States was the American Student Exchange, which was established in 1923 as part of the Institute of International Education in New York City.

Until 1932 the Academic Exchange Service applied itself energetically to the development of the exchange with the United States. Thereafter, the fate of the exchange between the two countries depended on the assessment of what Germany's new rulers considered politically opportune.[37]

A certain ambiguity in the goals of the German organizations promoting academic relations with other countries tended to reflect the differences in political views represented by the Ministry of Foreign Affairs and the Prussian Ministry of Culture. Some German organizations hoped to maintain a German presence upon the international scene in the interest of advertising German 'Kultur', others to promote an understanding between academic elites and foster the international character of science and scholarship, and still others to promote the acquisition of knowledge of foreign countries.

Relatively soon after the war, American students began again privately to pursue their studies at German universities, as did German students at universities in the United States. Starting in the summer semester of 1920, American students were once again enrolled at German universities. During the period between the wars, the number of American students in German universities rose to 800 (1932) and then declined to 166 (1939) (See Table 1.1).

A certain proportion of these students received scholarships provided by the Academic Exchange Service. The number of American students receiving scholarships went from 15 in 1925 to a maximum of 80 in 1931 and then down to 59 in 1937. In addition to these efforts on the part of the Academic Exchange Service, the Alexander von Humboldt Foundation awarded post-graduate fellowships to 21 Americans for study in Germany from 1925 to 1930 (Düwell, 1976, pp. 171 and 175).

Statistics are available on the number of German students attending universities and colleges in the United States between the two World Wars only for the period beginning with the academic year 1921–1922 and ending with 1930–1931. During this time, the number of Germans pursuing their studies in the United States rose continuously from an initial 49 to 415. Among them in 1924–1925 were the 13 students who comprised the first group invited to study in the United States on Duggan's initiative. They were followed by exchange students sent by the newly formed Academic Exchange Service.

Statistics and the record of institutionalized efforts can give an only very incomplete picture of the real extent of intellectual intercourse between the two countries. Here, too, the first stimulus was highly personal and came from outside Germany. At the urging of Chaim Weizmann, Albert Einstein, one of the few prominent opponents of the First World War in Germany and, in addition, a target of anti-Semitic harassment, toured the United States in 1920 giving lectures to promote the establishment of a university in Jerusalem. He was received enthusiastically, and his appearances gave the Americans reason to hope that a new Germany was emerging. In 1923 Nicholas Murray Butler offered him—in vain—a chair at Columbia University.

Table 1.1: Total Number of Registered Foreign Students and American Students at University-Type Institutions in the German Reich, 1925–1939, and in the Federal Republic of Germany, 1953–1980

Semester s = summer w = winter	German and foreign students	Foreign Students	
		total number	from the USA
German Reich			
s 1925	89,481	7,946	57
s 1926	94,584	7,422	92
w 1926/27	93,994	7,026	138
w 1927/28	101,681	6,861	139
w 1928/29	113,042	6,898	173
w 1929/30	122,391	6,939	259
w 1930/31	130,069	7,330	366
w 1931/32	129,741	7,060	500
w 1932/33	118,812	6,587	800
w 1933/34	103,454	4,655	399
w 1934/35	83,746	4,356	360
w 1935/36	74,246	4,568	393
w 1936/37	61,835	4,621	362
s 1938	53,917	4,302	252
s 1939	55,687	4,201	166
Federal Republic of Germany			
w 1953/54	121,392[1]	4,182[1]	469[1]
w 1960/61	239,481	19,826	1,299[1]
w 1966/67	322,709	22,418	1,683[1]
w 1973/74	589,413	34,010	2,605
w 1980/81	818,458	45,928	3,209

[1] Excluding students at Pädagogische Hochschulen.

Sources: Deutsche Hochschulstatistik, Vol. 7. Berlin 1931; and Vol. 8. Berlin 1932; Zehnjahresstatistik des Hochschulbesuchs und der Abschlußprüfungen, Vol. I. Berlin 1943; Statistisches Bundesamt: Studenten an Hochschulen 1980/81. Stuttgart and Mainz 1982 and earlier issues of the same series.

In the next decade, many German academics followed Einstein to the United States for various lengths of time. Among these were a few who remained in the United States permanently, such as the political scientist Carl Joachim Friedrich, who after having helped to initiate the first tour of the United States offered to German students, began his professorial career at Harvard in 1926. (In 1955,

Friedrich's *alma mater*, Heidelberg, provided him with a professorship, allowing him to alternate between Harvard and Heidelberg.) Another example is the political economist Joseph Schumpeter, who was given a chair at Harvard in 1932.

Among the American scientists and scholars who came to Germany after the First World War, some came to pursue their own education, such as the sociologist Talcott Parsons, who obtained a doctorate from the University of Heidelberg in 1928 with a dissertation on Max Weber. Others came in the name of international cooperation in scientific research, like the many natural scientists attracted to the great German centers of research, such as Berlin, Göttingen, Munich, and Leipzig. International seminars on both sides of the Atlantic also became a customary form of scientific cooperation during this time. The Deutsche Hochschule für Politik in Berlin, principally concerned with adult education, even numbered some Americans among its faculty members. These included Charles Beard and Nicholas Murray Butler, who taught there as Carnegie visiting professors in the 1920's.[38]

In spite of the recognition accorded to science and scholarship at German universities after the First World War, one vocal American admirer of Germany, Abraham Flexner, saw cause for concern because he viewed the German universities and the nation at large as confused. Nevertheless, he argued that:

> while aims have been to some extent muddled and obscured, lack of money is perhaps the most serious of the problems confronting the German university today . . . . Adjustments will be reached that will restore and perhaps even increase the efficiency of secondary and higher education.[39]

During the 1920's, Flexner's concern was shared by others in the United States with the result that American foundations and many individual Americans who had studied in Germany pitched in to help German science and scholarship financially. The most visible form taken by this aid was a large new building containing lecture halls at the University of Heidelberg; a sum of $500,000 was given for its construction in 1928.

Flexner concerned himself only with the organizational structure of German universities and the way these were traditionally administered. He did not become acquainted with the German professors of that period as Karl Barth came to know them. (The social scientists and the humanities scholars among them have been described by

Fritz K. Ringer in *The Decline of the German Mandarins*.) Had Flexner done so, and had he reflected upon the mentality and behavior of these professors, the portents of the moral and intellectual catastrophe which wrought havoc in German universities after January 30, 1933, could not have escaped his notice.[40]

Flexner's attitude toward the development of American universities, on the other hand, was very critical. He contrasted the extravagance, ignorance, and lack of understanding on the part of most American university presidents with the promotion of German universities by knowledgeable and understanding ministers and curators, state officials attached to German universities in a supervisory capacity. Giving their attention primarily to the organization of undergraduate education and the building up of professional schools, American university presidents neglected to foster science and scholarship the way this was done in Germany, by appointing to professorships the candidates best qualified in research.

But Flexner was not content just to criticize. Explicitly he invoked the ways in which scientific research and scholarship were being carried out at German universities and in the institutes of the Kaiser Wilhelm Society. He was especially impressed by the freeing of eminent scientists and scholars from teaching and administrative duties. He therefore initiated the efforts that led to the establishment of the Institute of Advanced Study in Princeton, and became its first director. Even before the collapse of the Weimar Republic, Flexner succeeded in persuading Albert Einstein to become one of the Institute's first members (Flexner, 1960, pp. 250 ff). Einstein came to Princeton in the summer of 1933 and remained there. His residence in the United States was a sign that the centers of research in the natural sciences and in other fields were beginning to shift to that country and became a signal to others to join the exodus from Germany.

1.6. Relations in school education and educational philosophy from 1919 to 1933

After the collapse of the old order, the democratic forces in Germany succeeded in anchoring the idea of a four-year common primary school for all children through the Weimar constitution. Details were spelled out in the Reich Law on the Primary School passed in April, 1920.[41] In June of 1920 a National Conference on Primary and Secondary Education took place. Preparations for this conference had begun under the former regime while the war was still going on; in view of the fact that great disparities existed between schools in the various German 'Länder', its purpose was to find a way to standardize the system of primary and secondary education in conformity with the new constitution. This conference constituted a sort of pedagogical parliament consisting of 650 professors, school administrators, and teachers from all types of schools. In short, its participants were prominent members of all the institutions concerned and of all the interested professional associations.

In this context, the conference is significant because its participants included a number of men who had visited the United States, among them von Harnack, Kerschensteiner, and Rein, as well as a few isolated radical reformers, who advocated an 'Einheitsschule', a kind of comprehensive school not based on the American model but rather designed to embody socialist principles. We shall have more to say about these reformers later. In the discussions of lengthy reports and proposals, only occasionally were foreign educational structures and experience mentioned. References to the educational situation in the USA were never more than incidental.[42] All in all, the majority of the participants in this representative gathering manifested clearly conservative attitudes. Neither the Great War nor revolution had shaken their nationalistic inclinations, or affected their traditional belief in the selective function of schooling.

By the time of the conference, the Weimar coalition, extending from the Social Democrats to the Catholic Zentrum Party, had lost its parliamentary majority. A center coalition, which did not include the now independent left wing of the Social Democratic Party, took control of the government on June 21, 1920. This shift in power put an end to the reform efforts that characterized the first year of the Republic. Because of the conflicts which from now on dominated political life in the Weimar Republic, only a few innovations could be effected that were legally binding throughout Germany. Among other things, a more academic professional training was introduced for teachers of the ubiquitous Volksschule, the lowest-ranking type of school, in all Länder except for Bavaria and Württemberg.

In the face of all vicissitudes, the Central Institute for Education (to which we shall return) continued to be active in the interest of reform up to the end of the Weimar period. From the fall of 1931 to the beginning of 1933, a commission established by the Central Institute worked out a plan for thoroughgoing reform of the middle level of the German school system, which included teaching guidelines that were in part uniform. In this reform plan, mention was briefly made of the organization of the American junior and senior high school. The plan, however remained for the most part merely on paper.[43]

Those concerned with primary and secondary education in Germany were, to be sure, interested in the educational systems of other countries. However, large organizations representing them, such as the Deutscher Philologenverband (Association of German Gymnasium Teachers), were fearful of excessive foreign influence, and agreed only in 1927, after long hesitation, to take part at least in the larger international meetings "in the interests of restoring cultural esteem and in counteracting the systematic cultural propaganda of other countries" (Rust, 1965, p. 97). The Allgemeiner Deutscher Lehrerverein (Association of German Volksschule Teachers) was more open to achieving international understanding in educational matters, but was in fact unable to link this enterprise to the daily activities of its members. Only the relatively small Reichsbund Entschiedener Schulreformer (National League of Radical School Reformers) and the even smaller German Section of the New Education Fellowship expressly made use of information and ideas from abroad in their own work. The effectiveness of these two organizations, which were small and internally riven, was due solely to the influence of some important educationists who belonged to them.

On the whole, however, both teachers and educationists were conservative in their outlook,[44] and the general political trend was inimical to educational reform. Therefore, viewing the decade from 1920 to 1930, one should not overestimate the importance of the popular literature about the United States that was finding a wide readership at this time. The same holds true for the Prussian Ministry of Culture's newly developed interest in foreign education, and the importance of individual educationists and teachers from schools and universities who endeavored to establish relations with the United States. From 1930 on, the worsening worldwide economic depression and increasingly uncontrollable political radicalism strangled all plans to modernize the German educational system.

In its transactions, the National Conference on Primary and Secondary Education availed itself of a handbook bearing the title *Die deutsche Schulreform* (German School Reform), that had been presented to it by the Prussian Central Institute for Education. This institute, established in 1915, developed into an important center which collected documents, journals and books and provided information. It also offered programs in continuing education, primarily for teachers, and became a source of impulses for reform efforts.

28

From 1924 on, the Institute began to gather and make use of materials from other countries, as well. After the end of Germany's international isolation in 1926, a special international section was built up under the direction of Franz Hilker.[45]

During this time, the International Institute of the Teachers College of Columbia University in New York City sent an invitation to the Minister of Culture, Carl H. Becker, asking him to select a suitably qualified person to come as a guest of the college for the purpose of studying the American system of primary and secondary education. An official in the Ministry of Culture, the educationist Erich Hylla, was chosen.[46] As a result of his visit, Hylla wrote a comprehensive description of the American educational system and its guiding principles. This book bore the revealing title *Die Schule der Demokratie* (School for Democracy) (1928); in it Hylla expresses his admiration for John Dewey. (His subsequent translation of Dewey's *Democracy and Education* into German appeared in 1930.) In his descriptions of American educational institutions, Hylla made numerous suggestions for improving the German educational system and for profitable educational research in Germany, which he felt had already fallen seriously behind that in the United States (Hylla, 1928). He directed the attention of German educational researchers above all to comparative research as well as to sociology and psychology.

From the vantage point gained by his experience in the United States, Hylla had a premonition of the catastrophe that was brewing in Europe, and especially in Germany:

Today the eyes of the world are upon America because of the feeling, which is correct even if it is as yet unclear, that for the next twenty, or perhaps even fifty or hundred years, the central events of world history will occur there, that there the fate of Western Europe will also be decided, if the latter does not in the last minute eliminate the gaping contradictions between its cultural substance and the forms of its political life by effecting a thoroughgoing reshaping of these forms. However, the prospect for such a reshaping is unfortunately not very favorable. (Hylla, 1928, p. iv)

Following Hylla's trip to the United States, the Central Institute for Education, acting in conjunction with the International Institute of Columbia Teachers College, organized a study trip in the spring of 1928. The trip began in New York City, where the group was greeted by Nicholas Murray Butler and John Dewey. The itinerary of the trip then led the German observers to primary and secondary schools, universities, teacher-training colleges, and other such institutions in the East and the Middle West. For example, Sebald Schwarz, chief school inspector in Lübeck, describes in enthusiastic articles the organization of primary and secondary schools in the United States as comprehensive schools financed by the local communities. With the exception of Schwarz, no school administrator took part in the study trip.[47] In the summer of 1929 a group of American educators returned the visit.

At German universities, study of the educational systems of other countries, and particularly that of the United States, gained ground during the Weimar period.[48] This was especially true among the members of the League of Radical School Reformers. The highly respected, widely traveled Peter Petersen was the successor in Jena of Wilhelm Rein (1847–1929).[49] We can assume that they drew students also from the United States. Friedrich Schneider taught at the universities of Cologne and Bonn.[50] Schneider, like Petersen, had visited George Peabody College for Teachers in Nashville, Tennessee, which at the time had a reputation for being progressive and for that reason attracted like-minded foreign educationists. In Munich, Georg Kerschensteiner remained active until 1931, while Karl Umlauf and Theodor Herbert Becker taught in Hamburg. In Berlin, Fritz Karsen, a reformist educator of socialist orientation, about whom we shall have more to say, lectured at the university from 1931 to early 1933 on foreign educational systems.[51]

The spread of comparative education was accompanied by an increase in publications on this topic in scholarly journals. Initially, articles from foreign authors about education in other countries had appeared primarily in the *Pädagogisches Zentralblatt*, published by the Central Institute for Education. Then in 1931 Friedrich Schneider in Cologne and Paul Monroe in New York City succeeded in establishing the *Internationale Zeitschrift für Erziehungswissenschaft— International Education Review—Revue Internationale de Pédagogie*. Participants in this enterprise were the Central Institute, the German Office for International Educational Relations (both in Berlin), the International Institute of Columbia Teachers College, and the Institute of International Education (both in New York City), as well as two other institutes in Münster and Geneva. The review appeared until 1934.[52] During the short time of its existence in its original form, it carried articles by almost 20 American authors on subjects having to do with education in the United States. They ranged from educational philosophy, and policies on primary and secondary education and education in general, to the improvement of teaching methods and examinations. Since these articles were written in English, the audience they found in Germany was necessarily limited.

From 1919 to 1933, a large number of articles in German educational journals were published on the educational systems of various countries; many dealt with aspects of the American educational system (see Zymek, 1975, pp. 237–238 and 356 ff.). On the whole, the articles and reports were predominantly devoted to giving information about national problems and institutions. Comparison of the United States with Germany was—if made at all—left implicit. American educational philosophy, especially that elaborated by Dewey, and reports on the organizational structures of American schools, especially of comprehensive schools, probably had an effective influence only on some radical school reformers and on some model schools.

There is no evidence of much American interest in the German educational system during this period, aside from the universities. Any policy interest was generally conditioned by American concern about the political and economic development of the young republic, and linked with the resolve that Germany should not become a Communist country. This is what was behind decisions on the part of the Carnegie Foundation for Advancement of Teaching and other foundations to provide a certain amount of financial support for science and education in Germany. The few discussions of German education by Americans tended to focus approvingly on progressive approaches, for example in regard to giving children and adolescents more freedom to develop their personalities and on reforms designed to democratize schools. There is no question about it, a relatively large number of innovations of this kind were introduced; but American visitors to Germany overestimated the effect of these impulses on the German system of primary and secondary education as a whole. Only to a limited extent, and, moreover, only for a few years, were German schools affected by these reform efforts.

During these years American interest in German education was probably strongest at the International Institute of the Teachers College of Columbia University, founded in 1923 in New York City. In collaboration with the Institute of International Education, it became, from the German point of view, the most important American educational research institute for the exchange of information and ideas with other countries, whether in the form of study trips, or of exchange of publications and contributions to international journals. Their intimate knowledge of Germany equipped the institute's professors, Thomas Alexander, George S. Counts, Isaac Leon

Kandel, and Paul Monroe, to deal intensively with German educational affairs.

Prior to and following the First World War, Alexander had been in Germany repeatedly. He had gone there as an exchange teacher and had written much about the problems of primary and secondary education in Prussia. Together with his young collaborator, Beryl Parker, he published in 1929 *The New Education in the German Republic*, in which many issues concerning primary and secondary education in Germany were critically although sympathetically discussed. They also examined a number of experiments in primary and secondary education, for example, the Lietz boarding schools in the countryside, other progressive private schools, and new approaches to education both inside and outside school. Their cautious reservations about the romantically idealistic impetuosity of the German youth movement notwithstanding, they conclude with the hope that there would be a successful transition in Germany from the traditional organization of education, which reflected marked social stratification, to democratic concepts and forms of education.

> Many teachers [they reported] have dared to venture into this new world of education where the child is really the center of the schools. (Alexander and Parker, 1929, p. 373)

In their pedagogical optimism and in their avoidance of any analysis of German schools and education in their general social and political context, the authors' approach reflected the positions of many German educational reformers.

In 1930, Carl Heinrich Becker, former Prussian Minister of Culture and chief author of liberal German 'Kulturpolitik' since the First World War, went on an extensive lecture tour across the United States, prepared by his kindred spirit, Nicholas Murray Butler. The tour ended at Columbia Teachers College, where he spoke on "The Present Educational Situation in Germany." In some ways Becker's lecture confirmed the impressions of the reforms in Germany which Alexander and others had brought back:

> American educational ideas have stood as sponsors for this reform. Many of the ideas championed by Professor John Dewey have been adopted, while others have had a direct or indirect influence in the actual reshaping of our system.[53]

In his critical summary of the German reform programs, Becker stressed, as had Alexander, that henceforth the child himself would be the focal point of the reforms. It would, however, be viewed from two perspectives: "The child is considered not merely as an individual but also as a member of society."[54]

But what "society" was Becker referring to? Could it set clear educational goals? Under the pressure of increasing economic need and an intensifying domestic political crisis, Becker, himself a tradition-conscious grand bourgeois who apparently had greater sensitivity to the nationalist political currents in Germany at that time than to the socioeconomic tensions underlying them, posed the question of the possibility of combining disparate goals of political education. He thus showed his American audience at least one critical aspect of the situation in the German context. Becker's own words were:

> The ideal of cultivating a spirit of peace and harmony among the nations must necessarily be a principle of our education.
> But every national system of education must also cultivate the ideal of national integrity. Hence the dualism of our present system. And its problem is to strike a balance which will be safer and more enduring than the positive nationalism which dominated the educational system of the old régime . . . . National self-consciousness rather than national self-assertiveness must be the watchword of our present educational policy.[55]

Nevertheless, three years later, in 1933, the watchword of German educational policy did become "national self-assertiveness."

Immediately before the Nazi seizure of power in Germany, Isaac Kandel published his *Comparative Education*.[56] In this extensive compendium of the education systems of six countries, he saw democracy and individual development as goals common to all the educational systems he discussed, but distinguished each case by its particular national consciousness and the particular task each faces. Kandel believed that he could glimpse the light of a new age:

> While the nineteenth century witnessed the cult of the spirit of nationalism in a sinister direction as the main-spring of prejudice and rivalry between national groups, the dawn of a new era appears to be in sight in which another concept, based on a desire for self-expression and self-determination, may be evolved and directed toward international co-operation and good-will. (Kandel, 1933, p. 5)

But the Great Depression and the concomitant political tensions forced him to make this assertion:

33

The nineteenth-century concept of nationalism has by no means disappeared and the high hopes of a new era of world peace and brotherhood which were entertained after the close of the War have proved illusory; there is, indeed, no lack of evidence of the introduction into schools of the worst forms of nationalism of the last century. (Kandel, 1933, p. 864)

With regard to Germany, Kandel fully acknowledged the many new theories of education and the considerable number of practical innovations, which together constituted "a complete departure from the absolutism which characterized German education before the War." (Kandel, 1933, p. 154) When time came to draw the balance, though, he arrived at a conclusion still more skeptical than that of Carl H. Becker two years before.

The great danger which today menaces German education is that the high ideal, which was set for it in the Constitution (Article 148), that it should be conducted "in the spirit of German national character and of international conciliation"—*Bildung zum Deutschtum und Bildung zur Humanität*—may be thwarted by conditions imposed upon the country by forces over which it has no control. A nation driven in on itself, with its future mortgaged for several generations to external powers, and without hope, torn by internal dissension, can hardly be expected to cultivate an educational ideal based on aspirations of friendship and peace within and without. (Kandel, 1933, pp. 154–155)[57]

The opinion he expressed was confirmed by the events which immediately followed the appearance of his work.

Kandel refrained from making any direct comparison between Germany and the United States. However, his final sentence on the educational system of his own country bears witness to American self-confidence. At the same time, it shows to what extent the prospects of education in the two countries already differed at the beginning of the new year, 1933. In Germany, Hitler stood *ante portas*; in the United States, Franklin D. Roosevelt, with the New Deal as his program, had been elected to the presidency in November 1932. Kandel stressed the importance of child-oriented public education and of a policy of social welfare as fundamental to a democratic community. Where such policies affect more than just the school system, they could, he concedes, be criticized as socialist, and makes the rejoinder:

Such criticism will have to be confronted with the fact that, in providing free education for all "from the gutter to the university," the United

States set an example of socialistic legislation which has not yet been matched by any other country in the world. (Kandel, 1933, p. 206)

However, in discussing reciprocal educational influence between the United States and Germany during the Weimar period, one must avoid giving the impression that at that time Dewey's philosophy of education already offered a common basis for both modern American education and German reformist educational theory. For Kandel—as for Dewey—education was part of the community's effort to integrate children, adolescents, and adults into society and also a means for shaping society and giving it stability. In contrast, German reformist educational theory, even when it invoked Dewey and took over his methods of instruction, proclaimed education's independence from society. This theory sought to transplant to Germany educational ideals oriented to the individual, i.e., an orientation in which children and adolescents are given their own space, their own 'Lebensraum', distinctly separate from the daily affairs of society and politics. There they were to be taught national ideals and social virtues and prepared for life in the 'Volksgemeinschaft', the community formed by the German nation.[58] In light of the two countries' different historical experience, social structures, and hopes for their political futures, the agreement in educational matters suggested by the invocation of John Dewey's name on both sides of the Atlantic proves to be more apparent than real. The difference between the United States and Germany with regard to the dominant philosophy of education in each country might be one of the reasons why, of the educational theorists advocating reform who emigrated from Germany after 1933, only a very small number chose to go to the United States.

1.7. Alienation between the United States and Nazi Germany in science, scholarship, and education from 1933 to 1945

The accession to power in Germany of the National Socialists on January 30, 1933, gave a new direction to German-American relations in the sphere of science, scholarship, and education. The destruction of the intellect in Germany extended from the burning of "subversive" books in May 1933, to the mistreatment and expulsion of intellectuals, including those who were "non-Aryan" or who were out of favor with the new government. It included the murder of political and "racial" opponents who remained in the country and

35

cast its shadow over all intellectual, scientific, and educational relations between Germany and the United States. We shall examine this process more closely, for it had a significant effect on the United States through the stream of refugees who fled before its ravages.

In contrast, the "normal" relations between the two countries need to be discussed only briefly. Germany brought itself into a state of "cultural isolation" (Rust, 1965, p. 109). Neither the German activities in the fields of science, scholarship, and education, which increasingly were placed at the service of Nazi propaganda, nor the ever more critical observations by American authors, made before a backdrop of anti-German public sentiment, can be considered as "mutual interaction" in the usual sense. Their peculiarity stemmed from the fact that former economic, political, and military competition had taken place within a singularly broad cultural frame, while now this competition extended into a conflict between two opposing cultural systems. In each country, education was a central ingredient, and copying became anathema. In this respect articles, pamphlets, and books attacking education in the other country, to which we refer later, are interesting but cannot be dealt with extensively.

Even after the Nazi take-over in Germany, American university professors and students continued to come there on scientific and scholarly exchanges and to pursue their studies. In addition, they were interested in the dramatic political changes that were taking place. Only with the passage of years did Germany become less attractive to most such Americans. Similarly, visits by Germans to the United States were continued after January 1933, but these, too, declined in number as German-American cultural relations became more strained (see Table 1.1).

Although the German Academic Exchange Service continued its activity (see the statistics given previously, pp. 23 f.), it soon came into conflict about political matters and about the scope of its authority. Conflicts arose with older and newly established ministries of the Reich government, and especially with the powerful organization of university students. In the aftermath of the events of June 30, 1934, the day on which Hitler bloodily settled accounts with some conservative opponents, Adolf Morsbach, the Catholic director of the German Academic Exchange Service and a member of an informal group of young conservatives, was arrested and replaced by a member of the National Socialist Party.

Increasingly, the Exchange Service became an instrument of cultural and political propaganda. As a consequence, relations between the Exchange Service and the International Institute of Education became increasingly problematic as the former attempted to bring the selection and supervision of grant-holders in the United States under its own direction and control.[59] Finally, contrary to the express wish of the International Institute of Education, the German Academic Exchange Service opened its own office in New York City in the middle of 1938 under the name German University Service. Barely six months later, the State Department ordered that this office be closed on suspicion of espionage. The director of the German University Service had called upon German exchange students to make note in their reports of their professors' political attitudes. In all likelihood, he was working for the German intelligence service (Laitenberger, 1976, pp. 125 ff.).

The Amerika-Institut in Berlin also continued its activity of documentation, collecting information and giving advice. To the extent that the few extant records pertaining to the Amerika-Institut permit reconstruction of this period, its behavior during this time exhibits an adaptation to the political situation that was characteristic of many organizations. As a rule, the Institut neither crassly stressed the National Socialist ideology in its dealings with foreigners, for that might have impressed them unfavorably or frightened them away; nor did its members allow foreigners to perceive clearly their own critical attitude toward National Socialism. Such an attitude might have endangered individuals, the Institut, or the accomplishment of the Institut's objectives. Thus it was possible to give a certain plausibility to an idea which respected American universities such as Harvard strove to make reality: International academic intercourse was to be kept free of political influences. Occasionally this policy of adapting to the situation proved successful—whether such "success" was advantageous on the long run, is an open question.

Apart from a few reports written by émigrés, the development of the German university system during this time appears to have been critically examined in the United States only in a book published by E. K. Hartshorne in 1937. The specific development of "National Socialist science and scholarship" and its intellectual contribution to the Holocaust was investigated in a study by Max Weinreich that appeared shortly after the war, in 1946.[60]

After they had come to power, the Nazis declared that, with regard to primary and secondary education and to educational theory, their goal was to "build the German school anew in accordance with the National Socialist 'Weltanschauung'." Proponents of international collaboration in education were condemned to silence; persons in important positions whose loyalty to the new order was doubtful were replaced (see Notes 45, 46, 47, 50, 51). The henceforth *German* Central Institute for Education became an "instrument for the forming of National Socialists." Relations between Germany and the United States in matters of education, science, and scholarship in which this institute had served as intermediary shrank to the point of insignificance.

In the name of the single valid 'Weltanschauung', the number of learned journals in Germany was severely restricted. Publication of the *Internationale Zeitschrift für Erziehungswissenschaft* (International Education Review) was carried on with new German editors and under an altered title (see Note 52). In general, the task of this journal was to continue observation of developments in education abroad, and particularly in the United States. According to Bernd Zymek (1975, Table 2d; see Note 58), almost all the articles on American topics which appeared in German journals between 1934 and 1944 were published in this review. Notwithstanding the Nazi commitment of the German editors, the journal aimed to have its opinions respected internationally. Remarkably, one issue of this review, published on the occasion of the 100th anniversary of the birth of William T. Harris in 1935, was devoted to the influence of this Hegelian on social life and philosophy in the United States. Also in this review, Eduard Baumgarten discussed Dewey's critical study of German idealism in three articles which appeared in 1936 and 1937 (see Note 29).

As educational relations with other countries were limited and subjected to as much centralized control as possible, comparative education withered away as a subject at German universities. V. D. Rust has established that the University of Hamburg was practically the only place where lectures were still given on foreign educational systems and educational theory, the focal point of which was "colonial pedagogy." The reason?: The German Reich was expected to someday recover its lost colonies.

After January 1933, the positive American interest in educational theory and politics of Germany that had developed during the Weimar Republic at a few institutions like the Teachers College at Columbia University and at Peabody College gave way to a critical observation of the events in Germany. Obviously, in Germany the effort to achieve understanding, exchange, and friendly relations with other nations on the basis of democratic social institutions gave away overnight to authoritarianism, to a racist ideology, and to nationalist hybris. Works of I. L. Kandel (published in 1935), Harold Taylor (1935), C. H. Bason (1937), J. Dambach (1937), Alind M.

Lindgren's study for the U.S. Office of Education (1938), and particularly the thorough study by George Frederick Kneller (1941-1942) — all these give evidence of the horrified effort to understand and find defenses against the threatening developments in Germany.[61] In 1938, Erika Mann, Thomas Mann's daughter, published a book with the unequivocal title, *School for Barbarians: Education under the Nazis*.[62]

As far as is known, visits by Germans during the period in question and publications like Theodor Wilhelm and Gerhard Graefe's pro-Nazi information booklet, *German Education Today*, published by the German Academic Exchange Service, did not call forth the intended positive reaction in the United States. Wilhelm was editor of the *Internationale Zeitschrift für Erziehung* and a department head in the German Academic Exchange Service, in which Graefe also had a post.

1.8. The immigration of German-speaking academics and its impact on science, scholarship, and education in the United States from 1933 to 1945

In the two centuries of its existence, the United States has grown culturally and socially from the vast numbers of emigrants from other countries. They have contributed, in turn, to the development of the greatness, wealth, and might of their new home. Until the First World War, the United States offered refugees from persecution, almost without exception, safety, freedom, and the opportunity to make a new start.[63]

However, no persecution had ever attained the proportions or erupted so brutally in the midst of the "civilized world" as that conducted by National Socialism. However, those who wanted to flee from it to the United States found themselves facing a different situation from that before the First World War. Because of the isolationist mood that had arisen in the United States, as well as for economic reasons, immigration had been limited since the end of the war to definite quotas for each country of origin. The size of the quota depended on the status accorded to the country in question.

In addition, applicants for permanent residence permits had to prove that their income was secured through employment or private financial guarantees. The difficulty for immigrants was acute, since the American middle class, even at liberal arts colleges and universities, was not free from anti-Semitism, and since immigration rules in the years 1930–1937 were especially restrictive as a result of the economic crisis. In these circumstances, the practical help necessary to overcome the barriers to immigration increased only slowly, in terms of finding jobs and financial support. But persecution increased. The burning of synagogues and the pogroms of November 1938 were particularly alarming. As the flood of immigrants grew, American willingness to smooth the way increased. Moral outrage over anti-Semitic excesses in Germany and the expulsion of "non-Aryans" helped to overcome the virulent anti-Semitism at many academic institutions in the United States. In this context, it is fortunate that academics, researchers, writers, and clerics—people expected to make a special contribution to education, science and, scholarship—could be admitted outside the normal immigration quotas. Moreover, the economic crisis of the 1930s was followed by an expansion of American higher education, thereby bringing new job opportunities for university teachers. The Emergency Committee in Aid of German (later Foreign) Displaced Scholars was particularly important in its role as facilitator. The activities of this committee began as early as May 1933, under the direction of Edward R. Murrow and Duggan of the International Institute of Education. The former was replaced by Betty Drury in 1935. The Committee continued its activities until 1945.

In retrospect, the immigration of academics, researchers, and other intellectuals between 1933 and 1945 is rightly appreciated as an important stimulus for the development of American science, learning, and art. But at the time, it was extremely hard for the people affected, with the exception of a few who were famous, to collect the necessary papers, obtain a visa, leave all or part of their belongings behind, and travel to the New World to find new roots. Like most other immigrants during this period, only a few had considered emigration prior to Hitler's rule. Many reports and autobiographies bear witness, in contrasting ways, of the needs and the help received, of the bitterness of exile and the satisfaction about a new beginning, of grief at losses and the formation of new, positive bonds. Immigrants achieved an existence between two cultures with varying degrees of success, generally dependent on personal circumstances, such as the age at which the immigrant had to make the unwanted transition from one culture to the other.

At first the refugees came from Germany, but with the expansion of Hitler's rule, they also came from Austria, German-speaking parts of Czechoslovakia, and finally from other European countries. For the period from 1933 to 1945, their number (including families) is

40

estimated to be 280,000. Over 220,000 are likely to have been "non-Aryans," i.e., people describing themselves as Jews (approximately 132,000) and persons of Jewish or partly Jewish origin.[64] By contrast, the number of refugees who left Germany "only" because they were political opponents of the regime, was small. This group consisted primarily of neo-Marxists, social democrats, and left-wing liberals. The number of academics —persons having completed a university education — among the immigrants from Germany and Austria is estimated to be just below 8,000 (excluding members of their families).[65] The number of refugees who reached the United States only after the end of the war is not known. All available evidence suggests that the number of those who returned to Germany permanently is small, especially among the intellectuals.

University-educated immigrants have made important contributions to the development, expansion, and improvement of many areas of cultural life in the United States. Science and scholarship received a significant stimulus, primarily in university teaching and research. The number of university teachers and scientists who had practised their profession before they emigrated was about 1,000.[66] This appears small when compared to the numbers quoted above and to the total number of American teachers in higher education at the time. But many were outstanding in their own field. A few statistics illustrate this: Twelve recipients of the Nobel prize found refuge in the United States. The 1944/1945 edition of *Who's Who* contains the names of 103 refugees. The 1944 edition of *American Men of Science* contains 220 formerly German scientists.[67] Thus, at a time of increasing impact of science on modern living, American universities gained people of world renown and many other well-qualified academics. The newcomers, in turn, helped to make particular institutes and universities into institutions of world renown, helping to attract students and researchers from other parts of the world. For example, when Albert Einstein moved to Princeton, the French physicist Paul Langevin is reported to have said:

> It's as important an event, as would be the transfer of the Vatican from Rome to the New World. The Pope of Physics has moved and the United States will now become the center of the natural sciences.[68]

Even if no other immigrant is accorded the same fame or the same influence as Albert Einstein, there are nevertheless important exponents of many disciplines who had a seminal influence on their subject area.[69] For an adequate appreciation of the work of many

41

specialists, we refer to the extensive literature available.[70] To attempt such an appreciation here would be presumptuous and go beyond the framework of this essay.

Immigrants forced to leave Europe arrived hoping to continue their academic work wherever the opportunity existed. This was significantly easier for those who were already established and known in their discipline as well as for those with professional contacts in the United States before 1933. With their knowledge, their methods, their way of teaching, the immigrants penetrated the American system of teaching and research, and contributed to the rise in the standard of American academic work. But, taking social science as an example, Rainer M. Lepsius has demonstrated how academic opportunities for immigrants were dependent on the standard of the institution at which they worked and on the scope of the position they were given. This applied to liberal arts colleges as well as to graduate schools. (See Note 66.)

There were some attempts to manage the problem of immigration by creating new academic institutions. These attempts differed greatly among themselves. Five examples can be considered here.

First there was the Institute for Advanced Studies at Princeton, already mentioned above. After attracting Einstein, Abraham Flexner, the head of the Institute, succeeded in creating a section for mathematics and physics, which included positions for other important immigrants. Thereafter a section for political economics, headed by Otto Nathan from Berlin, and then a section for humanities and art, headed by the archaeologist Ernst Herzfeld from Berlin and the art historian Erwin Panofsky from Hamburg, were formed. During the postwar period, the Institute gave many immigrant academics an opportunity to find their footing in the New World in congenial surroundings. At the same time it gave an important stimulus to the American system of science and higher education.

Alvin Johnson adapted the New School for Social Research, founded in 1919 as a liberal/progressive institute for adult education, into an institution to serve the integration of immigrant scholars through shared political and social convictions, and to make their work productive and effective.[71] As early as the summer of 1933, Johnson expanded the school by adding a Graduate Faculty of Political and Social Science. He created a "university in exile" whose staff in the early years consisted almost exclusively of German left-liberal immigrants concerned with social problems. In the fall of 1933 he started with 10 professors; three years later, there were 20. Characteristically, a number of them came from academic institutions whose aims were related to those of the New School. They were:

Hochschule für Politik (Academy of Political Science), Berlin;

Akademie der Arbeit (Academy of Labor), Frankfort;

Berufspädagogisches Institut (Institute for Vocational Education), Cologne;

Büro für Sozialpolitik (Academy for Social Policy), Berlin.

Those working at the New School included the economists Emil Lederer from Berlin, Gerhard Colm from Kiel, and Eduard Heimann from Hamburg; the sociologists Carl Mayer from Frankfort and Hans Speier from Berlin; and the psychologist Max Wertheimer from Frankfort.

While Princeton became more international through its integration into American scientific activity, the New School did remain a "German university in exile" for a long time. A significant reason for this marginal situation was that the institution provided an opportunity for its social scientists to avoid a reassessment of their own sociocultural background in disciplines which are closely tied to national culture.

Paul Lazarsfeld, on the contrary, did manage to make an impact on social research by working in association with existing institutions without giving up his independence. His Bureau of Social Research, in which no single political conviction was dominant, started in Princeton with support from the Rockefeller Foundation, and became a part of Columbia University in 1939. Since then, several generations of social researchers have been trained there.

A genuine institution in exile was the Institut für Sozialforschung (Institute for Social Research), of neo-Marxist outlook, which came from Frankfort University and was eventually attached to Columbia University. It is well-known for its extensive empirical research on the authoritarian personality.[72] Under the direction of Max Horkheimer and Theodor W. Adorno, it returned to Frankfort after the war. Certain individual members of the Institute, including Leo Lowenthal and Herbert Marcuse, remained in the States.

Robert M. Hutchins, president of the University of Chicago, followed an ideal of science and scholarship which was diametrically opposed to that of the New School for Social Research in his policy of employing new staff. He aimed at a university committed to the ideal of a humanist education modelled on the German tradition. He was against the usual high-school-like curriculum and instead envisaged general studies based on classical philosophy and other fundamental texts, to which the outstanding members of the graduate schools should contribute. To paraphrase Ringer (see Note 40), Hutchins' attitude fitted in well with that of many German mandarins. He employed a relatively large number of politically conservative immigrants, without fear of the criticism that he was creating an excessive and therefore unwelcome concentration of immigrants. Teachers in Chicago included Hannah Arendt (political science), Friedrich A. von Hayek (economics), Erich von Kahler (philosophy), Ulrich Middeldorf (history of art), Hans J. Morgenthau (political science), Max Rheinstein (law), Leo Strauss (political science), Eric Voegelin (political science), and Joachim Wach (religious studies).

In line with Hutchins' conservative views on university reform, a study group on German questions at the University of Chicago wrote a memorandum in October 1947, commenting on the "Report of the U.S. Education Mission to Germany." The memorandum was written by thirteen prominent immigrant professors, all of whom had passed through German schools before 1933. It rejected the American view that the tripartite German school system should be replaced by comprehensive schools of utilitarian outlook. Instead, it advocated an elitist system of education based on the ideology of the classical Gymnasium, with corresponding curricula and divisions in the school system. The signatories include a number of professors who returned to the Federal Republic of Germany after 1945, among them Arnold Bergsträsser (German cultural history), Hans Rothfels (modern history), Otto von Simson (history of art).[73]

Franz Neumann provides a comprehensive assessment of the impact of immigration reflecting the diversity of the various institutional initiatives for the reception of the immigrants, including those primarily helping individuals with their new life and work, and those primarily interested in attracting scholars for their scientific achievements and future contributions to teaching and research. In 1936, Neumann came to the Institute for Social Research from the Hochschule für Politik (Academy of Political Science) in Frankfort, via the London School of Economics. After the war he became professor of political science at Columbia University. In 1952, he wrote:

> It is quite impossible to assess the contribution of the German exile to the social and political sciences. The character of the Nazi regime caused — as I stressed — the emigration of scholars of radically different orientation, political and theoretical. Thus there is no comparison possible with the flight of Greek scholars from the Byzantine Empire in the fifteenth century. The extraordinary diversity of European refugee scholars makes it virtually impossible to determine their contributions

made to social and political science — in contrast to those in the natural sciences and, perhaps, in contrast to certain specialized historical and philosophical contributions such as art history, literary history, etc., the influences are too subtle, too diffused, to be easy identified or measured. (Neumann, 1977, p. 23)

Neumann's assessment is even more true in the field of education and school research that is of particular importance in the context of this essay. First, it should be noted that relatively few teachers and educationists emigrated to the USA, for three reasons:

1. Throughout the world, school systems are not as international in outlook as universities. Cultural as well as administrative difficulties impede a person's move from one system to the other. Although the number of teachers and school administrators in Germany was large, they had much less knowledge of foreign languages and foreign countries than university teachers, and far fewer international contacts that could be activated after 1933. As a rule, teachers thinking of emigrating were faced with the problem that the transfer to another educational system, assuming it succeeded, would require a high degree of adaptation, even to the point of total assimilation.

2. German Gymnasium teachers were overwhelmingly nationalist and conservative in their outlook. Even those who were interested in reform did not generally think in the liberal-democratic terms of progressive American education, but rather in socialist terms (see Section 1.6). Teachers in the Volksschule were more in favor of the Social Democratic Party. As political persecution increased, they were attracted to similar political camps in neighboring European countries, quite apart from the fact that access to these countries was much easier and cheaper. On the whole, it is likely that dismissal and persecution on political rather than racial grounds were relatively more widespread among teachers and school administrators than among university teachers, since Jews were less strongly represented in the school system.

3. The number of genuine educational theorists at German universities in 1933 was very small compared with other subject areas.[74] Here, too, advocates of reform were more in tune with idealist concepts of education than with education for democracy in the American sense. Few of them lost their posts under the National Socialists, and fewer still found their way to the United States.

There is more evidence of dismissal, persecution, and emigration to the United States in the fringe areas of educational activity, such as youth aid, social work, etc., as well as in the corresponding university departments, including child psychology. Here Jews were more strongly represented. As these activities were largely outside the organized mainstream of the education system, it was easier for individual immigrants to have an impact in the United States. A few managed to integrate their backgrounds with the new tasks they faced, and thus made original scientific contributions.

It is impossible to make a concise statement summarizing the work and influence in the United States of the whole group of immigrants from German education. As a group, even its most prominent members have not yet been treated in the literature and we can refer only to an extensive note listing names and fields of activity.[75]

1.9. Outlook

On May 8, 1945, Nazi rule and the German Reich were brought to an end. The area that was left of Germany was divided and occupied by the Allies. The Western Allies' zones of occupation were soon amalgamated into a single economic unit. In 1949 this became the new, sovereign Federal Republic of Germany. Similarily, the Soviet Union allowed its Eastern zone of occupation to evolve into the German Democratic Republic later in the same year. The latter moved so far outside the realm of German-American cooperation and interaction that a treatment of East German events is not attempted, neither here nor in the rest of this book.

In their own zone of occupation, the Americans made an early attempt at "reeducation," a thorough reform of schools and universities. A number of German refugees took an active part in reeducation. But the program was short-lived and foundered even before the establishment of the Federal Republic of Germany. American policies regarding Germany changed with the beginning of the Cold War. On the one hand, all thought of radical measures to change the socioeconomic and cultural structure was set aside. Instead, West Germany was given aid for physical reconstruction, so that it could rapidly become a strong and reliable ally in the confrontation with the Soviet Union. On the other hand, it became clear that without altering basic socioeconomic patterns, it was not possible to refashion the structures rooted in a country's cultural tradition according to foreign ideas, especially over a short period of time. Such external interference also ran counter to the ideals of liberal democracy and self-determination. Moreover, Germany lacked a sufficient number of suitable school teachers, university faculty, and administrators who could have undertaken reeducation efforts. Thus, in practice, schools and universities soon reverted to the structures and curricula which had been in use before 1933, with the exception of subjects directly affected by recent history. Education in the Federal Republic was set on its way, as described in the following chapters.

Since 1949, communication between the United States and the Federal Republic has increased beyond all expectations in education, in the sciences, the liberal arts, and all fields of scholarly research. To the extent that it can be measured statistically, Tables 1.1 and 1.2 (pp. 24 and 48), provide some evidence. After a period when German participation in international exchange had first been limited and then during the war nonexistent, new opportunities for study and information-gathering visits to the United States enabled Germans to acquaint themselves with the American way of life, democracy, and politics, and to take home the latest scientific and educational ideas and practices. This provided an important stimulus for social and political life in the Federal Republic, as it did for education, science, and scholarship there. American private and government organizations promoted these visits and funded them generously. From the beginning, they were concerned to help intellectual recovery and the rebuilding of schools, universities, and research institutions in the Federal Republic. This included the promotion of visits to Germany by American educationists, scholars, and administrators. Increasingly, immigrants took part in the visits, although the majority of them did not return to Germany permanently. Over the years, German institutions took part in organizing visits and meetings and in providing the necessary funds. In the years after about 1960, contacts intensified gradually and a normal international exchange developed. This has led primarily to each nation's reception of scientific ideas, discoveries, and methods from the other country. It has also been a stimulus for some experiments in school activities and curricula, especially in the Federal Republic. Further, developments in the mass media and the emergence of hitherto unknown levels of mass travel extended the dimensions of mutual exchange beyond the individual level, which had formerly been so important.

These developments ought to be studied in their own right, especially with regard to evaluating how much has been achieved beyond the immediate postwar need to become familiar with developments to which access was barred during the Nazi period and the war. Which of the more recent trends in education and scientific research in the United States have had a lasting impact on the

47

Table 1.2: German-American Exchanges in Education and Science, 1954 and 1978/79 (as Compiled by the Fulbright Commission)

Category	1954	1978/79
	German nationals in the US	
Students	759[1]	3,200
Professors/research scholars	} 48[2]	480
Teachers		30
Medical interns/residents	323	80
High school students	226[3]	880
Trainees	133[4]	330[4]
Total	1,489	4,970
	US nationals in the FRG[5]	
Students	778[6]	3,620[7]
Professors/research scholars	58	500
Teachers[8]	53	55
High school students	(?)[9]	220
Trainees	(20)[10]	320
Total	909	4,550

[1] Including holders of immigrant visa (appr. 30 %).

[2] Author has doubts on reliability of information: not included in 1954 statistics were scholars at independent research institutes; according to US experts, in 1954 probably between 80 and 120 German post-doctoral fellows were working in the US.

[3] "Teenage exchange" included high school students and other groups (4-H programs, youth leaders).

[4] Mainly short-term.

[5] In some cases including Canadians.

[6] Figure for 1955.

[7] Including 250 students in independent (non-integrated) Study Abroad Programs.

[8] Including language assistance at German secondary schools.

[9] No reliable data available; the estimates were below 15.

[10] Mainly working for US relief organizations.

Source: Littmann, U.: German-American Exchanges. A Report on Facts and Developments. Bonn: Fulbright-Kommission 1980, p. 6.

Federal Republic, what impacts — if any — can be discerned in
the opposite direction on the United States? How have the two
cultures' perceptions of each other evolved? Which of these cross-
influences could be viewed as a spreading and strengthening of a
modern international culture? At least with regard to the Federal
Republic, some of these issues will be touched upon in the chapters
that follow.

Two developments lend topical significance to such questions of
reciprocal influences:

1. Due to their age, most German emigrants to the United States
of both generations have gradually been leaving the scene; with them
a group has disappeared which was of crucial importance to mutual
understanding between the two nations. Despite the increasing current
contacts between the two countries, there is some concern that this
group's empathic mediation between the two cultures and peoples,
in a sense a living example of *Weltbürgertum*, will not be maintained
with equal commitment when they are gone.

2. The seriousness of this concern is evident against the background of growing international tensions, which force both the United
States and the Federal Republic to define their respective political
interests openly and explicitly. This raises the question of whether
the base of mutual understanding and trust is strong enough to
permit the elaboration of mutually agreed-upon strategies for action
or, if the need arises, to endure political conflict and divergence. Or
will the extreme danger facing the world of today force us all into
creating effective new concepts of democracy and sources of political
strength which surpass national borders? These questions point to
most urgent tasks for education and research in the United States
and the Federal Republic, and throughout the world.

Notes to Chapter 1

1. In his autobiography, G. Stanley Hall describes the readily apparent
change in attitude on the part of the Germans after the war against France.
He had observed the entrance of the victorious Prussian troops into Berlin:

> Most impressive of all, however, was the formal entrance of the army
> through the Brandenburger Thor when they came home crowned with
> victory, the Kaiser, von Moltke, and Bismarck leading. There could
> hardly be greater excitement. Every one was ecstatic. It was, indeed, a
> crucial moment for the Fatherland, for then it received a new soul, and
> the great transition from culture to Kultur, which has since brought her
> to grief, if not then actually begun, was accelerated greatly. The change,

too, was marked and instantaneous. Every Prussian seemed to stand more erect, was less 'gemütlich', and less respectful to foreigners, as one noted even in asking the way upon the street, for a new self-consciousness was born that day in the heart of every German. (Hall, *Life and Confessions of a Psychologist* (New York: Arno Press, 1977, (reprint of 1924 ed.), p. 195.)

Christian von Krockow gives a similar description of the rapid change of mood that occurred at the time of the German Reich's founding. He quotes the German historian Heinrich von Sybel, who wrote after the announcement of Paris' capitulation to the Germans in January 1871:

My eyes always return to the special edition of the newspaper, and tears flow down my cheeks. How have I earned God's blessing, to be permitted to witness such great and powerful things? And how will we live thereafter? What was for 20 years the object of all my wishing and striving has now become reality in such an infinitely glorious manner. Where shall I in my advanced years find another purpose for the rest of my life? (Krockow, *Scheiterhaufen: Grösse und Elend des deutschen Geistes* (Berlin: Severin & Siedler, 1983, p. 65).

The change in attitude on the part of the Americans has been characterized indirectly by Carl Diehl, who speaks of the American students who attended German universities before 1870 as "Innocents Abroad" (Diehl, 1978, p. 50), making use of the title of Mark Twain's well-known description of "the grand tour of Europe," which appeared in 1869.

2. In 1855, out of loose gatherings of American students in Göttingen emerged a formal fraternity somewhat modeled after a German 'Burschenschaft'. The group kept a chronicle that provides a glimpse of the lives of Americans in Göttingen beyond that covered by records of the university. (Buchloh, P.G., and W. T. Rix, *American Colony of Göttingen: Historical and Other Data Collected between the Years 1855 and 1888* (Göttingen: Vandenhoeck & Ruprecht, 1976).

3. See the lecture by J. A. Walz, *German Influence in American Education and Culture* (Philadelphia: Carl Schurz Memorial Foundation, 1936). Walz limits himself to the 19th century and is informative in this respect.

4. Henry Adams, *The Education of Henry Adams: An Autobiography* (Boston: Houghton Mifflin, 1918) pp. 61 ff. Nicholas Murray Butler (1862–1947) writes in a similar vein of his first impressions as a student in Berlin during the winter of 1884–1885. He was later a frequent visitor to Germany. As Columbia University's energetic president, as well as a prominent politician and member of the Republican Party, he became an important promoter of scientific and scholarly exchange between the United States and Germany. (See Butler. *Across the Busy Years: Recollections and Reflections*, Vol. 1 (New York: Charles Scribner's Sons, 1939), pp. 114–129).

5. J. M. Hart, *German Universities: A Narrative of Personal Experience together with Recent Statistical Information* (New York: Putnam, 1874).

6. Compare the list of selected names in Thwing, 1928, pp. 43 ff. and 78 ff. The immigration of scientists and scholars, as well as the university education of Americans in Germany can be researched with the aid of C.

A. Elliott, *Biographic Dictionary of American Science: The Seventeenth through the Nineteenth Centuries* (Westport, Conn.: Greenwood Press, 1979).

7. According to Diehl, 1978, pp. 52 ff. In addition to the enrolled students, a considerable number attended as registered visitors ('Gasthörer') or were not registered at all.

8. Königlich Preussisches Statistisches Landesamt in Berlin (ed.), *Statistik der Landesuniversitäten für das Studienjahr Ostern 1911/12* (Berlin: Verlag des Königlichen Statistischen Landesamtes, 1913), (Preussische Statistik, H. 236), p. 66; R. Schairer, *Die Studenten im internationalen Kulturleben: Beiträge zur Frage des Studiums in fremdem Lande* (Münster: Aschendorffsche Verlagsbuchhandlung, 1927), pp. 20 ff.

9. Königlich Preussisches Statistisches Landesamt, 1913, p. 53 (see Note 8 above).

10. Schairer, 1927, p. 28 (see Note 8 above).

11. Brocke, B. von "Hochschul- und Wissenschaftspolitik in Preussen und im Deutschen Kaiserreich 1882–1907: Das 'System Althoff'" in P. Baumgart, (ed.) *Bildungspolitik in Preussen zur Zeit des Kaiserreichs* (Stuttgart: Klett-Cotta, 1980), pp. 9–118; K. Düwell, "Science and Technology in American-German Interchange, 1880–1980" (manuscript, 1982).

12. One of the promoters of the Amerika-Institut (the foundation of which was also actively supported by the former President, Theodore Roosevelt) was Hugo Münsterberg. He supported Althoff's cultural political initiative, because, as he wrote in a letter to Friedrich Schmidt-Ott of the Prussian Department of Education and Culture on September 17, 1910:

the influence of German intellectual work upon the American universities, which are developing with incomparable speed, is in frightening decline.

As a Harvard Exchange professor he took it upon him to serve as a director and manager of the institute during its first year. The institute assumed the role of a center for documentation and information about the United States; it arranged for scientific connections and literary exchange. Soon it gained an importance in terms of Kulturpolitik which went beyond the academic realm, and in due course it was used as an instrument for German propaganda — especially during the Nazi period. (See Christian H. Freitag, *"Die Entwicklung der Amerikastudien in Berlin bis 1945."* Berlin: Dissertation, Freie Universität Berlin, 1977; M. Hale, Jr., *Human Science and Social Order: Hugo Münsterberg and the Origins of Applied Psychology* (Philadelphia: Temple University Press, 1980), pp. 164 ff.)

13. The founding of the Amerika-Institut in Berlin, as well as the academic exchange between Germany and the United States, was made possible largely through Jewish foundations, those established by Leopold Koppel in Germany and by James Speyer in the United States. In spite of this, the German and American academics, F. Althoff and N. M. Butler, who ultimately selected the participants in the exchange carried on a delicate correspondence. It was agreed that at most a few isolated Jewish professors of German origin —such as Hugo Münsterberg, the psychologist at Harvard, and Felix Adler, in social and political studies at Columbia — would be sent from the United States to Germany, and that on the whole the American professors chosen

would be confined to "native-born American stock." The exchange system was not, as the faculty members at the University of Berlin feared, "to fall into the hands of an international brotherhood." H. S. Wechsler, *The Qualified Student: A History of Selective College Admission in America* (New York: John Wiley & Sons, 1977), pp. 141 ff. and 179–180.

One should add to Wechsler's account that Münsterberg, a reliable German nationalist, is likely to have been found much less objectionable than Felix Adler (born in 1851 in Germany; emigrated to the United States in 1857). Adler was a radical whose strong position on social ethics was suspected of being socialist and pacifist. According to Friedrich Wilhelm Foerster, a visit by Adler to Berlin in 1894 led to the founding of the German Society for Ethical Culture. In view of these activities, the faculty of the University of Berlin, as well as the Prussian Department of Education, had reservations about his appointment. F. W. Foerster, *Programm einer Lebensarbeit* (Freiburg: Herder, 1961), p. 85.

14. Charles W. Eliot, "The New Education." *The Atlantic Monthly*, Vol. 23, 1869, p. 214.

15. H. J. Braun and W. Weber, "Ingenieurwissenschaft und Gesellschaftspolitik: Das Wirken von Franz Reuleaux". in R. Rürup, (ed.) *Wissenschaft und Gesellschaft: Beiträge zur Geschichte der Technischen Universität Berlin 1879–1979, Festschrift zum hundertjährigen Gründungsjubiläum der Technischen Universität.* Vol. 1 (Berlin: Springer, 1979), pp. 285–300.

16. H. Ebert and K. Hausen, "Georg Schlesinger und die Rationalisierungsbewegung in Deutschland." in R. Rürup (ed.), 1979, pp. 318–334 (see Note 15 above).

17. A. von Zahn-Harnack, *Adolf von Harnack* (Berlin: Hans Bott Verlag, 1936), p. 381.

18. Quoted from Emerson's *English Traits* (1856), which attracted new attention around the turn of the century; after P. Rühlmann, *Parteien, Staat, Schule: Zusammenhänge zwischen Imperialismus und Schulpolitik,* (Berlin: Gerdes & Hödel, 1905), pp. 21 ff. and footnote 10.

19. Memorandum: A. von Harnack, "Ew. Kaiserliche und Königliche Majestät . . . ." Denkschrift, Berlin, 21. November 1909, p. 6 (printed manuscript, Archives of the Max Planck Society).

20. Von Harnack points to the important physiologist Jacques Loeb (1859–1924), who went to Chicago in 1892 and later to Berkeley. He does not mention that Loeb was little known in 1892 and as a Jew had limited chances for an academic career in Germany.

21. Von Harnack, 1909, p. 8. (see Note 19 above).

22. "According to the 1910 census, close to 8.3 million persons considered Germany as their land of origin; 2.5 million of these were born in Germany, 4 million were born in the United States of German parents, and the rest had one German parent." H. W. Gatzke, *Germany and the United States: A "Special Relationship"?* (Cambridge, Mass.: Harvard University Press, 1980), p. 58.

23. C. Grieder and S. Romine, *American Education: An Introduction to the Teaching Profession* (New York: Ronald Press Co., 1965), p. 183.

24. Deutsches Pädagogisches Zentralinstitut (ed.), *Gedenkschrift zum 100. Todestag von Friedrich Froebel am 21. Juni 1952.* (Berlin: Volk & Wissen, Volkseigener Verlag, 1952), p. 43.

25. "Der Vorstellungskreis der Berliner Kinder beim Eintritt in die Schule." in *Berlin und seine Entwicklung: Städtisches Jahrbuch für Volkswirtschaft und Statistik*, Vol. 4 (Berlin: 1870), pp. 59–76; G. Stanley Hall, "The Contents of Children's Minds," *Princeton Review*, Jan.-June 1883, pp. 249–272.

26. Thus the further development of the kindergarten as a part of basic education went beyond Froebel's ideas of free play and working with simple materials. The kindergarten was consciously made into a place where children practice observing and learning from facts found both in nature and in their social environment. In this form, as a preschool kindergarten, it was brought back to Germany in the 1960's through German-American collaboration. (see N. Hoenisch, et al., *Vorschulkinder* (Stuttgart: Klett, 1969)

27. According to Bernd Zymek (1975; Tables 2a–2e), from 1871 to 1899 there appeared 41 articles on education in the United States, and from 1900 to 1918, 70 such articles.

28. Theodor Wilhelm, *Die Pädagogik Kerschensteiners: Vermächtnis und Verhängnis* (Stuttgart: J. B. Metzlersche Verlagsbuchhandlung, 1957), p. 54.

29. Some of Kerschensteiner's work appeared in the United States in English translations between 1911 and 1915. For his educational philosophy, see Ringer, 1969, pp. 369–374 and 408–409. Dewey's *The School and Society* (1899) was published in German in 1905. In contrast, his *Democracy and Education* (1916) became available in German only in 1930; Kilpatrick's presentation of the project method (first published in 1918) appeared in German in 1935; and other translations of Dewey's educational writing were not published in Germany until after the Second World War. The first attempt to communicate the basics of his philosophy was made by the philosopher and sociologist Eduard Baumgarten (1898–1982) in the second of his two books on *Die Grundlagen des amerikanischen Gemeinwesens* (1936 and 1938). From 1923 to 1928, he had been an exchange student and then assistant professor at the University of Wisconsin in Madison. However, on the whole, Dewey's extensive work has found only a belated and limited reception in the Federal Republic. (See F. Bohnsack, *Erziehung zur Demokratie: John Deweys Pädagogik und ihre Bedeutung für die Reform unserer Schule* (Ravensburg: O. Maier, 1976).

30. Theodor Wilhelm diligently shows Dewey's influence on Kerschensteiner (Wilhelm *Die Pädagogik Kerschensteiners, Vermächtnis und Verhängnis* (Stuttgart: J. B. Metzlersche Verlagsbuchhandlung, 1957). Kerschensteiner himself always acknowledged:

You have no need to fear that Dewey might be able to ensnare me with his pragmatism . . . . But I owe to Dewey much clarity in other matters, in almost everything which I myself wanted, and toward which I instinctively strove. (Georg Kerschensteiner to Eduard Spranger, March 21, 1915. In: G. Kerschensteiner and E. Spranger, *Briefwechsel 1912–1931*.) (München: R. Oldenbourg Verlag, 1966), p. 34.)

31. See Gatzke, 1980, pp. 52 ff. (see Note 22 above).

32. Dewey's reference to anti-Semitism reminds one that in Germany anti-Semitism was displayed openly and proliferated rapidly after the first enthusiasm of belligerent euphoria receded and as the burden of sacrifices incurred by war grew. Jews were suspected not to be serving in the military

according to their demographic proportion. Therefore, in October 1916, the war department ordered Jewish soldiers in the army to be counted. The result was published only in 1922; the suspicion proved to be unjustified. (See W. Jochmann, "Die Ausbreitung des Antisemitismus," in W. E. Mosse (ed.) *Deutsches Judentum in Krieg und Revolution, 1916–1923* (Tübingen: J.C.B. Mohr (P. Siebeck), 1971, Wissenschaftliche Abhandlungen des Leo Baeck Instituts, Vol. 25), pp. 421 ff.

33. Professor Eugen Kühnemann (1868–1946, University of Breslau), who was one of the early exchange professors and who traveled widely in the United States, wrote in his memoirs in 1937:

> In my own way, as a servant of the German spirit, I articulate here the meaning of the great turning in Germany's history, profoundly thankful and happy that I have been able to live to see this natural conclusion of my whole life's work.
>
> By bringing a *Volk* to follow him in his movement, Hitler made himself the master of the ultimate, primordial power needed to build any state. To those who followed him, the movement was home, fatherland, religion, and church. This enabled him to overcome all divisions that still stood in the way of the development of the unitary German state. (E. Kühnemann. *Mit unbefangener Stirn: Mein Lebensbuch* (Heilbronn: E. Salzer, 1937), p. 311.)

Another analysis by an American philosopher comparable with that given by Dewey is George Santayana's *Egotism in German Philosophy* (this work first appeared in 1915; in 1939 it was republished with a postscript; in 1968 a further edition was published under the title *The German Mind: A Philosophical Diagnosis* (New York: Thomas Y. Crowell, 1968). More recently Frederic Lilge has inquired into the historical background of German philosophy in his book *The Abuse of Learning: The Failure of the German University* 1st ed. 1948, 2nd ed. 1975 (New York: Octagon Books, 1975). Lilge criticizes Dewey's interpretation of Kant's work and of the effects it had on German philosophy (see pp. 158–162). The most recent work of German self-criticism is the book by Christian von Krockow (1983) (See Note 1 above).

34. For quotations and further source references pertinent to this topic, see von Krockow, 1983 (see Note 1 above).

35. Barth, Karl "Universitätslehrer — eine Gefahr? Briefwechsel zwischen Erich von Holst, Heidelberg, und Karl Barth, Basel." *Göttinger Universitäts-Zeitung*, Vol. 2, No. 15 (1946/47), p. 3.

36. The Department of Foreign Affairs was, moreover, restricted in its Kulturpolitik, just as it is today in the Federal Republic, by the fact that the making of educational policy was essentially a matter for the individual 'Länder'. This greatly limited the extent to which there could be a single representative cultural policy for the entire German Reich.

To increase its efficiency, Becker attempted to subsume Kulturpolitik under the authority of the central government of the German Reich, but to no avail. For him, Kulturpolitik was supposed not only to present German culture and accomplishments in international forums, but also to add to social and educational integration within Germany. His reference to American policy may be questionable:

> *Kulturpolitik is the conscious employment of spiritual values in the service of the people and of the state to* achieve *internal* consolidation and strength for *external* competition and struggle with other peoples. What have the Americans not done to hammer the idea of America into the variegated mishmash of their immigrants! They have created a new people [ein neues Volk] with a victorious idea. (C. H. Becker, *Kulturpolitische Aufgaben des Reichs* (Leipzig: Quelle & Meyer, 1919), p. 13.)

37. For details, such as distribution across the disciplines, see Laitenberger, 1976. A corresponding exchange was carried out from the American side by philanthropical organizations such as the Carnegie and Rockefeller Foundations. The extent to which they furthered scientific and scholarly exchanges between the United States and Germany has yet to be studied.

38. For a more detailed treatment of the Berlin Academy of Political Science see Peter Gay, "Weimar Culture: The Outsider as Insider." In D. Fleming and B. Bailyn *The Intellectual Migration: Europe and America, 1930-1960* (Cambridge, Mass.: Harvard University Press, 1969), pp. 43 ff.; an enlarged version of this essay was published as a book under the same title (London: Secker & Warburg, 1969).

39. Abraham Flexner, *Universities: American, English, German* (London: Oxford University Press, 1930), p. 360.

40. For the conservative concepts of education and culture see Ringer, 1969, mentioned above, particularly the chapters on "The Origins of the Cultural Crisis," pp. 253-304, and "The Crisis of Learning at Its Height," pp. 367-434.

41. Until 1920 the German school system was tripartite; it consisted of three parallel branches everywhere in the country, but with differences among the individual Länder in organizational particulars. To give a simplified overview, there were three types of school, all beginning with the first grade and each independent of the other two : the 'Volksschule' (grades 1 through 6, 7, or 8); the 'Mittelschule' (grades 1 through 8 or 9); and higher-level schools, including the 'Gymnasium', which prepared pupils for university study (grades 1 through 12, with differing emphases in their curricula). In many places, private instruction or private schools were provided at the 'primary level' (grades 1 through 3) as preparation for entry into a higher-level school.

From 1920 on, at the same time that the remnants of ecclesiastical school supervision were being eliminated, school regulations were established that had some degree of uniformity. Through the Reich Law on the Primary School, the 'Grundschule', attended by all pupils in the first through fourth grades, was established as an integral part of the Volksschule. The one restriction on the otherwise identical structure of all schools of this kind was that the law allowed for 'Bekenntnisschulen', i.e., separate schools for children from Lutheran and Catholic families. Other public or private forms of education at this level were almost entirely eliminated. Only for the Volksschule were parents not required to pay tuition. Pupils who were not to remain in the Volksschule could transfer to a 'Realschule' or a Gymnasium (see Chapters 8 and 9) only after completing the Grundschule. Not until 1964 were the Volksschulen divided into Grundschulen and 'Hauptschulen' (see Chapters 5 and 7). During the Weimar period the 'Reichsbund entschiedener Schulreformer' argued for the 'Einheitsschule' (common school).

42. Von Harnack stressed that the excellence of the humanistic disciplines in Germany was the foundation of its reputation abroad, and for that reason he advocated early instruction in Latin and hence retaining of the humanistic Gymnasium emphasizing classical antiquity (p. 705). His statements are characteristic of the conference's predominantly conservative mood.

Kerschensteiner noted the advantages of the shorter school hours in the United States and the value of the requirement that pupils repeat only the particular subject areas in which they failed, instead of a full school year. He also called attention to the course system in the American high school, which made possible the special promotion of technical training (pp. 125, 1017, etc.).

Rein, who had traveled in the United States in 1904, was critical of the elective system (p. 704) which was advocated by the radical school reformer Paul Oestreich (p. 704; see also note 49). A practical effect of previous German-American contacts appears most noticeably in the introductory report for the Committee on Pupils. With reference to the selection of students for the different occupations, the committee referred to the Taylor system and to Hugo Münsterberg's program of 'psycho-technics' for determining occupational aptitude as aids to the teacher in judging pupils. This, however, needed to be developed further (pp. 209 f). On the whole, however, remarks pertaining to education in the United States were so marginal that a perceptible influence of American experience and ideas on the results of the National Conference on Primary and Secondary Education cannot be claimed.

(All quotations from Reichsministerium des Innern: *Die Reichsschulkonferenz 1920: Ihre Vorgeschichte und Vorbereitung und ihre Verhandlungen.* (Glashütten im Taunus: Detlev Auvermann, 1972), reprint of 1921 ed.; also Rust, 1965, p. 63.)

43. Zentralinstitut für Erziehung und Unterricht (ed.) *Das deutsche Schulwesen: Jahrbuch 1930/32* (Berlin: E. S. Mittler & Sohn, 1933), pp. 125–266; especially pp. 255 f.

44. Once more reference is made to Ringer, 1969.

45. Franz Hilker (1881–1969) began as a teacher at a 'Realgymnasium'. After the First World War he was one of the founders of the League of Radical School Reformers. In 1923 he became a senior school inspector; from 1925 to 1933 he was a department head in the Central Institute for Education, and finally its director. In 1933 he was transferred out of this post. After the end of the war in 1945, he was active in the school system in Hesse and for a time president of the German section of the New Education Fellowship.

46. Erich Hylla (1887–1976) started out as a school teacher. He was discharged from the Department of Education and Culture in 1933 because he was considered politically unreliable. From 1935 to 1938 he was guest professsor for comparative education at Columbia and Cornell Universities. He returned to Germany prior to the outbreak of the war. From 1946 to 1951 he was German consultant to the Education Department of the U.S.

High Commissioner. In 1951 he established the Academy (later the German Institute) of International Educational Research, Frankfort. He also devoted himself intensively to school-related psychological research, drawing upon findings and theories from the United States.

47. Sebald Schwarz, "Was ist für uns in Amerika zu lernen?" and "Die Schulfahrt des Zentralinstituts nach Nordamerika." *Deutsches Philologenblatt*, Vol. 36 (1928), pp. 630 ff. and p. 556, respectively. Schwarz (1866–1934) worked toward the establishment of a comprehensive school for the intermediate grades (corresponding to American junior high school). Schwarz, a democrat though not a socialist, was forbidden to exercise his official functions by the National Socialists immediately after they seized power. On March 31, 1933, he was retired.

48. The following information has been compiled from the dissertation of Rust (1965, pp. 76–85), which also provided information for Section 1.6.

49. Peter Petersen (1884–1952), Rein's successor in Jena, was a German educational theorist with strong interests in the educational procedures of other countries. He was probably one of the most widely traveled German educationists of the interwar period. When he taught at George Peabody College in the summer of 1928, he set up an experimental class based on his views of educational organization, the so-called *Jena Plan*. In 1935 in a series of translations of foreign educational theorists, which had the support of the Central Institute for Education, he published a collection of essays by John Dewey and W. H. Kilpatrick, *Der Projektplan: Grundlegung und Praxis.* Petersen advocated a philosophy of education which had as its goal communitary education, and which was based on modern empirical research in the educational domain. His objective was "internal school reform," i.e., new forms of instruction and freer interaction between teachers and pupils in a 'general Volksschule', a school in which the members lived together as a community. Petersen doubtless found many elements in the American school system and in Dewey's philosophy of education with which he agreed and which stimulated him in his own work. For Dewey and Kilpatrick he had these words of praise:

In the realm of ideas, as well as practically, they prepared the way for the final act of liberation from Europe; indeed, they themselves energetically helped to effect this liberation. (Dewey and Kilpatrick, 1935, p. 212)

It is interesting to see how Petersen transformed American educational experience and philosophy when applying it to Germany. His thought and decisions might be characteristic of many ordinary German citizens as well as intellectuals during that time. On New Year's Day, 1935, he wrote in the postscript to the translation mentioned above:

In New England . . . the people continued to be responsible for the schools, and after the Declaration of Independence, freedom . . . really proved itself to be salutory in the United States. Thus there could arise here, even more purely than on European soil, a school system that is truly "Germanic" in character, free, and founded on the community of a 'Volksgemeinschaft' [a people united by language, culture, and race].

57

For it would be a total misunderstanding of the word "democratization" to think it referred to the forms of European democracy; it must be translated into German as 'Volksgemeinschaft' with precisely that meaning which we give this word today. (Dewey and Kilpatrick, 1935, p. 207)

Like other reform-minded educational theorists, Petersen did not think in political terms. For him the educational sphere was autonomous. In contrast to Dewey's position on this matter, he maintained that the content and forms of education should not be determined in relation to society. Petersen considered the school as a kind of preserve, sheltered from politics. Yet the quotation given above raises a few questions. Was Petersen so apolitical, did he understand Dewey so little, that he could seriously mean what he wrote? Did he want to ingratiate himself with the new regime? Did he understand the National Socialist ideology to be consistent with his own philosophy of education? Or did he want to make both the 'Weltanschauung' of German fascism and Dewey's theory consistent with his own ideas? Or did he use these catchwords only as camouflage, in order to publish in Nazi Germany a translation of writings by a passionate champion of Western democracy? The only literature he refers to is the noncontroversial book by G. Kartzke, *Das amerikanische Schulwesen* (The American School System) (Leipzig: Quelle & Meyer, 1928). He makes no mention of the significant and more outspoken work of Hylla, *Die Schule der Demokratie* (1928), who was removed from the Prussian Department of Education and Culture in 1933 (see Note 46).

Petersen retained his professorship during the Nazi period, although the experimental school linked with his Department had to be closed. In 1945, after the war, he became Dean of the newly established school of social education at the University of Jena, now in the Soviet zone of occupation. His experimental school resumed its activity. However, according to an indignant letter of December 27, 1945, written by the radical school reformer Paul Oestreich (1878–1959, a socialist, 1933–1945 discharged from school service and temporarily under arrest) Peter Petersen seems to have got along with the Nazis quite well. (Paul Oestreich: "Eine Anfrage an Herrn Professor Peter Petersen in Jena" with an introduction by H. König. In: Jahrbuch für Erziehungs- und Schulgeschichte. Volk und Wissen, Volkseigener Verlag, Berlin 1978, pp. 133–138). In 1950 the experimental school was closed, because it was "a politically dangerous island of capitalist pedagogy." W. Kosse, "Peter Petersen und sein Werk." *Pädagogische Rundschau*, Vol. 17 (1963), p. 700.

50. Friedrich Schneider (1881–1974) started his career as a Volksschule teacher. Beginning in 1923, he taught educational philosophy at the University of Cologne and the Teachers Training College in Bonn. He reports that his visit to the United States in 1928 was "of particular importance for his work as a researcher and teacher." F. Schneider, *Ein halbes Jahrhundert erlebter und mitgestalteter Erziehungswissenschaft* (Paderborn: F. Schöningh, 1970), pp. 17–23. In 1934 he was forced to retire from his post in Bonn; and in 1940 he was forbidden to teach at the University of Cologne. Schneider succeeded, however, as late as 1943, in publishing a book with the expedient title, *Geltung und Einfluss der deutschen Pädagogik im Ausland*

(Recognition and Influence of German Educational Philosophy Abroad) (Munich: Oldenbourg, 1943). In the foreword to this work, Schneider speaks of "German leadership and the victory march of German educational philosophy through the cultured nations of the world" (p. viii). Aside from such instances of sententiousness and exaggeration, the book offers a relatively thorough report, based upon the American literature, of the value of Pestalozzi, Froebel, Herbart, and Kerschensteiner, as well as of the German universities for education in the United States up to the 1920's. After the Second World War, Schneider taught first in Salzburg and then in Munich. He is considered the founder of the comparative study of education in Germany.

51. Fritz Karsen (1885–1951) began his career as a Gymnasium teacher. In 1919–1920 he was a cofounder of the League of Radical School Reformers. From 1921 until February 1933, he was the principal of the Kaiser Friedrich Realgymnasium in Berlin (renamed the Karl Marx Schule in 1930), a comprehensive school intended to serve as an experimental model. Study trips and guest lectures — such as those he gave at George Peabody College in Nashville, Tennessee, in 1927 — took him to many countries. In February 1933, he was removed from all his posts, left Germany, and went to Switzerland, France, and Colombia before entering the United States in 1938. There he taught at Brooklyn College and City College in New York City. From 1946 to 1948 he was Chief of Higher Education and Teachers Training in the Office of Military Government, U.S. Army (OMGUS), in Berlin. He died while on a mission for UNESCO in Ecuador (See G. Radde, *Fritz Karsen, Ein Berliner Schulreformer der Weimarer Zeit* (Berlin: Colloquium Verlag, 1973).

52. Publication of the journal continued with the overt political backing of National Socialist editors from 1935 to 1944. However, the term "Wissenschaft" was dropped from the German title, thus becoming the *Internationale Zeitschrift für Erziehung*. American coeditorship was preserved: Paul Monroe until 1937; Isaak Doughton until 1940. Schneider did not acknowledge this continuation: from 1947 to 1951 he edited the journal under its original title simply starting with Vol. 4.

53. Carl H. Becker, "School and Society," *Educational Review*, Vol. 32, No. 830 (1930), pp. 679 f.

54. Becker, 1930, p. 681 (see Note 53 above).

55. Becker, 1930, p. 687 (see Note 53 above).

56. Isaac Leon Kandel (1881–1965) studied with Wilhelm Rein at Jena in 1907. Kandel was Professor of Education and Associate in the International Institute of the Teachers College at Columbia University in New York City. He authored *Comparative Education* (1933) and *The Making of Nazis* (1935; reprint Westport, Conn.: Greenwood Press, 1970).

57. Article 148 of the Weimar Constitution says: "im Geiste des Volkstums und der Völkerversöhnung." The translation "in the spirit of German national character and of international conciliation" does not measure up to the specific German connotation of 'Volkstum' and 'Völkerversöhnung'. 'Volkstum' comprises common descent, language, and cultural heritage of a people. 'Völkerversöhnung' wants a conciliatory meeting between people representing different kinds of 'Volkstum'.

58. See, in this regard, Zymek, 1975, Section 4.2, pp. 180 ff.: "Das allgemeine Bewusstsein einer nationalen pädagogischen Reformbewegung." Zymek quotes a statement made in 1926 by the highly respected reformist and advocate of educational autonomy, Minna Specht (1879–1961), who lived outside Germany from 1933 to 1946:

"Neither do I fail to appreciate the dangers which hover above the youth of Russia, nor the clouds that darken the picture of American education. Both are under the dominion of the present ruling class in each country. The humanistic ideal, which under the leadership of von Humboldt formed the basis of German education, has found no official recognition in these countries . . . ." (Zymek, 1975, p. 192)

For a discussion of the relationship of reformist educational philosophy to fascism and of the partial continuation of the former by exiles from Nazi Germany see Hildegard Feidel-Mertz and H. Schnorbach, *Lehrer in der Emigration: Der Verband deutscher Lehreremigranten (1933–39) im Traditionszusammenhang der demokratischen Lehrerbewegung* (Weinheim and Basle: Beltz, 1981); Hildegard Feidel-Mertz, "Schulen im Exil." In *Jahrbuch für Lehrer*, Vol. 6 (Reinbek bei Hamburg: Rowohlt Verlag, 1981), pp. 341–351.

59. According to V. Laitenberger (1976), the International Institute of Education sought to remain loyal to the existing agreements and resisted intervention in its affairs. At the same time it was active in the effort to find posts at colleges and universities for German emigrants. (See Stephen Duggan and Betty Drury *The Rescue of Science and Learning* (New York: Macmillan, 1948).

60. Max Weinreich *Hitler's Professors: The Part of Scholarship in Germany's Crimes against the Jewish People* (New York: Yiddish Scientific Institute — YIVO, 1946).

61. I. L. Kandel, *The Making of Nazis* (New York: Teachers College, Columbia University, 1935); Harold Taylor, "German Education in the Republic and in the Third Reich." In Rexford G. Tugwell and Leon H. Keyserling (eds.), *Redirecting Education* (Vol. 2) *Europe and Canada* (New York: Columbia University Press, 1935), pp. 3–50; Thomas Alexander, *Training Elementary Teachers in Germany* (New York: Bureau of Publications, 1936); C. H. Bason, *Study of the Homeland and Civilization in the Elementary Schools of Germany* (New York: Teachers College, Columbia University, 1937); J. Dambach, *Physical Education in Germany* (New York: Teachers College, Columbia University, 1937); Alind M. Lindgren, *Education in Germany* (Washington, D.C.: U.S. Office of Education, 1939. Bulletin No. 15, 1938; George F. Kneller, *The Educational Philosophy of National Socialism* (New Haven: Yale University Press, 1942).

62. Erika Mann, *School for Barbarians* (New York: Modern Age Books, 1938).

63. In 1825, during the period of the Restoration in Europe following the Napoleonic wars, Charles Follen came to the United States from Germany to escape persecution for his political beliefs. A scholar of German literature, Follen became a professor at Harvard. He was followed in 1827 by the political scientist Francis Lieber, whose career ultimately led him to Columbia

University where he became a predecessor of John W. Burgess. In 1841 came Hermann von Holst, a historian of German origin who was born in Russia. After a career filled with vicissitudes, von Holst finally obtained a teaching post in Chicago. The list of names could be extended, for the failure of the bourgeois revolution of 1848 occasioned another wave of emigration by German academics to the United States. Around the turn of the century, anti-Semitic pogroms in Western Russia and bitter poverty in the eastern regions of the Austro-Hungarian Empire brought thousands of Jews to the United States, often after a sojourn in Germany.

For immigration following the German revolution of 1848, see: G. von Skal, *Die Achtundvierziger in Amerika* (Frankfurt am Main: Frankfurter Societäts-Druckerei, 1923); A. E. Zucker (ed.) *The Forty-Eighters: Political Refugees of the German Revolution of 1848* (New York: Russell & Russell, 1950); Carl F. Wittke, *Refugees of Revolution: The German Forty-Eighters in America* (Philadelphia: University of Pennsylvania Press, 1952).

64. See M. R. Davie, *Refugees in America* (New York: Harper, 1947), pp. 21, 37–46; L. W. Holborn, "Deutsche Wissenschaftler in den Vereinigten Staaten in den Jahren nach 1933," in E. Fraenkel, et al. (eds.) *Jahrbuch für Amerikastudien*. Vol. 10 (Heidelberg: Carl Winter Universitätsverlag, 1965), pp. 15 ff; H. A. Strauss, "Einleitung," in W. Röder and H. A. Strauss (eds.) *Biographisches Handbuch der deutschsprachigen Emigration nach 1933*. Vol. 1: *Politik, Wirtschaft, öffentliches Leben* (München, K. G. Saur, 1980), pp. xxix ff.

The figure of 280,000 quoted by Davie and Holborn relates to the period January 1, 1933 to June 30, 1944. The subdivisions, primarily the figure of 132,000 describing themselves as Jews, are based on figures by Strauss relating to the period 1933–1945 (p. xxix). Elsewhere, Strauss mentions 30,000 refugees for political reasons prior to the outbreak of the war (p. xxxviii).

65. See Radio Bremen, *Auszug des Geistes* (Bremen: B. C. Heye, 1962), pp. 16–17; also H. A. Strauss, "Reception and Acculturation of Refugee Intellectual." In H. A. Strauss and W. Röder, (eds.) *International Biographical Dictionary of Central European Emigrés, 1933–1945*, Vol. 2: *Sciences, Arts and Literature* (München: K. G. Saur, forthcoming).

66. In retrospect, it is easy to overlook the fact that those immigrants who only became active in their profession after they entered the United States are usually included among the immigrant scientists and scholars. Lepsius has recently tried to compile all the names of social scientists who emigrated from Germany, Austria, and German-speaking parts of Czechoslovakia. In total, he counted 322 persons, of whom 235 found their way to the United States either directly or indirectly. Of the U.S. immigrants, 20 returned home after 1945. Of the U.S. immigrants, 120 to 130 were too young to have graduated from a university before their arrival. In other words, they were at various stages in their education, but started work only once they were in the United States. Only a few immigrants were retired or about to retire. The immediate effect on the scientific community in the United States is likely to have come from the approximately 100 people in the age group of those actively at work. Only a few of these people are still alive today.

The task of the transatlantic linking of different academic traditions and perspectives has largely fallen on the younger generation born abroad, but immigrants at an early age, like the sociologist Reinhard Bendix (born 1916, today at the University of California at Berkeley) or the political scientist Kurt Shell (born 1920, from United States to Frankfort in 1970). As this generation also retires, a special phase of bilateral academic influences between the United States and German-speaking countries, brought about by the bicultural socialization of relatively large numbers of scholars, will draw to a close. The example of the social sciences is likely to apply similarly to other subject areas.

See M. R. Lepsius, "Die sozialwissenschaftliche Emigration und ihre Folgen," in M. R. Lepsius (ed.) *Soziologie in Deutschland und Österreich 1918–1945* (Opladen: Westdeutscher Verlag, 1981) (Materialien zur Entwicklung, Emigration und Wirkungsgeschichte, Sonderheft 23 der Kölner Zeitschrift für Soziologie und Sozialpsychologie), pp. 461–500 (Appendix: List of Emigrated Social Scientists).

67. Radio Bremen, 1962, pp. 16–17 (see Note 65 above).

68. See R. Jungk, *Brighter than a Thousand Suns* (New York: Harcourt, Brace, 1958), p. 46.

69. A partial list of the distinguished persons in the emigration would include:

Theology and the scientific study of religion: Richard Kroner, Paul Tillich, Joachim Wach.

Philosophy and social philosophy: Theodor W. Adorno, Gustav Bergmann, Ernst Bloch, Rudolf Carnap, Max Horkheimer, Erich von Kahler, Karl Löwith, Herbert Marcuse, Eugen Rosenstock-Huessy.

Classical languages and classical antiquity: Ludwig Edelstein, Hermann Fränkel, Albrecht Goetze, Werner Jäger.

Literature: Erich Auerbach, Alfred Kantorowicz, Leo Lowenthal, Leo Spitzer, Karl Vietor, René Wellek.

History: Hans Baron, Wolfgang Hallgarten, Hajo Holborn, Ernst Kantorowicz, Hans Kohn, Hans Rosenberg, Hans Rothfels, Veit Valentin.

History of art: Otto Benesch, Richard Ettinghausen, Walter Friedländer, Erwin Panofsky, Otto von Simson.

Sinology: Karl Wittfogel.

Law: Arnold Brecht, Hans Kelsen, Max Rheinstein.

Psychology: Egon Brunswik, Else Frenkel-Brunswik, Charlotte and Karl Bühler, Herta Herzog, Marie Jahoda, Kurt Lewin, William Stern, Max Wertheimer.

Psychoanalysis: Bruno Bettelheim, Erik H. Erikson, Erich Fromm, Heinz Hartmann, Wilhelm Reich, Theodor Reik.

Psychiatry: Kurt Goldstein.

Sociology: Hans Gerth, Paul F. Lazarsfeld, Hans Speier, Kurt H. Wolff, Hans Zeisel.

Economics: Peter F. Drucker, William J. Fellner, Gottfried Haberler, Emil Lederer, Adolf Löwe, Fritz Machlup, Jacob Marschak, Ludwig von Mises, Oscar Morgenstern, Hans Staudinger, Gustav Stolper.

Political science: Hannah Arendt, Arnold Bergsträsser, Otto Kirchheimer, Hans J. Morgenthau, Franz Neumann.

Mathematics: Emil Artin, Richard Courant, William Feller, Kurt Gödel, Karl Menger, John von Neumann, Hermann Weyl.
Statistics: Emil Gumbel.
Physics: Hans A. Bethe, Felix Bloch, James Franck, Victor F. Hess, Otto Stern, Eugene Wigner (all Nobel Prize winners).
Chemistry: Peter J. W. Debye (Nobelist).
Biochemistry: Konrad Bloch (Nobelist), Erwin Chargaff, Fritz Lipmann, Otto Meyerhof (Nobelist).
Genetics: Max Delbrück, Curt Stern.
Zoology: Richard Goldschmidt.
Pharmacology: Otto Loewi (Nobelist).
Architecture: Walter Gropius, Ludwig Mies van der Rohe.

70. The literature about emigration from Germany and German-occupied territories in the period from 1933 to 1945 and beyond is quite extensive. In addition to works quoted already, the following publications can be listed (in order of their publication date):

N. Bentwich, *The Rescue and Achievement of Refugee Scholars: The Story of Displaced Scholars and Scientists, 1933–1952* (The Hague: Martinus Nijhoff, 1953).

Franz L. Neumann, et al., *The Cultural Migration: The European Scholar in America* (Philadelphia: University of Pennsylvania Press, 1953; reprint New York: Arno Press, 1977).

H. Pross, *Die deutsche akademische Emigration nach den Vereinigten Staaten, 1933–1941*. Berlin: Duncker & Humblot, 1955.

L. Fermi, *Illustrious Immigrants: The Intellectual Migration from Europe 1930–1941*. Chicago: University of Chicago Press, 1968.

D. Fleming and B. Bailyn (eds.) *The Intellectual Migration: Europe and America 1930–1960* (Cambridge, Mass.: Harvard University Press, 1969). Includes a list of "300 Notable Émigrés" with biographical notes.

J. Radkau, *Die deutsche Emigration in den USA, ihr Einfluss auf die amerikanische Europapolitik 1933–1945* (Düsseldorf: Bertelsmann Universitätsverlag, 1971).

R. Boyers, (ed.) *The Legacy of the German Refugee Intellectuals* (New York: Schocken, 1972).

H. Stuart Hughes, *The Sea Change: The Migration of Social Thought, 1930–1965* (New York: Harper & Row, 1975).

M. Greffrath, *Die Zerstörung einer Zukunft: Gespräche mit emigrierten Sozialwissenschaftlern* (Reinbek bei Hamburg: Rowohlt, 1979, Das neue Buch).

H. A. Strauss, "Jewish Emigration from Germany: Nazi Policies and Jewish Responses," in *Year Book of the Leo Baeck Institute*, Vol. 25 (London: Secker and Warburg, 1980), pp. 313–361; and Vol. 26, 1981, pp. 343–409.

71. Alvin S. Johnson, *Pioneer's Progress: An Autobiography* (New York: Viking, 1952); B. Luckmann, "Eine deutsche Universität im Exil: Die 'Graduate Faculty' der 'New School for Social Research'," in M. R. Lepsius, *Soziologie in Deutschland und Österreich 1918–1945*, pp. 427–441 (see Note 66 above).

72. Theodor W. Adorno, Else Frenkel-Brunswik, D. J. Levinson, and R. N. Sanford: *The Authoritarian Personality* (New York: Harper & Row, 1950).

73. Report of the U.S. Education Mission to Germany, September, 1946 (Washington, D.C.: Department of State, 1946, European Series No. 16), (the so-called "Zook-Report"). The memorandum of the Study Group on German Questions is printed in German in Bayerisches Staatsministerium für Unterricht und Kultus (ed.) *Dokumente zur Schulreform in Bayern* (München. Pflaum, 1952), pp. 146–156.

74. In 1931, there were 2 professors emeriti, 16 professors with and 22 without tenure, 42 other faculty, mainly part-time. (Christian von Ferber, *Die Entwicklung des Lehrkörpers der deutschen Universitäten und Hochschulen 1864–1954* (Göttingen: Vandenhoeck & Ruprecht, 1956); (Untersuchungen zur Lage der deutschen Hochschullehrer, Vol. 3), p. 234.

75. I am grateful to Professor Hildegard Feidel-Mertz of Frankfort University (see Note 58) for permission to use source material from her own research in the selection of the persons listed below in order of date of birth. In the field of education proper, the following deserve mention:

Fritz Karsen (see Note 51);

Robert Ulich (1890–1977), James Bryant Conant Professor of Education, Harvard University;

Wilhelm Gaede, Professor of Education, Brooklyn College, New York.

Among teachers, two leading exponents of the 'Landschulheim' (country boarding school) deserve mention:

Max Bondy (1892–1951), head of Windsor Mount School, Lenox, Massachusetts;

Hans Maeder, founder and head from 1949–1974 of Stockbridge Boarding School, Massachusetts, who admitted black teachers and pupils from the start. Beyond his own school, Maeder was influential in removing racial barriers in boarding schools throughout New England.

The following were active as social philosophers and educationists:

Eugen Rosenstock-Huessy (1888–1973), Professor of Social Philosophy, first at Breslau University, then at Dartmouth College, Hanover, New Hampshire; he was active in training camp leaders for the Civil Conservation Corps;

Walter Friedländer (born 1891), a leading figure in social policy for the city of Berlin, lecturer at the Deutsche Hochschule für Politik (German Academy of Political Science), and then Professor of Social Welfare, University of California at Berkeley;

Hertha Kraus (1897–1968), a leading figure in social policy for the city of Cologne, then Professor at Bryn Mawr College; worked with Russell Sage Foundation and United Nations Relief and Rehabilitation Agency;

Ernst Papanek (1900–1973), social democratic educator and politician in Austria, then Professor of Education at Queens College and the New School for Social Research, active in many children's and youth aid organizations;

Gisela Konopka (born 1910), Professor of Social Work and founder of the Research Center for Development of Youth, University of Minnesota.

Finally, a number of psychologists, psychoanalysts, and psychiatrists deserve mention, whose achievements in their special disciplines are recognized in the literature, but who were also active in the field of education:

Kurt Lewin (1890–1947), Professor of Psychology and Child Development at Cornell University, the University of Iowa, and MIT;

Siegfried Bernfeld (1892–1953), renowned for psychoanalytical research into education, San Francisco;

Curt Bondy (1894–1972), Professor of Psychology, College of William and Mary, Williamsburg, Va.; returned to Germany 1950;

Erik H. Erikson (born 1902), Professor of Human Development, Harvard University;

Bruno Bettelheim (born 1903), Professor of Educational Psychology and Principal of the Sonia Shankman Orthogenic School, University of Chicago;

Else Frenkel-Brunswik (1908–1958), Research Associate at the Institute for Child Welfare, Berkeley, California.

Four other prominent immigrants who found refuge in the United States deserve mention, although they were too old to do much active work after their arrival:

Friedrich Wilhelm Foerster (1869–1966), Educationist and passionate pacifist (see Note 13);

William Stern (1871–1938), former Professor of Philosophy, Psychology and Education, Hamburg University;

Alice Salomon (1872–1948), previously head of the Soziale Frauenschule (Women's College for Social Work) in Berlin, founder of professional social work training in Germany;

Richard Hönigswald (1875–1945), once Professor of Educational Philosophy, Munich University.

Before and After the 'Wirtschaftswunder': Changes in Overall Educational Policies and Their Setting

2.1. A first glance

In the early 1980's the Federal Republic of Germany is clearly embedded in and affected by the overall socioeconomic trends common to most industrialized countries. For some years now, the world economic crisis has curtailed economic growth rates and worsened employment prospects there. All levels of government have accumulated huge debts, and there is growing uncertainty about what economic policies are appropriate and about what role the public sector should play. The renewed heightening of international tensions, especially between the two superpowers, has revived traditional ideological strains of the pre-détente era, while other concerns of more recent origin center on ecological issues and the question of individual self-fulfillment in modern society. A general feeling of uneasiness and uncertainty permeates public life and affects particularly those parts of the public close to the Social Democratic and the Liberal Party, which have dominated political life since the end of the sixties, when they brought to a close the Christian Democratic Party's two decades of ascendancy.

The 'Zeitgeist' certainly does not affect most of the daily routine of the educational system, but it has an impact on medium-term educational trends, partly causing, partly mirroring them. In this chapter we want to draw attention to some overall characteristics of the current state of education in the Federal Republic of Germany, and at the same time to summarize the evolution of some broad political and ideological issues relevant to it.

Figure 2.1 brings out two features of the Federal Republic's educational system which continue to set it apart from those of most other industrialized countries: first, the coexistence of three types of secondary school following a four-year primary level (cf. Chapters 4–9), and, second, the continued importance of a type of vocational education which is partly enterprise-based, partly school-based (the "dual system") (cf. Chapter 11).

Because of the particular mixture of centralized and decentralized educational responsibilities that one finds in the Federal Republic, the structures depicted in Figure 2.1 must be considered as a sort of national average that shows overall characteristics, but does not necessarily correspond to the specific features of the educational system in any of the 11 Länder making up the Federal Republic (cf. Figure 2.2, which shows the distribution of tertiary-level institutions in the Länder). The federal government has a limited and indirect say in education and science policy. In contrast, the governments of the 11 Länder are constitutionally vested with strong responsibilities in this regard, leaving open to the local governments and the individual schools only quite limited possibilities of participation in decision-making (for details cf. Chapter 3). The educational system of the Federal Republic is thus strongly decentralized when one considers it from the standpoint of the federal government, but it is fairly centralized at the level of the individual Länder.

The overwhelming majority of pupils and students attend schools which are both state-financed and state-organized. Privately run institutions, which are usually heavily subsidized from public funds, engage primarily in preschool and vocational education. Almost all German schools continue to be run on a half-day basis (8 a.m.–1 p.m.), leaving little time for "out-of-class" activities. Similarly, tertiary-level institutions were never very close to, and have increasingly diverged from the model of a "campus university" that integrates academic and social life.

The development of certain age-specific enrollment ratios over three decades shown in Figure 4.2 (Chapter 4), together with the structure displayed in Figure 2.1, presents a concise history of the major structural changes of the educational system. The most salient features of these changes are the following:

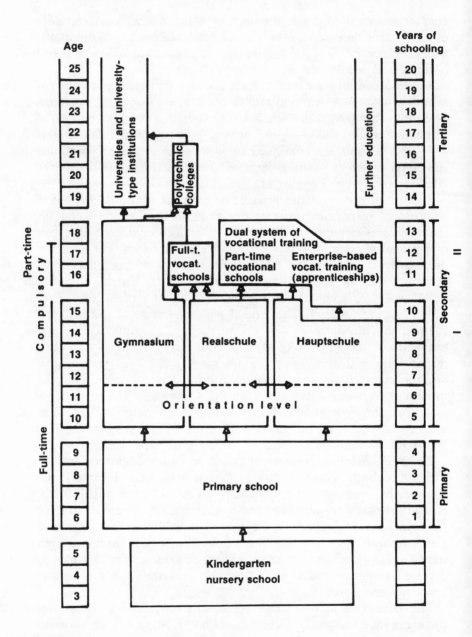

Figure 2.1. Chart of the Educational System in the Federal Republic of Germany, 1980

68

Figure 2.2. Location of Tertiary-Level Institutions in the Länder of the Federal Republic of Germany, 1980

- Taking the situation in the mid-fifties as a standard for comparison, there has been a three- to fourfold increase in enrollment in tertiary education (cf. Chapter 12).
- Partly as a precondition for the growth of tertiary education, there has been a tremendous change in the relative importance of the three types of secondary school. Until the early sixties, the great majority of 13-year-olds attended the Hauptschule, while only a minority of some 15 percent attended the academically oriented Gymnasium, and a still smaller fraction the intermediate level Realschule. Efforts to institutionalize a comprehensive type of secondary school throughout the Federal Republic met with only very limited success, and now, in the early eighties, less than 40 percent of the pertinent age group attend Hauptschulen, while a total of more than 50 percent attend Realschulen and Gymnasien.
- Although the fifties were far from being a completely static period, rapid and continuous structural change clearly began in the mid-sixties and has continued up to the present, losing some of its momentum in the late seventies.

From an international, comparative point of view, this overall pattern is noteworthy for two reasons. First, it shows that the Federal Republic of Germany was a late-comer to the process of change and expansion of secondary and tertiary level education that was typical of most other Western countries, as well as the industrialized socialist countries. Secondly, it shows that the Federal Republic eventually joined what came to be known as the "world educational revolution" of the last decades. So far, however, it has maintained two of its traditionally distinguishing characteristics, namely, the tripartite structure of secondary education and the dual system of vocational training.

The following chapters will describe in more detail the present situation and how it evolved. Here we will limit ourselves to giving a rough sketch of some of the overall ideological reasons why the Federal Republic was late in embarking upon educational reform, to highlighting the modernization push of the sixties and seventies, and to characterizing the current ideological definition of the present situation.

2.2. *Some reasons for the delay in educational change*

Although the fifties were more than merely a period of stagnation and restoration, it is undeniable that rapid and continuous overall change in education started much later in the Federal Republic than elsewhere. In our opinion, the extent of the physical destruction wrought by the war, the generally low living standards in postwar Germany, and the concurrent problems of reorganizing economic and social life are only partial explanations. After all, other continental European states had to face the same or similar problems (particularly the socialist states); nevertheless, they generally started earlier with their efforts to reform and expand secondary and tertiary education than did the Federal Republic, and their reforms transformed the structures of their educational systems in a more telling way.

In our opinion, the delay of educational reform in the Federal Republic of Germany was due to the particular constellation of a number of factors. These varied in nature, but were all related to the national catastrophe wrought by Nazi policies. One factor was the absence in the Federal Republic governmental organization of such legal and administrative structures as are necessary for nationwide implementation of educational policy. But more important were ideological factors that went to make up the general cultural and political climate which developed during the Federal Republic's first decade of existence either as a consequence of, or in reaction to: (a) the totalitarianism and chauvinism of the Nazi regime; (b) the reeducation efforts of the Allied occupying powers after 1945, to the extent that these had been contrary to what had been considered legitimate aspects of cultural tradition and national interests; and (c) the Stalinist policy of the Soviet Union and its German partisans prior to the establishment of the German Democratic Republic in 1949 and for a number of years thereafter.

A further reason for the delay of educational reform may be seen in the fact that in the first years of the Federal Republic there were large reserves of unemployed among both the resident and the refugee populations, and that in the following years there was a continuing influx of highly qualified refugees from the German Democratic Republic. Therefore before the end of the fifties there was no shortage of the educated and trained manpower required by the rapidly expanding West German industry. This large supply of highly qualified manpower meant that one of the main arguments in the international debate on expanding and reforming education was irrelevant for the Federal Republic in its first decade. Another central argument in this debate, namely that education should be made more egalitarian, was invalidated by the already mentioned political climate of the fifties. This climate was so potent that incipient reforms

71

of the structure of secondary education, which had been encouraged, not only by the Soviet Union, but by the Americans and the British in their occupation zones as well, could be undone, while the expressed intention to effect similar reforms that had figured in the early programs of various German political parties yielded to traditionalist views of educational policy.

This turn of events is comprehensible only when considered against its historical background. This background had several components. First, the traditionalism we have spoken of was not monolithic and clearly defined, but was rather an amalgam of different tendencies which nevertheless brought forth common views on some essential features of school and university structures, curriculum content, the status of teachers, and education in general. Second, the strength of this traditionalist policy consisted in the combined pressure exerted by various groups having vested interests in a hierarchically structured educational system. These groups were middle class parents, university and Gymnasium teachers, and employers who insisted on a hierarchical organization of the production process. The strength of educational traditionalism also came from the seemingly unassailable legitimacy of these interests.

Educational traditionalism was legitimated not only by insisting on its contrast to the policies of Nazism which had opposed religion and intellectuality and had been totalitarian in character, but also by the claim that the traditions in question were those of the German nation, or that they were traditions of the Christian West. Underlying these standpoints were normative premises derived, in some instances, from traditionalist views of society, or, in others, from traditional conceptions of an elite culture. Or they were derived from scientific theories according to which intelligence is a biological property determined by heredity and not by social environment and learning.

The third component of the historical background to the victory in the Federal Republic of traditionalist views in educational policy was what happened in the Soviet occupation zone in eastern Germany and, subsequently, in its successor state, the German Democratic Republic. The contradictions among the already mentioned tendencies in the Federal Republic were insignificant when compared with the difference between their shared goals and the educational policies in the eastern part of Germany. Communist ideology and the educational policy informed by it were used in the rest of Germany to make a rather facile political equation of any kind of egalitarian critique of traditional education with Stalinist, and Nazi,

72

attempts to enforce cultural uniformity and political conformism. This equation was the weapon with which earlier proposals for the establishment of comprehensive schools as an alternative to the tripartite secondary school system were defeated. Thus the early years of the Federal Republic cannot be understood without some slight knowledge of what was happening in the other part of Germany at that time.

In the Soviet-occupied zone, which became the German Democratic Republic in late 1949, the Communist conception of how a modern democratic society should be erected became institutionalized under the leadership of the Socialist Unity Party. This party harshly repressed any resistance and both negated and combatted any other kind of political, religious, or philosophical orientation. Educational reform and expansion was, in fact, from the very beginning one of the main thrusts of Communist reconstruction; the others were remolding and controlling the political system, and collectivizing industry and agriculture. Belligerently egalitarian and this-worldly in outlook, this régime took a strong stance against the churches, the bourgeois social strata, and the remnants of the landed aristocracy, the 'Junkers', all of whom it considered obstacles to its efforts to overcome inherited privileges, German nationalism, and racism. In education, the socialist comprehensive school was introduced to overcome the social-, class-, and sex-bias of traditional secondary education, with its tripartite structure; workers' and peasants' pre-university schools were set up to increase university attendance among the formerly underprivileged; a quota-system was institutionalized to assure equality of opportunity for women and the lower social classes; the curriculum was reorganized to stress the sciences and their technological applications and to reinterpret the national cultural heritage from a perspective that stressed the humanistic and socialist tradition of struggle for emancipation.

In the Western zones, the occupying powers—the United States, Great Britain, and France—also intervened in the educational system in a far-reaching way in the immediate postwar years. They attempted to remodel it to a certain degree on the basis of their own national educational systems as part of the overall campaign to de-Nazify and reeducate Germany. But their educational models and philosophies differed from one another, as did, incidentally, the extent of their determination to impose changes that were not really wanted by the Germans.

With the creation of the Federal Republic of Germany early in 1949, a pluralist and decentralized political and sociocultural system was established. Within the context of this system, political and administrative responsibilities were passed over to the Germans. By its very nature, this system did not favor a radical redefinition of the social situation, let alone a streamlined nationwide educational policy. Rather, it gave rise to regionally distinct political cultures, characterized in part by the preponderance in them of ideological traditions reaching back into the Weimar Republic and before, such as those of a politically organized Catholicism, of a liberalism inclined to secularism, and of social democracy. With the exception of openly fascist and, later on, communist orientations, the full ideological spectrum was permitted to participate in public life and bid for public support.

In this context it became possible to reassert "German ways of doing things" in opposition to the previous interference and influence of the foreign powers, which many had considered excessive. In fact, the issue of regaining full sovereignty and self-determination for the German nation in its entirety, and, if possible, within the prewar borders reaching eastward far beyond the borders of the German Democratic Republic, proved to be one of the strongest common bonds between all political factions. Thus, a defensive nationalism, nonimperialist and making no claims to racial supremacy but stressing the existence, the rights, the cultural heritage, and the dignity of the German people as a collectivity, lessened the cleavages between socialist and liberal-capitalist, secularist and religious orientations. It also, however, integrated, so to speak, those hidden undercurrents of political thought still close to the fascist past. Thus, the integrative power of the conception of the German people as bound together by fate, culture, and kinship contributed to a constellation of forces which made criticism of the educational system strongly suspect as a threat to one of the cornerstones of the reconstructed, fragile politicocultural German identity.

In the sixties, some of the salient ideological controversies of the fifties slowly subsided, in part, it appears, as the consequence of a newly found collective self-confidence, in part as a reaction to broader political and economic changes. Old wounds slowly healed and new challenges lay ahead. It was increasingly accepted that the partition of Germany would probably continue for some time, and the success of its economic reconstruction had enabled West Germany to reach or even surpass the highest standards of living its people had ever known. And by that time a fairly high level of mutual trust and understanding had developed between the Federal Republic, on the one hand, and its neighbors and the Western powers on the other,

74

the latter having become the Federal Republic's allies. In addition, the post-Stalin years had eventually brought about a slight easing both of the overall East-West confrontation and in the relationship between socialism/communism and the Christian churches. Slowly, the defensiveness toward both the Communist challenge and the threat of Westernization following the American model subsided and was replaced by a more self-confident attitude towards the future.

2.3. The modernization push of the nineteen-sixties and -seventies

By the end of the fifties, prewar standards of living had been reached again. In the following decade and a half, the Federal Republic succeeded in becoming one of the world's most dynamic and prosperous industrialized states, benefitting from the economic integration of Europe and favorable world economic trends. Politically, the transition from a long succession of federal governments led mainly by the Christian Democratic Union to an era mainly influenced by the Social Democratic Party (since 1969) marked the coming of age of German democracy. Internally, this change served as a spur to various issues and strategies concerned with improving the welfare state; externally, successful efforts were made to complement the political and economic integration of the Federal Republic with Western states by normalizing relations with its socialist neighbors. Thus the Federal Republic benefitted from and at the same time pushed ahead the overall process of East-West détente, the first signs of which had emerged in the sixties and were kept alive in spite of the Warsaw Pact's intervention in Czechoslovakia and the long involvement of the United States in the Vietnam War.

In more abstract terms, the modernization push of the period can be characterized in three dimensions. First, it consisted in stressing and strengthening the social position and the rights of the individual. This renewed emphasis on institutionalized individualism manifested itself in increased sensitivity to issues of equality of opportunity across boundaries of social origin, gender, and religious affiliation (cf. Chapters 4 and 10); a marked turn to a child-centered approach in normative conceptions of parental education and teaching strategies (cf. Chapter 5); efforts to extend associational principles of participation in decision-making in education, industrial relations, and community affairs (cf. Chapter 3); and, finally, changing conceptions of personal relationships and the women's liberation movement.

Secondly, and largely as a complement to the trend toward individual rights and not in contradiction to it, the conception of the state and its legitimate responsibilities and functions was extended. One of the ways this was done was through the general acceptance of planning and forecasting as legitimate activities of the state in its preparation and implementation of policy interventions, which had been largely indirect. With regard to the state's role as a trustee of the "common goods," there were, certainly, substantial differences in the interpretations of this role by the more socialist and the more liberal and conservative parts of the political spectrum. These interpretations differed, for example, with regard to the direction and the speed of educational expansion and reform. Nevertheless, there was broad consensus that there should be active state policies on the federal and the Länder level to further economic growth and to improve the social infrastructure.

Third, socially important value complexes were raised in ideological terms to a level of abstraction and generalization that allowed a further closing of formerly important cleavages, some fundamentalist outbursts of small neo-fascist and nationalist groups in the early sixties and again in the early seventies notwithstanding. The cleavages in question were those between the two important churches (the Roman Catholic and the Lutheran Protestant Churches) on the one hand, and between them and the political forces of traditionally more secularist orientation on the other.

In the sphere of education, this push for modernization found expression in the following ways:

(1) Arguments for overall expansion of education, but especially of higher education, at first stressed the significance of maintaining and improving the Federal Republic's scientific and technological potential vis-à-vis Western and socialist industrial competitors (late fifties/early sixties). These arguments were soon generalized and supplemented by emphasis on the school's role in the socially expanded definition of citizenship. The improvement of equality of opportunity for groups hitherto deprived of their full citizenship in this extended sense (children of workers, Catholics, segments of the rural population, girls) was sought through the introduction of pre-school programs, through extending compulsory education and lobbying for the comprehensive school, and, lastly, through the opening up of the formerly exclusive Realschule, Gymnasium, and university. These efforts to extend membership in the societal community also significantly reduced the stigmatization of handicapped children. On the other hand, it should be borne in mind that up to the middle

of the seventies the reinterpretation and extension of the concept of citizenship were for all practical political purposes concerned only with the ethnically homogeneous German resident population. Because of the Holocaust, and because up to the seventies immigration was negligible, the Federal Republic could avoid the challenge of responding to noticeable ethnic or cultural minorities (cf. Chapter 6).

(2) The stronger emphasis on science and education and on their role in social and economic development affected educational policy and philosophy on two levels. It had indirect effects by changing the traditional impact of the churches and by stirring up again the nature-nurture controversy over the bases of intelligence. With regard to the first effect, it was at this time that the formerly important 'Bekenntnisschulen' virtually disappeared (cf. introduction to Chapter 3). With respect to the second, the emphasis on the roles of science and education eroded the strength of received notions that stressed the organic and genetic bases of intelligence and thereby directly or indirectly legitimized the traditional school structure and, to some extent, curricula. The more direct influence made itself felt in efforts to modernize teacher education, the curricula, and instructional materials, and in a stronger emphasis on specialized instruction in the schools themselves. The overall philosophy behind these changes called for strengthening the cognitive orientation of education by replacing more traditional and diffuse orientations with the contents and procedures of the relevant academic disciplines, in appropriately modified form (cf. 4.10). These efforts encountered great difficulties and were most controversial in those subjects which were not only cognitive but also evaluative and expressive in nature, such as history, social studies, and music.

(3) In a very general sense, modernization implies for both collectivities and individuals a widening of their potential range of action and perception, achieved by the removal of limitations grounded in conceptual or technical traditions. However, for the additional degrees of freedom thus gained a price must be paid in the form of reduced stability and predictability. One prominent social mechanism for mediating the tension between stability and change is constituted by the legal complex, which extends from the Federal Constitutional Court, through the federal and Länder parliaments, to the courts and the legal profession. The function of the legal complex is not only to provide for the routine litigation of conflicts in the framework of existing juridical norms and procedures, but also to link up the more technical aspects of the law with changing ethical conceptions,

new social problems, and the ideological and political responses to them. Its components try to strike a balance between the rights and duties of individuals, on the one hand, and the need for effective collective action on the other. It strives to achieve a delicate balance between controlling the possible arbitrariness of state organs (the spector of Germany's authoritarian past is still much alive) and the possibly unduly particularist claims of the individual. Thus there has been a growing recognition of the need to include education more fully in the legal complex's realm of responsibility and authority (cf. Chapter 3, esp. 3.4). The strong responsibilities of the state in Germany have deep and sturdy historical roots, and education was traditionally one of the domains reserved to the state executive and the state administrative apparatus. These directly structured and controlled education, largely free from the influence of the legal complex.

2.4. Limits to growth and other strains

The oil price shock of 1973 and the ensuing prolonged world economic crisis did not spare the Federal Republic. True, it fared better than many other countries, partly, it seems, due to the flexibility and willingness to cooperate of state authorities, employers, and trade unions. Nevertheless, with real economic growth down over a number of years, unemployment rates rising markedly (at least by German standards), and public debt going up, the growth of various social welfare measures and other publicly financed programs has had to be curtailed since the mid-seventies, and in the early eighties has in some instances actually had to be reduced. In relative terms, education and science were hit hardest by this crisis, since public expenditures for them had skyrocketed in the period from 1960 to about 1975, surpassing by far, both absolutely and relatively, all other categories of public expenditures, such as defense, health, public housing, urban development, transport, and communication. Consequently, in the coming years education and science will have to operate within tight budgetary limits. The real impact of these financial constraints, however, will be softened by the fact that the school-aged population, in contrast to its substantial growth a decade ago, will remain stable at a lower level (cf. Figures 4.3 and 5.2 in Chapters 4 and 5, respectively).

But these are neither the only nor the most important dimensions characterizing the mood and the situation of the Federal Republic in the early eighties. Since the mid-seventies quite profound changes in the overall political climate have taken place, which, although perhaps not caused by the economic crisis, have nonetheless been associated with it and accentuated by it. In part these changes strengthened more traditional ideological positions, and in part they were manifestations of the search for new definitions of the social situation. A somewhat closer look at this political fluidity seems appropriate for two reasons. First, the fluidity might lead to an end of the era of the politically dominant coalition between Social Democrats and Liberals, which symbolized to some extent the drive and the optimism of the modernization push. It can be expected that the search for solutions to the new challenges will proceed along partisan lines, and at the present time it appears that they will have a more seriously disruptive effect on the left of the political spectrum than on the right or the center with their rather successful ability to sell old remedies as new answers. Secondly, and more important, the problems underlying the current state of affairs in the Federal Republic are not confined to this country, but are general throughout the world.

Although our reflections on these problems and challenges are of necessity both general and speculative, we nevertheless want to characterize them in three broad complexes.

First, beneath the current world economic crisis lie strong pressures for major structural changes in the decades ahead. These pressures are exerted by worldwide ecological problems which are intimately linked to both the levels and patterns of production and consumption in the wealthy countries, in the past as well as in the present. These problems are being intensified by the diverse consequences of the world population explosion, which have led to the call from many quarters for a New International Economic Order. Furthermore, the weight of these problems worsens the strains caused by technological innovation, such as the electronic revolution. While parts of the business community are reacting to these pressures positively, seeing in them new investment opportunities and chances for growth, others are calling for protective measures against new competitors and are lobbying for subsidies in the face of shrinking markets. From the trade unions and the ordinary citizens and voters there is, however, the danger of a less balanced response. The general effect of these pressures might be to tip the political scale toward a stronger nationalist and protectionist stance against the dangers to their prosperity posed by old and new economic competitors and by the demands from the poorest nations for increased support and special trade preferences.

Secondly, these worldwide problems seem to interpenetrate in a variety of ways with domestic matters. The social struggle around distribution of the social product in the face of shrinking real economic growth and the struggle about how the costs of economic adaptation will be shared have intensified in recent years and will continue to lead to bitter controversies. All this, however, is taking place against the background of a high standard of living. Some aspects of the crisis and some of the arguments being made are reminiscent of the period of clearly defined class struggle decades ago. But they merge with and are often subordinated to a new brand of reasoning: the transformation of the message of "Global 2000" —sold in great numbers in the Federal Republic—into what could be called the ideology of "Local 2000." The bitterness and even violence of political controversies over local ecological problems, over the need for new life styles, over nuclear policies, etc., is probably due to the fact that for a growing minority these issues transcend the community and even the nation, bearing rather on the human condition in general. Thus for a sizeable and articulate minority of the better-educated, of younger adults and of the middle-aged, the strengthened trend towards individualism has in fact gone hand in hand with acceptance of a more generalized and abstract conception of the "family of man" and of the ensuing obligations and bonds of solidarity. To a certain extent, this implies, of course, an erosion of the traditional presuppositions of legitimacy which provide the foundation for regionally and nationally oriented political parties and governments, even when the latter have been democratically elected.

In sharp contrast to these avant-garde minorities, there has been— especially since the end of the seventies—a small but undeniable resurgence of neo-fascism and, more important, a reassertion in the lower and the middle class of "healthy nationalism," which sometimes borders on xenophobia. The targets of this nationalism are, first and foremost, Turkish workers and their families, and, secondly, "economic refugees." These are mostly dark-skinned Asian and African applicants for political asylum. While the first group has been able to take advantage of Turkey's association with the European Economic Community, the second group tries to benefit from the laws on asylum (extremely liberal up to 1981), originally created in the fifties as a belated compensatory response to the plight of emigrants from Nazi Germany and, at the time, in fact mainly meant to benefit light-skinned, and Christian, refugees from European Communist countries. Rather late in comparison to the United States or the former European colonial powers, the Federal Republic has been confronted only since the mid-seventies with practical and symbolic issues arising out of the need to deal with cultural and ethnic minorities. Attitudes ranged from the minority position that rejects the foreigners, and adheres to a narrow conception of the German community, through a majority advocating immigration controls for and assimilation of the resident foreign population, to another minority that advocates the social inclusion of the foreigners and calls for a "multi-cultural" redefinition of the concept of "national community."

Third and last, the strains currently shaping political life in the Federal Republic take the form of the forces fearing, or declaring the end of, détente, on the one hand, and the Peace Movement on the other. There has been a pronounced return to viewing international events as confrontations which pit the "free world" against "communism." This turn of events is intimately linked to political crises connected with the two complexes outlined above, especially the changed response of the United States to international challenges since 1980. This world view is challenged and combatted by a peace movement which has its bases partly outside the traditional parties and is substantially anchored in the Lutheran and the Roman Catholic Churches, but which has also joined forces with the Old and the New Left and most of the emerging ecological movement. In the early eighties the old slogan, "Make love, not war," which had seemed to wither away at the end of the Vietnam War, is alive and doing well in the Federal Republic.

We believe that the main link between these general phenomena and education in the Federal Republic consists of the rejection of the close link between economic growthmanship and certain narrow interpretations of modernization in the sixties and early seventies. The pendulum has swung back, partly in the form of the seemingly "progressive" discovery of the relevance of Ivan Illich's concept of "deschooling" or of Paulo Freire's stress on political "conscientização", and partly in the German variants of the popular rediscovery of the importance of "value education," on the one hand, and of the instrumental relevance of the "three R's," on the other. Sometimes these reactions to the modernization push of the sixties and seventies are given fundamentalist interpretations. These reject the stronger cognitive orientation which underlay the preceding curriculum reform, as well as efforts to generally expand schooling. The common denominator of these critical perspectives seems, however, to have gained widespread acceptance in the form of a sensitivity to the need for a new equilibrium of cognitive orientations and standards, on the one hand, and expressive/affective and evaluative/moral orientations on the other. As could be expected, attempts to make the conception of such an equilibrium more precise differ greatly from one another, depending, among other things, on which level of the educational system it is intended for.

Empirically speaking, one way this search for a new equilibrium manifests itself is in a renewed emphasis on the multi-dimensionality of teaching and learning that attenuates somewhat the drive towards subject-matter specialization in the school curriculum and disciplinary specialization in teacher training (cf. 7.2.3 and 12.4.1). Certain subjects and fields of activity neglected during the period of reform and modernization now cause concern and are motivating efforts for change. These are sports, music and art, religion and ethics, the problem of "social learning," and the wide field of extracurricular activities, which is particularly underdeveloped in the Federal Republic's schools. Another form the search takes is the public political debate about value education and its ramifications for social studies and history and for the teachers of these subjects. On a somewhat different level, there has been growing interest within the research community in theoretical and empirical work on the sequences and the interdependence of the individual's cognitive, affective, and moral development.

It is an open question whether the social aggregate of these diverse forces will lead to the preponderance in the Federal Republic of regressive political tendencies of populist or neo-fascist character, or whether the cognitive thrust so prominent in the last decades will be complemented by a greater capacity for affective and moral generalization. But these social strains on the fabric of society, and the possible responses to them, are by no means peculiar to the Federal Republic of Germany. They are also to be found in other countries, be they Western or socialist in their political outlook.

CHAPTER 3

The Legacy of the Prussian Enlightenment: The State as Trustee of Education

"Whoever has the schools also has the future; and the Prussian State, for its part, intends to keep its schools." This pronouncement was made in 1850, a short time after the failure of the bourgeois revolution in Germany, by Ferdinand Stiehl, one of the department heads of the Prussian Ministry of Education. His lapidary statement was no more than a condensed formulation of a permanent characteristic of the educational system in Prussia and Germany, in the past as well as in the present: namely, that it is, to a large extent, state-controlled.

It should be made clear from the outset, however, that when we speak here of "state control," we do not mean the federal government in Bonn, but rather the governments of the 11 Länder. Although there were some centralizing tendencies in the Weimar period, and although National Socialism achieved a totalitarian centralism, there was in Imperial Germany, and there is now in the Federal Republic no centralized authority in educational matters. In fact, a Ministry of Education was established in the federal government only in 1969 and has more a coordinating function than decision-making power. State control of the educational system means, then, that the individual Länder have authority in matters pertaining to education.

Their sovereignty in this regard is a consequence of Germany's history. For the territory comprised, formerly, by Imperial Germany and now in part by the Federal Republic was controlled for a very long time by a varying number of independent states. Over the centuries, the major German states, the foremost of which was Prussia, gradually grew in size and in strength at the expense of other parts of the Holy Roman Empire, which ended in 1806, and of some neighboring countries. When the German Reich was created in 1871 by uniting the other German states under Prussia's hegemony, these states remained in many respects politically sovereign. Most of the Länder of the Federal Republic derive indirectly from these states.

The germ of state control of the German educational system lay in state-imposed compulsory school attendance, decreed first by Prussia in 1717. To be sure, the attempt to generally enforce this obligation succeeded in Prussia only toward the end of the 19th century. Compulsory school attendance was in the interest of the modern, absolutist state: it was to this state's advantage to establish the school as a state institution for disciplining the population and for strengthening the Christian religion, which provided the ideological foundation and safeguard for the state's dominion. However, the state's interest in this matter met with resistance from many quarters, most of all from the landed nobility in the hierarchically organized feudal society. The nobles had no reason to want either educated subjects and workers or intervention by the state that would also burden them financially.

In addition, from the middle of the 19th century on, other parties with an interest in education entered the arena with greater strength. It was against the efforts of these contenders—the churches, the communities, the teachers, and the parents—that the Prussian state wanted "to keep its schools." The churches in question were the Catholic and the Lutheran Churches, Germany's two dominant denominations. As far as the relationship of these churches to the state was concerned, there is little point in trying to distinguish between state and church administration of the schools in the first half of the 19th century, and even less point in looking for opposition by the churches to the state; the ecclesiastical administrations were part of the state administrative apparatus, although in a somewhat modified form in Catholic regions of predominantly Protestant states such as Prussia, and vice versa in Catholic states such as Bavaria. In this capacity they were commissioned to administer the state schools and later to superintend the community-sponsored schools. Only from the beginning of the 19th century on did the state build up, alongside its ecclesiastical administrative apparatus, its own school administration which gradually reduced the importance of the church school administration and displaced it.

Through the revolutionary events of 1848 and the Prussian Constitution of 1850, the ecclesiastical authorities gained a greater degree of independence from the state; they continued however, to have responsibility for the local superintendence of schools. The churches denied that superintending the schools was a privilege granted them by the state, and claimed that it was, rather, their traditional right. But after the founding of the German Reich, when Bismarck waged his 'Kulturkampf' to diminish the influence of the Catholic Church, the state once again made it clear that the schools belonged to it, and that the churches, specifically their local clergy, were merely commissioned by the state to superintend the schools. Only during the Weimar Republic, in 1919, was this local school superintendence by the clergy finally eliminated. A further point of contention was the question of whether the Volksschulen, state schools which provided basic education, should be 'Bekenntnisschulen'. These were also state schools, but were, at the least, characterized by the fact that most teachers and pupils of a particular school belonged to the same church. At the most, but rarely, instruction in these schools was penetrated by the creed of the church in question. The controversy was not easily settled. There were 'Bekenntnisschulen' in Prussia until the 1930's, in Bavaria and Baden-Württemberg into the 1960's, while in North Rhine-Westphalia at the present time more than one third of the pupils in the primary level attend such schools.

In addition to the churches, the cities and the rural communities also demanded more influence on the schools located in them. They were not content merely to administer the "external" school affairs, in accordance with the municipal directive issued by the Prussian government in 1808. In other words, they wanted to do more than construct and maintain buildings and appoint and pay teachers. They wanted to also have a hand in those "internal" matters which the state had reserved for itself, from the teaching guidelines, through the organization of instruction and the certification of pupils, to the training of teachers. Points of contention were local residents' demands for the transfer of local school superintendence in the cities and towns to school inspectors appointed by the municipal councils, and the state's demand for strict adherence to the teaching guidelines, the general regulative instructions laid down by the state. Furthermore, beginning in the second half of the 19th century, many municipalities undertook to extend their school systems. In so doing they brought into being the secondary sector of the school system and indirectly were able to wield considerable influence in questions of instruction and moral discipline. However, in the Prussian Constitution of 1850, the Weimar Constitution of 1919, and the Federal Republic's Basic Law of 1949, the tradition of the 'Obrigkeitsstaat', the state as the seat of centralized authority, succeeded in large measure in restricting the administration of schools by the cities and communities to the limits set in 1808. The communities, now as in the past, have immediate responsibility only for the noncurricular, "external" aspects of school affairs, in spite of the fact that their indirect influence has increased.

Third, and last, teachers as well as parents spoke up against the state domination of the school system. The teachers demanded, within a framework of state control, the internal administration of the schools and recognition of the special characteristics of the pedagogical enterprise and its institutions. The parents claimed the right of codetermination in fundamental questions of education (e.g., the choice between the 'Bekenntnisschule' and the community schools having a general Christian orientation, between the comprehensive school and the tripartite school system, etc.) and recognition of their conceptions of moral discipline and the implementation of their preferences in this regard. Whereas the teachers were able to increase their autonomy in pedagogical matters at the beginning of the 1920's and again at the start of the 1970's without having to call into question the principle of state control of the educational system, most of the claims of the parents were in the end rejected by the state.

In spite of the prolonged efforts of the churches and the communities, in spite of teachers and parents, state control of the German educational system was reestablished even after the Second World War, in both East and West Germany. This was done not just in spite of, but also in some ways, on account of the churches, the communities, the teachers, and the parents: State control was supposed to prevent open conflict between their contradictory and particularist interests and to reconcile them with one another by political means.

The well-established principle of state control was further strengthened when educational reform was planned and implemented in the 1960's (cf. Chapters 2 and 4). Once again it was the state that was supposed to—and wanted to—take action. It was the governments of the Länder that acted against the interests of the churches and to a great extent abolished the 'Bekenntnisschulen' in those Länder that had reestablished them after World War II; that succeeded in effecting the reform of the rural schools in spite of the opposition of the small communities (cf. Chapters 4 and 7); that facilitated increased attendance at Realschulen and Gymnasien (cf. Chapters 8 and 9); that introduced experiments with the comprehensive schools (cf. Chapter 10); that expanded the universities and integrated teacher training into them (cf. Chapter 12). And when university students and secondary school pupils demanded an enlargement of their rights of codetermination, even then it was expected, once again, that the state, acting against opposition from some of the professors and school teachers, would draw up and enact new university and secondary school statutes. Educational reform in Germany, then, still means not a reduction but rather an increase of the state's control and intervention.

But the state did not merely expand its sphere of control; it also underwent a change. Underlying the Federal Republic's constitutional law is a distinction between state and society. What happens in the society is settled in accordance with civil law, before which all citizens have equal rights, and watched over by those branches of the judicial system responsible for the administration of the civil law. What transpires between the state and citizens, however, has its legal basis in public law (i.e., in the legal codes pertaining to public administration, police, construction, education, etc.), in which not equality, but rather inequality of the actors obtains: the citizen is, in principle, subject to the sovereign state and its functionaries, the state officials, when these are executing the duties of their offices.

This relation of dominance and subjection between state and citizen, which is founded in public law, has, to be sure, undergone some considerable alterations since the Federal Republic's Basic Law was promulgated in 1949. These alterations, which are particularly relevant for the educational system (cf. 3.4), include the requirements that the state observe the law and respect the citizens' rights (including, of course, the Basic Rights), and the further elaboration of the Basic Rights. These rights no longer serve only to safeguard against infringements upon the citizens' liberties; they now also oblige the state to create the conditions necessary for exercising these liberties, and therefore to allow the citizens to participate in the state's decisions and activities.

In the Federal Republic, then, the state can no longer be understood as an 'Obrigkeitsstaat', an authoritarian state which is rigorously demarcated from the society and stands above it. Rather, the state is now rooted in a liberal-democratic fundamental order, in which the political system is democratized and placed under ultimate control of representative bodies. Furthermore, within this order the integration of the state's sphere of sovereignty into the society—a process which is still going on—has effected a quite strong interlocking of state and society. In particular, those reforms that were pushed forward under the banner of democratization of the educational system should be viewed as an outstanding example of this tendency.

Let us take a closer look at state control of the educational system: In what administrative entities is this authority vested? What are the exceptions to this principle? What legal status do the participants in the educational institutions have?

3.1. The political and administrative decision-making system

The educational system is not only state-controlled, it is also centralized. Again, the centralization does not obtain at the national level, but within the Länder: There are 11 centralized educational systems in the Federal Republic. The relationship between the national government and the Länder is governed by the principle of federalism (cf. 3.1.1 and 3.1.2). But the relationship between the government of an individual Land, on the one hand, and the communities as sponsors of schools, and the schools themselves, on the other, is characterized by centralization (cf. 3.1.3). The relationship between the Länder governments and the universities can also be described, in some sense, as centralized under state control (cf. 3.1.4). Private schools have a special status (cf. 3.2), as does enterprise-based vocational training in the "dual system" (cf. 3.3).

Figure 3.1 gives an overview of the decision-making system for educational matters. This diagram will be explained in the following sections.

3.1.1. Division of jurisdiction between the Länder and the Federal Government

The totalitarian Nazi state exercised centralized control over all of Germany. After its fall in 1945, federalism was reestablished as one of the most fundamental characteristics of the Federal Republic's political system. According to the Basic Law, the exercise of state powers and the carrying out of functions which are proper to the state are not tasks of the federal government, but rest, in principle, in the hands of the 11 Länder (Article 30). However, the Basic Law includes a considerable number of articles which specify areas in

88

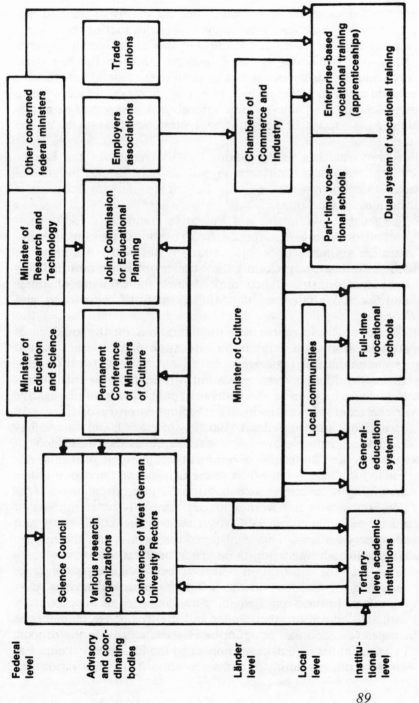

Figure 3.1. Decision-Making and Administration in Education and Research Policy

which the federal government has either the exclusive right to leg-
islate, or in which its legislative right supersedes that of the Länder
governments. As a result, almost all domains of critical importance
are subject to legislation by the federal government. But the Basic
Law has allotted hardly any authority at all to the federal government
in cultural matters. These include museums, libraries, theaters, opera
houses, schools, and universities. Educational policy and administration, as a matter of constitutional principle, are affairs of the
Länder.

But every rule has its exception. The sovereignty of the Länder
in cultural matters is limited in several respects, in part because of
various amendments to the Basic Law. The following restrictions
are the most important.

- The federal government has legislative competence for the important domain of enterprise-based vocational training. Administrative authority over this training is shared by a number of
  federal ministries, including the Ministry of Education and Science, the Ministry of Economic Affairs, the Ministry of Labor
  and Social Welfare, and the Ministry of Food, Agriculture and
  Forestry.
- The federal government sets the conditions on the granting of
  stipends from public funds for education and training, as well
  as the amount of these stipends.
- General or "framework" legislation pertaining to the institutions
  of higher education in the Federal Republic is also a prerogative
  of the federal government. The Federal Ministry of Education
  and Science and the Federal Ministry of Research and Technology
  have administrative authority with regard to this legislation.
- Furthermore, the federal government sets the general regulations
  that are the basis for the laws of the Länder and the communities
  pertaining to public service positions. By means of these regulations the federal government can establish the conditions of
  the careers of state officials, which include almost all school and
  university teachers. The Minister of the Interior has the responsibility for administering these general regulations.
- Since 1969 the constitution has recognized certain common tasks
  in which the Länder and the federal government may or must
  cooperate. In the overall planning and financing of the expansion
  of higher education, the Länder and the federal government are
  obliged to cooperate. In educational planning and in the support
  of research, the federal government and the Länder may cooperate
  on the basis of administrative agreements. This cooperation was

institutionalized in 1970 with the founding of the Joint Commission of the Federal and Länder Governments for Educational Planning and Advancement of Research (cf. 3.1.2).

Apart from these limitations, the Länder are responsible for their educational systems and especially for the schools. Their autonomy in educational matters was recently criticized by the Federal Minister of Education and Science, who argued that the federal government should have greater authority in questions pertaining to the educational system (Bericht der Bundesregierung, 1978). The Länder, however, objected unanimously and emphatically to this proposal.

3.1.2. Cooperation within the framework of federalism

As far as the cooperation between the 11 Länder and the coordination of their educational policies is concerned, the most important body is the Permanent Conference of Länder Ministers of Culture, organized in 1948 as a voluntary working association. This group handles matters of educational policy which are superregional in their scope, in order to guarantee a basic uniformity of the educational systems in the Federal Republic and to advocate the common interests and concerns of the Länder vis-à-vis the federal government. This conference works on the principle of unanimity; that is, only those recommendations become resolutions which have been approved by all the Ministers. But even unanimously passed resolutions are, of course, not binding on the legislators of the Länder. In spite of this limitation, almost all important aspects of the educational systems of all the Länder are based on resolutions of this committee constituted by their Ministers of Culture, for example, on length of compulsory education, the basic organization of the school system, the core curriculum, and regulation of transfers and examinations. All in all, one can say that the Conference of Ministers of Culture succeeded in establishing and developing a basic structure for the educational system that is common to all the Länder.

The Joint Commission of the Federal and Länder Governments for Educational Planning and Advancement of Research was established in 1970 on the basis of an administrative agreement between the Länder and the federal government. Like the Conference of Ministers of Culture, the purpose of this group is coordination among the Länder governments, but with the added participation of the federal government. The Joint Commission has the task of working out long-term comprehensive plans for the entire educational system, intermediate-phase plans, and partial plans and programs for meas-

91

ures to be implemented immediately. The commission is especially responsible for investigating the financial requirements of these plans. The agreement that established this commission raised high expectations: It was hoped that the commission's work would lead to a thorough rationalization of federal educational policy through planning; through the commission a link would be established between structural and financial planning. Thus the commission took over not only the task of assuring coordination between the educational administrations of the Länder, but also that of establishing a consensus among the Ministers of Culture and of Finance and between federal financial planning bodies and those of the Länder.

In 1973, the commission presented a comprehensive education plan which included a program for the structural development of the education system and its financial support. Subsequent efforts of the commission, however, faced a paralyzing polarization in matters of educational policy and were further restricted by a worsening shortage of funds (cf. Chapters 2 and 4). At the beginning of the 1980's, agreement on the continuation of the "General Education Plan" had still not been attained.

Public discussion of educational issues and political consultation among decision-makers in educational policy at the Länder and federal levels were and are conducted by central committees of experts that themselves possess no direct decision-making authority. One of these is the German Education Council (1965–1975), the successor to the German Committee for Education, the advisory body on school policy in the fifties and the early sixties; another is the Science Council (since 1957).

The German Education Council was founded in 1965 by an agreement between the Länder and the federal government. The council met for two terms, from 1965 to 1970 and from 1970 to 1975; the agreement was not extended after the second term as a consequence of political controversies. The Education Council consisted of persons prominent in public life, representatives of the school administrations, and researchers. These worked together to elaborate proposals for the extension and development of the educational system, especially of the primary and secondary sectors. Altogether, more than 50 expert opinion reports and 18 recommendations were published, the "Structural Plan for the Educational System" being probably the most noteworthy among them. In the reports, current scientific positions on various topics were compiled and explained. With its Structural Plan the Education Council laid the indispensable groundwork for the educational reforms that were carried out in the 1970's.

The Science Council was founded in 1957, also by an agreement between the Länder and the federal government. The Science Council works out recommendations for developing the structure and content of higher education and research. In addition, it has a special consulting function with regard to the geographical distribution, the construction, and the equipping of institutions of higher education. The Science Council consists of both researchers and representatives of the federal and Länder governments.

The close institutionalized collaboration of administrators and researchers may be the reason why the Science Council has been outstanding less for conceptual innovations than for practical suggestions which have generally met with acceptance. This is especially true of the Council's suggestions for the quantitative expansion of higher education and its gradual further development. The Science Council has presented a series of separate recommendations without achieving an all-embracing plan for the development of higher education and research. However, its recommendations for the expansion, structure, and organization of academic institutions have been pragmatic and capable of obtaining political support, and thus have been very effective. The Science Council's proposals have been the most important guidelines for the work of the Planning Committee for Tertiary Education Facilities, in which representatives of the federal and Länder governments have consulted with one another and made decisions on their shared investments in the construction of tertiary-level institutions since 1970.

3.1.3. The Länder governments, the community, and the school

3.1.3.1. Division of authority and responsibility between "Land" and community. The high degree of centralization of decisions in the educational system is shown most clearly in the supervision of the schools: "The entire educational system shall be under the supervision of the state." (Art. 7, § 1, Basic Law of the Federal Republic of Germany) Since the school system belong to the Länder's sphere of autonomy, that means first of all that the entire school system (including the private schools) is subject to supervision by the Länder administrations. As a collective term, school supervision historically has included the totality of the state's rights and obligations concerning the organization, planning, directing, and superintendence of the school system. These rights and obligations include establishing the way schools and instruction are organized, as well as determining the learning objectives and content of the courses.

93

Both the parliaments and the Ministries of Culture of the Länder participate in the supervision of the schools. The parliaments do so inasmuch as they are responsible for legislation on education and for planning the budgets of the Länder. The Ministries of Culture issue regulations and directives and plan the development of the school systems.

The legal domain of the Länder also encompasses the whole area of teacher training and personnel administration. Determining what form teacher training takes in the universities and the teacher-training colleges, and prescribing what kinds of examinations teachers have to take, falls under the authority of the Länder parliaments and their Ministries of Culture, as does personnel administration. This consists of the hiring of teachers, assigning them to schools, promoting and transferring them. Most school teachers are tenured officials of the Land in which they teach, and have concomitant rights and duties.

On the other hand, the school administration usually has neither authority nor responsibility in questions pertaining to the so-called external school matters. These have to do with the school buildings, the land on which they stand and the outfitting of the schools, (i.e., the furniture, the equipment for the laboratories and so forth, and teaching and learning materials), as well as with the nonteaching personnel necessary to run the school (e.g., the janitor and the school secretary). For these external matters the so-called sponsor of the school is responsible; this is, in most cases, the community.

The division of responsibility and authority according to whether a matter is internal or external to the school is, though, only useful as a general criterion. In fact, the school sponsor's competence is riddled by provisos requiring that the government of the Land approve certain kinds of measures, and its ability to take independent action is limited by the extent to which it needs the financial help of the Land's government. Thus the dictum holds without qualification: The community builds the schoolhouse; the master of the house, however, is the state.

3.1.3.2. Central administration and control of the school. How the Land and the community cooperate, and how the separation of external and internal school affairs function are, of course, important. Of greater importance for the every-day routine in the school, however, is the relationship between the school administration and the particular school. The organization of the school administration varies from one land to another, but in their basic structure the school administrations of the different Länder are comparable. Figure

3.2 shows, as an example, the organization of the school administration in Baden-Württemberg.

All of the Länder governments include a special ministry that is
responsible either for the school system alone or for cultural matters
in general, including institutions of higher education. According to
a decision of the Federal Constitutional Court, all fundamental

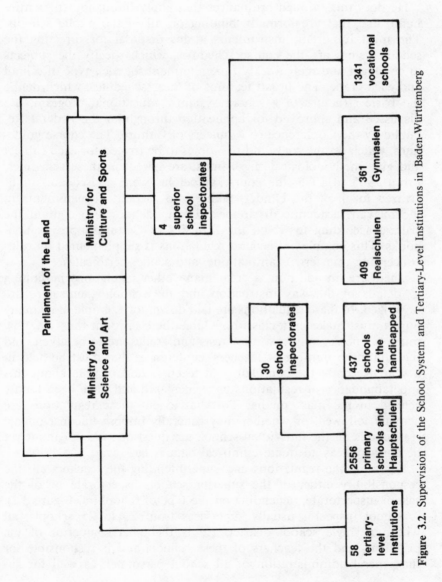

Figure 3.2. Supervision of the School System and Tertiary-Level Institutions in Baden-Württemberg

characteristics of the educational system of a particular Land are to be established by the laws passed by the parliament of the Land (cf. 3.4). Within the framework of these laws, the Minister of Culture is responsible for the more detailed regulation of all aspects of the organization of the schools, instruction, and the internal affairs of the schools.

He does this through ordinances that apply throughout the entire Land, and that are formally binding on all of the public schools. The most important instruments at his disposal for directing the school system are the course schedules, which specify the subjects to be taught and their weekly time allotment for each type of school and each grade. The broad features of these schedules, which define the basic structure of a school system's educational program, are discussed and approved for application throughout the Federal Republic by the Conference of Ministers of Culture. The course guidelines, which set the goals and the topics to be treated for each subject and give methodological suggestions, are based on these schedules. From 1965 to 1975, the course guidelines were revised and modernized in all of the Länder, taking into account developments in the relevant academic disciplines. The guidelines also contain the criteria according to which the Ministry of Culture approves textbooks. This complex of general regulations is supplemented by rules concerning transfers, examinations, and school certificates.

There are, in addition, a great many other regulations pertaining to details of the way instruction and the schools themselves are organized. In these regulations are laid down, for example, how many pupils must make up a class, how large the classroom must be, how much textbooks may cost, how tests and grades are to be given, and the minimum number of teachers' conferences that must be held in a year. Recently the complaints of teachers and parents about this superabundance of regulations have increased and have been loudly echoed in the mass media. To what extent these regulations are actually followed, or whether they generally impose unconscionable restrictions on the individual school, are questions which cannot yet be answered, as adequate empirical data is lacking.

Enforcing the regulations and superintending the teachers are the responsibility either of the superior school inspectorate or of the school inspectorate, depending on the type of school (cf. Figure 3.2). A school inspector usually supervises from 20 to 25 schools, all within a single school district. He is the official superior of the principals and the teachers of these schools and is responsible for the general administration of all school personnel, as well for superintending the teachers in the performance of their duties and ascertaining their competence in their disciplines. Supervision by the inspectors is limited, however, and is concentrated for the most part on important phases or points in teachers' careers. Intensive staff control is not practiced, if for no other reason than insufficient supervisory personnel. The ratio of teachers to supervisors in the Federal Republic is from three to ten times larger than in the United States. The number of teachers which a school inspector has in his charge ranges from 150 to 300. In the Gymnasium sector of the school system the number is considerably higher, sometimes exceeding one thousand teachers. In most of the Länder, however, the Gymnasium principal has more comprehensive powers than the principals of the other types of school and aids the inspector by functioning as an additional level of school administration.

Nevertheless, one should not underestimate the importance of the inspectors' supervisory activity, for the relatively few interventions of the school administration, especially when it is a matter of individual cases, have considerable symbolic significance and receive much public attention. Some of the important activities of the inspectors are the appointment of teachers to their posts after they have completed the requisite exams, assigning them to particular schools, promoting and transferring them. Primarily for these purposes, the school inspector visits the schools in his district and observes the courses in order to evaluate the professional performance of the individual teachers. Further, the inspector concerns himself with questions of school organization, regional and local development and the construction of school buildings.

In the 1970's, however, the relationship between the school administration and the individual school began to change. The trend of this development is toward greater latitude for independent action by the individual schools at the expense of the school administration's authority. Thus the school laws of some Länder have limited the authority of the school inspector or have at least laid some restraints upon him. Furthermore, the legal status of principals, teachers, pupils, and parents and the nature and scope of their interaction within the school have been redefined by new laws in most of the Länder.

The reform of the "school constitution," as these laws pertaining to the schools are called in the Federal Republic, was influenced by the student movement's demand for the right of codetermination as well as by general discussion about democratizing West German society which began somewhat later. To a certain extent this reform led to increased autonomy of the individual school. These laws

prescribe for all schools a relatively complicated system of conferences, i.e., decision-making bodies consisting primarily of teachers,
but including representatives of parents and pupils. These conferences
are established at the level of the school, the department, and the
grade.

Their decision-making power effectively reduced the influence of
the school administration, as well as the authority of the school
principal. The position of the latter is clearly different from that of
his British or American counterparts. The German school principal
is also a teacher, although with a reduced load, and in pedagogical
matters he is considered to be a *primus inter pares*, who is bound
by the resolutions of the school conferences and is obligated to carry
them out. In administrative matters, however, he is the immediate
superior of the teachers, who are subject to his directives. In some
Länder the school principal is able to a limited extent to exercise
functions of the school administration through his participation in
the evaluation of his school's personnel.

One can speak, then, of a relative autonomy of the individual
school as at least a tendency in the Federal Republic. But one should
still not overlook the fact that every school continues to be bound
by all laws, ordinances, and regulations of the school administrations.
This centralization guarantees a measure of standardization of the
school system that limits regional differences in the equipment and
organization of the individual schools. Nevertheless, there are for
any given type of school in any given Land, some individual schools
which have higher or lower prestige corresponding to their pedagogical effectiveness, social status and tradition.

3.1.4. State and university

The principle of state control applies not only to the schools, but
also to the universities, although in a somewhat different way. In
this regard, too, the principle has a long tradition. It was articulated
in Prussian Common Law as early as 1794 that schools and universities are establishments of the state. With regard to the universities
the state in question once again is essentially the Länder governments.
It is true that the federal government has a legal competence with
regard to the universities that it does not have as far as the lower
schools are concerned. This competence, though, is substantially
limited to setting general outlines for tertiary education by means
of federal laws. Other than enacting such framework legislation, the
federal government's activity in the realm of higher education—

aside from the two universities that it maintains for the armed forces—hardly goes beyond contributing to the costs of university building programs, when the federal budget can afford to do so.

It is the Länder, then, which establish and build universities and other institutions of higher learning. They also finance and control the critical parts of these institutions' budgets and decide how many and what type of academic and administrative posts the individual departments may dispose of. Furthermore, university professors, their assistants, and other academic members of the university staffs are for the most part officials of the Land in which the university is located. The universities in the Federal Republic are, then, without question state-controlled.

On the other hand, freedom in teaching and research has long been a cornerstone of the German university. This freedom was the foundation on which the University of Berlin was established in 1810. This university subsequently served as a model for all German universities. In the history of the German university, the principle of freedom in teaching and research is traditionally associated with Wilhelm von Humboldt (1767–1835), who was Privy Counselor and Director of the Education Sector of the Prussian Minstry of the Interior in 1809 and 1810. In Germany the contrast between state control of the universities and the maintenance of academic freedom has traditionally not been considered a contradiction, for the principle entrusts the state with the fiduciary responsibility of using its powers to control and influence the university in such a way as to protect university training, science, and research against the potential constraints of ideological and political partisanship and economic interests.

The constitutional principle of freedom in research and in teaching (Art. 5, § 3, BL) is succinctly explicated in the Federal Framework Law for Higher Education of 1976 (cf. Chapter 12). This law sets up a basic structure for detailed legislation on universities by the Länder and serves to establish some degree of uniformity in such legislation. According to this law, freedom in research encompasses in particular the choice of areas and problems to be investigated and the choice of the methods that will be used, as well as the unconstrained interpretation of research results and their dissemination. Freedom in teaching is the freedom to choose from the legitimate range of subject matters those on which courses will be offered, and freedom in determining the exact content of the courses and their methodological organization. As members of the academic community, students have an analogous freedom. It consists above all in the free choice of the courses they attend, as well as in the right to follow their own preference in selecting an area of specialization.

The university's autonomy also manifests itself in the faculty's influence over the selection and advancement of those who will succeed them. Both the procedure for obtaining the doctoral degree and the specifically German procedure for qualifying to lecture at a university, the 'Habilitation', are determined independently by the university faculties. As a rule, the qualifications of those who teach and do research at a university have previously been certified in a university.

A further domain of the university's autonomy is the appointment of its academic staff. The Länder governments, however, have reserved for themselves the right to decisively influence the appointment of university professors. When a vacant professorship is to be filled, the university presents a list of three candidates, in order of preference, to the Minister of Culture. As a rule, the Minister of Culture then offers the post to the first candidate on the list and, if the offer is accepted, appoints that candidate to the professorship. However the Minister is not bound to this procedure. He can choose another candidate from the list, or he can return the entire list and request a new one, and can do so repeatedly.

Besides academic appointments and budgetary questions, there is a third important area into which the state's fiduciary responsibility with regard to university affairs extends, namely the "state examinations." Roughly speaking, university study is certified in two ways: by academic degrees in the strict sense, such as the M.A. (Magister Artium) or the 'Diplom' (the lowest academic degrees, which require 4 or 5 years of study), the doctorate, and the Habilitation; and by state examinations. The requirements for the academic degrees are autonomously decided upon by the universities, but within a framework of ordinances which each university formulates for itself, and which must be approved by the Ministry of Culture. In contrast, the state examinations are regulated by detailed provisions set by the state for the purpose of ensuring that the practitioners of professions having particular social importance are suitably qualified. Lawyers, teachers, physicians, pharmacists, and a few others professionally trained must all take state examinations before they can legally practice their professions.

In the case of the first two professional groups, state examining boards, which include university professors, give the examinations for the individual Länder. As for the physicians and pharmacists, the procedure and the content of the examinations they must take are uniform in major respects throughout the Federal Republic. The examinations themselves are carried out by the academic personnel of the individual universities functioning as examiners commissioned by the state.

The system of state examinations—besides limiting and structuring the freedom of teaching and learning—has strengthened the academic system's tendency to qualitative uniformity. This tendency has also been supported by the Abitur as the qualification for entrance to university study, since the Abitur of any Land gives its holder the right to enroll at any university in the Federal Republic. Leaving aside the problem of enrollment restrictions (*numerus clausus*), every student can attend the university of his choice, as long as he received a passing grade on his Abitur exam (cf. Chapter 12).

Finally, it should be mentioned that the state's strong fiduciary responsibility for cultural matters continues to have an impact on the financing and administration of research. The most important sponsoring agencies for basic research are the German Research Society and the Max Planck Society for Advancement of Science. Although they are in essence funded by contributions from the federal and Länder governments, they autonomously determine their research policies. In addition, there are a number of private foundations which make a modest contribution to the available research funds (cf. Chapter 12, Table 12.1).

3.2. Private schools as exceptions to the rule

The centralization of the school and university system described above should not be misunderstood to mean that the state, i.e., the Länder governments, has a legal monopoly in the Federal Republic in the sphere of education. The constitution explicitly guarantees the right to establish private schools (Art. 7, § 4, BL). From language and technical schools to gymnastic and theater schools, there is a wide field for the activities of independent educational entrepreneurs. However, when it is a question of "substitute" schools, intended for children and juveniles subject to compulsory school attendance, then this right to establish private schools operates only under certain conditions. The Minister of Culture of the Land in question decides whether the conditions are fulfilled and must give his express permission for the establishment of such a school. According to the Basic Law, this permission is to be granted only if the private substitute schools are not inferior to the public schools in their educational aims, their facilities, and the professional training of their teaching staff. Moreover, segregation of pupils according to the means of their parents must not be promoted by the establishment of these schools. As long as these conditions are met, a private school has a legally justified claim to recognition as a substitute school.

From these provisions of the Basic Law it follows, then, that the precondition for this recognition is that the private substitute schools be equal, although not necessarily similar to the public schools. Therefore private schools, even when they are substitutes for public schools, have the right to determine their organization themselves, as long as equality with the public schools is maintained; the right to choose their teachers themselves, as long as the teachers' training and economic and legal positions are equal to those of public school teachers; and the right to selectively admit their pupils, as long as the financial means of the parents are not used as a criterion. The recognition of a private school as a substitute school also confers on it the right to financial aid from the government of the Land.

Quantitatively speaking, private schools play a minor role in education in the Federal Republic. At the beginning of the 1980's, less than 5 percent of all pupils in secondary level I attended private schools. At the primary level of the school system the proportion is even lower, since there are fewer private primary schools than secondary schools. This is so because the Basic Law imposes additional restrictive conditions on the approval of private primary schools. Generally speaking, private schools are quantitatively important only in the sphere of vocational training, where an extraordinary diversity of schools is to be found.

3.3 Enterprise-based vocational training

The private schools discussed in the preceding section are not the only part of the Federal Republic's educational system in which the influence of the federal and Länder governments is limited. The other is enterprise-based vocational training, which is quantitatively of great importance (cf. Chapter 11). About 40 percent of all juveniles 16 to 18 years of age are trained in the so-called dual system. As a rule, they attend a vocational school one day a week which is maintained and superintended by the government of the Land where the school is located. At the same time they go through an apprenticeship in a privately or publicly owned enterprise which employs them.

The basic conditions on the relationship between the apprentice and his employer were laid down in 1969 in the Federal Vocational Training Act. The fundamental features of enterprise-based vocational training are set by vocational training regulations which are uniform throughout the Federal Republic. These regulations are worked out, in collaboration with the employers, the labor unions, and the vocational schools, by the Federal Institute for Vocational Training, which is under the authority of the Federal Minister of Education and Science and located in West Berlin. The regulations are then issued by various federal ministers. But ultimately it is the privately or publicly owned firms offering the apprenticeships which are responsible for the enterprise-based vocational training and determine its content.

3.4 Parliament, the school administration, and the courts

The principle of state control of the school and university systems has been emphasized in this chapter. Yet which part of the state's power, as defined by Montesquieu, has primary control, the legislature, the executive, or the judiciary? Which has paramount authority over the educational system in the Federal Republic: the parliaments, the school administrations, or the courts? The relationship between these three functionally distinct parts of the state apparatus has changed in the last decades, on the one hand in favor of the parliaments, and, on the other, in favor of the courts.

Traditionally, the educational system in Germany was the exclusive domain of the state executive. Only compulsory school attendance and questions pertaining to the financing and maintenance of educational facilities have long been matters regulated by parliamentary laws. However, since the Basic Law came into force in 1949, the power of the executive in educational matters has been considerably curtailed in two respects. The legal status of school and university teachers, of pupils and students, and also of parents was strengthened by the Basic Law, which granted them fundamental rights. From these rights it follows that these parties can make certain claims on the state. They can demand that the state refrain from unnecessary intervention in their spheres of activity in the educational system. On the other hand, they can also demand of the state that it provide certain services. Further, the state executive was obligated by the

Basic Law to respect the strengthened legal status of those participating in the educational system, as well as to realize in the educational system the general goals set for the state by the Basic Law: democracy, social welfare, and the rule of law.

The achievement of democracy requires that, as a matter of principle, the internal organization of the educational institutions follow a participatory model which allows all of the parties concerned to have a voice in decisions. This principle also requires that within schools and universities freedom of opinion and expression, tolerance, and pluralism obtain; any and every form of indoctrination or discrimination is therefore forbidden.

Because it has the duty to look after the social welfare of its citizens, the state is obligated not only to provide an educational system as a public service, but also to give this educational system a form which corresponds to the demands of a modern society and to give those qualified adequate access to the system.

From the required lawfulness of the state's actions, it follows that the executive can intervene in the educational system only when it has been empowered to do so through laws enacted by the parliament. Furthermore, every citizen can make good his rights in court and can defend himself against actions of the executive that violate his rights. The realization of these two conditions for the law-bound state has been facilitated and accelerated in recent years by the increased activities of the complex of legal institutions. By this we mean the Federal Constitutional Court, the parliaments, the courts, and the legal profession, in their interrelated functioning as social mechanisms (cf. 2.2).

This aspect of the modernization of West German society in the last two decades also had an effect on education. One consequence is that the parliaments, more so than before, must now decide all essential questions concerning the educational system through the passage of laws, and thus draw the boundaries for the executive's activity. It is also part of this general development that more and more citizens are attempting to obtain their constitutional rights by bringing suit in court challenging actions taken by the state. Consequently, the significance of court decisions for the development of the educational system has considerably increased in recent years.

The extension of the legal complex's activity took place at both the federal and the Länder level. In 1976, the Federal Parliament passed the Federal Framework Law for Higher Education, which defines the tasks of the universities, the guiding principles for university study and teaching as well as for research, and the prerequisites for admission to university study. The law also determines the internal organization of institutions of higher education, the participation of their members in governing and decision-making processes, and the structure of these institutions' personnel. Prior to this law legal questions pertaining to higher education were settled primarily by the universities themselves. The Federal Law established throughout the Federal Republic a systematic and uniform framework for legislation by the Länder pertaining to higher education. A similar result was accomplished for vocational training in the dual system (cf. Chapter 11) through the Vocational Training Act of 1969, in which the rights and obligations of apprentices and of the enterprises providing the training, as well as the organization of the examination committees, were regulated throughout the Federal Republic.

As for the school systems, which are under the exclusive authority of the Länder governments, extensive legislation by the Länder parliaments began only after the courts had decided that also in the case of the school system all "essential" questions had to be settled by means of parliamentary laws. The Federal Constitutional Court played an especially important role with regard to these decisions. In addition to the conditions of compulsory education, these essential questions include general educational goals, the catalogue of subjects to be taught, the types of school and their basic organizational structure, admission to and expulsion from school, promotion, examination regulations, how pupils may be disciplined, and parents' and pupils' rights of codetermination in school affairs. As a result of these court decisions, the legislators of the Länder have systematically settled these questions in quite inclusive school laws.

Through these laws the activity of the school administrations is more tightly controlled and the legal protection of the parties involved is improved. As a result, the number of court proceedings having to do with school matters has considerably increased in recent years. More and more citizens are invoking their legally vested rights and do not shrink from pursuing them in court.

Since the educational system is subject to the authority of the state, school and university teachers are members of the state civil service: They are state officials. The legal status of the official in the Federal Republic has several distinguishing characteristics. When a person becomes a state official, he takes an oath and is then an official for life. As an official, he has a right to appropriate payment for his services and to appropriate funds for the provisions he requires to carry out his duties. In comparison with other employees in the Federal Republic, the social position of the official is a privileged one. He is appointed to his post for life, and consequently it is practically impossible to dismiss him from it. In case of sickness he receives special assistance from the government employing him, which gives him a privileged health insurance status, and he enjoys some privileges with respect to his salary.

On the other hand, he has an obligation, very narrowly defined by public law, to fulfill his duties and to be loyal to his superiors. He is also obligated to refrain from taking political stands and to be neutral with regard to all political parties when exercising his official functions. Finally, he is especially obligated to display political moderation in his actions and to be loyal to the constitution. Furthermore, every official is, as a matter of principle, bound by the instructions of his superior.

In this regard, however, special legal provisions are made for the universities and the schools. The rights and the duties of teachers in tertiary-level institutions are formulated in the Federal Framework Law for Higher Education and in individual laws of the Länder. These laws take into account the constitutionally guaranteed right of university teachers to freedom in teaching and research (Art. 5, BL; cf. Chapter 12). The laws governing schools also provide a special legal guarantee of the school teacher's "pedagogical freedom." Although this right of the school teacher does not extend as far as the university teacher's freedom in teaching and research, the law does state that the school teacher is to be restricted as little as possible by his superiors and administrative directives when teaching as well as when imparting moral discipline. From this pedagogical freedom it follows that both the teacher's superiors (the principal and the school inspectors) and the school conferences (consisting of all the teachers at a school) should make use of their power only sparingly and should not constrain the individual teacher's latitude for action unnecessarily or unreasonably.

CHAPTER 4

Modernizing the School System: The Challenge of Equality and Excellence

4.1. Starting points of educational reform in the mid-1960's

In the 1950's the primary and secondary school system in the Federal Republic was reconstructed following the organizational structures of the Weimar period. Before this time, immediately after the war and under the influence of the Occupying Powers, there had been attempts to replace the tripartite school system with one organized in several levels, similar to the American model. These incipient reforms were abandoned in the fifties, and measures which had already been implemented in some Länder were partially undone. These measures were, for example, the six-year primary school and steps taken toward an integrated secondary school established in opposition to the traditionally differentiated school system and comprising the entire range of obligatory education for all school-age children.

In this period there were, to be sure, reforms and school experiments, but in substance they did not go beyond the limits of the traditional basic structure of the school, which had been decided upon by the Länder in the Düsseldorf Agreement of 1955 on the standardization of the primary and secondary education system. Not until the Hamburg Agreement of the Länder governments in 1964 did the period of restoration give way to a reform phase, for the new agreement lifted the ban on school experiments which did not conform to the fundamental structure of the school system agreed upon in 1955. Nevertheless, it would be wrong to view the fifties as merely a time of stagnation, as their sobriquet "the decade of nonreform" would lead one to believe. During these years the severe shortages in school facilities and personnel caused by the war were finally overcome; the fundamental structure of the secondary school system was stabilized by increasing the number of schools of an intermediate type in all Länder; and the foundation was thereby laid for the quantitative expansion and qualitative improvement of the system. Without these achievements later reforms would not have been feasible.

Leaving out of consideration some deviations in Hamburg, Berlin, and Bremen, one can say, that, by the beginning of the sixties, the following basic structure of the school system had become firmly established (cf. Figure 2.1 in Chapter 2). Compulsory education began for all children at the age of six. After the four-year primary level of the Volksschule (called "primary school" from 1964 on), which all attended together, each pupil, aged 10 or 11, was assigned to one of the three different and completely separate types of secondary school.

Together, the three school types constituted the so-called tripartite or vertically structured system of secondary education. Most pupils remained in the Volksschule and attended its upper level (called the Hauptschule from 1964 on) for another four years, until they had completed their compulsory full-time education. In some Länder an additional voluntary school year was offered. A relatively small number of pupils successfully passed through a screening process and transferred from the primary school to the Gymnasium. This school conferred the intermediate certificate on them after six years of attendance, and after nine years the Abitur, which gave access to university study. Another group of pupils, also small in number, entered the middle school (called the Reaschule from 1964 on) at about 10 years of age; this school they completed after six years, obtaining the intermediate certificate, later renamed Realschule certificate. The overwhelming majority of pupils began to work or entered vocational training after attending the Volksschule for eight or nine years, or the middle school or Gymnasium for 10 years. Being subject to compulsory education to the age of 18, they attended part-time vocational schools, usually only one day a week, for another two or three years. Only a very small number completed the upper level of the Gymnasium and obtained the Abitur after 13 years of school.

However, a succinct description of the Federal Republic's school system at the beginning of the 1960's must also include at least the following characteristics, which are important for the later reforms:

(1) Schools in the Federal Republic are almost all half-day schools. The number of all-day schools is insignificant.

(2) They are under the superintendence of the Land in which they are located.

(3) Preschool institutions are predominantly supported and sponsored by the communities, churches, charitable organization, or parents' groups. They have almost no connection at all with the schools, and have not yet been discovered as an object of educational policy. This sector is extremely underdeveloped (cf. Chapter 5).

(4) Those types of secondary school granting at least a Realschule certificate, and so giving access to some sort of higher education, were also quantitatively underdeveloped. In 1963, 70 percent of the 13-year-olds remained in the Volksschule, 12 percent attended the Realschule, and approximately 15 percent was enrolled in Gymnasien. The state of this part of the school system is shown even more clearly by the relative sizes of the different groups of school-leavers. In 1965, from the pertinent age groups 17 percent left school without any kind of certificate; 53 percent earned a Hauptschule certificate; 19 percent obtained a Realschule certificate, and only barely eight percent managed to attain the Abitur.

In comparison with other industrialized nations, the Federal Republic was lagging behind considerably in the development of its secondary level I, as Figure 4.1 shows. Whereas in the Federal Republic, 24 percent of the relevant age group completed a tenth year of full-time schooling in 1960, in France it was 46 percent, in Sweden 55 percent, in Japan 74 percent, and in the United States 86 percent. However, if one takes into consideration attendance at part-time vocational schools in the Federal Republic—as a rule one or two school days per week—then the differences were not that significant.

(5) A further characteristic feature of the school system was the sharp delimitation from one another of the three hierarchically ranked types of secondary school with concomitant early and almost irrevocable channeling of the pupil into a certain educational track. Each of the three school types had its own educational philosophy and criteria for admission; and each differed from the others in its curriculum, in the prescribed number of weekly course hours in each subject, and in its course guidelines, which were set by the state school administration. Each type of school also used its own text-

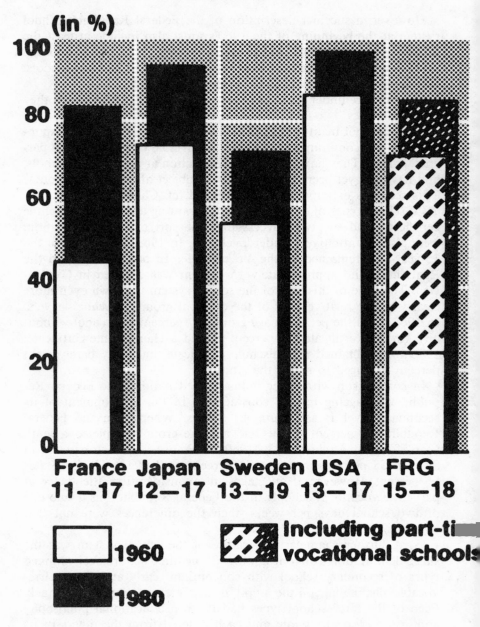

Figure 4.1. Pupils in Secondary Education in Selected Countries, 1960 and 1980 (as Percentages of Given Age Group)

books. Consequently, it was extremely difficult to transfer from one school type to another. After transition into the secondary sector at the age of 10 or 11, only a few pupils changed to a different type of school; in 1963, one percent did so. On the other hand, reassignment of secondary school pupils to a lower-ranking type of school occurred three times as often as did reassignment to a higher-ranking school.

Since in Germany careers were, and still are, to a great extent formally linked to academic certification, the encapsulation of the three school types vis-à-vis one another meant that one of the most momentous decisions affecting an individual's life chances was made when he was 10 or 11 years old. To be sure, it was, in principle, possible to obtain school certificates later in one's life by attending evening schools; this path, however, was very arduous, and taken by only a few (cf. Chapter 13). Consequently, this alternative was practically insignificant as a way of compensating for errors in the early classification of pupils.

(6) Finally, enrollments in the two higher-ranking secondary schools were heavily biased according to social background, region, and gender. These biases were the combined effect of certain features of the school system: the way it was organized, the content of its courses, its selection practices, and regional disparities in educational facilities. All these worked to the detriment of socially disadvantaged children, in particular children, especially the girls from working-class families and the rural population. The proverbial "Catholic working-class girl from the countryside" serves as a compendium of such disadvantages.

Discrimination and preference on the basis of social background played an especially important role. There are, though, no continuous statistics on this matter in the Federal Republic, the earliest official data now available being for 1965. This state of affairs is indicative of the strength of the belief that West German society had overcome class antagonisms and provided a middle-class standard of living for all its members. The discovery that this society is, in fact, socially stratified is relatively recent, and marks the beginning of efforts to counter this stratification.

Because adequate data is lacking, it is necessary to resort to the occupational status of the head of the family, usually the father, in order to determine which social stratum a pupil belongs to, and thereby to clearly show the educational disadvantages deriving from social background. Workers constitute the traditional lower stratum, while officials, who make up the greatest part of the employees of both the federal and Länder governments and of publicly owned enterprises, such as the Post Office and the Federal Railways, are an important occupational group of the middle stratum.

The statistical data for 1965 present the following picture of the educational advantages and disadvantages of belonging to the different social strata: Only 10 percent of the pupils in the tenth grade of the Gymnasium came from working-class families, whereas 25 percent were children of officials; at the same time, however, almost half of all employed males are workers, and only 9 percent are officials. Working-class children were, then, clearly underrepresented in the Gymnasium. Not only were these children at a disadvantage when it was decided who would enter the Gymnasium; the number of those in the Gymnasium was also further greatly diminished during the course of their study by reassignment to another type of school. In the last grade of the Gymnasium, the 13th, only 6 percent of the pupils were from working-class families, while the proportion of children of officials rose to 28 percent.

By the beginning of the 1980's, the educational disadvantages of pupils from the lower social stratum had not been significantly lessened, even though their attendance at the higher-ranking secondary schools has increased. Table 4.1 gives some idea of the extent to which the advantage of children from the other strata over working-class children has been maintained. In the long run, this gap between working-class children and those from the more privileged social strata will probably be reduced only as a result of a "saturation" effect: Practically all children from the higher social strata attend the higher-ranking forms of secondary education, and their rate of enrollment in these schools thus no longer increases, allowing that of working-class children to rise.

4.2. The reform plan of the German Education Council

In the middle of the 1960's there began a broad discussion of educational reform, the results of which were compiled in 1970 by the German Education Council (cf. Chapter 3) in its Structural Plan for the Educational System. In this document, the Education Council proposed a long-term plan for restructuring the educational system, all the way from the preschool level through the school system to adult education. According to the plan, the vertically divided secondary education system with its three types of school, and the separation of the upper level of the Gymnasium with its general

Table 4.1: Pupils Aged 13 to 14 According to School Type and Occupational
Status of Head of Family, 1972 and 1980 (in Percentages)

School Type, Year	Total	Occupational status of head of family				
		self-employed, incl. family business	officials	salaried employees	workers	other
1972						
Hauptschulen[1]	60.1	51.3	29.6	37.3	76.4	70.3
Realschulen	19.9	23.1	23.2	25.4	17.1	13.1
Gymnasien	20.1	25.6	47.2	37.3	6.5	16.6
Total	100.0	100.0	100.0	100.0	100.0	100.0
1980						
Hauptschulen[1]	45.7	39.8	20.5	25.5	62.4	61.7
Realschulen	25.5	28.9	25.0	30.5	22.7	18.7
Gymnasien	24.3	28.2	51.1	39.4	10.0	15.0
Comprehensive schools	4.4	3.1	3.4	4.6	4.9	4.7
Total	100.0	100.0	100.0	100.0	100.0	100.0

[1] Including schools for the handicapped.

Source: Statistisches Bundesamt (unpublished material of the microcensus).

education from the vocational schools, were to be replaced by unitary
secondary levels I and II. This plan was based on the considerations
set forth in the following paragraphs. (The further development of
the tertiary sector was not treated in the Education Council's plan;
this topic was the responsibility of the Conference of West German
University Rectors and the Science Council. It is discussed in Chapters 3 and 12. For vocational and further education, see Chapters
11 and 13.)

The Education Council stressed the importance of early learning
and recommended the expansion of the preschool level of the educational system. The intent of this recommendation was to ease
transition from play in the nursery school to systematic learning in

the primary school. In addition, the expansion of the preschool level was supposed to include measures which would compensate for the inequality of the children's preparation for schooling due to their differing social backgrounds.

The Council's recommendations concerning the structure of secondary level I are very cautious. To understand their caution, one must view it in its context. One year before coming to agreement on the Structural Plan, the members of the Education Council had recommended experiments with integrated comprehensive schools. The recommendation had clearly been reached by compromise. The advocates of the integrated comprehensive school were appeased by the approval of at least a few experimental schools; the school's opponents were willing to accept a restricted program of scientifically controlled experiments. In keeping with this compromise, the Structural Plan did not take a stand either for or against the comprehensive school. Rather, the Council emphasized the necessity of not making a commitment before the experiments had yielded conclusive results. Thus, the Council's recommendations concerning secondary level I were intended to be provisional. They included greater cooperation between the different types of school within secondary level I; the elaboration, as far as possible, of common curricula; and—with respect to new schools—an increase in the number of school centers, in which the three types of school are brought together in the same facility.

As far as the curricula are concerned, some convergence actually took place throughout the Federal Republic in all school types at secondary level I. This was particularly true for the fifth and sixth grades, which were reshaped into an "orientation level" in order to postpone the final decision on the assignment of pupils to one of the secondary schools. As for the later grades, curricula in the different types of schools have also become somewhat more similar. Still, they are far from being identical, and the tendencies toward convergence have recently encountered opposition from the governments of some South German Länder, which have again stressed the particular character of the Hauptschule. As to the recommendation that the different school types cooperate more, it has remained largely on paper.

Another reason why the convergence of the different types of school proposed by the Education Council occurred to only a small degree was that its recommendation on the length of compulsory full-time education has generally not been followed. Although the Council considered the lengthening of full-time education to 10 years as a basic precondition for raising the general level and quality of education in all forms of secondary school, only Berlin and North Rhine-Westphalia have done so. The remaining Länder still refuse to take this step even though more and more of their Hauptschule pupils are choosing to go on to a voluntary tenth grade. The Council also made suggestions for changing secondary level II, so that general and vocational education would be more closely interlinked in this educational segment. These suggestions met a fate similar to that of the other recommendations. The Education Council's plan has, then, been realized only in part.

4.3. Enrollments, the crest of the demographic wave, and educational policy

When it was first published, the Council's plan for restructuring the educational system met with rather general political approval. In the following years, however, the positions which provided the basis for the initial consensus were abandoned more and more in the face of the practical politics of education. Consequently, when the plan was to be implemented, serious differences of opinion emerged which could not be settled even in the General Education Plan formulated in 1973 by the federal and Länder governments, and which resulted in minority votes against the comprehensive school and the orientation level (cf. Chapter 3). Nevertheless, in the latter half of the sixties and again in the early seventies, measures were taken in all Länder, often within the framework of pedagogical experiments, to effect structural reforms.

At the same time, within the framework of the traditional tripartite division of the school system, decisive changes occurred. These changes were due in part to a long-term modification of the demand for education, and in part to the increase in the number of pupils as larger age groups from the baby-boom years reached school age; they were also in part the result of educational policy. To a very large extent, though, these changes were overshadowed by a few politically charged reform proposals, which for that reason had especially great visibility; foremost among these was the comprehensive school.

Since the beginning of the fifties, there has been an almost continually rising demand for the educational programs giving access to the tertiary sector, such as those offered by the Realschule and the Gymnasium. This demand levelled out somewhat in 1958, but rose again sharply from 1961 on—about three or four years before the "educational catastrophe" was declared in the Federal Republic and measures were taken to increase interest in education (cf. Chapter 2). Figure 4.2 shows the development from 1952 to 1980 of the enrollment ratios of 13-year-olds in the Hauptschule, the Realschule, and the Gymnasium. For the greatest part, these pupils were in the seventh or eighth grade; the percentages, however, refer to the age group.

In addition to the rising demand for education, from 1964 on increasingly large age groups entered secondary level I. Figure 4.3 presents the quantitative development of the groups of 6-, 11- and 16-year-olds, and thus approximately indicates the size of the groups entering primary school, secondary level I, and secondary level II. In 1971/1972 the first group with more than one million members was in the fifth grade. In 1977/1978, with the transition of the last group having more than one million members into secondary level I, the number of pupils in this level reached its peak, while from about 1976 on the declining birthrate became more clearly noticeable in the primary school.

This demographic trend and growing interest in more than minimal secondary education led to a rapid increase in the enrollments of the Realschule and the Gymnasium in the period from 1960 to the beginning of the 1980's. As for the Hauptschule, it was freed to a certain extent from demographic pressure by declining demand for the education it offered; the other side of the coin, however, was that it suffered all the more strongly from the negative selection of its pupils. In sum, in all three types of secondary school, shifts in enrollments and alteration in their social composition led to considerable changes.

If one were to assess the role played in this overall development by active educational policy and the school administrations of the Länder, the answer might be rather disappointing. This role probably consisted in no more than providing sufficient Realschule and Gymnasium facilities, so that expansion of their enrollments was not hindered. One can assume that this policy of increasing the capacity of these schools will have unplanned long-term effects which will once again greatly alter these schools' social composition. On the basis of what happened in the 1950's, it can be expected that from 1982 on, when the age groups entering secondary level I begin to diminish in size, the Realschule and the Gymnasium will exert a powerful attraction, and that consequently the ratio of enrollment in the Hauptschule will decline even further.

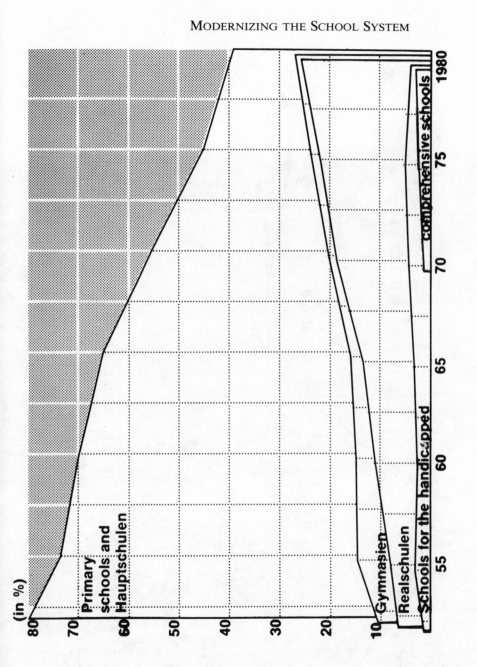

Figure 4.2. Enrollment Rates of 13-Year-Olds According to Type of School, 1952–1980

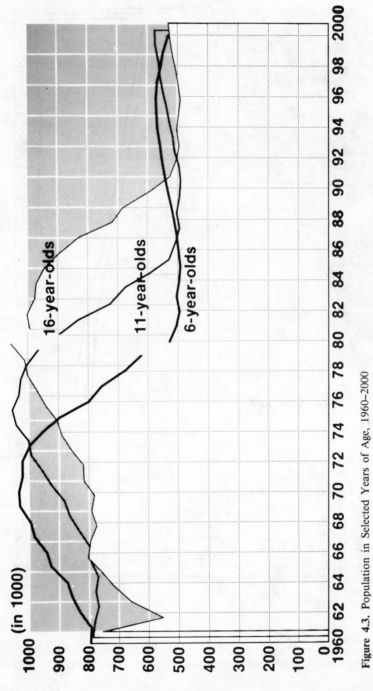

Figure 4.3. Population in Selected Years of Age, 1960–2000

In the last 10 years, reform of the nonvocational school system, i.e., those schools giving a general education (for vocational education, cf. Chapter 11), has focussed on matters which will be discussed in the later parts of this chapter, namely:

- expansion of the preschool level and reorganization of the transition into the primary school;
- modifying the transition into secondary level I through introduction of an orientation level in grades 5 and 6;
- secondary level I, to be expanded in the Realschule and the Gymnasium, reformed in the Hauptschule, given some degree of uniformity across all three traditional school types, and established in a new form through the introduction of the comprehensive school;
- the transition from secondary level I to secondary level II to be modified by offering a voluntary tenth grade of the Hauptschule and/or by establishing a program of basic vocational education lasting one year;
- and lastly, the reform of secondary level II in the Gymnasium.

Curricular changes, that is, changes in what pupils are supposed to learn in school, occurred at all levels of the educational system: Curricula and course guidelines were revised and new textbooks introduced; curriculum materials were developed by individual schools; and teachers changed their course plans.

4.4 Developments at the preschool level

Since 1960 the preschool level has been greatly expanded, with respect to both nursery school capacity and personnel (cf. Chapter 5). Since 1970 this improvement has been furthered by the declining number of children aged 3 to 5. In 1965, the available nursery school capacity was large enough for only 33 percent of the children then in this age bracket; in 1980, nursery schools were able to accomodate approximately 80 percent. It can be assumed that the situation will improve still further solely because of the declining birthrate. At the same time the differences between the Länder in available nursery school capacity and in the provision of personnel and supplies should diminish. (At the present time these differences are still considerable; for example, in 1980, Baden-Württemberg could provide enough nursery schools for 100% of the 3- to 5-year-olds, while Schleswig-Holstein had enough nursery schools for only 48% of the children in this age group.)

As for qualitative changes, they were made, and are currently being made, primarily in the transition from the preschool level to the primary level. On the one hand, nursery schools are attempting to prepare 5-year-olds for systematic learning in school through appropriate activities and exercises; on the other hand, primary school didactics are making increased use of play in the instruction of the beginning grades. The complementary developments in both levels were supported by a relatively extensive program of pilot projects, which aided in the elaboration of play and learning materials for 5- to 6-year-olds, and in which about 240 nursery schools throughout the Federal Republic participated. Furthermore, "threshold programs" or "preparatory classes" attached either to nursery schools or to primary schools were established to effect a smooth transition from the preschool level into primary school. In 1980, preschool institutions connected with the primary school were attended by between 2 and 30 percent of the 5- to 6-year-olds, depending on the Land. On the whole, the picture that emerges indicates that the abruptness of the transition to primary school, which was still quite pronounced in the sixties, has been moderated.

With regard to the preschool level, the task of the 1980's will no longer be its general expansion. Rather, it will be necessary to bring about a regionally balanced distribution of nursery schools. Other goals are increased attendance at nursery schools by children of foreign workers and socially disadvantaged families, and better provision of the particular kinds of care that these children need.

4.5. The transition from the primary level to secondary level I— introduction of the orientation level

The pupil's transition from the primary school to the secondary schools was and still is a critical threshold (cf. 7.1 and 5.4). With his entry into the Hauptschule, the Realschule, or the Gymnasium at the age of 10 or 11, a child's entire life is decisively channeled in a particular direction. This early classification has met with objections of considerable weight.

In the early screening of children many erroneous decisions are made, whether they are evaluated by their primary school teachers, or by admission tests, or on the basis of their performance during a trial semester. In some cases, pupils who have been accepted into the Realschule and the Gymnasium prove unable to meet the standards of these schools, and must then leave them before graduating.

However, a much more serious consequence of a rigorous selection at this age is that a large percentage of capable children are excluded from these schools. Finally, this early classification also implicitly discriminates according to social criteria.

To avoid these undesirable consequences, the German Committee for Education (cf. Chapter 3) proposed in 1959 that in the place of grades 5 and 6 a unitary school level be established with the same curriculum for all children. The children would be instructed not only in age-group classes which were heterogeneous with respect to ability, but also in some subjects, in homogeneous ability groups. In addition, special courses were to be offered which would help slow learners. There were a few experiments with this school level at the beginning of the 1960's in Hessia, and later the German Education Council made a similar recommendation. Finally, in 1973 the Joint Commission of the Federal and Länder Governments for Educational Planning and Advancement of Research issued its General Education Plan, which included its decision that different forms of the "orientation level"—the designation officially given—should be tested, and preparations made for introducing this new level throughout the Federal Republic, beginning in 1976.

As a step toward implementing the General Education Plan, the Permanent Conference of Länder Ministers of Culture agreed in 1974 on the nationwide introduction of the orientation level. Their agreement permitted two alternative models. The orientation level could be comprehensive, i.e., nonspecific with respect to the three types of secondary school, or it could be specifically coordinated with the Hauptschule, Realschule and the Gymnasium. Both forms of the orientation level presuppose the convergence of the three types of secondary school with respect to their curricula, their course guidelines and the number and distribution of their weekly course hours. The children who enter the nonspecific form of the orientation level are not assigned to one of the secondary schools at the end of the fourth grade. They are taught in heterogeneous groups, the members of which have different levels of performance, and, to the extent that this is possible, by teachers from the different secondary schools. However, the other form of the orientation level for two years puts to the test, so to speak, the children who have already been assigned to the secondary school in question. In this form of the orientation level, instruction is given only by teachers from the pertinent type of secondary school; throughout this level, however, the curriculum is the same, so that errors in the assignment of pupils to one of the secondary schools can be more easily corrected.

121

The agreement of the Conference of the Ministers of Culture has not been carried out in a uniform fashion in the various Länder. In 1980 there were not only variations between the Länder in the legal basis for the orientation level and in the procedures for transition into this level. There were also significant differences with respect to the parents' right to participate in the decisions on the assignment of their children to one of the secondary schools, as well as with regard to the extent to which the orientation level has actually been established. In some Länder the orientation level is quantitatively insignificant; in others it is attended by almost 100 percent of the pupils in the relevant grades. The discrepancies that have developed in this regard are due primarily to the fact that the various Länder governments judged the expansion of the Realschule and the Gymnasium from different political viewpoints.

It could be expected that the establishment of orientation levels would lead to further increase in the generally rising demand for those programs of study giving access to the tertiary sector (cf. Figure 4.2). In the Länder with a conservatively inclined educational policy, generally those with Christian-Democratic governments, the increasing enrollments in the Gymnasium were considered a threat to the quality of the education it offered and an undesirable future burden for the tertiary educational institutions. Therefore the governments of these Länder attempted to counteract this increase by channelling the great majority of pupils away from the Gymnasium early in their education. In these Länder, the tendency became more marked to establish only the school-type-specific orientation level and to use it as an observation period after which less successful pupils in the Realschule and the Gymnasium were reassigned to a lower-ranking type of school. An exception is Lower Saxony, which—even after its government had passed into the hands of the Christian Democrats—kept the nonspecific form of the orientation level, although not without some compromises with regard to the establishment of classes for highly gifted pupils.

In contrast, North Rhine-Westphalia, governed by the Social Democrats, has not yet introduced the orientation level either in the one or the other form. The reason, however, is completely different from that for the reluctance of the Länder governed by the Christian Democrats. Having the largest population of all the Länder, North Rhine-Westphalia had to plan the introduction of the orientation level far in advance. In 1977–1978, the government of this Land decided to link the introduction of the nonspecific form of the orientation level with the establishment of school centers (cooperative comprehensive schools). This policy was suspected of being an insidious way of introducing the integrated comprehensive school and was defeated in a referendum owing to a highly emotional campaign waged against it by the Christian Democrats, the 'Philologenverband' (an association, and interest group, consisting for the greatest part of Gymnasium teachers and tending toward conservative views), and parents' associations.

The introduction of the orientation level was susceptible to quite different, almost opposed evaluations. For some it was a very important although cautious reform of the Federal Republic's school system because it postponed the assignment of children to a secondary school by two critical years, from the end of the fourth to the end of the sixth grade. For others, it was merely a means to prevent the far-reaching school reform which they were striving to achieve, that is, the establishment of the comprehensive school.

Judged from both these standpoints, the introduction of the orientation level was not very successful in changing the school system for the better. In some Länder with Christian Democratic governments, the orientation level was introduced only in its school-type-specific form and has not changed in any fundamental way the early assignment of pupils to one of the secondary schools. Only in Hessia and Lower Saxony did the orientation level effect a thoroughgoing change in the structure of the schools.

4.6. Introduction of the comprehensive school

The most resolute step toward restructuring the school system was the introduction of the comprehensive school, in which the three traditional forms of the secondary school, the Hauptschule, the Realschule, and the Gymnasium, are combined with one another (cf. Chapter 10). At the beginning of 1969 the Education Council had suggested a program for establishing experimental comprehensive schools. In that same year, the Conference of Ministers of Culture agreed to carry out a program of experiments testing two forms of the comprehensive school: the integrated and the cooperative comprehensive school. In the integrated form, the three traditional types of secondary school are abolished and replaced with a flexible organization of instruction within the individual school. In the cooperative form of the comprehensive school the three traditional school types are joined together in a school center and connected with each other organizationally.

In connection with the agreement of the Conference of Ministers of Culture, experimental schools were established in all Länder, and preparations made for studies of these experiments by social scientists. The experiments, both the integrated and the cooperative comprehensive schools, run for either a half-day (8 a.m.–1:30 p.m.) or a whole day (8 a.m.–4 p.m.). They were financially supported by the federal government. Since the modification of secondary level I was most thoroughgoing in the integrated comprehensive school, scholarly and political interest has been and continues to be concentrated on this kind of school. In Berlin, Bremen, Hamburg, Hessia, Lower Saxony, and North Rhine-Westphalia, the integrated comprehensive school has been made a standard school, alongside the other traditional types of secondary school. In the remaining Länder the comprehensive school is still considered nonstandard.

The experiments with integrated comprehensive schools were carried out in the various Länder with very different goals in mind. In the Länder governed by the Social Democrats or by a coalition of Social Democrats and Liberals, the primary purpose was to determine whether this form of the comprehensive school might be the best model for the uniform secondary level I which the governments of these Länder intended to create. In the Länder with Christian Democratic governments, however, comprehensive schools were established on a purely experimental basis: These schools would have to prove their superiority over the traditional types of school before the establishment of more comprehensive schools would even be considered. Thus, the educational policies of the Länder also diverged with respect to the comprehensive school; and this divergence was accompanied by vehement political controversy within the Länder, especially in Hessia and North Rhine-Westphalia.

Across the nation, however, the integrated comprehensive school is only of slight quantitative importance. In 1980, 4 percent of all pupils in secondary level I were enrolled in comprehensive schools. In those Länder, on the other hand, where the reform of the school system through the establishment of comprehensive schools was strongly supported and correspondingly advanced, namely Berlin and Hessia, between 15 and 25 percent of all 13-year-old pupils now attend an integrated comprehensive school.

4.7. Establishment of the Hauptschule, modernization of the rural school system, and the question of lengthening compulsory full-time education

Before and during the structural reforms of the school system, great efforts were made to reform the traditional types of school.

124

The most ambitious program was the transformation of the upper level of the Volksschule into the Hauptschule. The latter was intended to be of equal rank with the Realschule and the Gymnasium and, like these, to open for its graduates paths leading to the tertiary sector (cf. Chapter 7).

The term 'Hauptschule' was introduced in 1964 in the Hamburg Agreement of the Länder governments on the standardization of the school system. In the same year, the Committee for Education published its recommendations on the establishment and organization of the Hauptschule. Five years later, in 1969, essential elements of these recommendations reappeared in an agreement on the Hauptschule concluded by the Conference of the Ministers of Culture; in this agreement the basic characteristics of this school were defined.

Associated with the Hauptschule reform was the goal of offering in one and the same school, and for the majority of the young, an initiation into scientific thinking and a more extensive preparation for employment after they finished compulsory education. To achieve this, the Volksschule had to be radically transformed. The new curriculum included a compulsory foreign language (English) and polytechnic courses (e.g., vocational orientation), as well as more demanding courses in the natural sciences and mathematics. Instruction was reorganized in order to offer courses differentiated according to levels of performance, a range of elective subjects, and specialized instruction in core subjects, in which teachers were henceforth to be specially trained.

The realization of these aims presupposed schools of at least a certain size, large enough, if possible, to have several classes in each grade. From these classes groups could be formed for the differentiated courses. Small schools in which pupils from different grades had to be taught at the same time in one room were obstacles to these plans. Thus the adherents of the Hauptschule reform and the advocates of eliminating, or at least mitigating, the differences between the city and the country with respect to Realschule and Gymnasium enrollments, and the availability of schools in general, were in agreement in their criticism of the miniscule village school.

But in order to provide better schools in the Länder that had rural areas, it was necessary to close many schools in the countryside and to forego the 'Bekenntnisschulen' in the Länder of Southern and Western Germany, where the Volksschule and the training of teachers still bore a religious stamp. The small Volksschulen, having often only one or two classes, were shut and replaced with school centers. In the intervening years it has been forgotten how momentous these political decisions were and how much they altered the structure of the educational system. In Bavaria, for example, beginning in 1967, the number of Volksschulen was reduced in a very short time from 7,000 to 3,000; and in North Rhine-Westphalia 6,000 upper levels of the Volksschule were replaced by 1,300 Hauptschulen, also in only a few years. Since then an extensive bussing system has, of necessity, been developed.

However, the reform which was intended to raise the educational standard of the Hauptschule and to stabilize its enrollment by making it more attractive as a self-sufficient school, collided, particularly in the cities, with the simultaneous growth of the Realschule and Gymnasium (cf. Figure 4.2). As a result, the enrollment of the Hauptschule steadily declined; in the large cities only a relatively small part of school-aged children now attend this school. (In Berlin, for example, 19.6 percent of all 13-year-olds attended the Hauptschule in 1980.) The present situation of the Hauptschule is, therefore, characterized in part by an internal contradiction: The improvement of the education offered by the Hauptschule, one of the reform's goals, is seriously hindered by the deterioration of the learning environment due to the large number of negatively selected pupils. Within the Hauptschulen themselves, this contradiction seems to be manifesting itself in the kinds and number of the certificates they confer. In the Länder where the Hauptschule offers a Realschule certificate after the completion of a tenth grade, more and more pupils are taking advantage of this possibility; at the same time, though, a considerable portion of Hauptschule pupils does not succeed in finishing the school's final grade and leaves it without a certificate of completion.

In connection with this trend toward obtaining the Realschule certificate, and a concomitant devaluation of the Hauptschule certificate, proposals were made to extend compulsory full-time education to 10 years. Up to now there has been considerable diversity of opinion among the Länder about how a tenth school year should be organized and what should be taught during it. In this debate it is primarily a question of the following alternatives:

- lengthening compulsory attendance at nonvocational schools, i.e., those giving a general education, to 10 years, hence adding a grade to the Hauptschule;
- making of the tenth school year a year of basic vocational training, while maintaining an organizational connection with the Hauptschule;

126

• introducing a year of full-time schooling in the vocational school system.

Berlin and North Rhine-Westphalia chose the first possibility and legally introduced the compulsory tenth school year in the Haupt-schule. The other Länder, however, seem to prefer the second or third alternative, although there is a discernible tendency to make the tenth year, as a year of basic vocational training, the responsibility of the vocational school system (cf. Chapter 11).

4.8. Contradictory trends in secondary level I

The way the reforms in secondary level I have proceeded in the different Länder give the impression that the reform of this school segment has led to considerable disparities in the Federal Republic's educational system, and that there is the threat of further divergence among the Länder in this regard. Moreover, there has also been divergence with respect to the orientation level, the comprehensive school, the tenth grade of the Hauptschule, the legal regulations pertaining to the transition from the primary level to secondary level I, as well as the regulations governing certification at the end of secondary level I. In 1978, in a report on the deficiencies of the educational system, the federal government pointed out problems which these shortcomings could cause for the uniformity of living conditions in the Federal Republic.

Despite these obvious discrepancies, there are a number of developments which point in the direction of a national standardization of secondary level I. All Länder were affected by the increase of the Realschule's and the Gymnasium's enrollments, which also changed the character of these types of school. In particular, the Gymnasium has lost its character of an elite institution (cf. Chapter 9). Concurrently with the expansion of enrollments in these schools, there emerged a trend toward obtaining the Realschule certificate, a trend which, as already mentioned, is also evident in the Hauptschulen.

This quantitative shift in the choice of secondary school also received support from measures taken by the school administrations of the Länder, which coordinated the curricula and the prescribed number of weekly course hours in the different school types with one another. In particular, raising the level of the education offered by the Hauptschule was a decisive step toward making the types of secondary school more similar; some Länder are consistently pursuing further improvement of Hauptschule education by attempting to develop uniform curricula and course guidelines for secondary level I, or curricula and course guidelines for this level in the three school types which are at least coordinated with one another. The convergence of the three types is furthest advanced in the elaboration of curricula and course guidelines for the orientation level, while its limits will most likely be revealed in the further development of the Hauptschule, for which the school administrations of some Länder are again making a concerted effort to secure a special status.

4.9. Reform of the Gymnasium's upper level and attempts to combine general and vocational education

In 1972 the Conference of Ministers of Culture agreed upon the reform of the upper level of the Gymnasium. This reform can be understood as a first, albeit small step toward developing a uniform secondary level II, or at least toward coordinating better with one another the different forms of this level in the several school types, as proposed by the Education Council in its long-term plan for restructuring the educational system. The reorganization of its upper level was supposed to enable the Gymnasium to better prepare its pupils for study at institutions of higher education, and at the same time to link the Gymnasium with the world of nonacademic occupations. It is too early to tell to what extent this linkage is really being effected (cf. Chapter 9).

At the heart of the reform is the replacement of the age-group class at the upper level of the old Gymnasium by a relatively complex system of basic and advanced courses, which is supposed to provide a common basic education while also allowing specialization. Under this system, Gymnasium pupils can fulfill the requirements for the Abitur with courses in different areas of concentration, which they choose themselves. In addition, evaluation by the traditional 6-point scale (cf. 5.4) has been supplemented by a cumulative point system. If he has accumulated enough points, a pupil can take the Abitur examination after two years in the upper level, instead of the usual three. The reform of the upper level has thus made it possible to shorten attendance at the Gymnasium by one year. Although they agreed upon a common framework for the reform, there are, nevertheless, substantial differences among the Länder in the way the reform of the Gymnasium's upper level has actually been carried out.

When the reform was implemented, a number of problems arose. With the abolition of the age-group class, pupils found it difficult to establish stable social relationships with one another in the changing groups in the courses in which the pupils were now taught; and coordinating course contents and maintaining temporal continuity among courses in the same subject turned out to be much more thorny problems than had been anticipated. The problems arising from the reform of the Gymnasium's upper level were exacerbated by the admission limitations imposed in certain fields at many institutions of higher education, for these made the Abitur grade of crucial importance. The competition to be among the number admitted to these institutions is threatening to make the pupils' interest in obtaining a high number of points decisive in their choice of courses, at the cost of their interest in the content of the courses.

More ambitious reform measures aiming at an integration of general and vocational education are being tested in several experiments with model schools, for example in a few vocational Gymnasien in Baden-Württemberg and in a number of 'Kollegschulen' in North Rhine-Westphalia. The latter schools consist of the upper level of the Gymnasium with additional vocational programs. Such forms of secondary level II are intended to permit their pupils to obtain the Abitur and vocational certification at the same time. In Berlin attempts were made on a larger scale to interconnect general and vocational education through so-called "upper level centers"; by the beginning of the 1980's, though, it has become clear that the success of these experiments was far less than had been expected.

4.10. Aspects of curriculum reform

The educational reform which began in the 1960's did not consist solely in the modification and further elaboration of the institutional framework of education. It was, in every instance, also reform of the curriculum, that is, reform of the goals and the content of education in the Federal Republic. In this reform, then, the opposition of curricular and organizational school reform, which had previously been treated as alternatives, was overcome through recognition that educational goals and the organization of educational processes are not independent of one another, but rather should be planned in close coordination with each other. Significant curricular changes did, in fact, always accompany the measures for institutional reform, such as the lengthening of compulsory full-time education to nine, and now possibily to ten, years, introduction of the orientation level and the comprehensive school, and reform of the upper level of the Gymnasium. The subjects included in the curriculum were changed, educational goals were revised, guidelines were streamlined and modernized, new textbooks were written, and new teaching methods were tried out.

A sweeping discussion of curriculum reform began at the end of the 1960's. For both educational and political reasons, there was vehement criticism of the traditional educational programs, such as were contained in the often antiquated course guidelines of the different Länder. At the same time, comprehensive proposals were made for systematically revising these programs. In this initial phase of curriculum revision, the research, development, and dissemination model elaborated in the United States played an important role. The United States also offered examples of immense efforts to provide institutional safeguards for the reform by establishing new research institutes, development centers, and educational laboratories.

Attempts to establish a similar institutional structure in the Federal Republic, however, miscarried at an early stage. For example, it was already clear in 1974 that the Länder would not jointly establish a central institute for curriculum development. An initiative made to found 60 Regional Pedagogical Centers (a compromise between the educational laboratories in the United States and the teachers centers in Great Britain) brought only two experimental institutes into being, one in Aurich, Lower Saxony, and the other in Bad Kreuznach, Rhineland-Palatinate, which are maintained today by these Länder as sites for in-service training of teachers. Big curriculum packages found but only a few supporters in the Federal Republic, while their critics were many, although seldom well informed. To be sure, a few important American curricula were adapted to the conditions in Germany (e.g., Lippitt et al., Social Science Laboratory Units, or Bruner, Man: A Course of Study); however, they are of significance primarily for teacher training, their diffusion and influence being otherwise slight. In recent years it has been contended by some that curricular reform has been a failure. This is true in the sense that the efforts to systematically reform the curricula through centrally planned reform measures have not been successful. Within the existing institutional structure of the educational system, however, many changes were made, some of them, of course, controversial.

An important factor in this process, and one having a lasting effect, was the development of subject-specific didactics at universities and teacher training colleges from about 1966 to 1976. During this period, didactics came to be accepted as an area of specialization within the various disciplines, and the new approaches elaborated by its proponents strongly influenced curricular reforms, through publications as well as through teacher training. In some cases, new didactic orientations have met with fierce resistance and provoked vehement political controversy; these new orientations have become widely known to the general public, although usually in a form distorted by policy debates. This is true, for example, of political studies, vocational orientation, mathematics, and German. In other subjects (e.g., English, geography, and the natural sciences), the new didactic orientations were quietly incorporated into course guidelines, schoolbooks and instructional materials.

The new subject-specific didactics affected most strongly the curricular reorganization of the Hauptschule. The courses taught in this school type were changed both in content and in character—at least programmatically. It is difficult to tell to what extent these changes were actually carried out. The courses at the Hauptschule had aimed at giving basic, practically oriented, nontheoretical knowledge about large subject areas defined without regard to academic disciplines; the shift was from this kind of instruction to one aiming at imparting a more theoretical knowledge and guided by scientific and academic conceptions of the various disciplines and their methods.

For a while at least, orientation to the scientific and academic disciplines was preponderant in curricular reform for all school types, bringing about a considerable degree of convergence with respect to course contents in the secondary schools. This was especially true for mathematics, the natural sciences, and the subjects derived from the social sciences. As for language-based courses such as German or English, there was a tendancy in all of the school types to make greater use of colloquially written texts and of everyday language in instruction.

Curricular reforms were most likely to be propagated throughout the school system when concurrent reforms of the school organization required new forms and new content of instruction. This was the case, for example, with the introduction of the comprehensive school and the orientation level, or the reform of the Gymnasium's upper level in all of the Länder. These changes obliged the school administrations to revise their course guidelines. Parallel to the reform of the course guidelines, the schoolbooks which were commercially available were also changed. The contribution of the schoolbook publishers to the curricular reforms was most conspicuous in the subjects in which new didactics had been developed. Long-established classics, which had been republished again and again with only a few small alterations, were replaced by new books, or were at least thoroughly reworked.

In view of all this, there is ample reason to claim that a revision of the school system's curriculum has taken place in the Federal Republic, a curriculum revision that is by no means concluded. To be sure, it was not a matter of a complete recreation, *ex nihilo* so to speak, of the total educational program; it was, rather, a step-by-step process of developing further what already existed, albeit sometimes only in rudimentary or inchoate form; of further developing such things as subject-specific didactics, course guidelines, schoolbooks, and teaching methods.

What occurred during the course of this revision, however, goes far beyond the modification of details specific to various individual subjects. For the first time in the history of Germany, the curricular reforms at the end of the 1960's and the beginning of the 1970's overcame to a certain extent the fundamental dualism between a popular education for the pupils of the Volksschule and Hauptschule and the education given to Gymnasium pupils to prepare them for university study. In spite of all the difficulties in realizing it, for example, in an endangered school type such as the Hauptschule, this beginning of a basic education common to all members of a highly industrialized society has taken firm hold and will not be undone.

CHAPTER 5

Setting Out: Preschool and Primary School

5.1. Entering school

Administratively, the school year begins on August 1 throughout the Federal Republic of Germany. All children who have turned 6 by the previous June 30 are considered to be of school age. This was one of the points established by the Hamburg Agreement, drawn up by the Länder in 1964 and again in 1971 to coordinate educational policy. Once a year, public notice is given that parents have to register their school-age children. At the time of registration, readiness tests are sometimes used to establish whether a child is in fact mature enough to enter school. Such tests are now administered less frequently, since a growing number of children attend kindergartens where their teachers can ascertain their readiness for the primary school. About half of the 6-year-olds and practically all 7-year-olds attend school. The vast majority of children go to the standard public, coeducational primary school, there being few private schools at this level. The primary school, also referred to as the primary level, consists of four grades in all the Federal Republic's Länder, save West Berlin, where it extends through the sixth grade.

The preschool level of the educational system includes nursery schools and kindergartens—in other words, all public or private institutions which provide half- or all-day care as a supplement to parental care for children from the age of 3 until they enter regular school. Parents' use of nursery schools is voluntary, and supervision of children there is carried out not by school teachers, but by personnel especially trained for this kind of work. Participation in kindergarten programs is also voluntary.

We can distinguish between two types of kindergarten, the "preparatory class" and the "threshold program." Both facilitate a gradual transition from home or nursery school to school proper. Organizationally, the threshold program may be attached either to the nursery school or to the primary school, as a one-year program for 5-year-olds or as a two-year program for 5- and 6-year-olds. In the latter case, only the first year is voluntary. The preparatory class, on the other hand, is an integral part of the primary school; for the most part, it serves those children whose sixth birthday falls after the cut-off date. The advantage of those preschool programs that are attached to a primary school is that sharing facilities is conducive to cooperation between preschool and regular teachers. These programs are thus particularly well suited to providing children with the continuous development of the learning process that educators consider desirable. In a number of Länder efforts are being made to expand these preschool programs.

Children whose sixth birthday falls in the second half of the year may, under certain circumstances, be admitted to school early. Conversely, a 6-year-old may be held back a year if, on the basis of readiness tests or his teacher's observations during the first months of school, it appears that he is not yet ready. Such children, as a rule, attend either a special kindergarten attached to the primary school, or a preparatory class, where they are given extra help in developing the abilities considered essential for success in school. In some Länder this attendance is compulsory. The school kindergarten thus occupies a special position between the preschool level and the primary level.

5.2. Capacity of preschool facilities and developments in the primary school

In 1960, nursery schools could accept, on an average nationwide, one child in three for the age group from 3 to 5. In 1977, they could take in three out of four children in this age group (cf. Figure 5.1). Since 1966, total nursery school capacity has steadily increased. Nursery education is still expanding throughout the country, and it can be expected that within the decade of the eighties nursery school facilities will be available for all children in the age groups concerned. Although nursery schools are still insufficient to accomodate all children who might attend such schools, there are considerable dif-

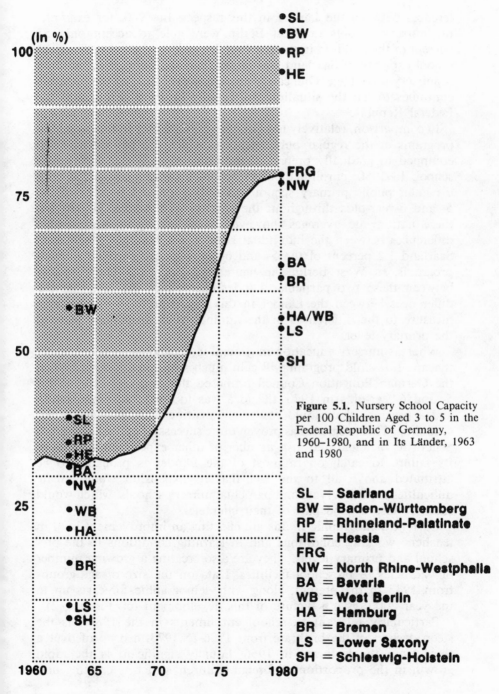

Figure 5.1. Nursery School Capacity per 100 Children Aged 3 to 5 in the Federal Republic of Germany, 1960–1980, and in Its Länder, 1963 and 1980

SL = Saarland
BW = Baden-Württemberg
RP = Rhineland-Palatinate
HE = Hessia
FRG
NW = North Rhine-Westphalia
BA = Bavaria
WB = West Berlin
HA = Hamburg
BR = Bremen
LS = Lower Saxony
SH = Schleswig-Holstein

ferences between the Länder in this respect. In 1980, for example, the nursery schools in West Berlin were able to accept only 55 percent of the children in the relevant age group, whereas the nursery school capacity of Saarland was larger than the number of children of nursery-school age. One can assume, however, that as the birthrate continues to fall the situation will rapidly improve throughout the Federal Republic.

In comparison, relatively few children are cared for in the preschool programs at the regular public schools, which are particularly well equipped to gradually prepare them from an early age for regular school. In 1980, enrollment in preschool programs connected with a regular public primary school was only some 5.5 percent of the 5- and 6-year-olds throughout the country as a whole. Underlying these nationwide averages, however, there are again considerable differences between the individual Länder; for example, whereas in Saarland 1.2 percent of the 5- and 6-year-olds are enrolled in such programs, in West Berlin the figure is 27 percent. The disparity between these two particular Länder exemplifies the fact that the differences between the Länder in this regard are also due in large measure to the differences in the number of facilities they have at the primary level.

Whereas nursery education in general is expanding, it is less likely that the threshold program will gain much additional ground. When the German Education Council proposed this two-year scheme for 5- and 6-year-olds in 1970, the idea was to create an organization and a program that would ease the transition from play to formal schooling. This program has proven quite successful at the Laboratory School in Bielefeld and at a number of other experimental schools. Its failure to catch on in most of the Länder is probably to be attributed above all to the fact that its expansion would create difficulties for the private and parochial nursery schools, which would stand to lose a good part of their clientele.

Current demographic trends are effecting an improvement both in teachers' working conditions and in learning conditions in the preschool and primary levels. They are also creating a growing number of vacancies in preschool facilities. Data on the size of age groups from 1945 to the present, along with demographic forecasts up to the year 2000, give a picture of this development (cf. Figure 5.2).

Particularly relevant to school enrollments in the 1980's is the steep decline in the birthrate from 1966 to 1973, a drop of over a third from the birthrate in 1966. Equally significant is the rapid growth in the proportion of foreign children, which is creating new

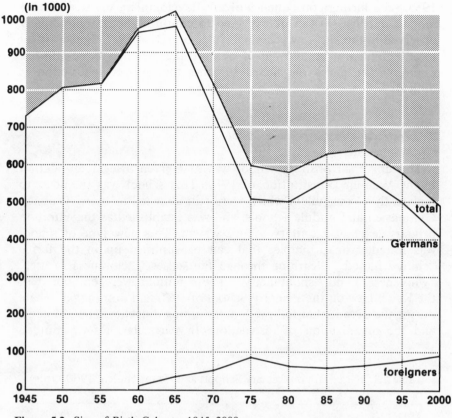

Figure 5.2. Size of Birth Cohorts, 1945–2000

problems for both preschool and regular school facilities (cf. 6.5). Yet, even taking the growing number of foreign children into account, the Federal Republic's primary schools will have a considerably smaller enrollment during the eighties than in the previous decade. Unfortunately, the improvement of the pupil-to-teacher ratio due to this decrease in enrollment will be undone in the near future. Because of financial constraints on the school system arising from the general economic situation in the Federal Republic, many teaching posts will be eliminated as teachers quit or retire.

As a result of the decline in the birthrate, the total number of children in primary school has dropped more than 30 percent, from some four million in the early seventies to roughly 2.8 million in 1980, and is expected to drop further, to less than 2.4 million in

1985. As a further consequence of this development, the size of both schools and classes can be expected to continue the decline already observed in the past few years (cf. Table 5.1). However, the statistical trend should not be allowed to obscure the fact that there still are numerous instances of classes so large that proper instruction is difficult.

5.3. Instruction in the primary school

The universal primary school was first given a legal foundation in the Weimar Constitution of 1919. This school was intended to replace the 'Vorschulen' which were still attached to many Prussian Gymnasien and middle schools, and was established as the common primary level of a unitary school system. This new type of school was founded on principles that can be summed up in the terms "child-centered," "learning through the senses," "closeness to life," "wholeness," and "spontaneity." These notions were embodied in the Reich Law on the Primary School of 1920 and dominated debate during the decade that followed, determining didactics, methodology, and the organization of instruction. In particular, reform-minded

Table 5.1: Basic Data on Primary Schools and Hauptschulen, 1960—1980

Year	Pupils	Full-time teachers	Pupils per teacher[1]	Pupils per class
	Primary schools and Hauptschulen			
1960	5,219,235	142,098	35.7	36.6
1965	5,565,778	161,115	33.1	34.7
1970	6,347,451	187,724	31.6	33.9
1975	6,425,116	235,042	27.5	30.0
1980	5,044,183	249,848	21.6	25.2
	Primary schools only			
1975	3,912,170	127,812[1]	30.6	29.6
1980	2,767,542	116,426[1]	23.8	24.1

[1] Including full-time equivalents of part-time teachers.

Sources: Statistisches Bundesamt: Bildung im Zahlenspiegel 1981; Kultusministerkonferenz: Statistische Veröffentlichungen, No. 54, September 1977, No. 75, October 1981.

educational theorists were intent on drawing a clear line between education in the new primary school and the authoritarian tradition of rote learning in the 'Lernschule' of Germany's past.

For a long time after the 1920's, the primary school was considered a school type in which all major reforms had been carried out, and for which the only remaining task was to consolidate the reform efforts in the individual schools. As late as 1962, a respected advisory body, the German Committee for Education, expressed the view that the primary school had found its proper form, more than any other level in the school system. In its "Master Plan" of 1959, a comprehensive program for the whole of the educational system, this advisory body defined the following objectives for the primary school:

- The primary school should shelter the child within and bind him to an external organizational order and an internal moral order;
- it should carefully guide the child from play into a readiness to work;
- it should introduce the child to life and the world around him in a way that is appropriate to him as a whole being, encouraging him to experience his surroundings directly and not merely exercising his verbal recall;
- it should help the child learn responsible social behavior;
- it should cultivate the child's active command of his native language, orienting him toward standard German;
- it should introduce the child to numbers and the written word, and enable him to read, write, and do simple arithmetic correctly and easily.

It was not until around 1970 that the primary school once again became the focus of pedagogical debate. This discussion took into consideration what had been learned about primary education from experiences in other countries, especially in the United States of America, and also drew from these findings incentives for changes in preschool education. Criticism centered on two issues, one being social integration in the primary level and the other equality of opportunity.

With regard to the former, it was felt that the integration of children of different creeds and backgrounds, Protestant and Catholic, rural and urban children, was insufficient. The school districts were considered too small and thus too homogeneous, and the usual four years at the primary school were held to be too short to effect satisfactory integration.

With regard to the equality of opportunity, it was thought that teachers were not sufficiently individualizing instruction to compensate for the particular deficits of children from homes which did not stimulate them to learn. Above all, however, the selection process that occurs at the pupils' transition to secondary school was criticized for taking too little into account the potential learning capacity of children disadvantaged in this way.

In 1970, the Education Council proposed a plan for the reorganization and development of education throughout the Federal Republic. This "Structural Plan for the Educational System" included a two-year transition phase for all 5- and 6-year-olds. This transition phase was based on recent findings in the field of child development showing that educability is especially great in early childhood. And since child-centeredness was no longer considered an appropriate criterion for instruction on the primary level, the Education Council made the following recommendations:

(1) Learning processes should be initiated in such a way as to render any subsequent change of their fundamental orientation unnecessary.

(2) Attention should be directed not merely to the subject matter to be learned, but just as much to the process of discovery and to developing individual initiative, ability to cooperate, and problem-solving skills.

(3) Individual factors that serve to promote or impede learning should be identified as precisely as possible.

(4) The simplified rudiments of science and social studies, as well as of modern mathematics and language theory, should be included in the instruction given in the primary school.

(5) More time and attention should be given to the acquisition of language skills, and language instruction should be revised.

(6) Instruction in art, music, and the crafts should stress the techniques typical of these subjects.

(7) Basic skills such as reading and writing should be taught in separate courses and thereby given a special place in the curriculum.

(8) New subjects—a first foreign language, for example—should be introduced.

The new principles which serve as guidelines for primary school education are individualization of instruction, its differentiation into basic and advanced courses, its orientation to basic concepts and methods of various academic disciplines, and compensatory education for the purpose of achieving greater equality of opportunity. These principles continue to be the objectives of primary education.

Although indisputable progress has been made in realizing them, much remains to be done.

These principles have not gone entirely unchallenged, however. It should be pointed out that, in particular, objections have been raised against the call for orienting instruction to the structure of academic disciplines.

Primary school instruction focusses on basic skills in reading, writing, and arithmetic. It also provides an introduction to the natural and social sciences through courses in a subject area encompassing both fields. Relatively few hours a week are devoted to the additional subjects: music, art, crafts, and sports. As a rule, children attend school during the morning hours, in 45-minute blocks. First-graders have a total of 17 hours of school a week, a load which increases to around 25 in the higher grades.

The subject matter to be taught in the primary school is set down in curricular guidelines by the school administrations of the Länder. These are more or less binding, depending on the individual Land. Whereas some school administrations stipulate exactly what is to be taught for the full school year, others allow teachers a certain number of weeks, which they can plan as they see fit. Yet other Länder view these guidelines as mere recommendations, allowing teachers considerable individual latitude in deciding when to present what material.

In addition to the regular classes, between one and three hours a week are set aside for instruction in small groups for those children who need special attention. Beginning in the second grade, special help is provided for dyslexic children in the form of remedial classes (cf. 6.2).

So far as methods are concerned, teachers are free to teach as they choose. For the most part, however, they still seem to prefer "frontal" instruction, in which the teacher stands at the center of all activity, asking questions, making corrections, introducing new material, announcing an exercise or review—in brief, determining in detail what the children are to do. Occasionally one encounters teachers who give the type of instruction recommended by the Education Council in its Structural Plan. These teachers apply methods which allow them to take better into consideration the children's varying individual aptitudes. For example, the children might learn something new by working together in groups on a project independently of their teacher, or they might work with changing partners. Teachers feel a strong need for techniques of this sort, but up to now their training, both at teacher-training colleges and at the uni-

141

versity, as well as during their first year of teaching, has not taken such innovations into account. Moreover, there are too few teachers with the appropriate experience who could serve as models (cf. Chapter 12). A further obstacle to the introduction of individualized instruction is the high pupil-to-teacher ratio (cf. Table 5.1).

The growing numbers of school-age children of foreign workers poses a special problem for the primary school and increasingly also for the different types of secondary school (cf. 6.5). The number of non-German children in the primary school and the Hauptschule tripled over the period from 1970 to 1978. In the 1979/1980 school year, 9.6 percent of all primary school pupils were children of foreign workers—most of them from Turkey, Italy, Greece, Spain, and Yugoslavia. Additional problems arise for the schools in those districts where there is a mixture of nationalities. It should be noted that the overall statistics obscure the fact that there are enormous variations within the individual Länder themselves, and that there are some schools in which non-German children are in the majority. The success of attempts to integrate these children into the school and give them a good education depends on the extent to which ghettoization can be avoided and various forms of differentiated and individualized instruction can be developed. Only by means of such instruction can a teacher take into account widely varying levels of knowledge, learning habits, and language skills, and thus give each child the specific help he needs.

5.4. Report cards, being kept back, and advancement to secondary school

Like all schools in the Federal Republic of Germany, the primary school is organized into grades. As a rule, the pupil advances year by year from a lower grade to the next higher one, promotion depending on satisfactory achievement. Report cards are issued twice a year, and the child's achievement in individual subjects is rated on a scale from 1 to 6. A "1" signifies very good, a "2" good, a "3" is satisfactory, a "4" is passing, a "5" means poor to failing, and a "6" means failing. A pupil whose performance in several subjects is poor to failing has to stay back and repeat the grade.

The proportion of children kept back a grade in the primary school was as high as 4.2 percent in 1976, dropping by 1978 to 3.2 percent. In dealing with the considerable differences that exist between children from different backgrounds, schools have until recently been inclined to favor having the low achiever repeat a grade early in his school career rather than later. Now, however, a number of Länder have introduced a policy of automatic promotion; all children advance together with their classmates, and any weaknesses are dealt with in special remedial classes. According to this policy, no child should, as a general rule, be kept back, especially in the first grade. In conjunction with automatic promotion, a limited number of schools in some Länder have replaced the traditional 6-point scale on report cards with detailed descriptive evaluations. This form of reporting, which is designed to pinpoint the child's individual strengths and weaknesses and suggest how best to help him, is not yet practiced on a scale wide enough to permit appraisal here.

There are considerable and growing differences in the way the various Länder deal with transition from the primary school to one of the four types of secondary school: Hauptschule, Realschule, Gymnasium, and comprehensive school. There is not even agreement on the specific point in time when the decision should be made on which type of secondary school a child should enter. In most of the Länder, selection takes place at the end of the fourth grade; in Berlin, it falls at the end of the sixth grade (cf. 7.1 and 4.5).

Quite apart from the problems that can arise, should a family, for instance, be forced to move from one Land to another at this critical point in a child's educational career, the transition process in itself places a considerable burden on the individual child. The main problem is that at this point the preparation of pupils tends to be concentrated one-sidedly on those subjects and skills which either are—or are considered to be—of crucial importance for the evaluation on which the recommendation for the one or the other type of secondary school is based. For example, some parents arrange for their children to be given special after-school tutoring in spelling and arithmetic for a while just before the crucial decision is to be made. Some schools even go so far as to drop altogether for a time in the fourth grade the few hours per week devoted to art and music so that more time can be spent on reading, writing, and arithmetic.

The selection process puts the child under great pressure to achieve, especially in those Länder where examinations are employed, or where the decision rests mainly with the teacher. As a rule, it is the parents who exert this pressure, many of them being prepared to make considerable sacrifices and go to a great deal of trouble to ensure that their children get the education that will give them the most advantages. The teachers, however, generally reinforce this pressure.

It would be easier to justify these disadvantages if the process of selection for the one or the other type of school were actually as accurate as it is supposed to be. Yet this appears to be doubtful, as a number of empirical studies on the reliability of the selection process have shown. The best guide in the decision on which type of school a child ought to attend appears to be parental preference, provided that the parents do not underestimate their child, a mistake that is made more often than their overestimating their child's ability. The use of the parents' assessment of a child as the primary criterion for his assignment to a secondary school minimizes the negative effects of this classification on primary school instruction and creates a new and more favorable learning environment in which children have a better chance of showing what they are capable of. In any event, grade point averages and written examinations measure only a small fraction of the abilities which are important if a child is to do well in secondary school.

CHAPTER 6

Integration or Segregation?
Children in Need of Special Attention

6.1. Groups with particular educational needs

Differentiated or individualized education in the schools has been a major preoccupation of reform in the Federal Republic in the last decades. In all types of school, different levels of achievement and different interests are taken into account, and children are helped to learn in a more personalized way. Still, the organization and the curricula of the ordinary schools are based on some assumptions about their pupils which do not apply for certain children. Several groups of children with particular educational problems can be identified in the school system of the Federal Republic. For some of them, special education is provided in separate institutions. Let us begin with a brief description of these groups.

There is no adequate general term for one of the most important of these groups. It consists of all the children who are considered slow learners, have ability weaknesses, are withdrawn, or have trouble adjusting. Their behavioral and learning difficulties vary according to the intensity of the problem and how long it has endured. In some cases, the behavioral problem is a temporary one and disappears with the specific conflict that caused it. But a considerable number of children have persistent learning and behavioral problems, often resulting from their home situation and the environment in which they are growing up. Teachers have always been expected to give these children particular attention. As long as the problem appears to be only deficient academic performance, the child belongs in an ordinary school. But in cases where a child proves unable to keep up with instruction in the main subjects, teachers and psychologists seek to determine whether he might not be better off in a special school.

In addition to those children whose progress is impeded by environmental and psychological factors, there are children who are incapable of following regular instruction because of a brain dysfunction or some sort of organic disorder or disability. While it is believed in the Federal Republic that mentally handicapped children should be educated in institutions of their own, it is also recognized that mental handicaps cannot be clearly delimited. Consequently, even in cases where brain damage is suspected, it has to be ascertained whether it is really necessary to place the child in the kind of special program that would isolate him from others.

A third group of children consists of those handicapped physically either from birth or as a result of illness or accident. This group includes the blind, the deaf, the paralyzed, and other physically handicapped children. Many of these children are highly motivated, but of course they need special facilities. Although these can sometimes be provided in ordinary schools, there is a strong tendency to place the physically handicapped in special institutions.

Psychologists, educators, and teachers in the Federal Republic have been concerned with these three problem groups for a long time. But in the late sixties attention was drawn to a new group of children whose difficulties in school are of an entirely different nature. Some Western European countries, and of course countries like the United States and Australia, have long been acquainted with the problems of immigrant workers' children. This was not the case in Western Germany, where the schools are now confronted with an increasing number of these children, who often cannot follow instruction because of their inadequate command of German. Besides being brought up in another mother tongue, these children also come from quite different cultures. The difficulties they have in school, as far as these are not of purely linguistic nature, can almost always be traced to the strain of adjusting to the new environment.

Educators, school administrators, and political authorities are in agreement that responsibility for these four groups of children rests with the educational system as a whole. As attested by their various statements and resolutions, the following goals are currently being pursued with regard to these groups:

146

- Children with learning disabilities, who often have behavorial problems in addition, should be given an opportunity to develop their capabilities more fully.
- Although most mentally retarded children cannot be expected to acquire the usual degree of formal education, they should be given all possible assistance in developing their abilities, in order that they may have a share in the normal life in the community.
- Physically handicapped children should be given the help they need to enable them to acquire the usual school certificates.
- The children of foreign workers should have the opportunity to acquire the same formal qualifications as German children. As a short-term objective, the school administrations would like them all to successfully complete at least the Hauptschule.

6.2. Special programs for children with deficient performance on the kindergarten, preschool, and primary school levels

Since it is the goal of public education to give all children the best education possible, kindergarten and preschool teachers throughout the country have sought to give special attention to those children who for one reason or another have been held back in their development. Some of these initiatives were inspired by American programs, but in addition the governments of the Federal Republic and the Länder jointly financed a major pilot project, while a considerable number of homegrown ideas were tried out in individual Länder or local communities. Until the early seventies, when a shift began to take place, the emphasis in preschool and kindergarten education lay on promoting language skills and cognitive abilities in general. Pressure to achieve is now considered harmful to such young children, and the prevailing notion is that their education should be founded upon their natural curiosity and their own experience, and that they should be encouraged to learn through guided play.

Many disadvantaged children need more help than a teacher can give them in the course of a regular school day. For this reason slow learners are given special help in small groups. On the primary school level, as a rule, two to three hours a week are set aside for remedial instruction, over and above the regular hours of instruction. Although this means more hours of school for the slow learner, such remedial classes often enjoy a certain popularity, for the teacher is more accessible and the atmosphere is more personal and friendlier than in the large regular classes. Of course, teachers have to take

147

care that the other pupils do not look down on the slow learners who are thus singled out.

6.3. The problem of special education

Special institutions for the handicapped have existed in Germany since the late 18th century, although there were very few such institutions then. In the Federal Republic, they have a definite place in the system of public education. In all the Länder there is a wide range of different types of special schools, extending from the pre-school level to more highly differentiated institutions on the secondary level. On the other hand, there has been growing concern about the fact that, despite significant improvements, these special schools still suffer from a rather poor reputation due to prejudice. Consequently, many teachers prefer to retain even a "problem child" in the ordinary school, to spare him a blot on his educational record that might have a negative effect on his future opportunities. They may find, though, that a handicapped child would be better off in a special school. In regular schools the teachers lack not only the time but also, as a rule, the specialized knowledge and experience they need to help such children.

Referral to a special school is problematic. Therefore the teachers do not alone determine whether a particular child has handicaps which necessitate special schooling. Diagnostic procedures vary, depending on the particular handicap that is assumed to exist, and from Land to Land. But in any case, referral to a special school is a complicated process, involving tests as well as statements and evaluations from parents, teachers, and the state school administrations (cf. Figure 6.1). Much effort is taken to identify the "problem cases," since wrongly placed children fail to receive appropriate encouragement and stimulation. Moreover, errors in placement are particularly painful in view of the persistent discrimination against graduates from special schools.

These considerations have raised the question of whether there ought to be special schools at all. There seems to be little doubt that in certain cases both mentally and physically handicapped children need to be looked after in special surroundings. Yet it has become apparent in the past few years that these groups, in particular, have not been the beneficiaries of the expansion of special education facilities. Up to now, the number of applicants for admission to special schools for these groups continues to exceed the number

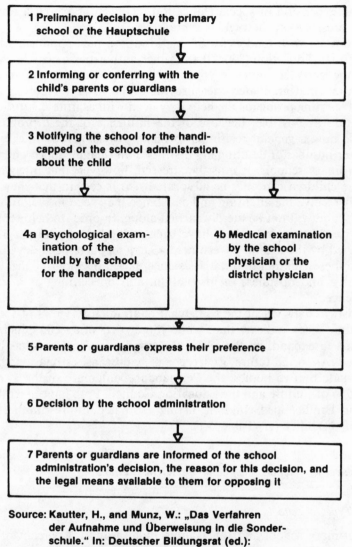

1 Preliminary decision by the primary school or the Hauptschule

2 Informing or conferring with the child's parents or guardians

3 Notifying the school for the handi-capped or the school administration about the child

4a Psychological exam-ination of the child by the school for the handicapped

4b Medical examination by the school physician or the district physician

5 Parents or guardians express their preference

6 Decision by the school administration

7 Parents or guardians are informed of the school administration's decision, the reason for this decision, and the legal means available to them for opposing it

Source: Kautter, H., and Munz, W.: „Das Verfahren der Aufnahme und Überweisung in die Sonder-schule." In: Deutscher Bildungsrat (ed.): Sonderpädagogik 3. Stuttgart 1974, p. 242.

Figure 6.1. Procedure for Referral to a School for the Handicapped

accepted. Special schools have been provided to a greater extent for the children with hard-to-define behavioral problems and learning difficulties. One conclusion that has been drawn from this fact is

149

that the expansion of special education has been above all a way of taking pressure off the regular schools.

In contrast with tendencies of this kind is a new approach which the German Education Council and other authorities have advocated since the early seventies. Typical of this approach is the recommendation that graduated measures be taken to give children with special learning problems the help they need with as little institutional separation as possible. Because of the influence of these proposals, there is now a general readiness to make provisions for integrating a greater number of emotionally disturbed and handicapped children into ordinary schools. It must be stressed, however, that integration of these children can only be advocated if it is certain that they will actually receive the attention and assistance they need in the ordinary schools, and will not be merely carried along. In order to help schools deal with this problem, there have been a number of pilot programs supported by the federal government. Curricula have been developed to give these children optimal assistance, based on individualization, flexibility, and openness of instruction, and on learning as a social experience.

Statistical data reflect the somewhat contradictory views of special education. They indicate that, while some parts of special education continue to expand, on the whole the trend toward growth has been reversed. As to the future occurrence of handicaps, estimations have been made by two bodies, the Permanent Conference of the Länder Ministers of Culture and the Education Council. Both have assembled data on handicapped children, listing estimated future numbers by type of disability (cf. Table 6.1).

6.4. Educating the handicapped in special institutions

6.4.1. Types of school

In primary school and the Hauptschule, around 4 percent of the children are found to be in need of more attention than they can receive in regular schools and are referred to one or another type of special school (cf. Table 6.2). In particular, special facilities are provided for children in the first three of the four categories defined at the beginning of this chapter: children with learning disabilities, the mentally handicapped, and the physically handicapped. Seven different types of special education are officially recognized; in some Länder and communities, however, the different facilities may be

Table 6.1: Children with Handicaps (Estimated Percentages of Birth Cohort)

Type of handicap	Permanent Conference of Ministers of Culture[1]	Education Council
Blind	0.015	0.012
Deaf	0.050	0.050
Mentally retarded	0.600	0.600
Physically handicapped	0.200	0.300
Learning disabled	4.000	2.500
Hard of hearing	0.180	0.300
Partially sighted	0.100	0.300
Speech impaired	0.500	0.700
Emotionally disturbed	1.000	1.000

[1] According to "Development Plan for Schools for the Handicapped in the FRG" ("Entwicklungsplan für das Sonderschulwesen in der Bundesrepublik Deutschland"), unpublished paper.

Source: Deutscher Bildungsrat: Zur pädagogischen Förderung behinderter und von Behinderung bedrohter Kinder und Jugendlicher. Bonn 1973.

located in the same building. There are schools for children with learning disabilities, for the emotionally disturbed and socially maladjusted, for the mentally handicapped, for the physically handicapped, for children with hearing defects, and for children with impaired vision.

Over the past two decades, special schools have more than doubled in capacity. Around four fifths of the pupils of these schools are in classes for the emotionally disturbed and socially maladjusted and for children with learning disabilities. The remaining one fifth is referred to classes for the mentally or physically handicapped. More recently, there has been a decline in the number of children entering schools for the learning-disabled. On the other hand, some schools for children with organic impairments have registered an increase in enrollment.

A year-by-year statistical analysis of the percentage of 10-year-olds attending special schools shows the development of enrollment in them. This development is the result of a number of superimposed factors: increases in capacity; more or less satisfied demand for admission; changes in size of the pertinent age groups; and teachers'

151

Table 6.2: Basic Data on Schools for the Handicapped, 1960–1980

Year	Pupils	Full-time teachers	Pupils per teacher[1]	Pupils per class
1960	142,945	6,237	20.1	20.4
1965	192,323	9,599	17.7	18.5
1970	322,037	19,399	15.3	16.7
1975	393,800	33,011	11.8	14.3
1980	353,885	40,365	8.7	11.9

[1] Including full-time equivalents of part-time teachers.

Sources: Statistisches Bundesamt: Bildung im Zahlenspiegel 1981;
  Kultusministerkonferenz: Statistische Veröffentlichungen, No. 75,
  October 1981.

referral practices. It is striking that, whereas the ratio of 10-year-olds enrolled in special schools to all children of that age increased up to 1969, since then the proportion has diminished (cf. Figure 6.2).

This is due not to any reduction in funds or staff, but rather to the fact that increases in special school capacity have not kept pace with the overall increase in the number of school-age children. An additional explanation is the inclination of teachers to avoid, if possible, referring a child with a learning disability or behavorial problem to a special school, unless the regular school proves absolutely incapable of dealing with him. Another tendency is to be noted in connection with the currently decreasing numbers of school-children: regular schools may try to assure that their enrollment does not fall below an economically defensible level by avoiding referrals to special schools whenever possible. This may, of course, work to the disadvantage of the child, should the regular school prove unsuitable for him.

6.4.2. Special schools for children with learning disabilities

Children with learning disabilities often start off in a regular primary school, and many of them even continue into the lower grades of the Hauptschule, where they are given supplementary instruction and other special help in an effort to carry them through. Those who nevertheless fail to keep up, gradually turn into "dead

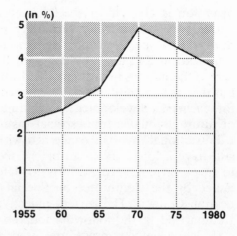

Figure 6.2. Enrollment Rates of 10-Year-Olds in Schools for the Handicapped, 1955-1980

weight," disrupting instruction for the rest of the class. Traditionally, in the German school system, these children were placed in what used to be called 'Hilfsschulen', separate remedial institutions which still had an ambiguous character in the years following World War II. Although there were certainly dedicated efforts to help these children, these institutions were often enough no more than catch basins for what were considered complete failures in the regular schools. Little distinction was made between the different causes of failure: Children with persistent learning difficulties (which in those days were little understood) were classified together in these schools with the mentally retarded, officially termed "idiots," and treated as such. Mentally retarded children now have separate facilities.

A large number of educators in special education believe that many of these children's difficulties can be traced to the fact that they have grown up in environments almost devoid of stimuli, or have experienced neglect or serious conflict in the family. Indeed, the proportion of children clearly suffering from the effects of such psychosocial damage appears to be on the increase; however, today schools for children suffering from learning disabilities are especially equipped to deal with such cases.

As a result of efforts on the part of educators to devise the appropriate didactic approach for each of the problem groups, there are separate schools for children with learning disabilities and for the emotionally disturbed and socially maladjusted. This shift to a new conception of special education goes back to around 1960. That the special school is not designed simply as an asylum or house of

153

detention is clear from special education's declared objective: preparing these children for gainful employment. Thus, pupils in this new type of special school are expected to attain a certain level of achievement and are provided with the skills they will need to take care of themselves in ordinary life. Initial results have been promising, but they are currently being threatened by cutbacks in appropriations for teachers, a development which dims the prospects for employment of future graduates from special institutions.

Educational theorists concerned with special schools feel that they still have a long way to go before special education is transformed to meet current needs. Efforts to date are documented in a report issued by the Committee on Special Education, set up by the Education Council. The current objectives of special education can be summarized in the following four points:

(1) The diagnostic procedures used in classifying pupils with learning disabilities and in evaluating their later progress should be made more effective.

(2) It should be made easier for children who are referred to a special school, and who show improvement, to return to primary school or the Hauptschule. (Up to now, only one in ten of the children referred to special schools has succeeded in returning to the regular schools.)

(3) Teaching methods should be developed which would allow a portion of the children suffering under more serious learning disabilities to remain in primary school or the Hauptschule and find help there. On this point the interests of special education appear to converge with those of educators who would like to see the primary school and the Hauptschule develop a more flexible organization of instruction. This has been attempted at only a few schools in West Germany, most notably in comprehensive schools (cf. Chapters 5 and 10).

(4) Contact should be promoted between pupils at special schools and children in ordinary schools in order to break down prejudice and resentment. The Education Council and the school administrations of many Länder consider this important, even though it appears strongly advisable to educate these children separately. A special school may now share the same building with a regular primary school without their children having any contact with one another. In certain areas, however, efforts are made to integrate children with learning disabilities and behavioral problems into the regular schools, or at least to organize visits back and forth between groups from special schools and Hauptschulen or Gymnasien.

6.4.3. Special schools for the physically and mentally handicapped

According to the Education Council, over 2 percent of any given age group is likely to be severely enough handicapped by a physical or mental disability so that their referral to a special school should be considered. At present, though, slightly less than one percent of any given age group is actually enrolled in such a school. Although the obvious feature of these handicaps is their strong somatic component, they are often compounded by emotional conflicts and social problems. It is frequently very difficult to assess the relative impact of primary and secondary factors. Educational theorists, in particular, are anxious to free themselves from definitions based solely on physical criteria, to take into account those consequences of a condition which are of pedagogical significance, or which could substantially impede a child in his exploration of his environment. This more inclusive definition of "handicapped" implies that a handicap has a sustained impact on the child's intellectual, emotional, and social development, and that help for these children should therefore not be confined to compensation for physical disabilities.

Since the various groups of handicapped children require facilities which are, to a considerable extent, especially equipped, providing appropriate education is very costly. For example, buildings used by the physically handicapped must be constructed to meet their needs, and small classes are needed for all handicapped children. Group size is smallest in the case of the blind, followed by children with hearing impairments and speech impairments. Expenditures on special personnel, materials, and equipment are considerable. Yet these children still do not receive all the help they need to enable them to lead a normal life, to the extent their handicaps would allow.

For this group, too, there are examples of successful integration of handicapped with nonhandicapped children. Experimental projects in Munich, integrating ordinary children and the handicapped in preschool and regular school classes, have received a considerable amount of publicity in the Federal Republic. As a long-term objective, the Conference of Ministers of Culture has considered allowing those handicapped children whose development is proceeding satisfactorily to attend regular comprehensive schools. In any event, it would be an important step if special schools for the handicapped could gradually be merged physically and, to some extent, organizationally with the existing educational and training centers.

6.5. Foreign workers' children in primary and secondary schools

In the early 1960's, West German industry began to recruit foreign workers, mainly from the less industrialized countries of Southern and Southeastern Europe, including Turkey. Workers from these countries and their families made up the bulk of the roughly 4.5 million foreigners registered in West Germany in 1980. Although the influx of foreign workers was reduced to a trickle after active recruitment in these countries was halted in 1973, children from families already settled in West Germany are entering school in increasing numbers (cf. Figure 6.3). In the main, these families come from Turkey, Italy, Greece, Yugoslavia, and Spain (cf. Table 6.3). In 1979, every tenth child under 15 years of age was non-German, and in the group under 6 the ratio was 1 out of 7. The proportion is likely to continue to increase, as, on the whole, the birthrate among foreign workers is higher than that of the German population. Moreover, foreign children are still entering the country, having been left behind until their parents had become settled in Germany. This applies particularly to Turkish families.

The education of these children is only one of a great number of problems created by this wave of economically motivated immigration, problems which initially were accorded very little attention. Nationwide, the proportion of foreign children in primary and general nonvocational secondary schools was 5.8 percent in the school year 1979/1980. They were overrepresented in primary schools (9.6%), in Hauptschulen (8.1%) and in special schools for the handicapped (6.4%). Their representation was below average in the Gymnasien (1.7%) and in the Realschulen (also 1.7%).

The educational disadvantage of the foreign workers' children is shown by a comparison of enrollment rates at the various types of secondary school. Whereas nationwide, only 38 percent of 13-year-olds attend the Hauptschule, for the foreign workers' children the figure is 78 percent. By contrast, among German children, 26.7 percent of the appropriate age group attend the Gymnasium but only 7.6 percent of the foreign workers' children. The latter figures are also approximately those for the Realschule. Comparison with other foreign children in the Federal Republic clearly shows that these proportions indicate a social-minority problem: for most of these others notably those from other Western European countries, the United States, and Japan, the situation is much more favorable.

Statistical averages for the country as a whole tend to obscure major regional differences. On the average nationally every sixth

156

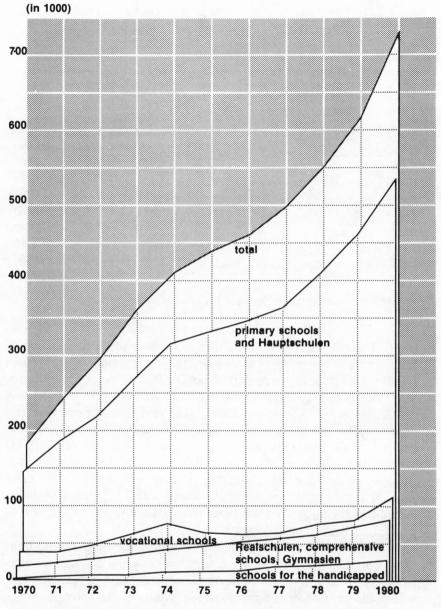

(in 1000)

Figure 6.3. Foreign Pupils in General and Vocational Education, 1970-1980

child under the age of 6 was born of foreign parents; in Berlin,
however, the ratio is 1 in 4, whereas in Schleswig-Holstein it is 1

157

Table 6.3: Foreign Pupils in General Education According to Type of School and Nationality, Federal Republic of Germany, 1980

Nationality	Primary schools and Hauptschulen	Schools for the handicapped	Real-schulen	Gymna-sien	Comprehensive schools	Total
Greek	42,484	1,465	2,498	3,740	503	50,690
Italian	62,295	5,995	3,759	2,956	1,104	76,109
Spanish	18,661	1,451	2,076	1,902	508	24,598
Yugoslavian	53,373	2,435	4,457	4,014	786	65,065
Portuguese	16,126	954	896	692	220	18,888
Turkish	286,041	12,956	8,072	6,195	4,072	317,336
Other	50,846	2,560	7,262	20,553	3,295	84,516
Total	529,826	27,816	29,020	40,052	10,488	637,202

Source: Statistisches Bundesamt: Fachserie 11: Allgemeines Schulwesen 1980.

in 16. Table 6.4 shows the resulting differences in the proportion of foreign children in primary school and the Hauptschule in the various Länder. The data for secondary schools other than the Hauptschule vary considerably, reflecting not only demographic patterns, but also differences in policy from one Land to the next. Comparable variance, depending on the Land, can be observed in the ratio of non-German children to German children in special schools. Attendance at special schools by immigrant workers' children varies also from one nationality to another. In 1980, the average nationwide enrollment ratio of foreign children in these schools was 7.8 percent, with the extremes ranging from 16.1 percent in Baden-Württemberg to 3.0 percent in Rhineland-Palatinate.

Within each of the Länder, the distribution of non-German pupils is far from being even. Average figures cannot show that a potentially explosive situation exists in certain industrial and urban districts, where the proportion of non-German pupils is far above average. In the Ruhr region, for example, which for many decades has been the center of Germany's coal-mining and steel industries, there are schools in which more than three fourths of the pupils are of foreign origin. In Berlin, as in other cities, foreign workers tend to be

Table 6.4: Foreign Pupils in General Education According to Type of School
and Land, Federal Republic of Germany, 1980 (Percentage of
Total Enrollment)

Land	Special kinder- gartens	Primary schools, Haupt- schulen	Schools for the handi- capped	Real- schulen	Gym- nasien	Com- prehen- sive schools	Total, general education schools
SH	8.2	4.4	3.1	0.9	1.0	2.3	2.9
HA	.a	17.4	10.4	3.8	2.7	4.8	9.4
LS	11.2	4.9	4.5	1.0	1.0	2.7	3.6
BR	24.3	12.1	6.2	4.2	1.5	4.1	7.9
NW	22.1	13.3	6.9	2.2	1.9	4.4	8.5
HE	31.9	12.3	9.4	3.2	2.5	4.6	8.2
RP	12.6	5.9	3.0	1.1	0.9	2.0	3.9
BW	18.2	14.2	16.1	2.9	2.2	4.5	9.1
BA	7.9	7.4	4.9	1.6	2.3	3.5	5.4
SL	14.8	5.5	5.1	1.6	1.1	3.8	3.9
WB	26.4	22.9	13.7	6.4	3.5	8.7	15.4
FRG	16.3	10.4	7.8	2.1	1.9	4.8	7.0

a Included in primary schools.

SH = Schleswig-Holstein, HA = Hamburg, LS = Lower Saxony, BR = Bremen,
NW = North Rhine-Westphalia, HE = Hessia, RP = Rhineland-Palatinate,
BW = Baden-Württemberg, BA = Bavaria, SL = Saarland, WB = West Berlin.
Source: Statistisches Bundesamt: Fachserie 11: Allgemeines Schulwesen 1980.

concentrated in certain districts, and their children in the schools
of these districts.

Often enough, neither these children nor their parents have a
sufficient command of the German language and so lack the key to
understanding many aspects of life in Germany. As a result, these
children have communication problems and adjustment difficulties
which greatly hamper their progress throughout the whole of their
school career, and result in disadvantages in later life. School grades
and qualifying credentials of all kinds are given great weight in the
labor market as well as in entry into vocational training programs.
Within this context it is significant that more than half of all non-
German children leave the Hauptschule without obtaining its final

certificate. In 1977, 46 percent of the non-German Hauptschule pupils in Bremen failed to obtain the certificate, and in Schleswig-Holstein the figure was 70 percent. The rate is, of course, even higher for those foreign children who more or less recently joined their families in Germany. By contrast, only around 11 percent of German children leave school after completing the compulsory number of years without obtaining the Hauptschule certificate. Of course, improvement can be expected in the results for the growing number of non-German children who were born in the Federal Republic or who have spent their early childhood here.

Available statistics are unsatisfactory and rather unreliable with regard to the number of non-German juveniles who attend the various types of vocational school (cf. Chapter 11). Roughly speaking, only around half of a given age group of non-German youths attends vocational school. About 65 percent had no vocational training whatsoever in 1977; 10.1 percent participated in programs of partial vocational training not leading to certification (the year of basic vocational training or the part-time vocational schools); and only 24.7 percent were enrolled in a vocational training program leading to full certification (7.1% in full-time vocational schools, and 17.6% in the "dual system" of apprenticeships and attendance at part-time vocational schools.). Due to this relative lack of training, the bulk of non-German youths have a still harder time getting a job than Germans of the same age.

It took the public and the government, including the school administration, a long time to recognize that minority problems were arising in the Federal Republic in connection with the foreign workers' children. Neither the Education Council nor the Joint Commission of the Federal and Länder Governments for Educational Planning and Advancement of Research in its General Education Plan of 1973 addressed this problem. As a result, foreign children and youths attend schools that were not prepared in time to deal with their problems. And at the same time, non-German children as a group have a considerable impact on the learning situation in a class. With the growing number of foreign-born pupils, more and more classes are "tipping over," the term some teachers use to describe the situation in a class when a third or more of the children are non-German. Most teachers feel that regular instruction is no longer possible under these circumstances. When a school is faced with this problem, all children suffer, not just the foreign ones.

Schools, teachers, and the children themselves do their best to cope with the present situation. As yet, no long-term solutions have been found. This is due in part to the fact that there have been such rapid changes in the numbers of children involved that the measures taken have continually lagged behind. At the beginning of the 1980's, for example, as a consequence of a family reunification program, authorities are expecting around three quarters of a million children, mainly Turkish, to arrive in Germany to rejoin their parents who are living here. Many of them are older children who have already begun their schooling and who will often enter school in the Federal Republic in the middle of an academic year without knowing a word of German. Moreover, measures adopted to help integrate foreign pupils have to take into account an extremely wide range of learning problems, arising because of the childrens' nationality as well as their family background and previous education.

One problem that has been affecting foreign children especially strongly is the uncertainty of their prospects. Unlike the United States and Australia, it has not been the policy of the Federal Republic to welcome immigration. Foreign workers are given a "guest" status, but not the full rights of a citizen. Most foreign workers arrived with the intention of returning home after working for a few years in this country. Hence, neither the German administration nor the parents involved saw any need to press for integration of foreign children into German schools.

As time went on, however, more and more foreign workers decided to remain in the Federal Republic, either for an indefinite period or for good. Often enough, it was not until the "second generation" grew up that the decision to stay was made. Years of indecision in such families often leave the children disoriented. However, disorientation may also result from parents' efforts to instill in their children the cultural values of their homeland, while at the same time placing value on a German education. In such a situation children attend special lessons after school in which they are taught the traditions of their countries of origin. For certain nationalities, a number of special schools have been established by the parents.

School administrations have worked out special programs to help foreign children adjust to German school life. The following are some of the ways in which help is given:
- Schools are given supplemental funds so that they may offer special assistance to foreign children who have difficulty following regular instruction. The children receive intensive tutoring in German and supplementary help in other subjects as the need arises.

161

- Schools which have particularly large contingents of foreign pupils may set up special preparatory courses in which groups of these children are prepared for regular, integrated instruction.
- Schools may recruit teachers from the pupils' countries of origin. These teachers take over part of instruction — for example in the children's native language or religion — and assist their german colleagues when language difficulties arise. They often function as interpreters between German teachers and foreign parents.
- Schools receive supplemental funds to purchase teaching materials especially designed for non-German pupils.
- Special courses are offered for teachers to prepare them to deal with the problems that arise in connection with the increasing numbers of foreign pupils.

Despite all these efforts, the chances for many foreign children to receive — and moreover to complete — a good education have not appreciably improved. These children have to acquire what sociologists call a "bicultural identity." Many of them seem to deal with the conflict astonishingly well. Nevertheless, there is no doubt about the strain these children feel because of their situation and the uncertain future it entails. This frequently leaves German teachers with an all but impossible task, well known to many of their colleagues in the United States and Great Britain, a task for which the teacher needs the qualities of a social worker in addition to those of an educator.

CHAPTER 7

Losing the Modernization Race: Reform and Decline of the Hauptschule

7.1. Secondary level I and the transition from primary school

In the preceding chapters, significant changes have often been mentioned that have been made in past decades in secondary education, and especially secondary level I, i.e., grades 5 through 10. One of these changes is that a completely new type of school, the comprehensive school, has found its place alongside the traditional Hauptschule, Realschule, and Gymnasium. Yet these schools, too, have changed to varying degrees in recent years. Another change, and not the least important one, affected the procedures by which pupils are distributed among the different types of secondary school upon completion of the primary school. The purpose of this change was to prevent cutting pupils off from educational opportunities by assigning them too early and irrevocably to the different educational programs.

There are considerable differences between the various Länder in the way the transition from primary school to the three types of secondary school is handled, differences which are widening. The decision on which type of school a child should enter is made in most Länder at the end of the fourth grade. In some Länder, however, this decision is postponed until the end of sixth grade, after a two-year orientation level encompassing all pupils in the fifth and sixth grades. Yet another practice obtains in Berlin, where the primary school lasts a full six years and the decision on which type of secondary school a child should attend is not final until after the first half of the seventh grade, the so-called "trial semester." The actual transition procedures vary as well, since in different Länder the parents, the primary school teachers, the teachers of the school in question, standardized tests, and the child's grades in primary school all play different roles in the initial assignment of a child to a secondary school. Since the 1970's, the differences among the Länder as to the time when primary school pupils are assigned to the different types of secondary school, and in the way this assignment is carried out, are so great that children are often seriously disadvantaged when their parents move from one Land to another (cf. 5.4).

Throughout the Federal Republic, considerably more children than in the 1950's now proceed to the two more prestigious types of secondary school, the Realschule and the Gymnasium, traditionally the only schools that give access to tertiary-level institutions. Although the Hauptschule has been upgraded, so that it might better compete with the Gymnasium and the Realschule, the trends in enrollment have resulted in the decline of the numbers of pupils in what used to be the "main school," attended by most children aged 13–15. This shift of enrollment among the school types accounts as much for the change that has taken place in recent years in secondary level I as do organizational and curricular reforms.

For all the attempts that have been made to put a stop to it with the help of educational policy, this trend has proved remarkably persistent. As a result, despite recent signs that some Länder are once again trying to counter the trend, there is no denying that the more or less "old" types of school now stand in a new relationship to one another at the lower secondary level. And the comprehensive schools, which are, to a large extent, the product of the reform that took place in the early 1970's, are in fact not an alternative, but rather have become an integral part of the complex secondary school system with its many divisions.

The more striking aspects of this new relationship include not only the great increase in the number of children attending the Gymnasium, but also the opposed trends in enrollment which, on the one hand, the Hauptschule and, on the other hand, the Realschule have exhibited since the early fifties (cf. Figure 4.2 in Chapter 4). There has always been a close relationship between these latter two types of school, arising from their historical roots and from similarities in the conception of the education they should offer and in the socioeconomic background of their pupils. In any event, they have more in common with one another than either does with the Gymnasium.

The present-day Realschule emerged out of the Prussian "middle school," established in 1872. On the whole, the different forms of this school lasted longer, were better equipped and had better trained teachers than the standard schools giving basic education at that time. In particular, they went beyond elementary education by teaching foreign languages and giving intensive instruction in the natural sciences. Nevertheless, for a long time the middle school generally did not succeed in becoming a higher-ranking school type which opened to its graduates the possibility of study in the tertiary sector. Educational policy excluded it from this status by giving it the task of carrying the academically weaker secondary school pupils.

This historical similarity between the Realschule and the Hauptschule — and its predecessor, the Volksschule — has not been lost. But the relative importance of its various aspects has been completely altered over the past two decades as a consequence of the completely different fates which these two school types have suffered. In 1952 around 80 percent of the relevant age group entered the Hauptschule, after which — apart from a temporary levelling-off around 1960 — the proportion fell to around 39.2 percent in 1980. During the same period of time, the Realschule, which, in contrast to the Hauptschule, may reject applicants not deemed suitable, registered a spectacular expansion of enrollment. The changes that have taken place in this, the middle-ranking type of secondary school, have encountered relatively little opposition and have gone relatively unnoticed. They occurred in the wake, as it were, of reform initiatives which attracted much official and public attention, such as those concerning the Gymnasium. Nevertheless, relative to its enrollment at the beginning of the fifties, the expansion of the Realschule exceeded even that of the Gymnasium, its share of the pertinent age groups rising from approximately 6 percent in 1952 to about 25.4 percent in 1980.

7.2. The Hauptschule

As a rule, the Hauptschule follows upon the primary school, beginning then with the fifth grade, or upon the two-year orientation level, consisting of the combined fifth and sixth grades and usually offering instruction intended as preparation for one of the types of secondary school. In the latter case, the Hauptschule offers three grades, thus bringing its pupils to the end of their compulsory nine years of full-time school attendance. Since compulsory school attendance was extended to 10 years in Berlin with the beginning of

165

the academic year 1979/1980, and in North Rhine-Westphalia with the beginning of the next academic year, the regular Hauptschule was lengthened there by an additional grade. In other Länder a noncompulsory tenth grade has been created, primarily for those pupils who want to obtain the Realschule certificate, but also as a response to the high rate of youth unemployment. The graduates of the Hauptschule generally go directly into a vocational training program or immediately begin to work, attending in either case a part-time vocational school one day a week (cf. Chapter 11).

The Hauptschule received its name formally in 1964, when this term was established by the Hamburg Agreement as the standard designation for what had theretofore been the upper level of the Volksschule (cf. Chapter 4). The name of this type of secondary school stands, in fact, for a whole program which contrasted sharply with the actual situation at that time: the upper level of the old Volksschule — which, despite its name, had never been the school for everyone, but only for the broad masses of the lower strata — was to be made into a secondary school which would be equal to the other types of secondary school. This program arose out of concern for doing away with traditional disadvantages in education, as well as from the recognition that the greater demands now being made on individuals by their jobs and by contemporary life in general necessitate improving the education of the population as a whole.

In addition, it was hoped that the increase of enrollment in the two selective types of secondary school could be halted or at least weakened by upgrading the least demanding kind of secondary education. The German Committee for Education, the "father of the modern Hauptschule," made this purpose explicit in a program draft in the late fifties: This type of school was to be made more attractive than the — in the opinion of some — then potentially overcrowded Realschulen and Gymnasien and hence capable of competing with them.

7.2.1 Educational improvements in the Hauptschule

In keeping with the Hauptschule's purpose of providing a considerably better education than its forerunner, the Volksschule, the innovations in its curriculum are particularly striking. Another improvement was the extension of compulsory school attendance from eight to nine years, which entered into effect in the largest part of the Federal Republic only in the sixties. Furthermore, changes in teacher training have made it possible to offer more courses by teachers who have specialized in the courses' subject matter (cf. Chapter 12). Finally, in the sixties and seventies, improvements in equipment and teaching materials, the merging of small schools, as well as various changes affecting the organization of instruction, created the preconditions for upgrading the education offered by the Hauptschule.

The guidelines for instruction in the upper level of the Volksschule, predicated upon a holistic conception of education, had stressed experience of the pupils' immediate social and natural environment. As far as possible, the content of instruction was to be kept in its concrete relationship to the pupil's everyday life and activity, not divorced from these in order to be inserted into a theoretical system of knowledge. It was, as a rule, considered undesirable that the study of natural and social phenomena go much beyond what the pupils could learn from their own experiences, or beyond the observation of elementary processes.

A complete break was made with this conception of "popular education" when the Hauptschule was established. The pupils of the Hauptschule were not be spared the effort of conceptual learning; the standard form of their instruction was to be the specialized course, modeled after one of the academic disciplines. It was the intent of this program to give the Hauptschule pupil access to basic methods of inquiry by teaching him to gather relevant information, pose questions, and test hypotheses, in order to develop step by step a basic conceptual framework for a given field of knowledge. The mode of instruction ranges from concrete operations to abstract thinking, depending on the age and mental development of the pupils. This type of education had been considered the preserve of the Gymnasium. These goals of redefining the subject matter of the courses and eliminating the sharp differences in the quality of education offered by the several types of secondary school, guided the changes that have been made in the Hauptschule's curriculum (cf. Table 7.1)

Although the higher standards of the Hauptschule manifested themselves in most of the subjects offered, their effect was strongest in the natural sciences and mathematics. That these subjects were made more demanding in the Hauptschule than they had been in the Volksschule is implicit in their changed designation. In contrast with the importance accorded to the natural sciences in the Hauptschule, elementary courses in general science played a minor role in the Volksschule's curriculum at the end of the fifties. These courses gave

Table 7.1: Hours per Week According to Subjects in Rhineland-Palatinate for the Upper Level of the Volksschule, 1957, and Secondary Level I (Hauptschule, Realschule, Gymnasium), 1977

Upper level of the Volksschule (1957)

Subject	Grade 5	6	7	8
Religion	4	4	4	4
Crafts	{ 2	2	2	2
Drawing		2	2	2
Physical education	3	3	3	3
Music	2	2	2	2
German	7	7	6	7
History	2	2	2	2
Civic education			1	1
Geography	2	2	2	2
Nature studies	3	2	2	2
Arithmetic and geometry	5	4	4	4
Total number of hours	30	30	30	31

Secondary level I (1977)

Subject	Grade 7 HS	RS	GY	Grade 8 HS	RS	GY	Grade 9 HS	RS	GY	Grade 10 (HS)[1]	RS	GY
Religion	2	2	2	2	2	2	2	2	2	2	2	2
German	4	4	4	4	4	4	4	4	4	6	4	4
1st foreign language	4	4	4	4	4	4	4	4	4	6	4	4
Mathematics	4	4	4	4	4	4	4	4	4	6	4	4
History	2	–	–	2	–	2	2	2	2	–	2	2
Social studies	1	2	2	1	2	2	1	1	1	4	1	1
Geography	2	2	–	2	2	2	1	1	1	–	1	1
Physics	2	2	2	2	2	2	2	2	2	2	2	2
Chemistry	2	2	2	2	2	2	2	2	2	2	2	2
Biology	2	–	–	2	–	–	2	–	–	2	–	–
Vocational orientation	3	–	–	4	–	–	4	–	–	–	–	–
Music	2	2	2	2	2	2	2	2	2	{ –	2	2
Arts (including crafts)	–	2	2	–	2	2	–	2	2	–	2	2
Physical education	3	3	3	3	3	3	3	3	3	3	3	3
Elective compulsory subjects[2]	3	5	5	3	5	5	3	4	4	3	4	4
Total number of hours	34	34	34	34	34	34	34	33	33	34	33	33

[1] The tenth year at the Hauptschule is voluntary.

[2] Hauptschule: arts, crafts and project groups. Realschule: see Chapter 8.3. Gymnasium: a second foreign language, see Chapter 9.

Sources: Amtsblatt des Ministeriums für Unterricht und Kultus von Rheinland-Pfalz, No. 7, 1957, No. 14, 1972, and Leitlinien und Arbeitsprogramm zur Weiterentwicklung der Hauptschule in Rheinland-Pfalz, 1977.

way in the Hauptschule to specialized instruction in physics, chemistry, and biology.

As for foreign languages, they were made part of the Volksschule's curriculum in a number of Länder in the years immediately after World War II. But, generally speaking, this took place only where trained teachers were available and schools were large enough to offer English courses, i.e., primarily in Hamburg, Bremen, and Berlin. However, not until the 1960's, in the Hauptschule, did English become a permanent part of the curriculum.

The courses in English and mathematics are each taught at two or three levels of difficulty to take into account the pupils' differing aptitudes. They are assigned to these courses semiannually, according to their level of performance. This kind of ability grouping was first introduced in the Hauptschule, and later adopted by the comprehensive school (cf. 10.2). The practice of ability grouping in the Hauptschule now makes it possible to offer academically respectable courses in English and mathematics to the better pupils which would not be feasible otherwise (cf. 7.2.3).

Another subject, unkown in the Volksschule, but which is characteristic of the Hauptschule, is vocational orientation. It consists of industrial arts, introductory economics, and study of the way the labor market functions, and was introduced to help acquaint the pupils of the Hauptschule with the world of business and employment. Achieving this goal turned out to be extremely difficult, however. Some of the Ministries of Culture have only recently formulated the guidelines for teaching this subject.

The final characteristic feature is that the Hauptschule offers elective subjects. According to his interests and inclinations, the pupil can choose among courses which are not part of the regular program of instruction. But this feature of the Hauptschule, too, has not been an unqualified success. The circumstances that have actually obtained in most Hauptschulen since the mid-seventies appear, as a rule, to militate against the elective courses (cf. 7.2.3).

Nonetheless, in comparison with the situation at the beginning of the sixties, it is clear that the innovations discussed above have brought about a complete transformation of curriculum and the organization of instruction in the Hauptschule. Whereas basic skills in the pupils native language were accorded the greatest importance in the upper level of the Volksschule, there is now a tendency toward a more balanced distribution of the weekly hours of instruction among the individual subjects or fields. If any subjects now have primacy, they are — leaving aside vocational orientation — the first foreign language, mathematics, and German, the three traditional main subjects in every school that qualifies its graduates to continue their education in the post-secondary sector.

The intent with which the Hauptschule was established could only be realized within an organizational framework such as was provided, at best, by the city-states, i.e., Hamburg, Bremen, and Berlin. In the sparsely populated and educationally often underdeveloped rural areas of the other Länder, it was first necessary to create the required conditions. One of these was the organization of the pupils into age-group classes, each of which consists only of pupils in the same grade. In the Volksschule such classes had been only rudimentary: At the beginning of the sixties, in the Länder with rural regions an average of only 42 percent of Volksschule pupils attended schools in which they were taught in separate age-group classes. These schools with their rudimentary grade structure had long been maintained by some school administrations that wanted to preserve the 'Bekenntnisschulen', which were, as far as possible, sexually segregated. In the sixties these schools more and more lost their importance, and since the middle of the seventies they have practically ceased to exist (cf. Figure 7.1)

Certainly it would be injust to dismiss these unsophisticated schools, most of which had no more than three classes, as simply inadequate judged from the standpoint of the present, for after the war they were the source of important innovations in teaching methods which carried over into other sectors of education. The educational reforms of the 1920's (e.g., integrative instruction, crafts, the project method, etc.) often found an especially ready acceptance in these schools, if for no other reason than because it was hoped that these reforms would ease the difficulties of overseeing several different grades simultaneously. Yet, because of its small number of classes, the Volksschule did not bear even an outward resemblance to the other two more elaborately structured types of secondary school. And because the different grades were gathered together in the same class, instruction and other activity within the school of necessity took on a form that rendered impossible systematic, specialized cognitively demanding instruction such as the Hauptschule is intended to offer.

The changes effected in this connection were of great importance, for another goal of the reform was the establishment of schools with parallel classes, i.e., two or more classes for each grade. As a result of the reform, the number of Volksschulen rapidly declined toward the end of the sixties throughout the Federal Republic, in spite of a continuing increase in the total number of secondary school pupils.

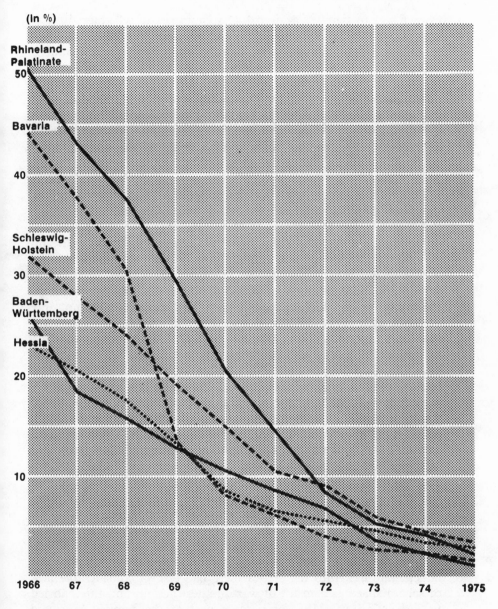

Figure 7.1. Percentage of Classes in Volksschulen Comprising Pupils of Different Grades in Selected Länder, 1966-1975

In the Federal Republic's most populous Land, North Rhine-West-phalia, for example, Volksschulen having an upper level were reduced

171

from 6,000 to barely one fourth that number (cf. Chapter 4). The large secondary schools that were created were a necessary precondition for the differentiation of instruction into basic and advanced courses, as well as for offering not only elective courses but also a range of such courses broad enough to permit pupils concentration on particular areas of study. The increase in school size also made it organizationally feasible to have in every school a ninth grade, the final grade necessary for the lowest ranking secondary school certificate. In the smaller schools, as a result of the normal dropout rate, not enough pupils reached the last grade to justify a ninth grade class in each of them.

This reform encountered special difficulties in rural areas where the main effort to improve secondary education had to be made. Preparations for the necessary "centralization" of the secondary schools, for the establishment of school centers, had already begun in some Länder at the end of the fifties. To pay the building costs of the school centers and to overcome the difficulties in administration and transportation of pupils arising from these new centers, the communities which financially sponsored them required not only the political and organizational help of the Länder governments, but also, and especially, their financial support. Furthermore, the 'Bekenntnisschulen' and the training of their teachers in separate institutions according to their church membership both were common in some of the Länder with extensive rural areas. These circumstances were incompatible with the merging of small schools necessary for the Hauptschule's establishment, as well as with the new educational program to be offered by this type of school. This hindrance, too, had to be eliminated by political means. All in all, the reform of secondary education in rural areas laid the necessary foundation for abolishing the disparities between the cities and the countryside that had emerged as soon as public education was established, and that, rather than diminishing, had deepened over the years.

In urban areas, too, the establishment of the Hauptschule required improvements in the organizational structure provided by the Volksschulen, in part the same ones as in rural areas, as well as new and larger buildings. Into the sixties there had been a considerable lack of school space as a result of wartime destruction, and this had led to instruction in shifts for a large part of the pupils. A related problem, and one having the same origin, was the large size of classes in the Volksschule. This was gradually reduced, but in the middle of the fifties one out of three Volksschule classes had, on a nationwide average, more than 40 pupils. Furthermore, in the schools with only a rudimentary grade structure, pupils in the same class were in different grades. In a few Länder, even classes with more than 50 pupils were not exceptional. The reduction of class size was doubtless one of the critically important conditions which made it at all possible to attain certain of the Hauptschule's goals, such as providing an active command of foreign languages or a deeper understanding of the natural sciences through experiments.

In this respect the situation of the Hauptschule at the present time is actually better than that of the Realschule and Gymnasium, which have traditionally had incomparably better teaching conditions (cf. 8.1, 9.3 and Table 5.1). Paradoxically, however, the reduction in the class size of the Hauptschule failed to have at least some of the positive effects usually associated with this kind of change. The reason is that the improvement also resulted from a decline in the proportion of pupils going on to the Hauptschule after completing primary school. Despite this decline, though, problem children, who need special attention, continued to enter the Hauptschule in disproportionately large numbers; and, in the opinion of many teachers, the current pupil-to-teacher ratio is still too high to permit them to give these children the help they require (cf. Chapter 6).

7.2.2. Vocational orientation and the different policies for the Hauptschule

As mentioned above, one of the particular characteristics of the Hauptschule is the new subject, vocational orientation. It serves to show the different policies the Länder have pursued in the course of the Hauptschule reform. It was originally intended that vocational orientation should combine theoretical instruction with practical work in shops located within the schools, and should be a particular characteristic of the Hauptschule as a third, self-sufficient pillar of the secondary education system. However, a number of Länder have attempted to shift the emphases contained in this conception of the Hauptschule. In these Länder, the way the curricular institutionalization of vocational orientation is being effected is intended to achieve two goals: making instruction that relies heavily on experience and is immediately practical in nature general throughout their Hauptschulen; and promoting the linking of these schools with vocational schools and the early assumption of an occupation.

Other Länder have taken an altogether different approach to the reform, leaving no doubt that they view the Hauptschule, both in its organization and its curriculum, as only an intermediate stage in

173

the development of an integrated system of secondary education. The Hauptschule's contribution to this system was supposed to be its technical and business training, which was more extensive than in the Realschule and Gymnasium. Consistent with this intent, serious efforts were made in these Länder not to confine vocational orientation to the Hauptschule, but rather to integrate the elements of its content into the entire system of secondary education. To the extent that this subject is offered at all in the Realschule, it usually appears among the elective compulsory courses, i.e., from which the pupils are required to choose a certain number. Here, however, vocational orientation is typically not as directly practical as in the Hauptschule. In the Gymnasium, on the other hand, this area is dealt with, if at all, generally in other subjects, such as social studies.

There is undoubtedly a connection between these differences in opinion about the appropriate policy regarding the Hauptschule and the fact that the original program for establishing this school has still not been completely implemented. The plan to extend the eight grades of the Volksschule to ten in the Hauptschule, a plan in existence now for a good many years, had been adopted by only two Länder at the end of the seventies — leaving out of consideration the extension of the Hauptschule introduced especially for the sake of unemployed juveniles. In some Länder it is not even possible for a pupil to continue voluntarily in the Hauptschule beyond the ninth grade, should he want to obtain a higher-level certificate. At the present time it appears that only a minority of the Länder are planning to add an obligatory full-time tenth grade to the Hauptschule. When North Rhine-Westphalia recently took this step, it was decided to give pupils the choice of spending the additional year of obligatory full-time schooling in the Hauptschule or in one of the programs of vocational training.

The discrepancy between plan and reality is nowhere more clearly evident that in the name 'Hauptschule' itself. Intended to be the main form of the secondary school, the Hauptschule now no longer serves the broad mass of the population for which it was established, as the "average" pupils choose to attend the other types of secondary school. It is precisely this state of affairs that hinders any further realization of the original plan. Of 11 Länder, only one, Rhineland-Palatinate, had more Hauptschule pupils in 1980 than in the other two secondary schools taken together. On the other hand, a number of Länder, notably Berlin, Bremen, and Hamburg, the proportion of pupils attending the Hauptschule has dropped to less than 30 percent (cf. Figure 7.2; for some further statistical data cf. Table 5.1). The consequence of this development has often been that the one-time "school of the majority" has the smallest number of pupils of all three major types of secondary school — leaving out of consideration the schools for the handicapped and the comprehensive school, which is more developed in the above mentioned cities than elsewhere.

Educational policy and the differences in policy among the Länder apparently had at best a very indirect influence on the shift of the educational preferences of the general population to the selective types of secondary school. In any event, the elaboration of the Hauptschule's organizational structure and the efforts to make it more attractive by upgrading its curriculum have proven to be ineffective as means to stem the "migration" to the Realschule and the Gymnasium

Two decades ago the differences among the various Länder appeared far less marked than now, at the beginning of the 1980's. There are, however, signs that, after a period of increasing controversy about educational policy, the differences in this regard have been diminishing since the middle of the seventies. The main obstacle to a convergence of the Länder's educational policies is not, however, differences of opinion, which, owing to the Länder's sovereignty in cultural matters, can result in differences in their policies on secondary education. Of greater importance in this connection are the geographical and social differences among the Länder. Thus, in view of the declining birth rate, which increases the difficulty of providing adequate schools precisely in rural areas, it will probably become more difficult to remedy the disparities in educational opportunities and in participation in education that still exist between the urban and the rural population. In the rural areas a considerably smaller proportion of the population achieves entrance in to the Realschule and the Gymnasium than in the cities; this ratio could become lower still, if the diminishing total number of secondary school pupils should make it necessary to reduce the number of schools and so increase the distance that pupils must travel. Nevertheless, there is no end in sight to the worsening trend toward a "shrinking" Hauptschule, a trend which is far more advanced in the heavily populated urban areas than in the countryside (cf. 8.4)

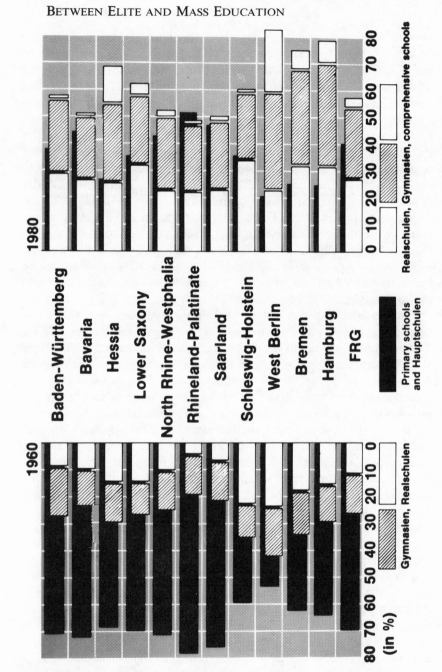

Figure 7.2. Enrollment Rates of 13-Year-Olds According to Land and Type of School, 1960 and 1980

7.2.3. The Hauptschule as victim of educational expansion

The reverse side of the educational system's expansion is the significant loss of importance of the lowest ranking type of secondary school. This development poses serious problems for educational policy and educational theory, problems which are difficult to resolve because their causes do not directly admit of political solution. The general rise in educational standards almost inevitably appears to place at a disadvantage all those who stand low in the hierarchy of social status or in the scale of ability, and who consequently become only poorly qualified. The social devaluation of the lowest level of educational qualification resulting from the higher standards of education affects not only the individual pupils but also the institution, the Hauptschule, lessening its attractiveness even further and thereby reinforcing the social processes which have devalued it. Because of its low prestige and declining enrollment, people have come to call the Hauptschule a "school for the leftovers," a name to which particularly the more committed teachers and policy-makers object.

The predicament in which the contracting Hauptschule finds itself is manifested above all in the school climate, which is often unfavorable to learning. Symptoms of the malaise are high rates of absence and disciplinary problems, and from time to time instances of vandalism. The minority of pupils engaged in such activity is obviously more strongly represented in the Hauptschule than in the selective types of secondary school. One reason is that, as more and more pupils choose to enter the Realschule and Gymnasium after completing primary school, children with problems of one sort or another are left behind, so to speak, as a residue, and are concentrated in the Hauptschule. Furthermore, it is clearly not easy to get pupils to accept the rules of an educational system that expects them to remain on the lowest level of achievement, rather than helping them to improve their life chances. In particular, problems must be expected with the integration into the Hauptschule of those pupils who must transfer from the Realschule and the Gymnasium in the seventh and eight grades because their scholastic performance was inadequate.

The situation is further complicated by the fact that the Hauptschule, contrary to all the aims of the reform, was not able to rid itself of its class-specific character. Indeed, the part of the social spectrum from which the Hauptschule draws the majority of its pupils has become narrower still. Among these, children from working-class families, and especially children of unskilled laborers, are disproportionately represented. The families of these pupils do not

177

provide the cultural background necessary for academic success, nor are they able to give the help with homework traditionally expected from German parents. A special problem in this connection are the children of foreign workers, who make up an increasing percentage of the Hauptschule's pupils, particularly in the urban areas (cf. Table 6.4). When one considers merely the number of pupils, as in Figure 7.2, the high proportion of foreign children in the urban Hauptschulen conceals the extent to which conversely enrollment of German children in the Hauptschule has declined.

A further indication of the seriousness of the problem, and one which renders it all the more acute, is the dwindling prestige of the Hauptschule certificate. From 1965 to 1976 the number of Hauptschule graduates dropped sharply. At the same time, the number of pupils who left the Hauptschule without graduating, after attending school for the compulsory number of years, did not significantly decline. It is thus likely that this latter group will have an even stronger influence on the character of the Hauptschule in its present contracted state. Because they are at a marked disadvantage in the job market, as shown by their high rate of unemployment, some members of this group obtain the Hauptschule certificate later. This they can do through Centers for Adult Popular Education, for example (cf. Chapter 13).

Another group of pupils, on the other hand, goes beyond compulsory minimum education by choosing to attend school for a tenth year immediately after completing the obligatory nine years at the Hauptschule. Contrary to some prejudiced assumptions, even in big cities, where most of the better pupils attend one of the higher ranking secondary schools, an astonishingly high proportion of the Hauptschule's pupils chooses to continue full-time schooling for a tenth year. However, only in a few Länder is it possible to obtain even the equivalent of the Realschule certificate by attending the Hauptschule for an additional year.

Where Hauptschule and Realschule have been joined, as in Hamburg, a way for Hauptschule pupils to obtain the equivalent of the Realschule certificate will probably be established in most instances. Elsewhere, a distinction is made between the "simple" and the "qualifying" Hauptschule certificate, the latter conferring a broader range of privileges, including access to further education. However, as long as a pupil does not actually obtain a generally recognized, higher ranking educational certificate, such as that from the Realschule, it seems doubtful that the expected improvement of his life changes will occur.

These negative repercussions are stronger or weaker, depending on the specific conditions obtaining in a given area. We have noted the differences between cities and the countryside, where more favorable conditions for the Hauptschule might exist, because a broader range of pupils is available there. The problem nevertheless appears to be a general one: The Hauptschule's curriculum is highly differentiated and makes considerably greater demands on the school's pupils than did the curriculum of the Hauptschule's predecessor; yet any attempt to put this more ambitious program into practice is, in effect, undermined by the changes the Hauptschule is currently undergoing — a process of shrinking enrollment accompanied by its narrowing range of pupils.

No reliable studies have been made on the extent to which this development is affecting instruction in the Hauptschule, and whether, for example, standards are being lowered in those Hauptschulen where a great many pupils have changed to the other types of secondary school. But the beginning of the 1980's, it is still true, generally speaking, that instruction in the Hauptschule is given much more often by teachers who have not specialized in the subjects they teach than in the other types of secondary school. Table 7.2 shows how things stand with the core subjects in this regard in North Rhine-Westphalia.

As one can see, the Hauptschule continues to be influenced by the tradition of the Volksschule, which offered a much more limited range of courses from instructors whose training was general, not specialized in any of the subjects offered. The relatively unfavorable situation in the natural sciences (in biology and chemistry even more so than in physics) shows how difficult it is to fill the long-standing gaps in the Hauptschule's teaching personnel. The new subject of vocational orientation is also currently being taught mostly by instructors who have not specialized in it, or who are, at best, only partially trained in it. Nevertheless, the figures do not simply show the inherited features of the old Volksschule. The lack of specially trained teachers in music, art, and physical education is common throughout secondary level I in all the school types and is, rather, a "modern" feature of the Hauptschule. The Volksschule was not faced with this problem, or at least not in this way, since the training of the Volksschule's teachers included these subjects, although often in reduced or ideological form.

When one considers the teaching situation in the Hauptschule when this school type was established, then it is clearly a significant achievement that now more than two thirds of all instruction in the

Table 7.2: Total Weekly Hours of Instruction at Hauptschulen in North Rhine-Westphalia According to Status of Teachers, 1981

Subject (selected subjects)	Hours of instruction per week				
	Number of hours scheduled	Percentage canceled	Percentage taught by instructors whose principal occupation is		
			non-teacher	teacher	
				not specialized in subject	specialized in subject
German	123,534	0.8	0.1	22.8	76.4
History, social studies	45,204	1.4	0.0	39.2	59.4
Mathematics	116,680	0.5	0.0	15.8	83.7
Physics	38,505	4.1	0.1	26.1	69.7
English	110,055	1.2	0.1	22.4	76.4
Music	19,526	15.8	0.1	34.1	50.0
Physical education	84,039	19.5	0.6	19.7	60.2
Vocational orientation	52,264	6.2	0.1	50.1	43.6
All subjects	832,914	5.3	0.4	27.5	66.8

Source: Kultusministerium Nordrhein-Westfalen (unpublished material).

Hauptschule is given by teachers specially trained in the subjects they are responsible for. And it is a signal success that more than three fourths of instruction in the core subjects of German, mathematics, and English is given by teachers specially trained in them. The progress that has been made since the middle of the 1970's is evidenced especially by the fact that hardly any use is made now of temporary teachers whose main occupation or official activity is other than teaching, and that it has been possible to considerably reduce the number of canceled course hours. As for the proportion of instruction given by teachers specialized in the subjects of their courses, however, the improvement since then has been, at best, slight.

The last circumstance is, in fact, a consequence of the current problematic situation in the Hauptschulen, which has been created by the increasing loss of pupils to the other school types. The number of specialized teachers available for the Hauptschulen is perhaps greater now than before. But the suggestion that more of them be assigned to this school has met with the response that this step would not resolve the disciplinary difficulties with problem pupils.

The Hauptschule teacher who is assigned to a class, and who, regardless of his specialization, teaches his pupils in several subjects, appears to have the advantage over his colleague who gives courses only in his special subject. His longer classroom contact with the difficult pupils strengthens his social relationship with them, and the strength of this relationship makes him a more effective teacher. For this reason it is characteristic of instruction in the Hauptschule that one teacher gives most, or at least several, of the courses a class takes. There might be a connection between this characteristic of the Hauptschule and the fact that of all the school types it has the smallest number of course hours missed by pupils. Finally, the relatively small size of the Hauptschulen is certainly also responsible for the continuing high proportion of instruction in some subjects by teachers not specialized in them, since their size makes it inefficient to recruit specialized teachers for subjects having relatively few course hours (e.g., the natural sciences). The steady decline of the number of the Hauptschule's pupils is dramatically reducing the size of its classes, but this will in the future exacerbate the kinds of problems caused by small school size.

Furthermore, teachers in the Federal Republic are tenured officials of the Land in which they teach, and as such they have, practically speaking, complete job security for the length of their working life. In addition, the declining number of pupils to a considerable degree will check the replacement of teachers who have resigned or retired and any increase in the number of teachers (cf. Chapter 5). Consequently, the gaps which still exist in the ranks of the specialized teachers will probably persist for a long time to come. On the whole, then, there is no reason to believe that the Hauptschule will be able to overcome its disadvantages vis-à-vis the other types of secondary school (cf. Tables 7.2 and 8.2).

CHAPTER 8

Upgrading the Norm:
The Success of the Realschule

8.1. Realschule and "middle school"

The way things changed in secondary education from 1950 on had aspects that were clearly disadvantageous to the upper level of the Volksschule and later to the Hauptschule. The Realschule, however, was able, for the most part, to profit from this development. There were no spectacular reforms of this type of school, nor were spectacular attempts to save it necessary; the important changes in the Realschule took place, as it were, on the quiet (cf. Table 8.1). Perhaps for these reasons the public and social scientists have shown relatively little interest in the Realschule.

Table 8.1: Basic Data on Realschulen, 1960–1980

Year	Pupils	Full-time teachers	Pupils per teacher[1]	Pupils per class
1960	430,683	15,389	23.0	32.4
1965	570,871	21,412	23.5	32.5
1970	863,450	34,117	23.1	32.1
1975	1,147,217	47,703	22.7	31.4
1980	1,351,071	63,142	21.5	29.8

[1] Including full-time equivalents of part-time teachers.

Sources: Statistisches Bundesamt: Bildung im Zahlenspiegel 1981;
          Kultusministerkonferenz: Statistische Veröffentlichungen, No. 75, October 1981.

Like the Hauptschule, the Realschule has borne this name through-out the Federal Republic only since the Hamburg Agreement of 1964, which established a degree of nationwide uniformity in the secondary school system. To be sure, in some Länder the name had already gained a measure of currency in the fifties as a new desig-nation replacing the traditional "middle school." But the name 'Realschule' harks back to a tradition that is almost as old as that of the Gymnasium and the Volksschule. This tradition encompasses a considerable number of different institutions established at various points in history, which, counter to the intentions that gave rise to them, evolved for the most part parallel to the old "humanist" Gymnasium and gave ever greater access to university study. In the last analysis, though, the tradition in which the Realschule stands has probably had its greatest effect through long-term curricular changes in general secondary education as a whole. In the course of these changes, natural and social phenomena, the so-called 'Realien' treated in mathematics, the natural sciences, history, and geography, gained in importance at the expense of the transmission of cultural traditions in Latin, religion, and German courses.

It was only after World War II that the term 'Realschule' could be made the standard designation for the intermediate level of qualification in the hierarchy of secondary schools, for then the remaining institutional vestiges of the earlier forms of the Realschule disappeared. Because they gave access to university study, these forms of the Realschule were also given the name 'Gymnasium'. Thus, this name no longer referred exclusively to a type of secondary school oriented to the classical languages, which were no longer considered prerequisites for higher education, and were in fact now given only a marginal place in the Gymnasium's overall curriculum (cf. Chapter 9).

Today's Realschule has ten grades, one more than required for compulsory minimum education, and its curriculum is more de-manding, both in quantity and in content, than that offered by the Hauptschule. The Realschule certificate used to be called the inter-mediate certificate, because it ranked between the Hauptschule cer-tificate and the Abitur. Whereas the latter gives its holder access to university study, the greater part of the Realschule's graduates im-mediately begin apprenticeships or take jobs; in either case, however, they also attend part-time vocational school. It is also possible for Realschule graduates to enter directly into full-time vocational schools, in most instances into the specialized technical secondary schools that have been in existence since 1969 and are considered the true

183

upper level of the Realschule. As specialized schools — for the industrial arts, economics, nutrition, and home economics, for example — they qualify their graduates, whose program of study usually lasts two years, for admission to polytechnic colleges. Furthermore, the Realschule certificate confers, in principle, the right to attend the Gymnasium and thus gain access to the higher education sector. Entrance into the Gymnasium, though, is usually made contingent upon a high level of academic performance, attested to in the Realschule graduate's certificate.

As already mentioned, most Realschule graduates go directly into an apprenticeship or immediately find employment. According to some experts, the number of those who do so is currently increasing. Nevertheless, on the whole — there are differences from one Land to another — they also make considerable use of the last two possibilities for continuing their education. For example, in 1975 about 17 percent of the Realschule graduates in Rhineland-Palatinate continued their general education in Gymnasien, and 20 percent went on to full-time vocational schools, while in Bavaria the figures were quite different. There, only about 3 percent of the Realschule graduates intended to take advantage of the possibility of continuing their education in the Gymnasium, compared to some 16 percent who wanted to attend specialized technical secondary schools and another 7 percent who intended to go on to other kinds of full-time school.

The differences between the two Länder indicated by the figures cited can be explained in part by differences in the secondary school curricula. Another factor is the differences between the Länder in the possibility for Realschule pupils to transfer to other types of school that open the way to the tertiary sector. For example, the possibility for Realschule graduates to enter directly into a specialized technical secondary school varies, depending on the importance attached to experience and occupational qualification for admission to this kind of school.

A multiplicity of institutional combinations has always been characteristic of the middle-ranking sector of the secondary school system, and this multiplicity is still a dominant feature of the Realschule. It encompasses four or six grades, depending, first, on whether a given Land has the two-year orientation level; second, on whether this level is part of the Realschule; and, third, on whether, as in Berlin, the primary school lasts six years. And a minority of Realschulen — a not inconsiderable minority in some Länder — are traditionally joined together with Hauptschulen. The shift of attendance, and importance, from the one type to the other is evidenced by the fact that, in Schleswig-Holstein for instance, what had been called "Hauptschulen with Realschule-tracks" have been renamed "Realschulen with Hauptschule-tracks." At the same time, the percentage of Realschulen incorporated into cooperative secondary school centers, which at present is still low, appears to be growing. Finally, there are also differences in what Realschule pupils must do to acquire their certificates of graduation; in four of the 11 Länder of the Federal Republic they have to take a special examination at the end of the tenth grade.

The dissimilar organizational forms to be found among Realschulen from one Land to another are manifestations of varying traditions. These traditions have also had a strong impact on the quantitative development of this type of school in the different Länder. In contrast to the course taken by the Hauptschule in its development, there was greater variation among the Länder in Realschule attendance in 1960 than in 1980, when relative attendance at Realschulen ranged from a low of 20.3 percent to a high of 32.4 percent (cf. Figure 7.2). In particular, the Länder of Southern Germany could offer little in the way of intermediate-level secondary education immediately after World War II, as the Prussian tradition of the middle school, starting in 1872, was to a large extent lacking there; and the rudimentary intermediate-level secondary schools that did exist often were private.

In this region, the function of such a school was often assumed by the lower and middle grades of the Gymnasium. Consequently, the individual Gymnasien here often did not have an upper level. When the Gymnasium functioned as an intermediate-level secondary school, a greater number of its pupils than usual left it after completing the tenth grade and having obtained promotion to the 'Obersekunda', as the Gymnasium's eleventh grade was formerly called. Only since the latter half of the 1950's did these Länder establish large numbers of middle schools or Realschulen.

The increase of enrollment in the Realschule that was general throughout the Federal Republic then proceeded especially rapidly in these Länder, as the newly established schools made possible the satisfaction of a demand that had already existed for a long time. These efforts did not, however, always succeed in overcoming the initial differences between these Länder and the others in the extent of the Realschule's development. On the other hand, in Länder where the Realschule has been traditionally more broadly established, such as Hessia and Berlin, the development of the comprehensive school has at least slowed down the expansion of its enrollment.

185

In seeking to explain this increase of enrollment, it is not enough to point out that the number and size of Realschulen were increased, although this expansion of the Realschule exerted a quite strong attraction. This it did especially in those regions which had been inadequately provided with schools, initially even at the expense of the Gymnasium. However, the slight extent of the Realschule's development as late as the beginning of the fifties is one indication that throughout the whole of its history up to that time the Realschule had not really been able to establish itself as an alternative to the other types of school.

The traditional vague designation "middle school" points up a serious weakness of this school's position in the educational arena. It was difficult for the Realschule to make good its claim to independence and a distinctive character vis-à-vis the Volksschule and the Gymnasium. The "psychological" and "sociological" explanations of the Realschule's raison d'être reflected this difficulty more than they helped to overcome it. These explanations postulated a special type of person, "practically and theoretically gifted," and a group supposed to have the occupational function of "mediating between planning and execution." The apologetic intention of these constructs was so obvious, though, that they failed to be convincing.

Furthermore, such appeals to the varying aptitudes of pupils and to differentiations in the societal system of occupational functions were so formal and general that they lent themselves to justifying almost any scheme for dividing secondary education into different sectors. Hence, it can be assumed that this line of argument was of interest mainly to the professional organizations concerned, and otherwise at most to those persons involved in making educational policy. As for the parents, what probably counted most was the curriculum offered by the Realschule, and above all whether their children's life chances would be improved by attending the school.

Even in the early years of its existence the middle school or Realschule was set apart by the fact that such subjects as business mathematics, English for commercial purposes, and typing were an integral part of its regular program. In this way the Realschule's curriculum, more than that of the other types of school, took into account the most likely employment prospects of a certain group of secondary school pupils. Especially after the war this feature of the Realschule was stressed, on rather dubious grounds, in the name of the school's historical tradition. Still, this proved not to be a solution to the Realschule's dilemma, its ambiguous position between two alternative possibilities—either to provide a more solid and comprehensive basic education, as in fact the Volksschule was supposed to do, according to earlier conceptions of educational reform; or to expand its curriculum and make its courses more demanding, and thus approximate a truncated version of the Gymnasium. When the latter course had been pursued, though, the middle school was regarded for a very long time as at most in only a very limited sense formally equivalent to the lower grades of the Gymnasium, and in fact not able to compete with the higher-ranking school.

The historical controversies about the intermediate certificate are clear evidence for the status of the middle school relative to the Gymnasium. It was a privilege of the Gymnasium to confer the right to serve in the military as a volunteer for one year in the place of three years of obligatory military service. Beginning in 1864, this right could be gained by successfully completing the tenth grade of the Gymnasium. During the second half of the 19th century, in addition to its significance for military service, the intermediate certificate acquired increasing importance as the entrance qualification for the middle level of the public service or of positions in the private sector. Accordingly, until after World War II a large part of the Gymnasium's pupils left school after finishing the tenth grade.

After World War I, because universal obligatory military service had been eliminated in Germany in consequence of the lost war, it became, in principle, necessary to redefine the intermediate certificate. It was not until the beginning of the 1930's, however, that a nationwide agreement about the intermediate certificate was made possible by the Depression and the fear that the economic crisis might lead an even greater number of persons to seek to improve their chances for employment through university study. In accordance with this agreement, the intermediate certificate could now also be obtained by completing the middle school's last year, the tenth grade. Nevertheless, promotion to the eleventh grade of the Gymnasium, formally equivalent to completing the middle school, continued to have clearly a far greater value than the latter. Moreover, the attempt made at this time to redefine the requirements for careers in the public service in order to take into consideration the new significance of the middle school certificate was unsuccessful. It was an admission of failure when the intermediate certificate was abolished in 1938, even though completion of the middle school in itself was now supposed to be the entrance qualification for a career in the public service. It remains questionable to what degree this effort was in fact really effective, since it was directed against the gradual raising of the level of educational qualification required for entrance into public service careers, and hence against the interests of the officials already in public service. Not until after World War II was the Realschule certificate able to overcome its traditional evaluation and achieve acceptance as equivalent to the Gymnasium's intermediate certificate.

8.2 The Realschule's success and its new function

In view of these circumstances, how does one explain the extraordinary success of this kind of school? Part of the answer lies in social developments in the Federal Republic over the last decades. To begin with, the Realschule fulfills a specific social function. School statistics suggest that the disproportionately large expansion of the Realschule is due to two social forces: the ambition of certain groups in the lower social strata to climb to a higher rung of the social ladder, and the desire of groups in the lower middle stratum to maintain their social status. In general, growing prosperity increased the interest and the participation of these groups in education, the increase benefiting the Realschule more than the Gymnasium, which is culturally and in its social character more alien to the members of these groups than the former type of school. As a result of their increased enrollment in the Realschule, the social composition of its pupils corresponds in large measure to that of the population as a whole.

The greater affinity to the middle school of groups which were previously underprivileged is the result of traditions that have been qualitatively changed through being perpetuated. The enrollment of girls in the Realschule has always been greater than that of boys. The middle-ranking secondary school served as the advanced school for most girls. In the course of the Realschule's development, the overrepresentation of female pupils increased further, while at the same time their disadvantage with respect to the Gymnasium disappeared. To the extent that the foreign workers who have, in effect, immigrated to the Federal Republic now constitute the lower status groups of the society, it seems likely that they, too, will turn to the Realschule as the educational means for their children's social ascent.

The large enrollments which the Realschule now enjoys are also to be attributed to the fact that, as the result of economic developments, its certificate has become more and more useful over the years. Since the Realschule certificate qualifies its holders to enter, as many of them do, the middle echelons of public administration and of management in the private sector, the shift that has taken place over the last two decades in favor of the service sector has certainly served to increase Realschule enrollment. In addition, the higher level of vocational training now required by industry probably also plays a role in this connection. These higher requirements are perhaps to be understood as a response by industry to the lack of skilled workers which continued until the mid-seventies. Be that as it may, throughout the period under discussion the employers' associations consistently supported the Realschule in their statements on educational policy.

Another reason why the Realschule certificate has acquired a special value is that it opens up considerably more educational opportunities than it did previously. In principle, this certificate now gives access to all higher levels of secondary education and their corresponding certification. Although the Realschule graduates wishing to transfer to the upper level of the Gymnasium must have achieved a high level of academic performance, the possibility of such a transfer has, in effect, made the Realschule equivalent to the Gymnasium's secondary level I. Continuing their education in the Gymnasium is one way for the Realschule graduates to gain access to higher education; another way is to go directly into a full-time vocational school, which, in addition to qualifying its graduates for higher-level jobs in industry, can also give them access to the tertiary sector of education, since at the end of their program of studies in such a school they usually obtain a certificate which allows them to enroll in a polytechnic college. Furthermore, the Realschule certificate is an important prerequisite for subsequent on-the-job training.

On the whole, the Realschule certificate has, for all practical purposes, replaced the Volksschule certificate as the commonly recognized criterion of a basic general secondary education. This is shown not least of all by the fact that a high percentage of secondary school pupils make the effort to earn this certificate or an equivalent of it, even though they have not attended a Realschule; this they do in vocational schools, for instance.

8.3. Organization, facilities, and program of instruction

A final reason for the Realschule's attractiveness to a broad range of pupils is the nature of its teaching staff and its curriculum. In contrast to the old Volksschule, which lacked the necessary facilities, the appropriate organization of instruction, and qualified teachers, the Realschule offers a general basic education consisting of a foreign language and a wide range of courses in science and mathematics.

Judging by the comparative expenditures per pupil for both types of school, the Realschule continued to enjoy this margin of superiority also vis-à-vis the Hauptschule up to the mid-seventies. From that time on, expenditures for primary schools and Hauptschulen together have increased disproportionately to their relative size, apparently in connection with the Hauptschule's particular circumstances. This increase has raised the outlay of money per pupil in the primary school and Hauptschule taken together above that for Realschule pupils. The Realschule is distinguished from the Hauptschule by the extent to which teachers at the two types of school are specialized in the subjects they teach. At the beginning of the eighties the Realschule undoubtedly had a considerably larger percentage of teachers giving courses in their subjects of specialization than the Hauptschule. In North Rhine-Westphalia, almost 80 percent of all hours of instruction provided for by the weekly course schedules were given by teachers specially trained in the subjects they taught (cf. Table 8.2).

The situation in the Realschule is nonetheless similar in a number of respects to that in the Hauptschule, since deficiencies are also evident in various subjects in the Realschule that are characteristic for secondary level I in the other school types. The natural sciences, as well as art, music, and physical education, continue to be the subjects taught most often by instructors not specially trained in them. For physics the situation in this regard is even worse in the Realschule than in the Hauptschule. As for the other two subjects mentioned, the Realschule is only slightly better off than the Hauptschule. In the Hauptschulen these subjects are frequently taught by teachers not specialized in them, but at least they are taught. In the Realschule, however, the more rigorous insistence that subjects be taught only by teachers specialized in them has resulted in a greater number of canceled course hours in these subjects.

In both types of school the use of temporary teachers is now insignificant in comparison with the situation that still obtained in the middle of the seventies. Interestingly, this is less true for secondary level I in the Gymnasium. There the percentage of canceled hours of instruction is also slightly greater than in the Realschule, although the percentage of instruction given by teachers specially trained in the subjects of their courses continues to be greater in the Gymnasium than in the other school types (83.6%). According to these data, then, the difference between the situation in the

Table 8.2: Total Weekly Hours of Instruction at Realschulen in North Rhine-
Westphalia According to Status of Teachers, 1981

Subject (selected subjects)	Hours of instruction per week			
	Number of hours scheduled	Percentage canceled	Percentage taught by instructors whose principal occupation is	
			non-teacher	teacher	
				not specialized in subject	specialized in subject
German	49,203	0.2	0.5	4.0	95.4
History, social studies	29,546	6.8	0.4	31.8	61.0
Mathematics	48,717	0.3	0.6	21.4	77.6
Physics	19,417	15.2	1.6	20.9	62.3
English	54,372	0.4	0.2	1.4	97.9
Music	12,774	26.8	2.7	20.3	50.2
Physical education	42,127	15.6	0.9	7.1	76.4
All subjects	399,293	6.5	1.3	12.9	79.3

Source: Kultusministerium Nordrhein-Westfalen (unpublished material).

Realschule and that in the Gymnasium appears to be, on the whole,
no longer very significant.

As late as the middle of the 1970's, it appeared that, as far as
education in secondary level I was concerned, the Gymnasium was
clearly distinct from the Realschule and the Hauptschule, which
shared many common characteristics. Now, however, it is clear that
the corresponding distinction lies between the Hauptschule, on the
one hand, and the Realschule and the Gymnasium on the other.

Even though the three school types have become more similar to
one another with regard to their curricula, the Realschule has been
able to preserve and develop a character of its own, not only in
contrast to the Hauptschule, but also vis-à-vis the Gymnasium. The
Realschule's unique character can be described as a combination of
general education with courses oriented to general occupational fields
designed to prepare the pupils for subsequent vocational training.
This is especially clear in the variety of elective compulsory subjects,
i.e., a group of subjects from which a pupil must choose a fixed

number. Since the end of the sixties, the range of these subjects has increased more and more in the Realschulen. At first, individual schools took the initiative in establishing this requirement; later, the Länder themselves adopted the elective compulsory subjects on a trial basis and increased their number. Since the late sixties, this curricular modification has been taken up by a large part of the Realschulen; at present, most of the Länder have formally instituted a program of this type, while in the others the prolonged trial phase is still continuing.

The purpose of this program of elective compulsory subjects is to give pupils in the Realschule's two upper grades, i.e., the ninth and the tenth — and in some areas, to a more limited extent, the seventh and eighth grades — the opportunity to design themselves at least part of their program of study. While these pupils must take courses in the obligatory core subjects, they have a certain amount of choice with regard to other subjects, within the framework of what can be called elective requirements. Within this framework they can choose to concentrate their courses in subjects other than those of the core curriculum. These elective compulsory courses comprise between 15 and 25 percent of the pupils' weekly course load, the variation depending on the Land and the subject of concentration.

Considering the program of the different Länder, one can roughly divide these elective requirements into five broad areas of concentration. Two such areas of concentration that are relatively clearly defined are foreign languages, with English as the obligatory first foreign language and French (less often Russian or Spanish) as an elective second foreign language, and the mathematics-science complex, with additional courses offered for students interested in deepening their knowledge in this area.

It is difficult to demarcate clearly the remaining three areas because of the close ties between the subjects that make them up. Of these, the area of concentration constituted by economic and social studies is quantitatively the most important. Included in this area is the broad subject of vocational orientation — industrial arts, introductory economics, and elementary study of how the labor market functions — as well as courses in business mathematics, bookkeeping, shorthand, and typing. Sometimes a group of subjects falling under the general classification of social pedagogics is distinguished from the area just mentioned. Social pedagogics embraces courses in subjects pertaining to social work and home economics, and also courses in the arts. Recently, however, the trend has been toward separating the arts from social pedagogics and establishing them as an independent field of elective compulsory subjects. Where this field has been established, it has a special organizational status, the purpose of which is to remove subjects such as art, crafts, and music from competition with other such fields. Pupils must then take some courses in the arts in addition to the other areas of concentration, fewer courses being required in the former field, though, than in the latter.

The organization of elective compulsory subjects into fields such as those described above is not practiced in all Länder. In Bavaria, for example, a concentration in foreign languages is not possible, while provision for the arts has not yet been established in the majority of the Länder. Moreover, the full range of elective fields is far from being offered in every single school, because many schools lack the necessary equipment and facilities or specially trained teachers, or because there is insufficient interest on the part of the pupils. On the whole, however, by offering their pupils a range of choices, schools can, in large measure, take into consideration the pupils' individual propensities and preferences and also prepare them for subsequent employment or vocational training. Furthermore, through their choice of courses, pupils can take the needs of the local labor market into account. Most important, however, the Realschule's comparatively broad range of elective compulsory subjects makes it possible for this school to organizationally combine academic and vocational study programs, something the other traditional types of secondary school have not succeeded in doing.

The recent reorganization of the upper level of the Gymnasium has not altered the fact that any pupil wishing to transfer from the Realschule to this level of the Gymnasium must have learned a second foreign language or have had intensive preparation in mathematics and the natural sciences in order to do well in the Gymnasium's secondary level II. Yet it is not these fields, but rather economic and social studies that most Realschule pupils choose as their area of concentration, their choice reflecting more modest educational aspirations and entailing reduced life chances. It is an open secret that the choices permitted by the differentiation of elective compulsory subjects in effect divide the Realschule pupils into groups according to their levels of academic performance. The heterogeneity of the Realschule pupils in this regard has become greater as their number has increased.

In connection with the school's continuing expansion, some Realschule teachers have maintained that the quality of education offered by their type of school has already generally declined. To many who agree with this view it seems doubtful that the Realschule can in the long run preserve the character it has traditionally had, a character arising from the readiness to adapt and the desire to learn that have been especially strong qualities of Realschule pupils. In the course of the school's development these qualities are becoming palpably weaker among it pupils. In sum, the success of the Realschule has brought problems in its train which have cast a shadow on the satisfaction and vindication felt by the school's proponents.

8.4. Outlook

Apart from the internal difficulties already indicated, the success of the Realschule has also created a problem, inasmuch as it is, in fact, no longer a "middle school" because of the size of its enrollment and its prestige within the secondary school system. Owing to its curriculum, the Realschule also seems in many respects to have achieved, in an exemplary fashion, an integrated secondary level I, just as the Realschule certificate has, to a large extent, achieved the status of the standard for a basic education. The Realschule thus appears to be a model, as it were, for a type of school that should be made universal. In view of its achievements, it is significant that some Länder have already begun to incorporate the Realschule into cooperative school centers. It can be expected, however, that further steps in this direction will encounter resistance because the Realschule is so well established in its own right and enjoys considerable support in the general population. Nonetheless, the interest of parents' and teachers' associations in preserving the Realschule could be thwarted by the decline in the number of children entering the secondary school system in the eighties due to demographic causes. This decline may make it difficult for the Realschule to maintain on its own the degree of internal differentiation which it has been able to achieve (cf. Figure 4.3).

It is already evident that the competition which now exists between the Realschule and the comprehensive school will become more intensive under the pressure of a general and continuing decline in the number of school-age children. The present basis of the competition is the fact that the two types of school not only embody similar conceptions of education, but also draw upon much the same social strata for their pupils. And in those areas where the comprehensive school has been widely introduced and has been established to some extent as a standard school, parents have not shown the readiness to accept this type of school as equivalent to the Gymnasium that is necessary for its success. In the cities, at least, the result of this rejection has been that the comprehensive school is entering into competition with the integrated Hauptschule/Realschule (cf. Chapter 10).

It is questionable that this state of affairs will change when the number of pupils in secondary level I declines. One can, however, predict with certainty that the children of foreign workers by themselves will give rise to very different situations in different regions. Because these foreigners have a higher birth rate than the Germans, the percentage of the school-age population coming from the former group will increase further, particularly in the urban areas where foreign workers and their families are concentrated. At the same time it is to be expected that in the long run these children will progressively adapt to the living conditions in a highly industrialized society, and that they will then enter in increasing numbers the secondary schools opening the way to the post-secondary level.

Different factors conditioning the development of school enrollment in the 1980's are thus manifesting themselves. Nevertheless, the choice between the comprehensive school and the triparatite school system, which affects especially the Realschule, will in all likelihood continue to be of importance. There is much evidence in support of the contention that, as the number of secondary school pupils on the whole declines, it is probably the comprehensive school which, because of its organizational flexibility, will be able to continue to offer the individual pupil the wide range of subjects and courses which it has managed to achieve. For the school administrations of the Länder, the comprehensive school offers an alternative to merging schools of the same type, and thus leaving some areas at an educational disadvantage; the comprehensive school makes it possible to join the different educational programs together under one roof. For this reason, not a few Länder will probably favor this solution, while in the others the school administrations apparently believe that joining the Hauptschule and the Realschule holds the best promise for the future of secondary education.

The combining of the Hauptschule with the Realschule, regardless of whether or not it in fact integrates them, raises once again the question of the relationship to one another of these two types of school, which had so much in common at their inception. Nevertheless, it is probably the Hauptschule, the school already faced with the greatest difficulties, which will be most seriously affected by the problems arising from the declining number of school-age children.

CHAPTER 9

Democratizing Elite Education: The Emergence of the New Gymnasium

9.1. The Gymnasium: the concept and the program

In the first years after the founding of the Federal Republic, the types of secondary schools which went beyond the obligatory full-time school attendance in force at that time differentiated themselves greatly from one another in the course of their development. This differentiation was due to a number of factors. The most important of these were: the effects of the differing legal regulations enacted by the three occupation powers concerned, the United States, Great Britain, and France; the differing goals of the educational policies of the Länder governments; and different regional traditions.

In 1955, in an attempt to bring their school systems into accord with one another, all of the Länder of the Federal Republic concluded the Düsseldorf Agreement. One of the provisions of this agreement was that every form of the secondary school which qualifies its graduates for admission to the university was to be called a Gymnasium. The purpose of this step was not merely to reintroduce the designation of a type of school with a long and highly respected tradition in Germany. This provision of the Düsseldorf Agreement was above all the expression of a program which was the modernized version of the ideas embodied in the Prussian Gymnasium reform at the beginning of the 19th century. According to this program, the general educational task of the Gymnasium was the preparation of its pupils for study at a university.

The notion that "gifted" pupils should be brought together as early as possible, that is, at the age of 10 or 11, and led to the portals of the university through a nine-year-long unitary program of education was not as self-evidently valid in the first years of the Federal Republic as it appeared later, after the Gymnasium had been consolidated, and as it probably appears even today to many German parents. The triumph of this position was a victory for the champions of the German Gymnasium, who had organized themselves well in various organizations relatively soon after the end of the war. It was the victory of the tradition of the Gymnasium against the "Basic Principles for Democratization of Education in Germany," which pointed in the direction of a horizontally structured school system similar to the American model, and which were decreed in 1947 by the Allied Control Council, consisting of the Supreme Commanders of the British, French, Soviet, and United States Armed Forces.

Yet the restoration of the traditional conception of the Gymnasium contradicted to a large extent the institution's reality: less than half of those who began the Gymnasium in the fifth grade succeeded in obtaining the Abitur, and a large part of the Gymnasium pupils reached their educational goals with the "intermediate certificate," equivalent to the present-day Realschule certificate (cf. 8.1), after completing the sixth grade of the Gymnasium, that is, after 10 years of school. However, the public became generally aware of this contradiction only a decade later.

9.2. The types of Gymnasium

The use of the single term 'Gymnasium' conceals a differentiation within this kind of school that gradually develops in its lower and middle levels (fifth to tenth grade) and by the ninth or tenth grade, at the latest, results in the demarcation of several different types of Gymnasium. The three best known types of Gymnasium are those whose principal orientation is to the classical languages, to modern languages, and to mathematics and the natural sciences. The decisive criteria for this classification are the kind, number, and sequence of foreign languages taught in these schools.

Gymnasien, of course, have a core of subjects common to all of them, i.e., German, two foreign languages, history, geography, social studies, mathematics, the natural sciences, art, music, and sports. The number of hours of instruction which are to be given per week in each subject for each grade is set in schedules issued by the Länder school administration. Most of the larger Gymnasien have more than one class per grade; and even when their names designate them as a certain type of Gymnasium, for example as a "humanist" (i.e., classical-language) Gymnasium, they include at the present time branches of other types of Gymnasium.

After nine years of attendance and a successful Abitur examination, the pupils of these Gymnasien obtain the so-called "general qualification for university study." This gives the right to study any subject offered at any institution of higher learning, no matter which type of Gymnasium the pupil attended.

By 1978 the reform of the upper level of the Gymnasium (grades 11–13) had been introduced in all Länder on the basis of an agreement of the Permanent Conference of the Länder Ministers of Culture reached in 1972. This reform changed the system of institutionally fixed variants of the Gymnasium into a system of individual educational programs through the introduction of a greater range of choices. Consequently, one can no longer meaningfully speak of different types of the Gymnasium's upper level.

Nevertheless, these types retain importance even for the reformed Gymnasium. Some Länder—for example, Bavaria or Baden-Württemberg—have retained in the middle level of the Gymnasium the programmatic concentrations in a number of areas that are intended to prestructure the combinations of courses in the upper grades. In grades 7 to 10 in these Länder, one still speaks of the classical-language, the modern-language, and the mathematics-and-natural-science Gymnasium. By contrast, other Länder (Berlin, Hessia, North Rhine-Westphalia, Rhineland-Palatinate, and Lower Saxony), in addition to reforming the upper level, have also revised the weekly schedule of courses for the middle level, abandoning the division of the Gymnasium into types, or at least reducing their number. The purpose of this revision was, first, to enlarge the fundamental education common to all Gymnasium pupils, and to thus create a counterweight to the strong differentiation at the upper level, and, second, to create greater possibilities of differentiation for the certificate obtained after completing the tenth grade (the Realschule certificate) by means of a spectrum of elective courses which pupils can take, up to a fixed number of hours per week.

Be that as it may, the traditional types of Gymnasium in fact still provide fundamental models for the core curriculum of the contemporary Gymnasium. Nevertheless, the elective courses among which the pupils can choose make possible new variations of these patterns. Figure 9.1 gives an overview of the most important types of Gymnasium and of the sequence of language courses characteristic of each one.

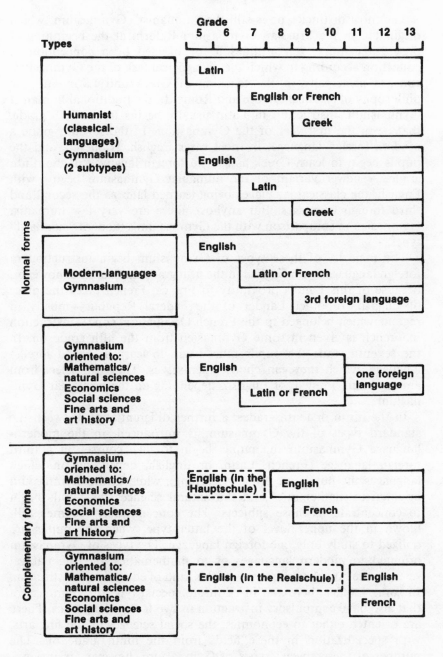

Figure 9.1. The Types of Gymnasium and Their Compulsory Language Sequences

The most distinct type is still the "humanist" Gymnasium, which originated in the Prussian Gymnasium Reform at the beginning of the 19th century. It continues to be molded by a conception of education according to which the pedagogical task of the Gymnasium consists principally in the teaching of Greek and Latin and the philosophy of classical Greece and Rome. In the traditional humanist Gymnasium, instruction in Latin usually begins in the fifth grade, that is, in the first year of the Gymnasium. In the seventh grade a modern foreign language, in most cases English, is offered, and the pupils begin to learn Greek as a third foreign language in the ninth grade. A newer variant of the humanist Gymnasium begins with English, the classical languages being learned later as the second and third foreign languages. But anyhow, there are very few humanist Gymnasien in comparison with the Gymnasium's modern "standard" types.

The majority of these types of Gymnasium begin instruction in foreign languages with English in the fifth grade. In Saarland, however, because of this Land's proximity to France, French takes the place of English. In other Länder of the Federal Republic—mostly in regions which belonged to the French Occupation Zone—instruction in French is given in some Gymnasien from the fifth grade on. In the seventh grade the pupils must begin to learn a second foreign language, which they can choose themselves. They can select from among Latin, French, or English, depending on the particular Gymnasium.

In the ninth or tenth grades, a further differentiation between the standard types of the Gymnasium is introduced: in the modern-language Gymnasium the pupils begin to take courses in a third foreign language (French, Latin, or English, depending on which languages the pupils are already learning), while in the Gymnasium oriented to mathematics and the natural sciences the pupils begin to concentrate in those subjects. The concentration becomes full-blown in the upper level of the latter type, when the pupils are obliged to study only one foreign language. The types of Gymnasium oriented to modern languages or to mathematics and the natural sciences are now the main types of this kind of educational institution. In some Länder there are, in addition, special types of Gymnasium that also have compulsory instruction in two foreign languages. These are oriented either to economics, the social sciences or the fine arts, with specialization in these fields from the ninth grade on. The number of these special types of Gymnasium, however, is insignificant.

As mentioned above, some Länder recently eliminated or restricted the different types of Gymnasium when they reworked the weekly schedules for secondary level I. These Länder require that pupils learn two foreign languages, beginning in the fifth and seventh grades. The specialization in the ninth and tenth grades, which was previously prescribed for the traditional Gymnasium types, now takes a more flexible form as a part of the schedule that allows curricular differentiation through elective subjects. This part of the schedule was elaborated differently from Land to Land and from school to school. In Table 9.1 the weekly schedules of Lower Saxony and North Rhine-Westphalia for grades 9 and 10 are used to exemplify the changed curriculum of the Gymnasium.

9.3. Complementary forms of Gymnasium and the second path to the Abitur

Some pupils who do not enter the Gymnasium directly from the primary school later want to transfer to it from the Hauptschule or Realschule. In order to make such a transition possible, most Länder have added the so-called 'Aufbaugymnasien' to the normal or the long forms of the Gymnasium, which last seven or nine years. These Aufbaugymnasien are intended to complement the education given by the other kinds of schools and begin, as a rule, after the seventh grade for pupils of the Hauptschule, and for Realschule pupils after the tenth grade (cf. Figure 9.1). They are usually attached as a separate branch to a Gymnasium of the normal form. By attending such a complementary Gymnasium for three or six years, depending on whether the pupil entered from a Realschule or a Hauptschule, a pupil obtains the general qualification for university study.

It is possible, furthermore, to obtain the qualification for university study, the Abitur, by following the so-called "second educational path" (cf. Chapter 13). Those who are employed full-time, and who have the Realschule certificate, or its equivalent, can obtain the Abitur by attending an Evening Gymnasium; or, if they can afford to stop working, they can attend a 'Kolleg', a special secondary school which prepares adults for university study. Even though more and more people are taking advantage of the complementary forms of the Gymnasium and the alternate path to the Abitur, these possibilities for rectifying the unsatisfactory course of one's schooling have had numerically insignificant results in comparison with regular Gymnasium education. In 1980, for example, of 150,000 persons

Table 9.1: Hours per Week for Subjects in the 9th and 10th Grades of the Gymnasium in North Rhine-Westphalia[1] and Lower Saxony[2]

Subject	9th grade		10th grade	
	North Rhine-Westphalia	Lower Saxony	North Rhine-Westphalia	Lower Saxony
	Number of hours per week			
German	3	3	3	4
1st foreign language	3	3	3	4
2nd foreign language	3	4	3	4
Music	} 2	2	} 2	1
Art		2		2
History	} 4	2	} 4	2
Social studies/political studies		2		1
Geography		1		2
Religion	2	2	2	2
Mathematics	3	4	3	4
Physics	} 5	1	} 5	2
Chemistry		2		} 2
Biology		2		
Physical education	3	2	3	2
Elective subjects	4	2/3	4	2/3
Total hours of:				
obligatory courses	32	32	32	32
obligatory and elective courses		34/35		34/35

[1] Circular order of March 23, 1972; published in: Gemeinsames Amtsblatt des Kultusministeriums und des Ministers für Wissenschaft und Forschung des Landes Nordrhein-Westfalen, 1973, p. 199 ff.

[2] Weekly schedule I (excluding the classical-language Gymnasium), order of the Minister of Culture of June 6, 1978; published in: Schulverwaltungsblatt Niedersachsen, 1978, p. 197 ff.

who had obtained the general qualification for university study, only 7,000 had attended an Evening Gymnasium or a Kolleg.

While the educational programs named above give those who complete them access to any course of university study, the so-called 'Fachgymnasien' certify their graduates for admission to specific courses of study at universities and other institutions of higher education. Most of them are specialized in fields such as the technical sciences and economics, and the overwhelming majority are three-year complementary Gymnasien. Fachgymnasien require only a single foreign language for admission to them, and their pupils are expected to specialize in particular subject areas, in most instances for vocational purposes. In some of these Fachgymnasien, the general qualification for university study can also be obtained by taking a supplementary examination in a second foreign language.

All forms of the Gymnasium must be distinguished from the specialized technical secondary school intended to provide both general and vocationally oriented theoretical knowledge and skills. All Länder, with the exception of Baden-Württemberg, have introduced this kind of school, which one could call the upper level of the Realschule (cf. 8.2; and Figure 2.1). Two years of attendance at a specialized technical secondary school in the eleventh and twelfth grades certifies one for admission to a polytechnic college with a primarily vocational orientation.

9.4. The reformed upper level of the Gymnasium

In the last 10 years, as the result of policy decisions, two important changes have taken place in the Gymnasium. The first was the introduction of the orientation level in grades 5 and 6, the first two years of the Gymnasium, which was decided upon by the Conference of Ministers of Culture in 1974. This orientation level is explained in more detail in Section 4.5. The second change was the reform of the upper level of the Gymnasium.

The reform of its upper level (i.e., grades 11–13) doubtless constitutes the most decisive intervention in the Gymnasium up to the present time. The resolution to effect this reform was passed by the Ministers of Culture in 1972; after a period of testing, the reform was to be introduced in all Gymnasien at the beginning of the academic year 1977/1978, at the latest. The Gymnasium continues in part to be divided into different types in grades 9 and 10. However, the reform of the upper level replaced the rigid division into types

203

of Gymnasium, which had hardly permitted transfer from one type to the other, with a flexible system of obligatory and elective course offerings.

In secondary level II of the Gymnasium, each subject is now taught both in less demanding basic courses and in more demanding advanced courses. This measure is intended, on the one hand, to preserve a common basic education, and on the other hand to make possible an individualization of a Gymnasium pupil's program of study in these years. Some Länder carried out the reform very rapidly, without first trying it out for a number of years as an experiment; Berlin, which implemented the reform in 1973, was one of these. Other Länder, for example Bavaria, drew upon the results of the testing of the reform measures, while yet other Länder complied only reluctantly with the agreement concluded by the Ministers of Culture.

The heart of the reform is the replacement of the age-group class, all members of which are in the same grade and take courses together as a unitary group, with variable combinations of the basic and advanced courses mentioned above, each of which the pupil takes for one semester. The combination of elective courses and choice of the course level permits the Gymnasium pupils to pursue in these grades a broad range of subject matters with differing degrees of concentration in various areas. This possibility, however, in no way prejudices the pupil's qualification to study any discipline at any tertiary level institution.

The reformed upper level begins in the eleventh grade with an introductory phase which lasts one semester or an entire academic year, depending on the Land. During this introductory phase the pupils are made familiar with the elective possibilities of the course system. In most of the Länder, the pupils still receive instruction during this period either completely or partially in age-group classes. However, by the beginning of the twelfth grade, at the latest, the course system is fully developed in the Gymnasien of all the Länder. The last two years, formerly called the "Lower" and the "Upper Prima," are divided into four semesters. At the beginning of each semester the pupil composes his individual schedule from the courses offered by his Gymnasium. The courses form large thematic units which are classified according to their subjects. A course generally comprises either two to three or else five to six hours of instruction per week. Each semester, a pupil registers for a total of approximately 30 course hours per week.

The reform of the upper level broadened the palette of available subjects in comparison with what the traditional Gymnasium offered, and made possible a greater range of course combinations. Areas of study entered the curriculum which had previously been offered only in some special forms of the Gymnasium, for example, an introduction to jurisprudence, psychology, sociology, economics, and data processing; in addition, art, music, and sports were accorded more importance.

The subjects offered in the reformed upper level of the Gymnasium are divided into four examination areas:

- languages, literature, and art;
- the social sciences;
- mathematics and the natural and the technical sciences;
- sports.

The pupil must choose courses from each of these areas. The possible choices and combinations are, however, limited by regulations, sometimes differing from one Land to another. These regulations prescribe which subjects are compulsory, the group of subjects from which the pupil must choose a certain number, and the minimum number of course hours per week for each category of subject. The differences between the Länder in this respect are considerable, as the framework for the reform agreed upon by the Conference of Ministers of Culture contains only minimal directives (cf. Table 9.2).

Most of the Länder go beyond this framework in their regulations. They require an additional compulsory subject, e.g., art and music, or they increase the minimum number of courses required in German, foreign languages, and mathematics, in order to assure a greater continuity of learning. In order to make the content of the courses chosen by the pupils more coherent, courses have also been bound together in "packages." However, in all the Länder the range of admissible subjects is so broad that even very large Gymnasien can only offer a selection of these subjects. The choices open to the pupils of the Gymnasium are, then, not only limited by legally binding regulations, but also by the individual school's area of pedagogical concentration, as well as by its facilities and the areas of competence of its personnel.

The fact that in each subject two courses are supposed to be offered, one more demanding and the other less demanding, sets especially difficult organizational tasks for the Gymnasium. The latter courses meet two or three hours per week and treat their subjects less thoroughly than the advanced courses. These meet five or six hours a week and are intended to give thorough preparation for the

205

Table 9.2: Course Distribution Requirements in Grades 12 and 13 of the Reformed Upper Level of the Gymnasium

Examination area (Subjects are classified according to each Land's regulations; Lower Saxony's classification is used here as an example)	Minimum number of weekly course hours in 4 semesters	Required courses	Minimum number of courses in 4 semesters
1. Languages, literature, art (includes: German, 6 foreign languages, art and music)	22	German: a foreign language: literature, art or music:	2 courses 2 courses 2 courses
2. Social sciences (includes: social studies, history, geography, philosophy, economics, psychology, sociology, pedagogics, vocational orientation, etc.)	16	set by each Land:	usually 3–4 courses for social studies
3. Mathematics, natural sciences, technology (includes: mathematics, computer science, accounting, physics, chemistry, biology, technology, etc.)	22	mathematics: natural sciences:	2 courses 4 courses
4. Physical education	8		
5. Religion	set by each Land		

Source: Framework Agreement of the Permanent Conference of Ministers of Culture of the Länder; published in: Sammlung der Beschlüsse der Kultusministerkonferenz.

university study of the corresponding disciplines and to impart extensive specialized knowledge. By the end of the eleventh grade, at the latest, each pupil must choose two subjects in which he will take such advanced courses. One of them must be either a foreign language, or mathematics, or a natural science. By the time he reaches the Abitur examination, the pupil must have taken four advanced courses in each of these subjects. In his final examination, the Abitur exam, he is tested in the two subjects in which he has taken advanced courses and also in two subjects in which he has taken basic courses. These examination subjects must cover all three examination areas.

The final or exit examination of the Gymnasium, the Abitur, is given annually in most Länder. To be admitted to the examination, a pupil must have completed the prescribed number of the prescribed kinds of courses, and must have attained a certain total number of points with his grades. In the Abitur, the Gymnasium pupil is examined in four subjects. For three of them the test is written; in the fourth subject, he is examined only orally. In two Länder, Bavaria and Baden-Württemberg, the topics for the examination essays are set by the state school administration. In the other Länder, the teachers propose several topics or problems in their own subjects; from these the Länder school administration makes a selection, such that comparable standards are established for all schools.

In order to achieve a standardization among the various Länder, the Conference of Ministers of Culture worked out a list of uniform standards for the Abitur examination, which defines the purposes of this examination, what areas of knowledge the different subjects encompass, and what forms the problems set for each subject may take. These standards have been criticized, certainly not without justification, because they officially reward and thus encourage broad superficial knowledge on the part of the Gymnasium pupils. The reason for this attempt to achieve a nationwide standardization of the Abitur was the procedure introduced at the beginning of the 1970's which regulated admission to university study of overcrowded disciplines, entrance to which was to be restricted to a set number of students (*numerus clausus*; cf. Chapter 12). The decisive criterion for a pupil's admission to such a discipline was the average of the grades he received on the Abitur examination. Differences of a tenth of a grade point could thus definitively determine the subsequent course of a Gymnasium pupil's life.

The reform of the upper level of the Gymnasium was initially carried forward by the momentum and the consensus of the reform era in the Federal Republic. In the last few years, however, this reorganization has become the focal point of intense controversy among educators and experts on education, as well as in the sphere of general political discussion. The criticisms were directed above all against the expansion of the Gymnasium pupils' opportunities to select their own courses and to specialize in the secondary school, but also against the elimination of the age-group class and its replacement with the course system. An observer from the Anglo-American educational tradition who is familiar with a more strongly differentiated organizational model of the secondary school might find this debate surprising. It becomes understandable, however, in light of the fact that the reform of the Gymnasium's upper level struck at the school's philosophical foundation, namely at the identification of general preparation for university study with the education proper to a cultivated person.

The history of the Gymnasium is also the history of its institutional ramification into different types, each with a different emphasis. But with every establishment of a new type of Gymnasium, the problem of the continued self-identity of Gymnasium education, and of the possibility of preparation for a wide range of specialized university study through a canon of a few traditional subjects (e.g., Latin, Greek, mathematics/natural sciences, history, and literature) became a topic of debate. Although these questions have periodically become topical again, the evolution of the Gymnasium up to the present time has not dispelled belief in the fundamental unity of the Gymnasium as an institution, and in the concomitant homogeneity of preuniversity education.

Until the reform of the upper level of the Gymnasium, this belief had, to some extent, a factual basis in a set of obligatory subjects, which, in spite of varying emphases, were common to all Gymnasien, and which were ordered in a generally recognized hierarchy according to their importance and prestige. This hierarchy was able to give the impression of a unitary but internally differentiated canon, and thus promoted simple definitions of general education and preparation for specialized university study that were accepted as valid throughout West German society. The Abitur certificate attests to the completion of this general education, for at the German university there is no general undergraduate education as at American colleges and universities; rather, German students at post-secondary-level institutions specialize in a few subjects from the beginning of their university studies (cf. Chapter 12).

The Gymnasium role in general education was broken up by the reform of the Gymnasium upper level into individually chosen programs of study. The reform thus aggravated in the extreme a problem that had plagued the Gymnasium throughout its history, namely, the problem of providing homogeneous preparation for university study in a wide range of disciplines and so maintaining its institutional identity. Not surprisingly, it is precisely the universities which regard the Gymnasium reform with skepticism and demand that a broad range of subjects again be made compulsory in the upper level of the Gymnasium, for the universities give only specialized training and thus have a self-image which is incompatible with formally providing general education. Consequently, they cling to the belief that homogeneous preparation for university study is possible. The Ministries of Culture in some Länder have already yielded to the universities' demands and have restricted the possibilities of specializing in the Gymnasium's upper level, to the benefit of the traditional main subjects of the canon.

Within the school system the restructuring of the upper level also brought with it a number of problems which have not been easily resolved. The elective system of the upper level necessitated a revision of the traditional hierarchy of subjects, since this system is based on the assumption that all of the subjects offered are, in principle, of equal value. The inevitable consequence has been friction and resistance. On the one hand, long-established belief in the greater and lesser importance of different subjects cannot readily be abolished. On the other hand, especially strenuous efforts are demanded from the teachers, who previously taught traditionally subsidiary subjects in courses usually meeting two hours a week (e.g., biology, geography, history, music, and sports), and who must now offer an advanced course meeting six hours a week without having the necessary books and other materials.

Furthermore, "trivial" problems of organization are a persistent source of irritation. In order to offer a certain range of courses, small and medium-sized Gymnasien must extend the usual half-day of instruction into the afternoon, with the consequence that the schedules of teachers and pupils are no longer continuous. In schools which have a teachers' room, but no place where teachers can work without distraction, which have no rooms or libraries where their pupils can read and do their written assignments, which have hardly any facilities for extracurricular activities, which do not even have a cafeteria—in these schools such discontinuous schedules must of necessity produce strain and dissatisfaction.

A further cause of controversy is the dissolution of the familiar age-group class and the resulting attenuation of social relations among the pupils—a consequence which must certainly be more serious at a half-day school with only a rudimentary peer culture than at an all-day school where extracurricular activities are well developed. The individual pupils have probably felt their isolation all the more clearly and oppressively because of the effects of the *numerus clausus* procedure restricting admission to the universities. The quota system has led to competition among the pupils in the upper level that puts the individual pupil under more intense pressure to do well in his courses. In order to prevent such isolation, an effort has been made, following the example of the comprehensive schools, to systematically provide tutors and counselors for the Gymnasium pupils.

9.5. The Gymnasium as preparatory school for university study

After the Second World War, attempts were made to change the structural divisions of the German educational system into horizontal ones, or at least to make it easier to transfer between the three parts of the vertically divided system by means of a more pragmatic and less academically oriented conception of the Gymnasium. In spite of these attempts, during the fifties those for whom the purpose of the Gymnasium lay in qualifying its graduates for university study carried the day. This turn of events was clearly expressed in the Tutzing Abitur Catalogue of 1958, the authors of which had been commissioned by the Conference of Länder Ministers of Culture and by the Conference of West German University Rectors to define the minimum requirements of qualification for university study and thereby establish the core of the Gymnasium's curriculum. This catalogue was followed in the sixties by further attempts by the universities to specify more precisely what they wanted the Gymnasium to accomplish.

Making it the purpose of the Gymnasium to prepare its graduates for university study presupposes that the Gymnasium and the university are considered to be a single educational unit. This conception of the relationship between the two institutions derives from the educational theory of Wilhelm von Humboldt (1767–1835). According to this theory the schooling in the classical languages and philosophy given by the Gymnasium was to be immediately complemented and continued by the philosophical education offered by the university, the center of which at the beginning of the 19th century was the unitary Philosophical Faculty. A harmonious transition from the Gymnasium to the university was, however, very quickly made impossible by the development of disciplinary specialization in the university from the first years of the 19th century on.

Because of this specialization the Gymnasium found itself in a dilemma, as it attempted to replicate to a certain extent in its curriculum the disciplinary divisions of the university, and at the same time to make good its claim of giving a general education in the classical languages and classical philosophy. It was, in other words, caught in the contradiction of wanting to provide a basic education in philology and philosophy and at the same time to offer a curriculum which was a microcosm of the system of academically recognized disciplines. It was caught also in a conflict between the opposing goals of providing, on the one hand, a broad modern general education and, on the other, specialized preparation for the study of a few subjects at the university.

As shown by the controversy about the reform of the upper level, two fundamental problems of the Gymnasium result from this contradiction and conflict, problems which have not yet been satisfactorily resolved. It has become increasingly difficult to justify the predominance in the Gymnasium of instruction in foreign languages to the exclusion of other areas of learning, while concurrently the profusion of the material to be treated in each individual subject presents an ever more serious problem, for which no rational solution has been found.

The Gymnasium still remains a language school, especially in secondary level I. This is perhaps most obvious in the ruling that Fachgymnasien, which give instruction in only one foreign language, but which might offer a quite wide range of courses in the natural sciences, for example, are not allowed to confer the general qualification for university study, while an Abitur-holder who has learned three foreign languages but has only scant knowledge of mathematics and the natural sciences may pursue the study of any natural science at the university. The schedule of courses set for the Gymnasium pupils by the school administrations shows more exactly the preference given to language instruction.

Thus in Baden-Württemberg, according to the schedule issued in 1972 and in force until 1979, the pupils of the modern-language Gymnasium as well as those of the mathematics-and-natural-science Gymnasium have 14 hours per week of language courses in the eighth grade, in contrast with eight course hours per week in mathematics and the natural sciences. When the pupils begin to concentrate in the ninth grade, i.e., the fifth year of the Gymnasium, the ratio of course hours per week in languages to those in mathematics and the natural sciences is 15 to 7 in the modern-language Gymnasium, and 11 to 9 in the mathematics-and-natural-science Gymnasium. Only when a pupil in the Länder which have recently issued new weekly schedules (for example, Bavaria, Hessia, North Rhine-Westphalia, or Lower Saxony) chooses at the end of secondary level I to concentrate in mathematics and the natural sciences, does the distribution of course hours in his weekly schedule shift to a slight predominance of these areas.

Attempts in the fifties to overcome the fundamental dilemma of the Gymnasium by establishing new forms of this institution succeeded as little as did the efforts to argue theoretically for the special educational value of individual subjects or areas of knowledge. Special types of Gymnasium, such as those having economics or the social sciences as the focal points of their curricula, did not gain enough support to be established in significant numbers. And the Gymnasium was unable to answer the question, why economics, law, the social and the technical sciences were represented hardly at all in its program of studies, and why the fine arts and art history play, for the most part, only an insignificant role in its curriculum.

An important result of the discussion of the secondary school reform in the Federal Republic during the last two decades appears to be a reformulation of the problem of secondary education in general. According to this new understanding of the problem, the educational task of the secondary school, and hence of the Gymnasium, does not consist in orienting all instruction to preparation for specialized university study, nor in instruction balanced between such preparation and general education. What is required is, rather, a new definition of the role of specialized instruction in the established disciplines within a more comprehensive conception of general education.

If the problem is understood in this way, then it should no longer be so difficult for the proponents of the Gymnasium to consider its pupils' departure before the Abitur as legitimate, and to adjust their conception of the Gymnasium to the fact that a large percentage of its pupils traditionally have left school without obtaining the Abitur. They considered these pupils to be accidents, rather than a challenge to the conception of secondary education embodied by the Gymnasium. Today between 20 and 30 percent of Gymnasium pupils still quit school after completing the tenth grade and obtaining the Realschule certificate; of the Gymnasium pupils who do obtain the Abitur, more than 30 percent do not intend to go on to the university. The Gymnasium education must provide these groups of pupils with a foundation for vocational training which is nonacademic in nature (cf. 9.7).

As part of its program, the reform of the upper level dissociated the Gymnasium to some degree from the conception of its serving as a preparatory school for the university. The purpose of the reform was not only to make a better preparation for university study possible; it was also the intention of the Ministers of Culture that, as a result of the reform, the secondary school should enter into a more dynamic relationship with social reality. To be sure, whether this reform is bringing into being a firmer path to vocational training or employment remains an open question. Up to the present time there have been only a small number of experiments in the secondary school which have tried to combine vocational preparation with the general qualification of its graduates for university study (cf. 4.9).

9.6. Expansion of the Gymnasium

Up to the middle of the sixties, the Gymnasium was still a highly selective school, with which notions of educating a socially homogeneous elite were highly compatible (cf. Figure 4.2). In 1965, about 15 percent of all 13-year-olds attended the Gymnasium, and in the same year 7.5 percent of the appropriate age group obtained the Abitur. Several studies from the sixties show that less than half of those pupils who began the Gymnasium in its lowest grade succeeded in obtaining the Abitur. And as for the Gymnasium pupils who persisted until the Abitur, between 30 and 50 percent of them had to repeat a grade.

Moreover, through the combination of restrictive admission regulations, a curriculum emphasizing languages and a regional imbalance in its distribution, the Gymnasium was, in effect, discriminatory in a number of ways. It disadvantaged children of poor and socially underprivileged families, especially working-class children, children from rural areas, and girls. Thus, in 1965, 10 percent of the pupils in the tenth grade of the Gymnasium came from working-class families, while 25 percent were the children of state officials; at the same time, however, workers made up 55 percent and state officials barely 7 percent of gainfully employed males. In addition to being discriminated against at the time of entry into the Gymnasium, a disproportionately large number of working-class children failed to complete all grades of the Gymnasium. The ratio of working class children to the entire class dropped to 6 percent by the 13th grade of the Gymnasium, while that of the children of state officials rose to 28 percent.

In the period from 1965 to 1978, however, this highly selective Gymnasium underwent dramatic changes, and the number of Gymnasium pupils approximately doubled (cf. Table 9.3). Since the building of new Gymnasien was alone not sufficient to contain this flood of pupils, the existing Gymnasien "exploded." Their enrollments expanded, on the average, by 60 percent. This expansion of the Gymnasium is a consequence of, first, the fact that large age groups reached the secondary school (cf. Figure 4.3), and, second, an increased demand for Gymnasium education. Thus the attendance at Gymnasien of 13-year-olds rose during this time from 15.8 percent to almost 25 percent of that age group (cf. Figure 4.2). Correspondingly, the ratio of the pupils obtaining the Abitur in the appropriate age group rose from 7.5 percent in 1965 to approximately 20 percent in 1979. Selection within the Gymnasium had obviously become less rigorous, and the proportion of those who successfully completed the Gymnasium had become considerably higher.

Yet although all social strata participated in the expansion of the Gymnasium, the social composition of the entire body of Gymnasium pupils did not change significantly (cf. Figure 9.2). Similarly, regional disadvantages in connection with attendance at Gymnasien were only slightly diminished. Nevertheless, the expansion of the Gymnasium resulted in a considerably greater heterogeneity among its pupils as far as the educational background of their families was concerned.

Table 9.3: Basic Data on Gymnasien, 1960–1980

Year	Pupils	Full-time teachers	Pupils per teacher[1]	Pupils per class
1960	853,437	46,033	17.4	28.2
1965	957,871	50,424	17.9	27.7
1970	1,379,455	69,748	18.8	31.6[2]
1975	1,863,479	89,706	18.9	32.1[2]
1980	2,118,014	116,071	17.4	30.3[2]

[1] Including full-time equivalents of part-time teachers.

[2] Without grades 11–13, for which data are incomplete.

Sources: Statistisches Bundesamt: Bildung im Zahlenspiegel 1981;
Kultusministerkonferenz: Statistische Veröffentlichungen, No. 75, October 1981.

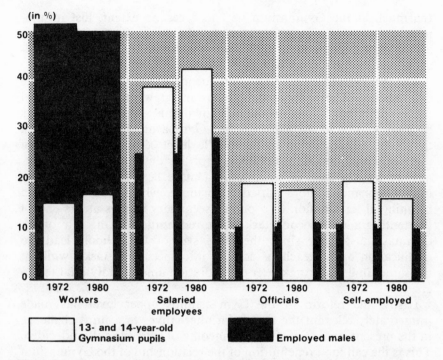

Figure 9.2. Gymnasium Pupils Aged 13 and 14 According to Occupational Status of Head of Family, 1972 and 1980

9.7. The challenges

The most apparent result of the expansion described above is that the Gymnasium ceased to be an educational institution of the elite. The schools themselves became larger, and the backgrounds of their pupils became more heterogeneous. Thus the significant changes which the educational system in the Federal Republic had been undergoing since the beginning of the sixties also seized upon the Gymnasium, perhaps even to an especially large degree. The process of transformation posed three serious challenges for this school which have persisted into the eighties.

The first is the continuing development of other types of school, and above all of the Realschule, for the heart of these changes in the German educational system was that instruction intended as preparation for university study was no longer confined to the Gymnasium. Today many Realschulen have a program of study which leads, via the upper level of the Gymnasium or the specialized technical secondary school, to the university (cf. Chapters 8 and 11).

215

Inasmuch as the Gymnasium has, to a certain extent, lost its monopoly over education preparatory for the university, it has become all the more necessary to reexamine the bases of Gymnasium pedagogy and to reflect on how it can best fulfill its educational task.

The second challenge is a consequence of the expansion of the Gymnasium. The individual Gymnasium grew rapidly—1,000 and more pupils per school is the rule in urban areas—and its pupils became more varied, although the Gymnasium did not attain a degree of differentiation in its middle level comparable to that of the Realschule, for example. Because of this development, the Gymnasium has the task of elaborating a more flexible organization of instruction and a more varied curriculum, which would permit a meaningful termination of a pupil's secondary studies at the end of the tenth grade. A second task is the redefinition of the role of the Gymnasium teacher since the large size of the schools leads to ramification of the teachers' activity into specialized tasks, while at the same time requiring closer collaboration among individual teachers.

Lastly, the reform of the Gymnasium's upper level has made immediately relevant the search for alternatives to a third challenge in the present state of affairs, the outcome of which is still undecided. This is the call for a redefinition of the relationship of the Gymnasium to the university and to society as a whole. On the one hand, the reform of the upper level can be viewed as a possibility of more strongly specialized preparation for university study. Or it could be developed into a measure for abolishing the symbiosis of the Gymnasium and the university, and for opening the Gymnasium to the larger world of nonacademic occupations.

CHAPTER 10

The Mighty Midget:
The Comprehensive School

10.1. From experiment to standard school

Even at the beginning of the 1980's, after a good 15 years of development, the comprehensive school is still a midget among the Federal Republic's secondary schools. Nevertheless, no other reform of the educational system in the past two decades was the focus of such vehement dispute as the comprehensive school, or found so many committed champions and so many determined opponents. The controversy over the comprehensive school, a symbol of all the reform efforts, appeared at times to divide the nation into two hostile camps. The comprehensive school did, in fact, embody almost all important innovations — and fashionable trends — in secondary education, and thus both challenged and exerted a persistent influence on the traditional school system.

The comprehensive school was the response to the deficiencies of the tripartite secondary school system. From the beginning of the 1960's onward, the traditional school system had become increasingly an object of public attention and criticism. The criticism had concentrated on the emphasis placed by the schools giving access to post-secondary education, and especially by the Gymnasium, on principles of selectivity which thus seemed to contribute to the waste of an urgently needed "store of talent." Another criticism was that the premature assignment of pupils to established educational programs hindered the development of their differing abilities, and at the same time placed children from the working class and from the countryside, as well as all girls, at a disadvantage (cf. 4.1). In answer to these criticisms, the comprehensive school, in accordance with the Federal Republic's general and accelerated process of modernization and democratization in the sixties, offered the following program:

- raising the general level of education, and enabling as many pupils as possible to obtain the Realschule certificate;
- providing all its pupils with a common basic education that would help them to understand the underlying principles and the fundamental structure of any field of knowledge;
- taking better into consideration and furthering the inclinations and abilities of the individual pupil by differentiating the courses offered according to the pupils' differing interests and their differing levels of performance;
- delaying the decision on the educational career of pupils until the end of secondary level I, if possible, in order to avoid the consequences of the early assignment of pupils to the different educational programs;
- and lastly, contributing to the social integration of a stratified society by providing school experiences which the members of the rising generation all share.

In 1964, the Hamburg Agreement of the Länder Governments reopened the possibility of structurally modified experimental schools which had been obstructed 10 years before in the Düsseldorf Agreement on the standardization of the school system (cf. Chapter 4). Soon thereafter preparation was begun in some Länder for isolated experiments with comprehensive schools. Such initiatives, which were sponsored in part by the Ministries of Culture and in part by various associations and communities, arose especially in Berlin, Hessia, and North Rhine-Westphalia. The planners of these experiments drew upon already existing nonstandard schools with characteristics similar to those of the comprehensive school and upon the results of experiments with "orientation levels" (grades 5 and 6) comprehensively organized to avoid early selection (cf. 4.5); or they used the British and Swedish comprehensive school as a model to which they could orient themselves. The regional beginnings of reform were given consistency and a systematic basis by the German Education Council's recommendation in 1969 that at least 40 experiments with comprehensive schools be undertaken throughout the Federal Republic. In the same year, the Permanent Conference of Länder Ministers of Culture concluded an agreement on an experimental program which would include two variants of the comprehensive school, namely the integrated and the cooperative comprehensive school, as well as all-day and half-day schools.

In the integrated comprehensive school the three traditional types of the secondary school are abolished. Instead of the rigid vertical structures of these types, there is a flexible and more diverse organization of instruction within the school. This organization takes several complementary forms: the age-group class, elective courses, and obligatory courses to which pupils are assigned according to their performance in the various subjects. In the cooperative comprehensive school the three traditional types of secondary school are preserved. However, they are housed together in a single "school center," that is, in one building, and organizational and curricular provisions make it easier for the pupils to transfer from one school type to another. Following the agreement of the Ministers of Culture, experiments with model schools were conducted in all Länder with the financial support of the federal government and preparations were made for evaluation of these experiments by social scientists.

The comprehensive school stands now, at the beginning of the eighties, at the end of its experimental phase (cf. Table 10.1). Different conclusions are drawn from the experiment depending on what school policy is favored by the government of a particular Land. In five Länder — Berlin, Bremen, Hamburg, Lower Saxony, and North Rhine-Westphalia — the comprehensive school is a standard school alongside the three traditional types of secondary school. Baden-Württemberg and Bavaria, on the other hand, are inclined to either eliminate the experimental integrated comprehensive schools or transform them into cooperative comprehensive schools. In Rhineland-Palatinate, Saarland, and Schleswig-Holstein the situation remains unresolved; it is expected, though, that the continued existence of the experimental schools will be guaranteed. Considering the Federal Republic as a whole, the comprehensive school is still not of great quantitative importance. Only about 8 percent of all secondary school pupils attend an integrated or cooperative comprehensive school. However, in the Länder which resolutely pursued a policy of school reform, up to 24 percent of secondary school pupils attend an integrated school and up to 76 percent a cooperative school center (cf. Table 10.1).

The heart of the innovation program was and continues to be the experiment with the integrated comprehensive schools. They were, moreover, always used as a standard for measuring the success of the cooperative schools. A description of the basic structure of the integrated comprehensive school should begin with a reminder that

Table 10.1: Basic Data for Comprehensive Schools, 1980/81[1]

Länder	Integrated comprehensive schools		Co-operative comprehensive schools	
	number of schools	7th grade pupils in proportion to all 7th grade pupils	number of schools	7th grade pupils in proportion to all 7th grade pupils
Baden-Württemberg	6	1.2	5	0.9
Bavaria	2	0.5	11	2.0
Bremen	5	9.1	39[2]	76.0[2]
Hamburg	23	7.3[3]	1	0.8
Hessia	65	16.0	103	27.5
Lower Saxony	13	2.4	17	3.9
North Rhine-Westphalia	34[3]	2.9[3]	–	–
Rhineland-Palatinate	3	0.6	3	1.6
Saarland	2	2.4	–	–
Schleswig-Holstein	2	0.9	3	1.8
West Berlin	30	23.5	–	–
Total FRG	185	3.8	182	4.3
of these:				
all-day schools	80 (43.2 %)	•	9 (5.0 %)	•
schools with upper level of Gymnasium	75 (40.5 %)	•	52 (28.6 %)	•

[1] Excluding Waldorf Schools (based on Rudolf Steiner's teachings).

[2] In Bremen secondary schools of the traditional types are being joined together in co-operative school centers.

[3] Expected to increase in the next years due to new schools or expansion of old ones.

Sources: Gesamtschul-Informationen, Vol. 13 (1980), No. 4; Jahrbuch für Schulentwicklung, Vol. 2 (1982).

the basic features of the program of instruction in all secondary schools are established by the school administrations of the Länder (cf. 3.1.3). As a result, the regulations concerning the program of instruction differ within certain limits from Land to Land. For every type of school the weekly schedules of courses set the canon of subjects to be taught, as well as the official length of time for instruction in each subject. For every grade, guidelines define in greater or lesser detail the general goals of courses and the broad outlines of their content. Only those textbooks may be used which have been approved by the Ministry of Culture for each type of secondary school.

In general, the experimental schools are also subject to the centralized authority of the Ministries of Culture over their programs of instruction. At the beginning of the experiment, however, the newly founded comprehensive schools had relatively greater freedom in most of the Länder in organizing the instruction they offered. They were only urged to take as their general model the varying regulations for the traditional types of secondary school. There were no weekly schedules of courses "harmonized" for secondary level I, no common guidelines, and practically no textbooks or teaching materials specially tailored to the requirements of the comprehensive schools. The lack of appropriate instructional materials was felt especially strongly in those subjects for which ability grouping was introduced.

Consequently, some of the first comprehensive schools invested much time and effort in superregional cooperation in elaborating their own instructional materials. At the beginning of the 1970's, some comprehensive schools developed, so to speak, into curricula-producing workshops. A wealth of curricular units, differing greatly in duration and in quality, was developed. The heterogeneous material represented by these units could seldom be connected, though, to form meaningful sequences or complete courses of instruction. Since then, however, integrated guidelines for the comprehensive school and even for the entire secondary level I have been developed or at least outlined. These guidelines define a common basic obligatory education for all pupils of secondary level I and establish the differentiated supplementary requirements for the Realschule certificate and for transition into the upper level of the Gymnasium.

There has also been improvement in the textbook market, in part as a consequence of the fact that the traditional types of secondary school have been made more similar to one another. This improvement is, however, also due to the increased number of comprehensive schools, which thus can now increasingly make use of commercial textbooks. This development has probably diminished to a certain degree the variation among the secondary schools of a given Land in their programs of instruction.

On the whole, a similar process of standardization can be observed in grouping practices in the integrated comprehensive schools. In the course of their evolution, the comprehensive schools have worked out, tested, and then modified quite a number of models for grouping pupils, with the result that one could, and in some Länder still can, find a relatively wide diversity of organization in these schools. In recent years, however, these efforts in some Länder have resulted in basic models which all comprehensive schools follow.

There are some fundamental features common to almost all comprehensive schools. The programs of instruction in these schools are organized chiefly in two ways: grouping according to the pupils' level of performance in particular subjects (the British "setting" system); and grouping according to the choices that the pupils can make. These choices are of two kinds: the choice of wholly elective subjects and the compulsory selection of a fixed number of subjects from a set group.

10.2. Grouping in the comprehensive school

10.2.1. Grouping according to level of performance

Most comprehensive schools distinguish between the subjects taught to the heterogeneous age-group class and the subjects taught at different levels of difficulty in a number of courses. The subjects taught in undifferentiated courses generally include history, geography, social studies, and vocational orientation, as well as music and art, and, up to the end of the eighth grade, also the natural sciences. The subjects taught in courses differentiated according to varying levels of performance are: English, mathematics, and German, and, from the ninth grade on, the natural sciences.

With regard to the latter subjects, differentiation according to level of performance is usually introduced gradually. These subjects are taught at first to the age-group class, then in courses at two levels of difficulty which can later be differentiated into as many as four levels. The time at which the assignment to courses at such different levels begins varies from subject to subject, from Land to Land, and often from one school to the other. Similarly, there are differences in the number of such courses offered. However, a tendency seems to be emerging to begin this grouping as late as possible, perhaps not before the seventh or eighth grade, and to limit it to two or three levels.

The classification of pupils according to performance level is done separately for each subject, in order to take into consideration the variation of a pupil's performance from one subject to another. Thus a pupil can, for example, attend the most demanding course in mathematics, while in English he has been assigned to a lower level course. When courses are differentiated according to performance levels, it is important that the content of the courses in any one subject be so organized and coordinated that a change from one level to another is possible. The opportunity to change courses is generally offered semiannually.

Until the ninth grade, as empirical studies have shown, a considerable number of pupils take advantage of this possibility. In some schools a change of courses is facilitated by supplementary "elevator courses," which are intended to help in the transition to a course at the next higher level. From the ninth grade on, however, the "mobility" of the secondary school pupils declines. Moreover, after this point many schools in some Länder group pupils together according to the program of education they are expected to complete. In connection with these groups one then speaks of the formation of Hauptschule, Realschule, and Gymnasium tracks.

Within the system of course differentiation according to performance levels, the comprehensive schools have developed additional possibilities of helping individual groups of pupils. For example, the number of pupils in the lowest level courses is intentionally kept small to make it possible for the teacher to give more individual attention to the pupils; or remedial courses of limited duration are offered to give pupils threatened by reassignment to a lower level course the chance to catch up with the group they are in.

At some schools, efforts have been made to diminish ability grouping in order to preserve for the slower learners the more stimulating learning environment of the heterogeneous group. In these schools the attempt has been made to replace the homogeneous ability groups, which are relatively stable over time, with more flexible kinds of grouping. One kind, termed temporary grouping, consists in temporary subgroups formed according to very clearly defined criteria, such as problems with reading or spelling. The other kind is thematic or methodological differentiation within the instruction given to the age-group class, and is referred to as internal differentiation. Both of these kinds of differentiation, however, require that the teacher be thoroughly grounded in his fields, and that he have highly developed diagnostic and methodological abilities. They also necessitate instructional materials which take into consideration the various goals of these kinds of differentiation.

A special variety of flexible grouping is the "small-group-team-model," which is being tested at some comprehensive schools and publicized more and more by the association representing the interests of comprehensive school teachers (Gemeinnützige Gesellschaft Gesamtschule). In this model, about 90 pupils are united in a reference group, the members of which remain in large measure the same for several years. This group is looked after by a team of from five to seven teachers, the members of which do not change, and who together plan the instruction for the group as a whole. This large group is internally differentiated by the formation of subgroups which are made as stable as possible: core groups, each consisting of 30 pupils who are taught together by one teacher; tutorial groups of approximately 15 pupils; and "table groups" consisting of four to six pupils, which can be tended temporarily by an additional teacher when necessary. One of the basic problems of this form of organization is that it results in a relatively large proportion of instruction by teachers not specialized in the subjects of their courses.

10.2.2. Grouping according to choice of courses

The second basic form of the organization of instruction is grouping pupils according to the choices of courses they are allowed to make. This type of organization is to be found in all comprehensive schools and exists also in the traditional secondary school system. At set points in his school career the pupil must make a choice among certain subjects offered by his school. As a rule, the most important decisions about these elective compulsory courses are made in the seventh grade, between a second foreign language and, for example, augmented vocational orientation courses. In many cases this decision has the effect of determining in advance the level at which the pupil will conclude his education, since two foreign languages are prerequisite for the Abitur. (Pupils who initially chose vocational orientation as their elective compulsory subject must later begin to learn a second foreign language, should they subsequently want to transfer to the upper level of the Gymnasium.) With regard to elective compulsory courses, a second choice must be made by the pupil in his ninth school year from a range of offerings: a third foreign language, increased study of mathematics and the natural sciences, augmentation of social studies, etc. In the part of his study program in which he has completely free choice, the pupil selects from among additional offerings at his school, for instance a foreign language, study groups on different topics in various fields, projects, etc. In all-day schools this program is supplemented by extracurricular activities.

The variety of the program offered by the comprehensive school makes it possible for the pupils to elaborate — within the framework of preestablished basic structures — individual profiles with respect to the subjects they take and to their own performance. However, to be admitted to the upper level of the Gymnasium, or to obtain certification that he has completed an entire program of study, the comprehensive school pupil must satisfy minimal requirements. These are intended to ensure that certification by the comprehensive school is equivalent to that of the traditional secondary school system. Just as the pupils in the traditional types of secondary school, the pupils of a comprehensive school obtain the Hauptschule certificate, the Realschule certificate, or the qualification for admission to the upper level of the Gymnasium.

10.3. Organizational preconditions and comprehensive school policy in the Länder

As a result of the large increase in the number of pupils in secondary level I (cf. Figure 4.3), most of the comprehensive schools could be established in newly constructed buildings. This was a highly favorable condition for the inchoate comprehensive school reform. In Hessia, where to a large extent existing schools were converted into comprehensive schools, it was possible to make use of the relatively good facilities of the recently established central schools, which served quite large rural areas. In spite of deficiencies in isolated cases, one can say that the architecture and equipment of the schools offer favorable preconditions for an exacting and differentiated education. Thus the rooms provided in the schools generally permit variation in the size of the groups in which pupils are taught. Demonstrations made before the pupils in a large group can be supplemented by work in small groups or by individual work. The equipment with which the schools are furnished makes it possible to give technical instruction in the workshop or to teach the natural sciences by means of laboratory experiments, and the teaching aids available in these schools contribute to broaden the range of the instruction offered.

All comprehensive schools include at least grades 5 to 10 (in Berlin, 7 to 10). In the Länder where the "orientation level" has already been introduced, grades 5 and 6 of the comprehensive school have been combined as the orientation level and are subject to the legal and administrative regulations pertaining to the orientation level (cf. 4.5). A number of comprehensive schools, however, have a primary school attached to them, and about 40 percent have their own upper level of the Gymnasium, which conforms to that of the traditional secondary school system. A school complex, which offers a primary school, the orientation level, a comprehensive school, and the upper level of the Gymnasium, combines the experimental school with the standard school, so that only grades 7 to 10 are part of the comprehensive school experiment.

General secondary education in the Federal Republic normally takes place in half-day schools. With the construction of new buildings for the comprehensive schools, though, some Länder (Berlin, North Rhine-Westphalia, and Lower Saxony) have made the change to all-day schools (8 a.m.–4 p.m.), while other Länder have at least begun experiments with a limited number of all-day schools. On the one hand, the length of the school day at these schools makes them attractive especially to parents both of whom are employed; on the other hand, the duration of their school day turned out again and again to be a new source of problems. It demanded from teachers, whose principal activity had been teaching, and who had as a rule left the school at one o'clock in the afternoon, a fundamental re-orientation in their thinking without the help of traditions and accumulated experience to fall back on. As for the status of the all-day school at the present time, it is becoming apparent that its development will come to a halt in the 1980's. As a consequence of the decline in the number of pupils due to demographic factors, new comprehensive schools can, practically speaking, be established only through joining together existing schools that generally do not offer the prerequisites for all-day instruction.

As a rule, pupils are not assigned to comprehensive schools. Rather, their parents have the choice between the comprehensive school and one of the traditional types of secondary school. This means that the comprehensive schools must prove their value to the pupil's parents in competition with the traditional system of secondary education. In this regard the comprehensive schools seem to have been successful up to now: Even though they have increased in number and size, their capacity is not sufficient, on the average, to meet the demand for admission to them. At present, about 1 out of every 5 applicants must be turned away. The situation is different, however, in urban areas, where many diverse types of school are available, and where the competition between them is correspond-ingly intense. In Berlin, for instance, the limit of the demand for admission to the comprehensive school seems to have reached with approximately 20 percent of the relevant age group. In that city the existence of some comprehensive schools is already threatened, and several others are finding it difficult to maintain an academically balanced body of pupils.

In selecting their pupils, the comprehensive schools are, in general, careful to maintain a balanced distribution within the body of pupils with respect to both scholastic performance and social and economic criteria. A standard is provided for the social composition of a school's body of pupils by the statistical relationship of the social strata in the Land or in the area from which the school draws its pupils. In judging their applicants' ability, the comprehensive schools are guided by the evaluations of the child given by his teachers when he finishes primary school.

However, the extent to which pupils of varying evaluation from their primary schools are in fact represented in the comprehensive schools varies from school to school according to the school's reputation and the area in which it is located. Comprehensive schools in decidedly upper middle-class areas, especially if they were founded in the vicinity of a long-established Gymnasium, have difficulty in obtaining a sufficient number of pupils recommended for the Gymnasium by their primary school teachers. Comprehensive schools in socially disadvantaged areas have hardly any difficulties in this regard, but they in turn are faced with the problem of refusing applications from parents who expect that the comprehensive school will assume a great deal of responsibility in matters of social education, or that it will function simply as a custodial institution for their children. Up to now the comprehensive schools have probably benefited from the existence of the Hauptschulen, as they could, to a certain extent, count on these to accept the "problem cases." On the whole, then, the body of pupils attending the comprehensive schools probably deviates in its composition from that of the general population, the pupils having the highest and lowest levels of performance being underrepresented and the middle range of pupils being somewhat overrepresented.

The experiments with the comprehensive school were carried out in the various Länder with quite different political goals in mind. In the Länder governed by the Social Democrats or by a coalition of Social Democrats and Liberals, the policy on comprehensive schools clearly had the long-run aim of standardizing secondary level I. The central purpose of these experiments were therefore conceived to be obtaining information which would be useful for gradually changing the structure of the existing school system to a "horizontal" one. Or, if they were not intended from the outset to be part of the de facto introduction of the comprehensive school, they were supposed to allow the development of a defensible and generally applicable organizational model. The educational policy of Hessia at the beginning of the 1970's, for example, had as its goal the introduction of the comprehensive school generally throughout that Land's territory by 1980, if possible. The number of comprehensive schools there increased very rapidly at first. Then, before the status of a standard school had been legally secured for the integrated comprehensive school, this growth came to an abrupt halt because of the Hessian parliamentary election of 1974, the results of which were threatening to the Social Democratic Party. In contrast, Berlin was content to establish at first only four model schools in the 1960's. From these schools a basic model was developed; the comprehensive school was legally safeguarded as a standard educational institution; and only after this consolidation had been achieved was the number of comprehensive schools increased.

In contrast, in the Länder with conservative governments comprehensive schools were established as an open experiment, in accordance with the recommendation of the Education Council. The integrated comprehensive school was supposed to prove its superiority, or at least demonstrate that it was a vehicle for attaining important educational goals, for example, optimal conditions for the self-development or the social integration of its pupils. Only then would an expansion of the comprehensive school be considered.

Differences in the goals of the various Länder with respect to the comprehensive school led to the development of divergent policies and to heated political controversies. These disputes often completely lacked an objective basis, and sometimes, especially in Hessia and North Rhine-Westphalia, bore a resemblance to wars of religion. The result of this polarization is shown in Table 10.1: Enrollment in the comprehensive school varies among the Länder from 2 percent to 85 percent of the relevant age group.

10.4. The problems of the comprehensive schools and what has been learned from them

Ten years ago, the opinion was quite widespread that the secondary school system of the Federal Republic could be given a new institutional structure by a single organizational reform which would be immediately and completely effective. It is safe to say that today this position is not maintained in any Land. Even in the Länder which are striving to achieve a strongly horizontal organization of the secondary school system, the prevalent opinion is that this goal will be attained only by a slow process of change in which the comprehensive school is merely one element. In view of this situation, it is important to go beyond the controversy about the comprehensive school, and to point out that many organizational features generally considered peculiar to the comprehensive school were taken up by the traditional secondary school system quite some time ago.

Ability grouping has been implemented in the Hauptschule and, in modified form, also in the upper level of the Gymnasium. Furthermore, in all types of secondary school, the effort is being made to achieve a broader differentiation in the pupil's program of study through the choice of courses he is permitted; flexible measures for promoting the pupil's self-development have found acceptance in the Gymnasium. Forms of specialization by teachers and of cooperation among them which originated because of the structural constraints of the comprehensive school's organization are now developing also in the large Gymnasien and Realschulen. Similarly, the comprehensive school seems to be serving as a model for the introduction of teacher-trainees and young teachers to teaching practices in other kinds of school. One could also mention a number of other matters (for example, teachers' contact with parents and union organization), in which the comprehensive school was and still is the precursor of developments within the traditional secondary school system.

There is no doubt that in the course of the comprehensive schools' evolution, problems appeared which were in part limited to individual schools, and in part consequences of changes in the school structure. But these problems were also partly the result of accumulated reform measures — grouping experiments, the all-day school, curricular reform — and of the superimposing on these reform measures of political and cultural tendencies, such as the trend to anti-authoritarian education at the beginning of the 1970's, especially noticeable among the teachers in the comprehensive schools, who were, as a rule, very young. This trend thus had stronger effects in the comprehensive schools than in the other types of secondary school and, because of the comprehensive school's relatively complicated organization, more problematic ones. Another problem was fostering the development of precisely the weakest pupils' abilities and individual personalities. This need posed a special task for the

229

comprehensive school, as did, in another way, the organization of social life in the school, which had suffered from the dissolution of the age-group class.

When the comprehensive school was designed, few provisions had been made for the development of a satisfactory community among all members of these schools. In all likelihood such provisions could not have been made because the experience necessary for formulating them was lacking. In the all-day schools, special attention could, of course, be given to the extracurricular sphere as a counterweight to the formalized learning process, as well as to the general development of the capacity of all concerned for social interaction in the school. In these respects, though, the comprehensive schools had few models in the Federal Republic, and there was no tradition which they could draw upon. Rather, it was necessary to first learn from experience. Only gradually were forms of interaction among the members of the school elaborated which proved viable, and which in time came to be taken for granted. Even now, at the beginning of the eighties, the fact that the school is open until 4 p.m. is believed to be one of the chief causes of the comprehensive school's social problems.

The comprehensive school pupil was faced not only with the cognitive emphasis of an upgraded program of basic education. He was also confronted with a complicated grouping system which made it difficult for him to establish friendships. For many pupils these two facets of the comprehensive school combined with one another in such a way as to reinforce each other.

The inconstancy of personal relationships was seen as an especially sore point in the comprehensive school because, generally speaking, in the traditional types of secondary school the age-group class constitutes a stable social frame of reference. With the exception of those pupils who quit school or have to repeat a grade, the age-group class remains the same for years at a time. In the new schools there were no social conventions that one generation of pupils could pass on to the next. This unavoidable lack of tradition together with the complicated organization of instruction and the concomitant inconstancy of personal relationships led in some cases to obvious signs of social malaise.

The problems of social integration in the comprehensive school have, however, been recognized, and a number of possible solutions have been worked out; among these are tutorial systems, advisers for the pupil about his program of study, and institutionalized discussions between a counselor and each pupil. Many of these solutions have already been proven successful and can now be passed on, together with what was learned in applying them, to the reformed upper level of the Gymnasium.

At the beginning of the experiments with the comprehensive school, there were neither course guidelines prepared specifically for the comprehensive school, nor textbooks or other instructional materials. The experimental schools took this situation as a challenge to initiate a comprehensive general reform of the curriculum for secondary level I. For a time it was believed that the organized exchange among the comprehensive schools of curricular units which they had developed themselves would be able, to a large degree, to permanently replace the commercial production and sale of these kinds of material. With this belief was joined the hope that the individual school would become more autonomous vis-à-vis the Länder school administration. Since then, however, the curricula of the comprehensive schools have again been more strongly standardized by the school administrations in all Länder. More recent commercial textbooks, appropriate for the comprehensive school, are again being used in these schools after being approved by the school administrations. As a consequence of this standardization of the comprehensive school, though, the pioneer élan may diminish in some schools, but on the other hand a stabilizing and supportive routine will emerge.

Whenever the social organization of the comprehensive school is discussed in the Federal Republic, the size of the individual school comes again and again to the fore. "Mammoth schools," "teaching factories," these were the catchwords of the comprehensive school's critics from the very outset. These critics' standard of comparison was the size of the primary and secondary schools in the Federal Republic in the middle of the sixties, which were on the average still relatively small. In 1965, the average number of pupils per primary school was 185, per Realschule barely 370, and per Gymnasium approximately 500. In the course of the last 20 years, however, all school types have undergone considerable growth, resulting in a doubling of the average size of the school with a concomitant increase in the heterogeneity of the individual school's pupils. The range of the comprehensive schools' size is less than that of the traditional types of secondary school; they usually have at least four classes in each grade (thus they have between 700 and 800 pupils in grades 5–10). However, "large" Gymnasien with more than one thousand pupils have also become the rule. The fundamental problem now facing all types of secondary school is how large schools can be "made small" through organizational measures. Attempts to subdi-

231

vide large schools by means of such measures have been undertaken most resolutely in comprehensive schools.

10.5. Findings of studies of comprehensive schools

By the beginning of the 1980's the comprehensive schools had reached the end of their experimental phase. In 1982, the Joint Commission of the Federal and Länder Governments for Educational Planning and Advancement of Research is making public its evaluation of the comprehensive school experiments. In this report the results of empirical studies of these experiments by social scientists, as well as the reports of the individual schools and of the school administrations of the various Länder, will be systematically combined and summarized. During its barely 15-year-long history, the comprehensive school has become, without question, the best-researched school type in the history of German education. The results of this research now available present the following picture.

Even after the expansion of the educational system, comprehensive school pupils still attain the Realschule certificate in greater proportion than the pupils of the traditional school types. Correlatively, the value of the Hauptschule certificate is declining. Finally, the proportion of pupils who quit school without completing any program of study and obtaining the corresponding certificate is clearly smaller than before.

The correlation between social background and school career has been attenuated in the comprehensive school, but not eliminated (cf. Table 10.2). As for discrimination by sex, girls are not disadvantaged in this type of school (this is now also true of the tripartite school system after its expansion). And in rural areas, where it contributes to the improvement of educational opportunities, the comprehensive school helps do away with regional disparities in secondary education.

The available studies comparing the academic performance of comprehensive school pupils with that of pupils in the traditional tripartite school system have not yielded exhaustive results. However, the following general findings emerge from these studies. The variance in academic performance among the individual schools is in every case greater than between the comprehensive school and the traditional school system. In some Länder the comprehensive schools were run as relatively autonomous experimental schools for quite a while and were not standardized in accordance with a basic model.

232

Table 10.2: Social Selectivity in Expected Certification from the Hessia Comprehensive Schools and in the Tripartite School System, 1977 (Percentages)[1]

Social stratum	Type of school system	Level of certification			
		Gymna-sium	Real-schule	Haupt-schule	total
Upper stratum	tripartite system	44.7	27.9	27.4	100.0
	comprehensive school	39.2	34.5	26.3	100.0
Middle stratum	tripartite system	32.4	37.4	30.2	100.0
	comprehensive school	34.7	37.3	28.0	100.0
Lower stratum	tripartite system	13.6	35.7	50.7	100.0
	comprehensive school	21.7	37.4	40.9	100.0

[1] Distribution of a sample of 9th graders.

Source: Bongers, D.: Bildungsniveau und Chancengleichheit. Konstanz: Universität Konstanz 1978.

At least a partial decline in the achievement scores of comprehensive school pupils is found in these Länder, due to a shift of emphases in the educational goals and a lowering of the standard of performance in individual schools.

As far as the personal well-being of the pupils is concerned, the comprehensive school seems in many respects to offer a more favorable learning environment than the traditional school system. Comprehensive school pupils have less test anxiety; they enjoy being in school more and feel more bound up with their school than do their counterparts in the traditional school system; and they feel themselves less under pressure to do well in their courses. However, within the comprehensive school, as in the traditional school types, the findings in this regard vary with the level of performance of the pupils: The pupils who perform most poorly to a greater degree display adverse effects from school attendance.

The results of an empirical study conducted in a school district of Hessia, where the comprehensive school had been introduced throughout the district, indicate that these differences between the comprehensive school and the traditional schools become smaller when the comprehensive school is a standard school type and is widespread. This study also showed that comprehensive schools do not have to cope with more serious discipline problems than the traditional kinds of school. On the whole, the great majority, both of parents of comprehensive school pupils and of pupils who have attended a comprehensive school, are satisfied with this kind of school.

10.6. The outlook for the comprehensive school

At its outset, the comprehensive school reform benefited from favorable public opinion about the necessity of an educational reform, and was further aided by the new school facilities made necessary by the growing number of pupils in secondary level I. At the end of the seventies and the beginning of the eighties, public opinion changed. A conservative counter-current, which began to gain strength in the middle of the seventies, directed its attacks especially against the comprehensive school and its curricular organization, so that the establishment of new comprehensive schools became politically more difficult. Concurrently, the beginning of a shift to smaller age groups entering secondary level I prevents the construction of new schools. The consequence of these developments is that from now on new comprehensive schools can be established only by modifying already existing schools.

Now, at the beginning of the 1980's, four typical constellations are emerging in the development of the comprehensive school in the Federal Republic. In Berlin and Hessia, the comprehensive school is quantitatively significant, and at the present time it is expanding rapidly in Hamburg. Although the quantitative importance of the comprehensive school is still slight in North Rhine-Westphalia, a cautious expansion can be expected there. In Berlin, Hamburg, Hessia, and North Rhine-Westfalia the comprehensive school has the legal status of a standard educational institution.   A second constellation can be found in Bremen. This "city-state" is attempting to avoid a dualism between the system of comprehensive schools and the traditional school system. Only a few experiments with the integrated comprehensive school are being conducted there, and, following a long term plan, the traditional school types are being linked by making their curricula more similar to one another and by the establishment of school centers. It is not clear, however, if, and if so when, the comprehensive schools and the traditional school system will converge into a single model.

In a third group of Länder, the comprehensive schools although limited in number, function as a stimulus to the traditional school system. Here they can rely on a political guarantee of their continued existence, but neither their number nor their importance will be increased. This holds true for Lower Saxony, Rhineland-Palatinate, and Schleswig-Holstein. In the Saar, the situation is still unclear.

A fourth constellation occurs in the South German Länder of Bavaria and Baden-Württemberg, where the school experiments were univocally condemned by the Länder governments. These governments intend either to eliminate them or to transform them into cooperatively functioning school centers.

All in all, it is clear that the development of the comprehensive school in the Federal Republic will henceforth proceed more slowly. In all probability it will not come to a complete halt, as there is still an unmet demand for the education this school offers. Moreover, in view of the declining numbers of secondary-level pupils, the comprehensive school is the optimal school type for thinly populated rural areas. However, the availability of this kind of school will presumably be increasingly regulated by parents' interest in sending their children to it.

CHAPTER 11

Learning a Trade:
Initial Vocational Education
and the Dual System

11.1. Independence of initial vocational training from the general-education system

Vocational training at the skilled-worker level takes place outside both the general-education secondary schools and the tertiary sector. Although secondary level II encompasses initial vocational training, the latter is clearly separated from general education and from preparation for study in the university. The pupils in the Gymnasium can continue their education in the school's upper level, and the majority of them choose to do so. By contrast, Hauptschulen and Realschulen end with the ninth or tenth grade, and their pupils thus normally leave the general-education system at the age of 15 or 16. (cf. Figure 2.1).

These young people must then choose one of the paths shown in Figure 11.1. They must decide whether they want:
- to find employment immediately as unskilled workers (although even in this case they remain obligated to attend a public vocational school one or two days a week until the age of 18);
- to undergo vocational training within the "dual system" consisting of enterprise-based apprenticeships together with part-time attendance at public vocational schools;
- or to participate in other forms of vocational training, the spectrum of which stretches from training programs in full-time vocational schools, some lasting several years, to courses which

in a few months prepare their participants to perform simple tasks in the production process (as do, for example, some of the programs offered by the Federal Employment Agency).

Should these young people choose to undergo vocational training, the form most readily available to them is enterprise-based training in an apprenticeship. This training takes place in both privately owned and state-owned-and-operated enterprises and is complemented by instruction given in part-time vocational schools financed and run by the state. This form of vocational training in the workplace as well as in school is the product of an historical evolution and has been designated since the middle of the 1960's as the "dual system." It constitutes the bulk of all initial vocational training offered in the Federal Republic. About 40 percent of all juveniles between 15 and 18 years of age receive training in this way. Through apprenticeships they learn an occupation that is officially recognized as requiring training, and become skilled workers, clerks, or journeymen in the various trades. The successful completion of this training not only qualifies them for employment corresponding to their training, but also entitles them to attend various vocational schools (cf. 11.3). However, vocational training in the dual system does not give access to schools in the tertiary sector.

Together, secondary schools leading to the Abitur and the universities or other tertiary level schools give those who attend them uninterrupted preparation primarily for academic professions, while the system of vocational schools and training programs qualifies its participants for less prestigious occupations and for occupations of a subordinate nature. As for returning to the general school system and so gaining access to tertiary-level education, this is, to be sure, possible, but only at a considerable cost in terms of time and effort. This path leads via vocational extension schools, specialized technical schools, specialized technical secondary schools, and polytechnic colleges to the university and finally to academic professions.

The separation between vocational training and education preparatory for study at tertiary-level institutions is by no means the product of an internally coherent conception of education or of an educational policy based on this conception. Rather, this separation is the result of historical development. Three factors have especially contributed to this development:

- a particular interpretation of the educational theory of neo-humanism, the best known representative of which is Wilhelm von Humboldt (1767–1835);

237

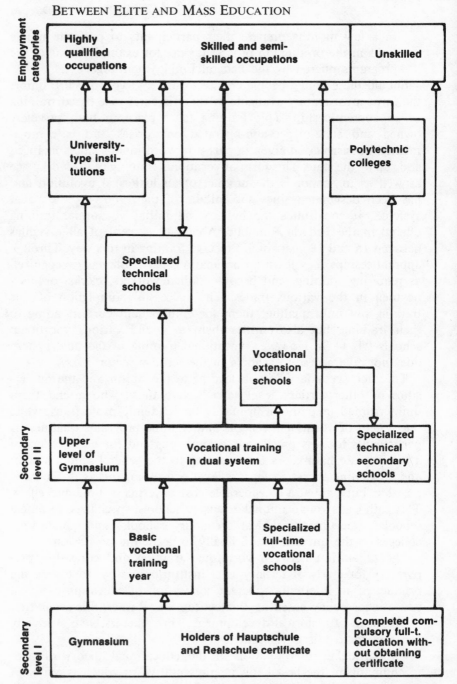

Figure 11.1. Selected Paths through the Educational and Vocational Training Systems

- the persistence and further development of the tradition of the master craftsman's training of apprentices in his trade, and the taking over of this kind of training by industry;
- the elaboration of the system of vocational schools supported and administered by the state, which are attended concurrently with participation in enterprise-based training in an apprenticeship, and which complement the latter.

According to the neo-humanist conception of education which was dominant in Germany in the 19th century, general education and specialized training, that is, the acquisition of skills and knowledge for the sake of their direct application in an occupation, were supposed to be institutionally separated and undergone succesively rather than concurrently. According to this view, only schools giving general education contributed to the cultivation of an individual's humanity, whereas those institutions which served to qualify their pupils for the practice of an occupation specifically did not. The separation between general education and vocational training corresponded to a distinction between the social strata which partook of this education and this training.

Initially, members of the lower social strata had access only to industrial employment and apprenticeships in the trades as ways of acquiring the skills and knowledge required by a particular occupation. The industrial apprenticeship had its origin in the apprenticeships established by the medieval guilds, in which the training and moral instruction of the apprentices were carried out by a master craftsman in his own home. After completing an apprenticeship lasting several years, the apprentice was advanced to journeyman, and he then had — as he still does today — the possibility of becoming an independent master in his trade.

11.2. Enterprise-based vocational training

11.2.1. The dual character of enterprise-based vocational training

In the 19th century, the apprenticeship in the home and the workshop of the master craftsman was complemented by a school for general further education. It was the purpose of this school to be a continuation of the Volksschule and to give its pupils more extensive abilities than the latter provided in reading, writing, and arithmetic. At the beginning of the 20th century, the school for the general further education of apprentices evolved into a school for

239

specialized further training in the various trades. This school in turn developed into the present-day part-time vocational school. This last kind of school, which was defined and legally established throughout the German Reich by the Reich Law on Compulsory School Attendance of 1938, now accompanies and complements apprenticeship training in the workplace with one or two days of instruction per week. (In what follows the term "enterprise-based vocational training" always refers to apprenticeship training in the workplace complemented by part-time attendance at a public vocational school.)

Of central importance as a precondition for this development was the classical theory of vocational training, the most prominent representatives of which were Georg Kerschensteiner (1854–1932) and, later, Eduard Spranger (1882–1963). In the theory of vocational training which they founded, the separation between general education and vocational training, between an individual's education and his occupation, was overcome, at least conceptually. They considered the occupation as the medium of education: The road to general education, according to Spranger, goes by way of one's occupation and only by way of one's occupation.

Kerschensteiner, though, had also argued that vocational training and occupational socialization were significant instruments for the social integration of the lower social strata. He advanced this thesis in the context of an intensifying conflict in the last decades of the 19th and the first decade of the 20th century between the government of Imperial Germany and a growing Social Democratic labor movement. By teaching them to be good citizens, the vocational school was supposed to integrate the young adults who passed through it into the existing political and social order, and to support the privately owned firms in the socialization of their apprentices.

Today the laws of the Länder compel all juveniles who attend neither a general nor a vocational full-time school to attend the part-time vocational schools provided by the state, even if they are not engaged in an apprenticeship. This compulsory part-time school attendance lasts until the age of 18, or until a juvenile has completed his apprenticeship. However, initial vocational training in the dual system takes place primarily in the workplace; the instruction which apprentices receive in a part-time vocational school is only an accompaniment to their training in a firm. Three or four days in the week the apprentices go to work in a factory, say, and one or two days a week they go to the vocational school. The exact division of time between factory and school is determined by the school laws of the particular Länder and according to the occupation chosen by the trainee.

Since the 1960's, the term "dual system" has entered into general use as the designation for enterprise-based vocational training. This name, however, has several dimensions of meaning. First, it points out the complementarity of the two learning sites: the school and the workplace. Second, the term expresses the fact that enterprise-based vocational training has two sponsors. The Länder governments establish and finance the vocational schools, while providing and financing apprenticeships is the affair of the particular privately and publicly owned enterprise. Lastly, the term "dual system" can refer to the twofold supervisory structure of enterprise-based vocational training. The Ministers of Culture of the individual Länder are responsible for organizing and superintending the training programs in the vocational schools. Responsibility for training in the workplace, though, lies with the individual firms and the industrial, commercial, and craft chambers (cf. 11.2.2). The organization and supervision of apprenticeship training by these chambers and the individual firms must remain within guidelines laid down by regulations of the federal government. Figure 11.2 gives an overview of the institutional framework of the dual system.

11.2.2. The institutional framework of the dual system of vocational training

The character of the education given by the general secondary schools is determined by their status as institutions governed by public law. In contrast, initial vocational training in the dual system is, to a large extent, not subject to control by the state. Participants in this form of vocational training have, to be sure, a double status: they are, at the same time, both pupils and apprentices. The legal status of their training is correspondingly twofold: Inasmuch as it takes place within state-sponsored schools it falls under public law, while the relationship between the apprentice and the firm training him falls under the jurisdiction of civil law. However, training time is unequally divided, and the possibilities of exerting control over the content and the financing of the training are distributed unequally between the two partners in the system. As a result, vocational training in the dual system is, to a high degree, subject to the influence of the privately and publicly owned enterprises which offer the apprenticeships, and to the influence of those persons who represent the interests of these enterprises.

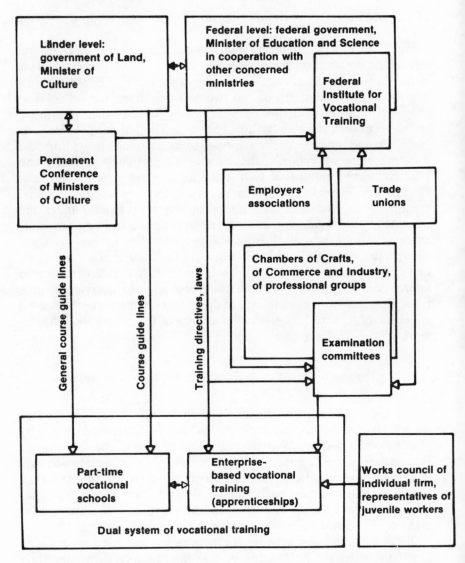

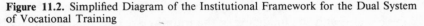

Figure 11.2. Simplified Diagram of the Institutional Framework for the Dual System of Vocational Training

These enterprises essentially determine what the apprentices learn, and when and where they learn it. They finance the training workshops located on their premises, the training personnel and the teaching and learning materials which they provide. The apprentices are thus primarily under the authority and control of the firms which give them their practical training. To be sure, the Intra-Enterprise Labor-Management Relations Act, passed in 1972, grants rights of codetermination to the representatives of juvenile workers (up to 18 years of age) and to the shop stewards who make up the works council, which a company must have if it has more than a certain number of employees, regardless of whether it is unionized. These rights of codetermination, though, are limited in comparison with the power of the firms. Consequently, the views of the latter are predominant in the shaping of the vocational training they give their apprentices.

These firms have two chief interests: first, that the apprentices develop the desired skills and virtues, as well as loyalty to their employer; second, that the costs of training the apprentices not exceed the necessary minimum. The latter goal is achieved by limiting the training to skills required for the occupations in question, or to the requirements of the firm providing the training.

The firms' latitude for determining the vocational training they give is limited by the training directives issued by the relevant ministries of the federal government for the individual occupations, as well as by more general federal laws, such as the Vocational Training Act of 1969 and the Employed Minors Protection Act. The most recent version of the latter dates from 1976. This law sets the length of work time, minimum vacations, and certain work conditions for minors, while the Vocational Training Act requires that the skills and knowledge necessary for the occupation in question be, in fact, imparted to the trainee. However, the federal government's monitoring of enterprise-based vocational training is restricted to ascertaining whether the firms observe the norms laid down by the Employed Minors Protection Act.

As for the supervision of the training itself, and of the maintenance of suitable training workshops and training personnel, it is the prerogative and responsibility of the chambers of commerce and industry, of the crafts, and of the professions. These chambers, which are provided for by law, are associations, the purpose of which is the autonomous self-administration of the groups in question. Members of these groups are legally obligated to belong to the appropriate chamber. One of the most important functions of these chambers is to appoint the members of the committees that examine the apprentices at the conclusion of their training. It should be emphasized that these committees include examiners who have been delegated by the trade unions, and who are equal in number to the examiners associated with the employers. Each examination committee also includes among its members at least one vocational school teacher.

11.2.3. Enterprise-based vocational training and the market economy

Unlike the general school system, enterprise-based vocational training in the dual system functions according to the laws of the market economy. The structural development of this kind of vocational training is not guided by comprehensive plans worked out to implement vocational training policy concerning the numbers of apprentices training in the various occupations. Rather it is regulated by supply and demand in a market of training opportunities. The supply of apprenticeships is, therefore, dependent on the willingness of the individual firms to provide training to apprentices. In other words, it is dependent on the cost-benefit calculations of the individual firms. Juveniles do not have a right to an apprenticeship, nor do the enterprises, whether privately or publicly owned, have an obligation to provide such training. Thus a youth who wants to be trained within the dual system must find a firm that is willing and authorized to provide training for apprentices in the occupation he wishes to pursue.

To this end juveniles and their parents turn to the vocational counseling offered by the governmental Employment Offices, or they look for apprenticeships on their own by making use of personal contacts and by reading newspaper advertisements or publicly posted notices. Large firms are especially attractive as apprenticeship sites because they generally offer better training. Consequently, these firms are increasingly using examinations and standardized aptitude tests to screen applicants for the apprenticeships they offer. If an applicant is accepted on the basis of his school certificate, his grades in school, the test results, and the personal impression he made, then he and the firm must conclude an apprenticeship contract. This contract is largely standardized throughout the Federal Republic; in it the firms commit themselves to instill and teach the specific proficiencies and knowledge laid down in the respective training directives. Further, the contract covers remuneration and vacation arrangements negotiated by the trade unions and employers' associations.

The state has only slight influence on the supply of and the demand for apprenticeships. It can change the institutional and legal framework encompassing enterprise-based training, or it can, and does, try to channel juveniles' choice of an occupation, and so regulate

244

demand for apprenticeships. This it does with the help of the vocational counseling given by the Employment Offices on the basis
of forecasts of the supply and demand of labor by occupations.

To be sure, the choice of an occupation is subject to many different
influences, including the conditions obtaining in the market for
training opportunities and, in particular, the actual supply of apprenticeships at any given time. Thus, when the apprenticeships in
certain occupations are in short supply, the effective demand for
apprenticeships in these occupations is determined by the number
of them available. This supply of apprenticeships is, in turn, dependent not only on the demand by the individual firms for new
or additional workers in the occupations in question, but also on
the costs and benefits of apprenticeships to these firms, on the trend
of the economy, and on the regional economic structure, as well as
the tendencies in the structural development of the various occupations and branches of economic activity. The influence which these
factors exercise upon the decisions of the individual firms at a
particular time determine the number of apprenticeships which they
offer and the distribution of these among various occupations. Ultimately these factors also determine, through the firms' decisions,
the supply of skilled workers in the labor market.

The coordination between the economy's need for skilled workers
and the supply of such workers provided by the vocational training
system is, however, not completely successful. The consequence is
that some of those who complete apprenticeships find that the firms
which trained them no longer have jobs for them, or that they cannot
obtain employment at all in the occupations for which they have
been trained.

11.2.4. The occupational character of enterprise-based vocational training

In an apprenticeship, a young person is trained for a quite specific
occupation, and this is usually accomplished through the execution
of tasks that are typical of the occupation in question. An apprenticeship is possible only in one of the occupations which are officially
recognized as requiring training; at the present time these number
slightly more than four hundred.

What skills and knowledge are required for each occupation is
determined by the Federal Institute for Vocational Training, in
collaboration with representatives of industry and commerce and of
the trade unions. The resulting description of an occupation is
codified in training directives issued by the Federal Minister of

Education and Science, sometimes together with the Federal Minister for Economics, or in consultation with other federal ministers; these directives guide the enterprises in their training of apprentices. In addition to the description of the skills and knowledge required for the occupation in question, the training directives regulate the length of apprenticeships, instructions on dividing the content of the training into time segments according to the nature of the material taught (a vocational training framework plan), as well as general instructions on examination requirements. The training in an apprenticeship is of relatively long duration, lasting an average of three years, during which time complex packets of qualifications, which follow quite narrowly delimited and standardized models, are transmitted to the trainees.

The occupational character of vocational training in the Federal Republic is the reflection of the occupational organization of work there. Occupations are the fundamental building blocks of work organization, and workers trained in the various occupations are the backbone of production in industry and in the crafts in West Germany.

This is so because the methods of "scientific management" (i.e., Taylorism), which include the scientific analysis of the labor process into its smallest constituent units, have not yet seized upon the industrial organization of labor in the Federal Republic to the same extent as in the United States of America. Consequently, the specialized sectors of the overall labor market which are reserved for trained workers in the various occupations have kept a somewhat greater importance in the Federal Republic than in Frederick Taylor's homeland. And therefore occupational certification in the form of the skilled craft worker's certificate, the journeyman's, or the clerk's, is an essential prerequisite for access to more privileged positions of employment, such as, for example, foreman, department head (requiring the rank of master in the pertinent occupation), master craftsman, or technically skilled salaried employee (e.g., technical illustrator).

However, certification in an occupation is by no means a guarantee of employment in that occupation, or of employment corresponding to the level of one's certification. This is made evident by the lot of many workers, highly trained in the crafts or in commercial occupations, who have had to change their occupation, or whose occupations no longer require high skill, while many others are unemployed, or have had to accept underemployment.

246

In recent years, technical innovations such as microprocessors and industrial automation, as well as modern, Taylorist methods of work organization seem to be increasingly destroying occupations in the Federal Republic, too. The importance of the labor market for unskilled workers and of firms' internal labor markets seems to be growing at the expense of the labor markets for particular occupations. In other words, the qualifications of workers that are specific to particular occupations are being supplanted in the labor process by the qualifications of the unskilled worker, and by qualifications which are specific to individual firms.

The declining importance of work organization based on the different occupations has brought forth a call for a new conception of vocational training. Thus schemes for graduated vocational training have been introduced which organize training in a sequence of steps or phases, with a corresponding sequence of certificates. To acquire the complete vocational training of the skilled worker, it is necessary to go through all steps of this training program, the initial certificates attesting only to the qualifications of semiskilled workers.

Another innovation was motivated by concern about the increasing incidence of change of occupation and by the growing importance of occupational mobility. These have made it imperative, in the opinion of many, that a year-long program of basic vocational training be made available to young people to give them a broad fundamental preparation which they can use in a number of related occupations. Both this and the already mentioned training program make initial vocational training less specialized. Their step-by-step introduction constitutes, in effect, a dismantling of the system of occupations and is leading to a weakening of the occupational character of enterprise-based vocational training.

11.2.5. The combination of work with learning

Whereas learning in the general nonvocational schools and in the institutions of the post-secondary sector is divorced from the work process, enterprise-based vocational training is characterized precisely by an intimate linkage of working and learning. Originally, working and learning could hardly be distinguished from each other in an apprenticeship; apprentices learned through working, not by passively listening to the explanations of a teacher. Vocational training in the Federal Republic today is deviating more and more from this conception, as enterprise-based training increasingly takes on the character of schooling. Training is separated more and more from the production process and takes place in training workshops and class-rooms within the factories, in the case of industry, or, in the case of the crafts, in training workshops maintained cooperatively by a number of craft establishments. The reasons given for this turn of events are the declining opportunities to learn while participating in highly mechanized and automated production processes, and the rising costs and risks associated with training through participation in the modern production process.

Nevertheless, practical vocational training in the workplace and in the work process still predominates in the firms offering appren-ticeships. Here training consists of demonstration and imitation of simple operations accompanied by brief explanations. In small and middle-sized firms the apprentices are instructed either by the de-partment head, who is a master in his occupation; or by workers who have completed training in their occupations, for example, journeymen, skilled workers, or, as often happens, by older appren-tices. Larger firms provide their own training personnel especially for the instruction of apprentices. Opportunities to learn and the quality of the training the apprentices receive in the workplace often depend less on a firm's training plan than on its production program at a given time.

In contrast to true on-the-job training, vocational training in train-ing workshops and in classrooms tends to be more systematic and to take the usual form of school instruction. Such training firms usually provide elaborate teaching media, expensive teaching and learning materials, and teachers trained both pedagogically and in the relevant occupation. In this training, the traditional didactic principle of combining work and learning, a principle to which contemporary pedagogical theory has again assigned a central role, is honored more often in the breach than in the observance.

11.2.6. The part-time vocational school as complement to training in the workplace

For many apprentices the days on which they attend school are days of rest, in comparison with the days spent in training in their workplaces. Instruction in the school usually lasts from 8 a.m. to 1:30 p.m.; the number of hours of instruction per week varies according to the occupation. If they spend less than five hours in school, then the apprentices must go to work in the afternoon.

The instruction given in part-time vocational schools is intended to provide a theoretical foundation for the practical training the apprentices receive in their workplace and also to continue and broaden their general education. However, the portion of the teaching devoted to particular occupations is greater by far than the part given over to general education.

The instruction is based on course guidelines and weekly schedules of course hours issued by the Ministries of Culture of the Länder (cf. Figure 11.2). In these guidelines and schedules, a distinction is generally made between subjects which pertain to particular occupations and subjects falling under general education. To the latter category belong German, political and social studies, religion, economics, and physical education. The subjects belonging to the former category vary, depending on the occupation in question. These subjects are usually divided into two subgroups: those dealing with the practical aspects of the occupation, and those dealing with its theoretical aspects. In the vocational school the prevalent forms of instruction are the lecture, the use of questions as a means of leading the pupils to an understanding of the subject matter, demonstration by the teacher, and practice by the pupils of what they have learned.

11.3. Full-time vocational schools

In addition to the dual system, a broad range of diverse schools and programs is available for vocational training. These do not, as a rule, substitute for enterprise-based vocational training; rather, they either prepare their pupils for such on-the-job training, or they continue and deepen such training. These were not established systematically. As needs arose for new kinds of vocational training new types of vocational schools or programs were set up to meet them. The resulting congeries of schools and programs and their labyrinthine nomenclature are confusing even to many Germans.

To the first group belongs the year-long program of basic vocational training (cf. Figure 11.1). According to the conception of vocational training underlying this program, such training should be divided into a less specialized basic training for an "occupational area"—a range of related occupations—and specialized training for a particular occupation building upon the former training. This program is considered the first stage of vocational training. In one year it is supposed to impart to its participants a basic vocational training as well as general knowledge of German, social studies, and physical education. An ordinance issued by the Federal Minister of Economic Affairs established a total of 13 occupational areas, for example, economics

249

and administration, metal technology, and electrical technology. To ensure a common approach between the Länder, the Permanent Conference of Ministers of Culture has passed general course guidelines for the occupational areas. The program of basic vocational training is open to all youths who have completed their nine years of compulsory general education, and is offered both as a full-time school and as a cooperative form of part-time schooling in conjunction with training in the workplace.

In the first form of the program, all of the training takes place in a school, either in a vocational school or in a vocational school center with training workshops. This form of vocational training is legally considered equivalent to the training given in the dual system. It is, of course, quite controversial if and to what extent formal schooling can qualitatively fully substitute workplace-related practical training. In spite of considerable opposition from some employers, parliament has, however, decided to treat both forms as equivalent. The firms offering apprenticeships must therefore count the basic vocational training received in a school as part of the term of an apprenticeship. In other words, these firms must shorten enterprise-based training by a year for apprentices who have completed the year of basic vocational training.

In the cooperative form of the year-long program, by contrast, the vocational training takes place both in school and in the workplace. This program includes more instruction in the school (2–2½ days) than the first year of training in the dual system. Further, basic vocational training also covers an entire occupational area. Thus, the pupils participating in this program only have to decide upon an occupational area rather than a particular occupation. However, they must also conclude a training contract with the firm responsible for their training in the workplace.

The number of participants in the year of basic vocational training confined to the school has recently greatly increased. Nevertheless, this form of vocational training is of no great importance when one considers the total number of pupils in vocational schools in the Federal Republic. As for the cooperative form of the year-long program, from the purely quantitative point of view it plays only a negligible role. Some Länder have introduced the in-school year of basic vocational training, at least in some occupational areas, throughout the extent of their territory and have made it obligatory for all juveniles who leave school after completing their compulsory general education. A further expansion of the program is planned.

More important by far than the year of basic vocational training are the specialized full-time vocational schools (cf. Figure 11.1 and Table 11.1). A course of study at these schools lasts at least one year and consists of both specialized training in a particular occupation and general education. The usual prerequisite for admission is the Hauptschule certificate; in some cases, though, the Realschule certificate is required, for example, when it is a matter of training for more demanding occupations.

There are three kinds of specialized full-time vocational schools. Some offer complete training in occupations officially recognized as requiring special training, and can therefore take the place of the training given in the dual system. Others offer training which can be accounted part of a corresponding apprenticeship. A third group of these schools provide training in occupations not covered by the dual system; their training programs take place entirely within the schools.

The length of the training programs at the specialized full-time vocational schools varies between one and three years, according to the occupation chosen. By attending a two-year school of this kind, a pupil, who must already have the Hauptschule certificate, can obtain the Realschule certificate. This certificate is the prerequisite for admission to some schools that lead to the post-secondary sector, such as the specialized technical secondary school, which consists

Table 11.1: Pupils in Vocational Education According to Type of School, 1960–1980

Year	Part-time vocat. schools, incl. basic vocat. training year	Vocat. extension schools	Specialized full-time vocat. schools	Specialized technical secondary schools, vocat. oriented Gymnasien	Specialized technical schools	Total
1960	1,661,911	–	139,160	–	141,772	1,942,843
1965	1,780,044	52,999	167,546	–	145,914	2,146,503
1970	1,599,840	40,382	205,022	58,973	167,483	2,071,700
1975	1,635,968	27,786	294,964	118,675	211,105	2,288,498
1980	1,967,839	21,712	352,158	133,689	190,492	2,665,890

Source: Statistisches Bundesamt: Bildung im Zahlenspiegel 1981.

only of the upper secondary level (cf. 8.2 and 9.3; and Figure 11.1). Specialized full-time vocational schools are organized into departments according to subject areas; the most important departments are economics, nutrition/home economics, and industrial/technical occupations. Even though the number of specialized full-time vocational schools has increased greatly, the number of those training programs which provide complete training in an occupation, and which are thus fully equivalent to enterprise-based vocational training, is relatively quite small. Enterprise-based vocational training thus still constitutes the core of initial vocational training.

The schools and programs discussed above, with few exceptions, prepare their pupils for vocational training. In contrast, the vocational extension schools presuppose that their pupils have already undergone vocational training. The purpose of these schools is to deepen both the general education and the occupational training of their pupils. Under certain conditions the certificate conferred by the vocational extension school is equivalent to the Realschule certificate and gives access to the specialized technical secondary school (cf. Figure 11.1, and Table 11.1). In the latter type of school, which comprises grades 11 and 12 of secondary level II, three kinds of courses are offered; nonvocational courses having a general content; those treating the theoretical aspects of particular occupations; and those dealing with the practical aspects of particular occupations. Successful completion of the specialized technical secondary school in turn gives access to the polytechnic college (cf. Chapter 12).

In the Federal Republic's system of vocational training, the specialized technical schools are of great importance (cf. Figure 11.1 and Table 11.1). These schools do not provide initial vocational training, but rather form a part of further education (cf. Chapter 13). Admission to them presupposes the Hauptschule or Realschule certificate, completed training in an occupation, and usually several years of experience in the pertinent occupation. They are intended to deepen the specialized vocational training already acquired and to advance the pupil's general education. Transition from the specialized technical school to the polytechnic college is possible, on the one hand, via the specialized technical secondary school. On the other hand, some of the specialized technical schools offer courses which make it possible to transfer directly into a polytechnic college.

11.4. Vocational training under scrutiny

The development of the present-day system of enterprise-based vocational training began after World War I. During the reign of

National Socialism in Germany this kind of training was consolidated. After the founding of the Federal Republic of Germany in 1949 it was continued in that part of Germany, while in the German Democratic Republic in the east the development of vocational training followed a different path. There, efforts to modernize vocational training began somewhat earlier. The first step was to substantially reduce the overall number of occupations for which training is offered and to devise a scheme for graduated vocational training that imparts general qualifications in its early phases, before the onset of occupational specialization.

Until the end of the 1960's the apprentices in the Federal Republic were a "forgotten majority." Then the enterprise-based vocational training of the apprentices became increasingly subject to criticism. The criticism extended from simply pointing out individual deficiencies of the training to finding fault with the principles of its institutional framework. Underlying the variety of the criticism, however, was unanimous agreement that vocational training in the school and in the workplace had been sorely neglected and would now have to be improved.

Many of the criticisms were confirmed by empirical studies. These showed that enterprise-based vocational training was often incomplete, that is, it imparted to the apprentices only some of the skills and knowledge specified in the training directives for the different occupations. In addition, the training was often not organized into instruction periods according to its content, as prescribed by law. The enterprises offering apprenticeships seldom provided training workshops and classrooms. To an excessive extent, apprentices had to perform menial, trivial, or routine tasks; and their instructors seldom combined both pedagogical and technical competence. Rather they were often instructed by fellow workers or even by older apprentices. Further, these studies clearly showed that the quality of training in enterprises varied greatly, according to the occupation and the size of the enterprise providing the training. They also established that in many small and middle-sized enterprises profits were made by exploiting the cheap labor of the apprentices in training for certain occupations, while in large enterprises training was very costly and brought only small returns.

The state-run part-time vocational schools were also criticized, no less than the enterprises offering apprenticeships. Both social scientists and representatives of the enterprises concerned found fault with the small portion of time given to the vocational school in the dual system and with the corresponding neglect of theory in the training

253

of the apprentices. They denounced antiquated course guidelines, the shortage of teachers and suitable classrooms, and insufficient teaching materials and teaching aids.

The causal analyses of these deficiencies and the suggestions for reforms based on them varied as greatly as did the criticisms of the dual system. The minimum reform proposal called for changing only some details in order to improve the quality of enterprise-based vocational training. At the other extreme were the claims that a radical reform of the entire dual system of initial vocational training was necessary. Those who saw the roots of the problems primarily in isolated deficiencies demanded, for example, that coordination between the two components of the dual system be improved, and that the training directives be modernized. They also called for better trained teachers in the enterprises, more thorough counseling and supervision of the enterprises offering apprenticeships, development of training in supraenterprise training centers, and the introduction of a broadly conceived basic vocational training.

Other critics considered the structural characteristics of the dual system to be the cause of the diagnosed defects. In their recommendations, they proposed drastic modifications of the institutional framework of initial vocational training, going as far as calling for the elimination of the dual system. Instead, they suggested that either the state or other self-administered collective bodies should take over responsibility in order to replace the supposedly one-sided and short-term economic orientation of the dual system with more generalized and long-term criteria. Somewhat along this type of reasoning were some reforms suggested by the German Education Council in 1974, when it proposed the integration of vocational training and general education preparatory for university study (cf. 4.9).

In the same year, the Commission of Experts on the Costs and Financing of Vocational Training, appointed by the Federal Minister of Labor and Social Welfare, proposed that the financing of apprenticeships by the individual firms be replaced, or at least supplemented, by a system of collective financing. What they had in mind was that the state should provide financial support for apprenticeships, or that a fund should be created into which all or some enterprises would pay money, and which would be placed at the disposal of the firms offering apprenticeships for the financing of their training programs. In 1973, the federal government expressed its intention to limit the control of the firms over enterprise-based training and to strengthen the influence wielded by the state on vocational training through training directives, examinations, and its supervision.

Against these proposals for fundamental reforms the objection was made that more "big government" would not necessarily guarantee the modernization, flexibility, and efficiency of the vocational training system. In any case, the adherents of these proposals did not succeed in getting even one of them carried out. Thus the dual system still continued to be independent, and general education was still de facto separated from vocational training. Training in the workplace continued to be financed by the individual firms, and the discretionary power of the publicly and privately owned enterprises over enterprise-based vocational training remained as unlimited as before.

This state of affairs was first modified in 1976 by the Apprenticeship Promotion Act. When the supply of apprenticeships exceeded the demand by less than 12.5 percent, then the financing of apprenticeships by the individual firms offering them was to be supplemented by a supraenterprise fund. Contributions from all enterprises paying more than 400,000 marks (DM) annually in wages and salaries were supposed to provide assistance for endangered, newly established, or additional apprenticeships.

Yet, although the legally defined conditions for this governmental intervention obtained, no use was made of this regulation. Rather, in view of the economic crisis the federal government confined itself to threatening to implement this law and to making appeals, to which employers—above all craft establishments and small firms— responded by offering more apprenticeships. This law was subsequently abrogated, having been declared unconstitutional by the Federal Supreme Court for formal reasons: The required approval of the representatives of the Länder governments had not been obtained. However, since then another law has been passed, the Vocational Training Promotion Act, identical with the Apprenticeship Promotion Act except for the provisions concerning a potential supraenterprise fund, which were dropped. This law entered into effect in 1982.

Since the beginning of the seventies, however, many measures have been taken, which, while not altering the organizational and institutional framework of the dual system of vocational training, have improved training conditions both in the schools and in the enterprises. In 1972, for example, an ordinance on the qualification of instructors was issued by the federal government which requires that the instructors provided by the enterprises have the pedagogical knowledge appropriate for vocational training, and that they demonstrate this knowledge in an examination. Three years later, in 1975, the Joint Commission of the Federal and Länder Governments for Educational Planning and Advancement of Research agreed upon a plan, in accordance with which instruction in part-time vocational schools is being extended to 12 hours per week, and supraenterprise training centers are being further developed. In addition, in recent years many of the training directives applying to training in the workplace have been reworked, and new course guidelines have been drawn up for the part-time vocational schools, and in some cases coordinated with the directives applying to training in the workplace.

11.5. Problems and tendencies in initial vocational training

Economic growth since the founding of the Federal Republic, the shortening of the workweek, and the entrance of numerically smaller age groups onto the labor market—all of these resulted in a persistent shortage of German workers in the 1960's that led to the increased employment of foreign workers. Against this background, and because it was assumed that in the future higher qualifications would be required of workers, the discussion of the vocational training system at the beginning of the 1970's focussed primarily on improving the quality of training and on coordinating training and employment possibilities.

This situation changed as a result of the 1973 oil crisis and the resulting modifications of the competitive positions of various nations in the international market. From the end of 1973 on, quite serious economic difficulties arose which were at first considered temporary, cyclical phenomena that could be neutralized for the length of their duration. The passage of time showed, however, that it was a matter of a long-term crisis arising from the structural adaptation of the Federal Republic's economy to the changes in the world economic system, a crisis that has continued to the present. There was only slight economic growth, and unemployment rose to a level that was disturbingly high by the standards of the Federal Republic.

The crisis especially affected the job markets for those seeking employment for the first time. These are, of course, predominantly minors. New entrants into the labor market are, in general, particularly hard hit by the contraction of the supply of jobs, since companies are more inclined to reduce the numbers of their personnel by hiring fewer new workers, than by discharging older ones. Furthermore, social welfare measures, such as protection against unfair dismissal and against job loss due to rationalization of the production process, have an unfavorable influence on the employment opportunities of minors. Another factor, which exacerbated the effect of the first two, was that the number of juveniles finishing school, and hence the supply of young workers, rose substantially from 1974 onwards.

However, it was the connection between the unemployment of juveniles and the system of vocational training, particularly enterprise-based vocational training, that was especially stressed, because the demand for apprentices had substantially declined at the beginning of the seventies. Opinions about the causes of this turn of events and their interaction differed considerably. Part of the blame was laid on processes of economic concentration and rationalization which had eliminated many of the small and middle-sized firms that had provided a large number of apprenticeships. Other elements of explanation referred to diminished learning opportunities in the work process due to intrafirm changes in work organization and due to increased interfirm specialization; further, the costs and risks of workplace-specific education seemed to have risen. That is why the tightening of training regulations and of supervision of the enterprises offering apprenticeships, measures which had been intended to improve training in the workplace, were also held responsible.

It was against this background that the concern about worsening quantitative problems since the middle of the seventies began to replace some of the older reform preoccupations. The federal and Länder governments, the Federal Employment Agency, craft and industrial associations have all developed a plethora of programs and measures intended to provide more positions for young workers, primarily by increasing the number of apprenticeships. One of the ways the federal and Länder governments undertook to achieve this goal was through subsidies and other forms of financial support for additional apprenticeships, through promoting supraenterprise training centers and attempting to provide more apprenticeships in the public service. At the same time, the federal government followed a policy of abandoning reform concepts and relaxing the regulations governing the training and employment of minors, and of enforcing them more laxly. The activities of the federal and Länder governments were paralleled by the efforts of the principal employers organizations, such as the National Union of German Employers Associations, the National Association of German Industry, and the National Association of German Industry and Commerce. These organizations conducted intensive advertising campaigns among their members, urging them to make full use of their existing training capacity and to enlarge it.

These endeavors to invigorate the supply of apprenticeships were further accompanied by training measures that resulted to a certain extent in an easing of the pressure on the markets for jobs and apprenticeships. On the one hand, the supply of full-time vocational schools was expanded by increasing the number of specialized full-time vocational schools, by the introduction of a whole year of in-school basic vocational training (cf. 11.3), and by establishing a school-based additional vocational-preparation year for weak students. On the other hand, most Länder lengthened attendance at the Hauptschule by a voluntary or a compulsory tenth year. Finally, the Federal Employment Agency financed training programs that gave their participants elementary preparation for employment, and that also had the effect of easing the pressure on the job and apprenticeship markets.

All of these mesures working together produced a considerable effect. Above all, the supply of apprenticeships responded relatively quickly and flexibly to these measures. But the price paid for the speed of this response were concessions with regard to the quality of training and a certain increase of less expensive apprenticeships in occupations with little prospect for employment, such as the crafts; even before this time, half of those who completed an apprenticeship in a craft had to change to another occupation. Nevertheless, as a result of these measures, the number of new apprenticeship contracts concluded each year rose continually from the middle of the 1970's on, and at the present time the dual system is absorbing more juveniles who have completed their compulsory full-time education than ever before (cf. Table 11.2). It is clear that this development is preventing an even higher rate of youth unemployment.

As for the current level of youth unemployment, it is probably to be explained more by the general contraction of the job market, the difficulty that new entrants onto the labor market have in obtaining employment, and a higher job turnover rate among young workers, than by the inadequate capacity of the vocational training system, inadequate training, or training in the wrong occupations. This thesis is supported by the fact that youth unemployment and general unemployment have been developing almost parallel to one another, and to a large degree are concentrated in the same occupations (cf. Figure 11.3); that one quarter to one third of all registered unemployed juveniles have already completed an apprenticeship; and that skilled workers are also having difficulty finding employment. Up

258

Table 11.2: Apprenticeships and Pupils Completing Full-Time Compulsory Education, 1965–1980

Year	Apprenticeships							Pupils	
	Industry and commerce	Crafts	Agriculture	Public service	Other sectors	Total	Beginning apprentices (included in total)	Completing full-time compulsory education with less than Realschule certificate	with Realschule certificate
1965	752,373	468,039	37,277	23,719	50,540	1,331,948	·	563,223	143,353
1968	769,219	478,584	49,805	22,945	71,682	1,392,235	·	501,710	164,164
1970	724,898	420,936	38,133	20,172	65,981	1,270,120	·	481,104	200,039
1972	722,173	434,130	27,786	30,557	88,105	1,302,751	·	504,363	202,333
1974	664,554	486,531	27,404	47,189	105,090	1,330,768	405,888[1]	509,376	258,011
1976	611,173	510,356	37,361	43,850	113,822	1,316,562	422,966[1]	464,649	277,271
1978	691,985	614,905	45,176	51,726	113,581	1,517,373	621,016	531,962	342,703
1980	786,917	702,331	46,791	53,816	122,861	1,712,716	669,901	505,550	319,484

[1] In first year of apprenticeship.

Sources: Statistisches Bundesamt: Bildung im Zahlenspiegel 1974 and 1981; Fachserie 11: Allgemeines Schulwesen 1980 and Berufliche Bildung 1980.

to two thirds of all registered unemployed workers in the quantitatively most significant occupational groups have completed a program of vocational training. Moreover, a large portion of the skilled workers is also underemployed because, contrary to earlier predictions, once-skilled occupational requirements have often fallen to the level of semiskilled work operations.

Nevertheless, the claim is made that there is a shortage of skilled workers. The validity of such general claims is dubious, but it is true that there is a shortage in some occupations, in some branches of the economy, and in some regions. In large measure, responsibility for this discrepancy has been laid at the door of the vocational training system, whereas in fact it is due to a number of factors which influence the supply of and the demand for skilled workers. Among these are: limits in the regional and occupational mobility of workers; the level of wages; the hiring criteria and the working conditions in the pertinent firms; and the previous training practices of the firms in question. In this regard, the organization of the work process also plays a role, for structural change can eliminate the jobs of large numbers of workers, or it can modify the demand for skilled workers in a way that is difficult to satisfy in the short term.

However, criticism of the vocational training system because of the state of the job market for skilled workers raises again the old question of whether it is possible to effectively coordinate vocational training with the employment opportunities actually offered by the economy. Such coordination can be viewed from two standpoints. With regard to the occupational life chances of the individuals concerned, its purpose would be to avoid training them in an occupation with little or no prospect of employment, to avoid change of occupation, downward social mobility, placement in jobs not making use of skills, etc. The second standpoint is whether, and to what extent, the labor market can be provided with the appropriate number of skilled workers. The latter point of view is of considerable importance for the second half of the eighties, when relatively quite small age groups will enter the labor market. In general, a strengthening of broad basic vocational training, which could serve as a basis for numerous possibilities of further training or of retraining in a new occupation, could contribute to respond effectively to such strains.

An especially difficult challenge to the system of initial vocational training has been posed in recent years by the employment in the Federal Republic of large numbers of foreign workers. It is becoming more and more imperative that young foreigners living in the Federal

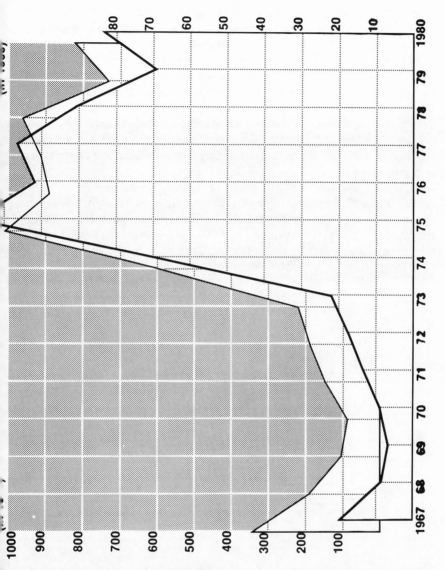

Figure 11.3. Total Number of Unemployed and Unemployed Under 20 Years of Age, 1967–1980

Republic be given vocational training that is as extensive as possible in order to facilitate their social integration. It is expected that by 1990, on a yearly national average, more than 15 percent of the juveniles leaving school after completing their compulsory full-time

261

education will be foreigners. In the urban and industrial areas where the foreign workers are concentrated, the percentage will, of course, be considerably higher, and the problem more severe. At present, foreign juveniles often take jobs as unskilled workers immediately after finishing school, or they remain unemployed. Their rate of unemployment has been much higher than that of German juveniles; their rate of enrollment at vocational schools is only half that of their German contemporaries—in spite of the fact that they, too, are legally obligated to attend the part-time vocational school until the age of 18; and there is a strikingly large difference between the two groups in the percentage of their members having apprenticeship contracts. These all reflect the precarious situation of foreign juveniles in the Federal Republic. Finally, the training of foreign youths is accompanied by language difficulties and social problems. These necessitate special instruction and social support for the foreign apprentices and must be taken into account both by the firms offering apprenticeships and by the vocational schools.

CHAPTER 12

The Core of the Cognitive System: University Expansion and Growing Professionalization

12.1. Some general characteristics of the tertiary education system and its recent evolution

Judging by such statistical indicators as the relative and absolute numbers of students, one can say that the Federal Republic of Germany, like other Western industrial nations, has a modern, democratically open post-secondary system. Figure 2.2 in Chapter 2 above shows how tightly woven the regional system of academic institutions has become in the past two decades. The number of universities has grown from 19 in 1960 to 61 in 1980; further, there are 27 other university-type institutions, 26 art academies, and 115 polytechnic colleges. This wave of expansion and reform lasted from the early sixties to the mid-seventies, following a period of reconstruction in the wake of World War II. The year 1975 marked the beginning of what may be called a period of stabilization. Superficial parallels, however, tend to obscure a number of peculiarities in West German higher education that even today distinguish this system from the British and American models. We shall deal with a number of these features.

Since the end of the 19th century, German universities have, for the most part, been a combination of research institution and professional school. In other words, the main purpose of the university was not to provide a continuation of general education, but rather to be both a center for research and a place where one could acquire the academic qualifications for such specialized professions as engineering, medicine, law, education, and theology. Higher education's enormous expansion and the increase in the number of students between 1960 and the late seventies may be traced primarily to a widening of the spectrum of professional schools by means of establishing new institutions and expanding existing ones, and through the inclusion of engineering schools in the system of higher education and of teacher training in the university curriculum. In other words, the expansion was not the result of an exploding undergraduate population partaking in general education, as in the United States, but was due, rather, to an increase in the age-specific ratio of enrollment in post-secondary level institutions in conjunction with a general upgrading process.

The traditional definition of the German university's role continues to exercise an influence on the way German society defines the university student, as well as what is customarily expected of the university and its staff. Analogous to one aspect of "academic freedom," there still exists the notion of 'Freiheit des Studiums': the student's freedom to draw up his own course of studies and pursue it—perhaps at more than one university—as he sees fit, deciding for himself when he is ready to be examined, and who his examiners will be. In many respects, this image has been an idealization for some time, particularly for those courses of study which lead to qualification in one of the established professions. Still, the ideal had a certain vitality and served during the seventies as a brake on efforts at university reform.

The student's role, then, is that of a preprofessional adult. In view of the age of the group concerned, any other role would clearly be inappropriate. At the present time the Abitur is seldom obtained before the age of 19.5 years, and university study usually lasts at least six years (cf. 12.3). Consequently, only about 15 percent of the students in the Federal Republic were younger than 21 years of age in 1978, whereas roughly 25 percent were over 25. It is in keeping with the student's role that German universities have no function *in loco parentis* or any other general custodial responsibility.

This has always been the case. Thus, there has never been anything like the American university campus or residential college in Germany. The focal point of the German student's social life lies outside the formal learning situation. Since World War II, traditional fraternities—'Korporationen'—have had little relevance, and the sorority is unknown in Germany. The primary function of student housing, much of which was built in the course of the expansion of higher education, is not social but instrumental: it provides a place to sleep. Thus in 1979 some 22 percent of the students continue to live with parents or relatives, while 64 percent rent rooms or apartments off-campus, and only 13 percent live in dormitories. All in all, patterns of social life among students tend to be diffuse; as a rule, a student's private life and much of his group activities go unnoticed both by faculty and by fellow students. On the other hand, political and religious associations have always served as an important focal point of students' social life, and this has been especially true during the past fifteen years.

The predominance of public—not private—forms of organization and finance is a further salient feature of the German system of higher education, and for that matter of higher education in all of continental Europe. The core of the tertiary education system are the full-fledged universities. These are state financed, but—as shall be explained—autonomous public legal entities (cf. 3.1.4.). Most of the polytechnic colleges and all of the remaining teacher-training colleges are also state-financed, and the former do not enjoy the full privileges of academic autonomy, which means, among other things, that they cannot award advanced degrees. There are, in addition, a number of small theological seminaries and private but state-accredited polytechnic colleges, all of which receive public support. In all these cases, the primary responsibility for financing rests with the Länder governments and not the local or the federal governments. Finally, the publicly funded system of financial assistance to needy students has been considerably extended over the last decade.

There is a strong pressure in the Federal Republic for uniformity of standards. The state is, to a large extent, entrusted with responsibility for maintaining professional standards—and this is done by imposing uniform standards of education. The Abitur certificate, which, in principle, is the necessary and sufficient entrance qualification for university studies, has the same value throughout the country. The counterpart to this is the official assumption that the universities all provide education of the same quality. Despite modifications of admission procedures introduced in the seventies when applications for admission began to exceed the universities' capacity in some fields, individual academic institutions are still not allowed to set their own standards for selecting students.

When one considers the overall role and position of higher education within the broader context of research and development activities and institutions, its structural stability is striking (cf. Table 12.1). Over the past 20 years the total research and development effort—measured in gross national expenditures on research and development at current prices—has increased more than sevenfold; in real terms—i.e., after allowing for inflation—the increase was considerably smaller, about twice the level in the early sixties. On the performance side of these total expenditures, the post-secondary sector still accounts for about 17 percent and the private non-profit institutions for around 12 percent—both with a slight tendency to decline over the past two decades. In contrast, the share of business and industry-based research and development has increased to about 64 percent. On the financing side, the overall share of Länder and federal contributions decreased to 45 percent, but they remain the dominant sources of funds for the university and private nonprofit sectors. For functional reasons, basic and theoretical research still tends to be concentrated in these two sectors.

12.2. A sketch of institutional features in higher education, and the political debate since 1945

At all levels, German education is essentially public education; the extent of state control, however, varies with the level (cf. 3.1.4). Being state institutions, the German universities do not enjoy the degree of independence that the autonomous British universities or the many private institutions in the United States have. Yet, on the other hand, they do not fall under the kind of tight fiscal and administrative control which the Länder governments exert over elementary and secondary education. And although university teachers are just as much state officials as the other teachers in public education, they are not subject to the same types of regulations. In other words, they enjoy the freedom to teach and conduct research as they see fit. This academic freedom is specifically guaranteed in Article 5 of the Basic Law of the Federal Republic. The rights enjoyed by the university teachers, in teaching and research, and by students, in their choice of university and course of study, have a parallel in the universities right to administrative autonomy.

Each university has its own constitution, in conformity with the laws of the Land in which it is situated and which provides the university's budgetary resources. Among other things, this constitution regulates the election of representatives to the administrative bodies of the various organizational levels in the university, from institute or department to the entire university. It is in these bodies that decisions are made on curriculum and research, as well as on

Table 12.1: Gross Expenditures on Research and Development by Performing Sector and Source of Funds, 1962 and 1980

Performing sectors, sources of funds	1962		1980	
	Amount (million Deutsch Marks)	Percent of gross national expenditures	Amount (million Deutsch Marks)	Percent of gross national expenditures
Gross expenditures	4,490	100.0	34,720	100.0
Business enterprise sector[1]	2,450	54.6	22,000	63.4
financed by				
Government sector	340	7.6	4,600	13.2
Business enterprise	2,110	47.0	16,730	48.2
Private non-profit s.	–	–	20	0.1
Foreign sector	–	–	650	1.9
Government sector[2]	240	5.3	1,600	4.6
financed by				
Government sector	220	4.9	1,550	4.4
Business enterprise	5	0.1	20	0.1
Private non-profit s.	15	0.3	30	0.1
Private non-profit sector[3]	700	15.6	4,130	11.9
financed by				
Government sector	638	14.2	3,680	10.6
Business enterprise	15	0.3	50	0.2
Private non-profit s. and foreign sector	47	1.1	400	1.1
Higher education sector	910	20.3	6,040	17.4
financed by				
Government sector	900	20.1	5,930	17.1
Business enterprise	10	0.2	110	0.3
Foreign sector	190	4.2	950	2.7
financed by				
Government sector	180	4.0	830	2.4
Business enterprise	10	0.2	120	0.3

[1] Business enterprises and private co-operative R&D institutions.

[2] Scientific institutions of the federal and Länder governments, including scientific museums, libraries and archives.

[3] Mainly government financed R&D institutions (Max-Planck-Society, Fraunhofer Society, 'big science' technological development centers).

Source: Bundesministerium für Forschung und Technologie: Informationen, No 1, 1981.

267

personnel and organizational questions. Staff appointments are made by the pertinent Land's Minister of Culture on the basis of recommendations submitted by the university. As a rule, the list contains the names of three candidates, the first of which is the one preferred by the university. The minister, usually, but not always, chooses the preferred candidate.

In the course of efforts to reform higher education over the past two decades, the individual Länder have introduced various sorts of legal measures with the aim of revamping the university's organizational structure. One of the main changes introduced in the early seventies consisted in eliminating status differences among professors with respect to decision-making rights. Further, temporary junior faculty, technical and clerical staff, and students gained certain rights of representation and participation in decision-making.

Leaving aside two precedent-setting decisions handed down by the Federal Constitutional Court, it was not until January 1976 that legislation was enacted on the national level establishing a framework for subsequent detailed regulations affecting higher education (Federal Framework Law for Higher Eduction), thereby binding Länder legislation and administrative regulations to a national standard. Along with new Länder laws, university constitutions, and Constitutional Court decisions confirming the hegemony of tenured academic staff in matters of research, appointments of academic staff and curriculum, this national framework legislation is itself the product of a reform process which has considerably altered the face of German higher education, and which, indeed, from time to time took on a revolutionary character.

By the early sixties, the situation at the universities had become ripe for reform. The principal bone of contention and an obstacle to reform was not the principle of academic freedom as such, but rather the fact that it had come to be identified exclusively with traditionalism and a rigid academic hierarchy, all of which appeared to be standing in the way of efforts to come to terms both with the Nazi past and with contemporary problems.

The Third Reich and the Second World War left deep wounds in the academic community. Apart from material destruction, Nazi rule had dealt the very integrity of the university and academic study a severe blow. In the thirties, Socialist and Jewish scholars and students were driven out of the universities in the name of "German science and scholarship"; certain scientific and philosophical approaches were declared taboo; and both research and teaching were made to toe the fascist line. The number of students declined between 1932 and

1939 from 121,000 to 56,000, a decline largely due to demographic factors, but to some extent also caused by the political climate. The result was a loss of intellectual vigor, indeed, a deterioration in the humanities and above all in the social sciences, whereas the reputation of German science and engineering was only confirmed by their close association with war-time technology.

After 1945 efforts were made to heal these wounds. Parallel to the rejection of the Nazi past, a conscious effort was made to revive liberal ideals and prewar academic traditions—in particular that of the "unity of research and teaching" and even stronger "academic freedom" than in the 19th century. Developments in the Soviet Occupation Zone, later to become the German Democratic Republic, only reinforced this liberal orientation.

There, policy on higher education and research was characterized by administrative regimentation of courses and course content, as well as the imposition of college-style organization of teaching and learning. Furthermore, government policy in East Germany sought to increase enrollments as early as the fifties, and higher education was centrally planned by the national government in accordance with economic requirements and the political objective of rapidly establishing women's equality and improving the position of educationally underprivileged groups in society. A further characteristic of East German education was the attempt to subject research to thoroughgoing centralized planning, as well as to exert political control over teachers and students. Such control was originally justified in the name of rigorous de-Nazification, and was subsequently employed as a means of pressuring teachers and students into identification with the aims and methods of the governing Socialist Unity Party. Symbol of opposition to this East German policy is the Free University of Berlin, established in the western sector of the city in 1949 by professors and students in reaction to Communist pressure on the Humboldt University (founded in 1810), located in the Soviet sector of Berlin.

But, whereas in the fifties, the East German measures served in the main as a deterrent to similar reform measures in the West, by the late sixties some of these measures had taken on the character of an undeclared model. This is true in particular of East Germany's efforts to increase secondary and post-secondary level student enrollments, as well as of its early and largely successful policy of reducing class- and sex-specific discrimination in secondary and higher education—a success due to a rigorous implementation of a quota system still in effect today. On the other hand, the recent East

German policy, in effect since 1971 and designed to stabilize university enrollments and indeed reduce them to less than 10 percent of a given age group, has received practically no attention in West German educational circles.

The twofold challenge posed by the Nazi past and the postwar policies in the other part of Germany had a decisive impact on the resumption of academic and scientific studies and the reestablishment of a system of higher education in postwar West Germany. Developments there were marked by a number of peculiar contradictions, a lack of uniformity, and a degree of complexity however, can also be seen in a favorable light, namely as the expression of a striving for diversity and freedom from tutelage.

The West German constitution does not provide for any centralized authority in matters of research and education policy. It does, however, call for freedom of research and scholarship and does not seek to orient these to any specific societal objectives (cf. Chapter 3). In line with the principles of free enterprise and freedom to choose one's occupation, any overt attempt to steer young people into specific occupations is considered unacceptable. As this shows, the constitutional provisions tend to restrict and limit the state's influence in an effort to guarantee the autonomy of higher education and research. The function of the parliaments and governments of the Länder has been to create the legal framework in which science and scholarship can administer themselves and flourish, free from external influence.

Thus far, we have been discussing science and scholarship in abstract terms. Concretely, these enterprises are carried on by the following groups of persons and institutions. At the top of a traditional hierarchy of institutions is the university, and in the university, the top rank in terms of influence and status consists of the 'Ordinarien', the full professors appointed for life who often head one of the institutes which traditionally make up the faculties, or schools, of a university or—after the reform—the departments. One rung lower—below the professors—is a group of middle-level university teachers who have earned the doctoral degree and in many cases the Habilitation, a more advanced academic degree which is the traditional qualification for a professorial appointment. At the lowest level in this academic hierarchy stand the assistants, who either have the doctoral degree or are candidates for it. There is, in addition, a nonacademic staff.

Save for the uppermost echelon, this classification has never been particularly uniform. Things became even more complicated during the sixties, when higher education, and in particular middle-ranking teaching personnel, underwent expansion and the various Länder parliaments enacted differing legislation on higher education (cf. Figure 12.1). The Federal Framework Law for Higher Education of 1976 established a uniform structure for university faculties by defining four categories of personnel and fixing their modes of representation and participation in university life: the professors, the university assistants, teachers for special purposes, and other full-time or part-time academic personnel. To these groups of persons engaged in teaching and research (who, in addition, have administrative duties), we must add the students, who are also considered members of the university.

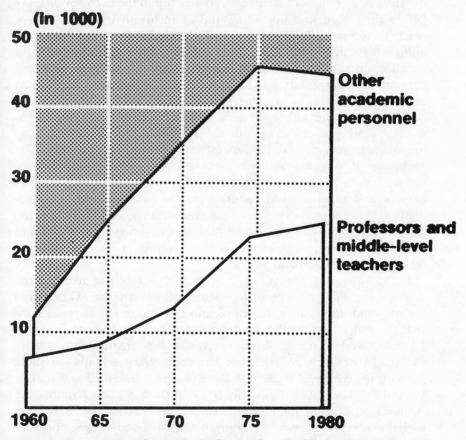

Figure 12.1. Positions for Academic Personnel at Tertiary-Level Institutions (Excluding Polytechnic Colleges), 1960–1980

271

Before the reform of higher education, the university self-governance rested for the most part in the hands of the full professors. Their personal judgment was the determining factor in decisions on personnel and on curricula and research in their institutes and departments. Other staff members had little or no say in these matters. Until recently, the same might be said of the role of the students, whose activities were confined to associations on the university and departmental level in which they had limited discretionary authority in purely student affairs, notably those connected with student welfare.

A further instrument of university self-governance is the Conference of West German University Rectors, an interuniversity coordinating body representing all universities (up to the early seventies—before their academic upgrading and/or inclusion in universities—teacher-training colleges were virtually excluded from this body). In addition to this cordinating body of the universities, we should mention the German Research Society, which channels financial support to a large number of mostly smaller research projects at universities, as well as the Max Planck Society for the Advancement of Science, an organization which maintains about 50 research institutes, mainly scientific, outside the universities. Both organizations are funded primarily by the federal and Länder governments. The exchange of students and scholars between German and foreign universities is handled primarily by the German Academic Exchange Service and the Humboldt Foundation. A national students' association, the 'Verband deutscher Studentenschaften', which had played an active role in educational politics in the sixties, but which had vanished in the turbulence of student unrest at the end of that decade, was reestablished in 1975.

In the fifties, only the universities combining teaching and research enjoyed the full privilege of academic self-governance. These were the fifty-odd universities, technical universities, and theological seminaries, which all together had around 130,000 students in 1955. Excluded were a number of nonuniversity-type institutions, notably the teacher-training colleges and the engineering schools. In these schools, the course of study was more closely regimented and shorter than at regular universities. Only some of these schools required the Abitur qualification for admission, and the teachers often had no higher academic degrees and enjoyed few of the privileges normally accorded their colleagues in the traditional universities. These institutions were also not empowered to confer academic degrees such as the 'Diplom' (the lowest academic degree, requiring four or five years of study), the Ph.D., or the Habilitation.

It is against this background of a reestablished postwar German academia that one must consider all the debates, reforms, and changes that took place during the sixties and early seventies. It all started when it became apparent that the expansion of higher education was by no means keeping pace with the growing demand for university education, nor doing justice to the growing importance of research, with the result that the university system as a whole was threatening to break down. Whereas enrollment had doubled in the fifties, the number of university teachers had increased only by around one-third. The result was that in some university institutes the ratio of students to full professors was between 250 and 300 to 1 in 1960, in contrast to an average of around 37 to 1 in 1928. This development was accompanied by two distinct phases of critical debate and reform initiatives. The first, lasting from the mid-fifties to roughly 1967, centered on the economic and social aspects of education policy in general; the second phase coincided with the student revolt in the years 1967 to 1970 and was characterized by arguments and demands that were in part more radical attacks on higher education policy and specific positions in science and scholarship, and in part general political claims, mostly of leftist and egalitarian orientation.

The criticism voiced by educators and policy-makers during the first phase pointed to a certain inherent weakness in Germany's traditional system of higher education and advanced studies: academic and scientific autonomy—'Freiheit der Wissenschaft'—carried with it the danger that neither the university nor the government would recognize and act on contemporary challenges and demands in higher education. It was generally felt that more planning was needed, as well as more effective support for science and technology and an increased number of university students and graduates in order to keep West Germany competitive in science and scholarship, and to enable it to hold its own in the international economic and political arenas. With its outdated structures, higher education appeared to be standing in its own way: the professorial freedoms that characterized the 'Ordinarienuniversität'—the traditionally structured university dominated and run by the permanently appointed professors as an aggregate of autonomous academic entrepreneurs—were attacked not just for being an annoying anachronism, but also because they were seen as the reason why German research in certain fields was lagging behind.

273

As time went on, however, criticism focussed more and more on the social effects of traditional higher education, whose self-recruitment mechanisms continued to perpetuate a small economic, social, and political elite. In the early sixties, only 7 percent of university students were what is termed "lower class," whereas almost 60 percent came from the upper middle class. These figures represent almost the complete opposite of the actual numerical relations in the population as a whole (cf. Chapter 4).

All in all, these arguments militated against the original idea of restricting admissions in order to raise academic standards. Instead, what emerged was a policy in accord with public demand for higher education; in other words, a policy designed to open up higher education to a greater number of students. At the same time, academic training was to be made more rigorous, while research and development were to be promoted more vigorously and effectively.

The student movement of the late sixties and early seventies took up many of the same positions, but in more radical form. The students flatly rejected the 'Ordinarienuniversität' with its antiquated power structures, refusing any further allegiance for reasons that were at once moral, theoretical, and—in the practical sense—political. They called for internal reforms, justifying this demand by contending, among other things, that the university has a more general political responsibility to society. They now called for an independent, "critical" approach to science and scholarship. Advocates of this position felt that setting research priorities and running the university in accordance with the principle of academic self-governance should not be reserved to the professors (and politicians), but rather that nontenured faculty, students, and nonacademic staff should have a voice in the administrative and decision-making bodies.

The worldwide indignation over the war in Vietnam developed into a youth protest movement not just against American policy, but also against political conditions at home. The ossified power structures in the universities, which had for so long resisted reform, crumbled under the force of this protest movement. Many universities responded directly and reformed their statutes, and in the course of time the law bearing on higher education were brought up to date in all the Länder, with the already mentioned Federal Framework Law for Higher Education of 1976 serving as the nationwide standard. An additional effect of the student movement was a political polarization in the universities, which for a time virtually paralyzed many of the reformed administrative committees and other decision-making bodies. Indeed, in a few instances the movement politicized research and teaching, too.

The revival of socialist and radical democratic values in the years from, say, 1968 to 1974 provoked a powerful political reaction outside the universities, ostensibly in "defense of the constitution" and "to preserve loyalty to the constitution." This reaction resulted in a crisis which bore some similarities to the American experience during the McCarthy era in the early fifties. Informing on students and university teachers and other practices poisoned and further politicized the climate in the universities, and the term 'Berufsverbot'—"professional proscription"—was coined to designate the practice of investigating the political background of prospective government employees, including teachers, with the intent of eliminating politically disagreeable applicants.

Political rearguard skirmishes with the heirs of the "Revolt of '68" were still going on, when, around 1974, new ideological constellations began to take form. Characteristic of this new trend is skepticism about the viability of traditional ideological blueprints for industrial society, be they socialist or liberal-capitalist in orientation. A new sensibility has developed, partly religious—in the broadest sense—and partly ecological in orientation, and characterized by continued attentiveness to the rights and needs of the individual. The most important consequence of this new ideological trend—leaving aside all its "fundamentalist" aspects, including the rejection of present political structures—appears to be a blurring of the traditional cleavages between the left and the right.

12.3. Quantitative changes in higher education

Looking back on developments since the fifties, we can see that it is not just the universities, but indeed the whole of post-secondary education that has undergone change. This applies to its political and social function just as much as to its structure and size.

With regard to the more formal aspects of governance and finance, an outstanding feature of the last decades has been the stronger involvement of the federal government and the attempt to establish a system of policy-coordinating mechanisms between the federal and the Länder governments, on the one hand, and the institutions of the post-secondary sector on the other. This has to be seen against the background of the constitutionally guaranteed jurisdiction of the Länder in matters of education, one aspect of their more comprehensive "cultural sovereignty." (For a more extensive discussion of these issues, cf. Chapter 3.)

The federal government's stronger involvement dates from the late fifties and has consisted primarily in participation in financing new university buildings and equipment, funding research, and providing financial aid to students. Initially, federal involvement was based on agreements with the individual Länder, but in light of the Basic Law this was an awkward arrangement. In 1969, the Basic Law was amended to take account of patterns that in the meantime had evolved and become established. The federal government is now entitled to play an active role in devising policy guidelines for higher education and research, while at the same time the Länder governments in effect retain a veto in virtually all matters of educational policy.

This left power substantially in the hands of the Länder governments (local governments having practically no say in educational policy). Toward the end of the seventies, the Länder were picking up the bill for over 90 percent of expenditures for higher education, providing half of student assistance, and almost one third of public funds for research. This means that, in contrast to the multifaceted American situation, educational decision-making in the Federal Republic is concentrated at the Länder level, where it is dependent on the established mechanisms of party politics.

Two important matters which call for coordination among the various Länder have been the expansion of higher education and the allocation of admissions in those fields where the demand is greater than the universities' capacity. Since 1957, the Science Council, formally an advisory body, but in fact a politically very influential organ composed of representatives from the federal government, the Länder, and the universities, has regularly drawn up prognoses and expansion programs to aid governments and parliaments in deciding on appropriations (cf. 3.1.2).

But despite a considerable expansion of university facilities, by the early seventies applications for admission by far exceeded capacity in a number of fields. Since then, a quota system—*numerus clausus*—has been established and a central placement office set up to distribute admission to these fields among students throughout the Federal Republic. Since a certain restriction on the basic principle of free choice of education is apparently unavoidable for the time being, the objective is to make the distribution of available resources as fair as possible.

From the early sixties up to around 1975, personnel and physical capacities of universities expanded at a very rapid pace (cf. Figure 12.1). Since then, the expansion has slowed down considerably, and is only partially responding to the still rising demand, which, for demographic reasons, is not expected to abate until the end of the decade. Although the international economic crisis has been in progress since 1974, it was only toward the end of the seventies that the general public realized that the crisis was seriously affecting middle-range planning in Bonn and the Länder capitals. Over the next few years cutbacks can be expected to affect the tertiary-level institutions' teaching and research functions, the latter, however, less than the former.

Figure 12.2 gives an idea of the quantitative development of enrollments in higher education over the past two decades, together with a projection of future developments. The total number of students in 1980 was around one million, a fourfold increase over 1960. This is the combined result of four groups of factors. The first of these, and the most important one, is the growth in the number of eligible persons, the result of the increase in the enrollment in schools or tracks preparing pupils for study at the tertiary level. A second factor is the expansion of engineering and advanced technical schools and the upgrading of their academic status which took place in the early seventies, when these were formally established as polytechnic colleges. A third reason is the steady growth of the demographic base from the mid-sixties on into the late eighties, but which is expected to drop off abruptly after 1990 (a proxy variable for this is the size of the cohort of 18-year-olds; cf. Figure 12.2). Fourth, and last, the increase in the average length of study at tertiary level institutions affects the absolute number of students; this in turn is partly due to the rising number of students who actually, or at least formally, continue their studies to avoid the uncertainties of the labor market. (The average length of study is currently more than 6 years at universities and a little less than 4 years at polytechnics.)

There is, of course, a considerable element of uncertainty in projections of future enrollments. Thus the projection of the number of students anticipated in the eighties had to be substantially revised downward over the past few years before reaching the level depicted in Figure 12.2. One reason is that there was a substantial drop in the propensity for further study by the Gymnasium graduates from somewhat above 90 percent in the late sixties to some 70 percent in the early eighties (cf. Table 12.2). This in turn is the result of a

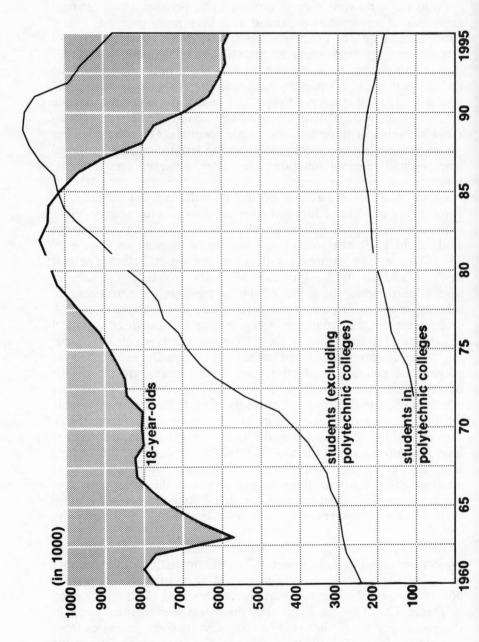

Figure 12.2. Students in Higher Education and the 18-Year-Old Population, 1960–1995

variety of influences, notably the overall deterioration since 1974 in job opportunities for university graduates, as well as the excess of applications for admission over the universities' capacity in a number of disciplines, which often substantially delays the beginning of university study.

Although low by international comparison, unemployment rates of between 4 and 5 percent have been a constant feature of the West German economy ever since the onset of the economic crisis (cf. Chapter 11). Unfortunately, this overall slump in economic activity coincided with an increased output of graduates from the expanded system of higher education and a sharp drop in demand for highly qualified manpower, especially teachers, in the public sector. As a consequence, the employment crisis has not spared academically trained manpower, and recent graduates in particular. The total number of graduates and consequently of entrants into the academic labor markets rose substantially from 1965 to the end

Table 12.2: Candidates for Abitur and for Certificates Giving Access to Polytechnic Colleges According to Educational Goals, 1972–1981

	Year					
	1972	1974	1976	1978	1980	1981
Total number of candidates (in 1000)	126.4	163.3	183.2	204.2	200.7	234.2
Intend to enter tertiary sector (total)						
Number (in 1000)	113.3	138.2	137.9	141.5	137.1	160.9
Percentage of total	89.7	84.6	75.3	69.3	68.3	68.7
Intend to enter tertiary sector and become teachers						
Number (in 1000)	•	38.2	22.4	22.7	17.9	18.7
Percentage of total	•	27.6	16.2	16.1	13.1	11.6
Are undecided about educational goal						
Number (in 1000)	7.8	15.2	28.3	37.6	42.7	49.9
Percentage of total	6.2	9.3	15.4	18.4	21.3	21.3
Do not intend to enter tertiary sector						
Number (in 1000)	5.3	9.9	17.0	25.1	20.8	23.4
Percentage of total	4.2	6.0	9.3	12.3	10.4	10.0

Source: Statistisches Bundesamt: Wirtschaft und Statistik, No. 10, 1981.

of the seventies, from around 65,500 graduates to some 120,000. Mainly as a result of the large age groups entering higher education in the eighties, the total number of graduates is expected to continue to grow to some 150,000 by the middle of the decade and to roughly 180,000 by its end. Up to the early seventies, graduates faced an attractive seller's market. Since the mid-seventies, however, labor market conditions have deteriorated substantially as a result of the overall slump.

In the case of teachers, there is reduced demand as a consequence of reduced secondary school expansion and a substantial and persistent decline in the size of the cohorts reaching school age. Public warnings ever since the early seventies about expected difficulties as well as the temporary application of *numerus-clausus* restrictions on teachers' training had the cumulative effect of substantially reducing the percentage of prospective university students opting for a teaching career (cf. Table 12.2). One form this adjustment took was a recommendation to make teacher training polyvalent, i.e., to conceive of it as a preparation for a variety of careers besides teaching.

It is important to note that such counterpressures to the process of professionalization have not proven successful. Yet there is pressure from the labor market to adapt, and—with some differences—this pressure has affected virtually all categories of graduates. Although manifest unemployment has been kept comparatively low, the waiting period before entering employment has lengthened substantially. Since no rapid return to high and sustained rates of economic growth is likely in the years to come, the way out of the general employment crisis is likely to take the form of a redistribution of worktime; such a course is already being pursued on a limited scale in the form of early retirement opportunities and an increase in part-time employment as a stopgap measure for stretching employment opportunities for prospective teachers.

In this connection it should be pointed out that the introduction of the *numerus-clausus* restrictions and the establishment of a central admissions office for the disciplines under heavy demand were not officially intended as mechanisms by which to regulate manpower supply. An explicit exception in this respect were the quantitative restrictions operating in teacher training. Restrictions on enrollment in medical schools have been imposed mainly because of the particular shortcomings in medical education: a student-to-teacher ratio that is far too high, lack of adequate clinical facilities, extremely high building costs for new clinics with modern equipment; the fears of the medical lobby that the still highly remunerative medical professions might become overcrowded may also play a role. But the *numerus clausus* generally has been justified as a temporary mechanism for alleviating supply shortages in the education market; in principle, it does not infringe on the constitutionally guaranteed right to a free choice of education. It is supposed to leave the market forces, as these operate on both education and the labor market, as little affected as possible.

Nevertheless, on average higher education in general operated at between 25 and 35 percent overcapacity during the seventies and is expected to continue to do so until around the mid-eighties. Therefore, quotas are being applied to entrance into various disciplines. The strictest form of *numerus clausus*, essentially based on a combination of Abitur marks, test results, and "waiting time," currently applies only to applicants for medical studies (where the available placements make up some 10% of the total number of admissions to higher education possible each semester). An intermediate form, essentially based on Abitur marks and waiting time, applies to applicants for, among other subjects, architecture, biology, pharmacy, psychology, and teacher training (some 40% of the university capacity available each year). Another 40 percent of places in a variety of disciplines is subject to a partial *numerus clausus* designed to overcome regional disparities between supply and demand by allotting the available places on a nationwide basis. There are no restrictions for the remaining 10 percent of applications.

Generally speaking, the expansion of the system has led to modifications in its patterns of selectivity, with the result that it is coming somewhat closer to the ideal of a democratically open system of mass higher education. So it is that the ratios of enrollment in institutions of higher education in the pertinent age groups have increased substantially over the past thirty years, and in particular in the past fifteen (cf. Table 12.3). While women's enrollment has more than doubled over the past twenty years and now stands at around 40 percent of overall enrollments, it is still concentrated in the liberal arts and education; this concentration is diminishing, however.

Nevertheless, although the system's social selectivity has lessened, it still remains very pronounced (cf. Figure 12.3). Thus even though the percentage of students from working class backgrounds increased from 8.5 percent of all beginning students in 1967 to 14.6 percent in 1979, workers themselves make up some 47% of the labor force. By contrast, the percentage of students whose fathers are tenured

Table 12.3: Enrollment Rates of German Students in Tertiary Education
According to Age and Sex, 1952 and 1980

Age	Enrollment as % of age-specific population					
	1952		1980			
	university-type institutions[1]		university-type institutions		polytechnic colleges	
	male	female	male	female	male	female
18	0.1	0.1	0.1	0.1	0.2	0.1
19	0.7	0.4	2.2	4.3	0.5	0.9
20	2.1	0.8	6.4	8.3	1.6	1.8
21	3.2	1.0	10.0	9.1	3.1	2.3
22	3.6	1.0	11.9	9.1	4.3	2.2
23	3.7	0.9	12.7	8.9	4.8	1.8
24	3.0	0.7	12.6	8.0	4.4	1.3
25	2.4	0.5	12.2	6.4	3.6	0.9
26	2.0	0.4	10.5	4.7	2.6	0.6
27	1.6	0.3	8.6	3.4	1.7	0.4
28	1.3	0.2	6.7	2.6	1.1	0.3
29	1.1	0.1	5.3	2.0	0.8	0.2
30	0.8	0.1	4.0	1.6	0.5	0.1
31	0.6	0.1	3.1	1.2	0.4	0.1
32	0.5	0.0	2.4	0.9	0.3	0.1
33	0.4	0.0	1.8	0.8	0.2	0.1
34	0.3	0.0	1.3	0.6	0.2	0.1

[1] Including teachers' colleges.

Source: Calculations based on data of Statistisches Bundesamt.

state officials dropped from 27.2 percent to 21.6 percent. Yet their
fathers account for only 12.9% of the male labor force.

Worth mentioning in this connection is the considerably less
pronounced social selectivity in the polytechnic colleges, which is in
part a reflection of the fact that they continue to be the "junior
partner" in the system of higher education. As was the case with
their predecessors, access to these institutions is possible without the
Abitur; their courses of study are highly structured, shorter, and
more practically oriented; and teaching loads for the professors are
twice as heavy as is the rule in the universities.

The limited success of efforts to improve educational opportunity
in higher education can be traced in part to certain dominant features

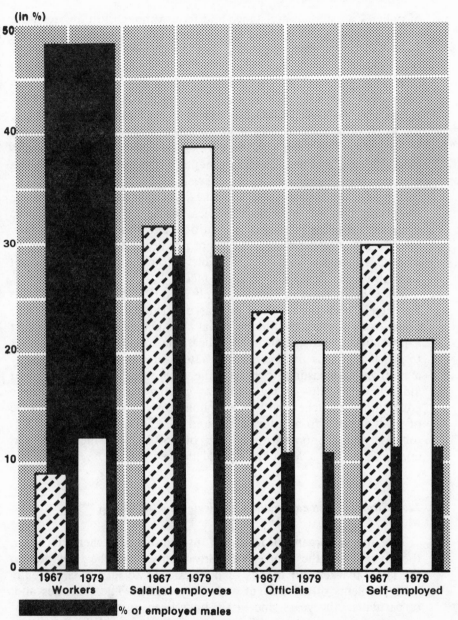

Figure 12.3. German Students in First Year of Higher Education (Excluding Poly-technic Colleges) According to Fathers' Occupational Status, 1967 and 1979

283

of policies on student assistance and fees. Although tuition fees were already very low by United States standards, they were abolished altogether in the early seventies, and the scheme of public stipends then applied—the "Honnef Model" of 1955, which used as a standard of eligibility a combination of social criteria and academic performance—was expanded and revised. This program, the Federal Education and Training Promotion Act of 1971, bases assistance solely on social criteria. The reform of the student aid scheme amounted to an increase in cash subsidies for lower-class and lower-middle-class students, and thus was instrumental in drawing greater numbers of them into higher education, as well as into secondary level II. But in addition to these cash subsidies, the quantitatively even more important flow of invisible subsidies has to be considered. These invisible subsidies consist of the tuition fees that no students now have to pay. On the whole, the more privileged social strata benefit disproportionately from this invisible subsidy, since students from such strata are heavily overrepresented.

Since the increase in student numbers during the last two decades has largely been the result of increased participation of middle- and upper-class women, the hidden social class bias of the system against a pronounced redistribution of educational opportunities continues to be strong. This has been accentuated since the mid-seventies by a number of measures to reduce the cash subsidies of the student aid scheme, while—at least so far—leaving the principle of "free education" untouched (with direct public costs for a completed course of study ranging from a low of around 18,000 Deutsche Mark (DM) for law and economics to a high of 250,000 for medicine, and averaging 80,000 DM at the end of the seventies).

12.4. Structure of the disciplines, curricula, and professions

The internal organization of the institutions of higher education, the diversity of the courses of study offered, and their relation to the labor market and modes of political and social life continually pose problems of adjustment and readjustment. The seventies and, in particular, the years since 1978 have been unique as a period of particularly pronounced efforts at reorganization. While the late sixties and early seventies were characterized by legislative measures redefining the overall structure of higher education (which involved, among other things, the inclusion and upgrading of teacher-training colleges and engineering schools), subsequent efforts have been directed toward reorganizing curricula and examination requirements. Special commissions have been set up for this purpose. The Federal Framework Law for Higher Education of 1976 provides for commissions on two levels. One type of commission is organized by field of study on the national level and consists of experts delegated from the various academic institutions, as well as representatives from the federal and Länder governments and from professional organizations. The second type of commission is organized on the Länder level and has a similarly mixed composition, though without federal participation. It is charged with working out details for the individual institutions, which subsequently have to be submitted to the Länder Ministries of Culture for approval.

These efforts have to be seen against the background of more long-term qualitative trends which, with some variations, appear to be affecting most industrialized countries. We shall treat three of these. The first is the emergence and consolidation of a "new" body of theories and set of disciplines: the social sciences. Connected with this trend is a second one: the two-pronged process of generalization and relativization of the concepts of science and cognitive rationality. The third trend is increasing professionalization of occupations.

The main line of intellectual development throughout the 19th and into the 20th century was the progressive emancipation of the exact and biological sciences from older, religiously or philosophically grounded explanations of the nature of the world. Thus the theories and methodologies of disciplines such as physics, chemistry, and biology, together with their practical application in various branches of engineering and modern medicine, became virtually synonymous with science as such and with its application. By contrast, the cognitive status of the arts and humanities became more dubious. In these, the boundaries between practical performance and theoretical generalizations, between moral, normative commitment and objective rationality continued to be blurred. This was true not only of theology and philosophy, but also of the forerunners of the modern social sciences, law, and economics. More specifically, theorizing about society and social processes was either—in the idealistic tradition—an extension of normative religious or philosophical explanations or—in the "scientific" tradition—an extension of biological arguments or organicistic analogies. It was only in this century, in particular in the decades following World War II, that theories of society and social processes were broadly institutionalized, which stressed the relative autonomy of social structures and processes from their physical and organic, as well as cultural, environments. It should be noted that this process of scientific differentiation and evolution is, empirically speaking, the combined effect of two factors: first, the availability of "new" systems of ideas, theories and, methodologies and, second, their quantitative diffusion and the degree of their institutionalization in an academic system, and indeed in society at large.

Well into the sixties—and in some respects even up to the present—German experience with the evolution and institutionalization of the modern social sciences was a delayed and particularistic one, for both quantitative and qualitative reasons. On the qualitative side, in consequence of the reign of fascism and its emphasis on racist or organicistic theories, the then nascent social sciences fell into intellectual and political discredit. The reconstruction period in the first decade and a half of post-war West Germany saw mainly a renaissance of the essentially idealist and normative tradition of social science. It was only in the late fifties and sixties that developments in British and American social science began to be assimilated on a large scale, and it was then, too, that the continental European and specifically German traditions of Marxist, Weberian, and Freudian thought were rediscovered. Quantitatively speaking, the increase in numbers of students and in academic staff in the sixties and seventies gave this process considerable impetus.

One aspect of the differentiation and stronger institutionalization of the social sciences is what can be called the two-pronged process of generalizing and relativizing the concept of science. In Germany—as in other Western countries—a fairly pronounced split had developed between the "natural" and "exact" sciences on the one hand—the hallmarks of cognitive rationality and instrumentalism—and the humanities and arts on the other. It can perhaps be said that the sixties marked the high point of this development, yet at the same time it brought forth forces which helped to offset the natural sciences' claim to preeminence. The evolution and institutionalization of the social sciences was important as a means of bridging the gap between the sciences, on the one hand, and the humanities and arts on the other.

Finally, the substantial expansion and reorganization of higher education over the past twenty years can be seen as an integral part of an intensified process of professionalization. When we speak of "professionals," we mean academically trained practitioners, specialists whose working conditions and social outlook are substantially structured by their orientation toward their particular discipline.

Typically, training for the professions involves combining various bodies of theory and knowledge with emphasis on practical, inter-disciplinary problem-solving. In this sense, professional schools and professional training as functions of the system of higher education are distinguishable from pure research and academic training, as well as from general education and from ethical and normative concerns. For many decades, engineering, medicine, and law have been considered the established professions.

As already pointed out, the expansion and reform of German higher education has thus far not led to the inclusion of general education as a formal university function. (In a very tentative way, discussion is just beginning on the possible role of tertiary-level academic institutions in general education, something which may become relevant when the numerically smaller age groups begin to enter higher education after 1990.) Rather, concern has been focussed on the question of redefining or establishing clusters of professions and—as a slightly lower priority—on problems relating to graduate training and research organization (the stronger emphasis on the problems of professions is understandable, since only a minority of students remains in academic research or in university teaching). Thus the commissions set up to draft reforms of courses of study and examinations have been intent, first, on mapping out more or less broadly defined areas of prospective gainful employment for graduates and, second, on translating these into programs of study which combine the basics of a number of different disciplines and possibly a certain amount of structured practical experience.

The upgrading of former advanced vocational schools into poly-technic colleges and their inclusion—as the "lowest stratum"—in the academic system meant, first of all, that the fringe of semi-professional occupations surrounding the core of the established professions moved closer to and became more integrated with the latter. The most important, quantitatively, are the clusters of technical and engineering professions focussing on activities and concerns relating to physical and organic systems; these account for some 60 percent of the student body of the polytechnic colleges. Second in importance, each group accounting for some 20 percent, are professions focussing on functions deriving from social systems, namely a cluster of welfare professions (including nursery school teachers and social workers) and a cluster of administrative, legal, and economic professions.

In quantitative terms, the most important occupation to be subjected to this process of professionalization over the past decades has been that of teaching. This process has occurred not only parallel to, but as part of the more general process of institutionalizing the social sciences. Essentially, the term "professionalization of teachers" refers to two complementary efforts: first, the attempt to change the focus of university-based teacher education for Gymnasium teachers and for the secondary level in general, moving it away from the traditional narrow academic specialization, and giving it a more clinical, multidisciplinary, and practical orientation. The second effort is to upgrade primary and lower secondary level teacher training—which traditionally was based in teacher-training colleges, not in universities—by lengthening the course of study and widening the spectrum of academic disciplines in the curriculum, as well as by increasing the weight of a combination of these academic disciplines in the student's course of study.

12.4.1. Teacher training

Teacher training both for the regular school system and for vocational schools is carried out in two phases: the first phase consists of academic training at a university and is completed with an external examination, the first state examination. The purpose of the second phase is to provide the graduate with practical experience in a school; at this stage he has a short-term contract. This second phase concludes with a second state examination, which qualifies the examinee for appointment as a tenured state official.

As the name implies, the state examinations are administered by the Länder governments, functioning as gatekeepers to the teaching profession (cf. 3.1.4). The first state examination is conducted by university professors, acting as members of a commission headed by a state examiner. The examination procedures are fixed by a set of government regulations with slight variations between the different Länder, sometimes giving more weight to the university influence, sometimes less. University teachers play no part in the second state examination. It is conducted by the state school inspector in conjunction with experienced teachers who have supervised the candidate's training.

In general, training varies according to the type of school the student is preparing to teach in. The academic phase of preparation for primary school teachers, as well as for teachers at the Hauptschule and Realschule, lasts a minimum of six to seven semesters. Up to the mid-seventies, students interested in taking these courses enrolled in a teacher-training college. Such colleges now exist only in the

Länder of Baden-Württemberg, Rhineland-Palatinate, and Schleswig-Holstein. Elsewhere, they have been integrated into universities or the few comprehensive universities, essentially a combination of polytechnic colleges and standard universities. Gymnasium teachers, on the other hand, have always done their academic training at the university, where their studies are more or less confined to the subjects, usually two, which they will later teach. Their course of study lasts a minimum of eight semesters (the actual average is 10 to 12 semesters). The same kind of specialized training is required of those preparing to become teachers at vocational and commercial schools.

As we have seen, jurisdiction over education rests with the 11 individual Länder—a fact that makes itself felt especially strongly in teacher training. In some Länder—for example in Hamburg, Hessia, and North Rhine-Westphalia—students training to teach at the Realschule and the Hauptschule take the same course of studies. In other Länder, training for the Realschule is more demanding, corresponding to the higher starting salary these teachers receive in contrast to their colleagues at the Hauptschule. Berlin is in a category of its own: Here there are two separate teacher-training programs in addition to that of Gymnasium teachers; in one, the student has one major, and in the other he has two. In theory, teachers with both types of training can be employed in all types of schools, but in fact teachers with only one major find jobs only in the Hauptschule. This list of variations and exceptions could be extended at some length.

The General Education Plan of 1973 in fact proposed a different system of teacher training, one structured not according to school types, but rather to school levels. The Länder governments and the Federal Ministry of Education and Science were then in agreement that teacher training should be specialized according to level: the primary level, encompassing grades 1 through 4; secondary level I for grades 5 through 10; and secondary level II for grades 11 through 13. The Länder governed at that time by Christian Democratic governments agreed to this scheme only on condition that a distinction be made in minimum academic training between teachers in secondary level I (6 semesters) and those in secondary level II (8 semesters), with a corresponding distinction in salary classifications.

The nationwide switch to level-oriented training foundered on a fundamental difference of opinion between Christian Democratic governments and those run by a coalition of Social Democrats and

Liberals. Only Bremen and North Rhine-Westphalia have managed to put a scheme into practice that comes close to the original plan for level-oriented teacher training. But even in these two Länder training differs considerably on some points—for example, only in Bremen do all prospective teachers have the same amount of academic training—all in all, 8 semesters. In no other Land is there a tendency toward doing away with separate programs of teacher training according to school type—that is, apart from the sort of combination practiced in Berlin.

Until recently, the practical phase of training varied in length—from one and a half years to two years—and in employment status, depending on the type of school a trainee was preparing for. By the end of the seventies the second phase was standardized in almost all the Länder. While the interim status for teachers-in-training has so far made it possible for the Länder to offer opportunities for practical professional training to virtually all applicants, employment prospects after the second state examination have worsened considerably over the last years. The teacher-in-training has a teaching load of between five and 11 hours a week (versus the normal load of between 23 and 27 hours a week). In addition, he spends around 18 hours a week in seminars conducted by experienced teachers. In this two-phase training program, the prospective teacher is brought face to face with the practical aspects of his professional only at a relatively late point.

Professional orientation in the first, academic phase of training varies considerably. Studies have tended to be more practically oriented and more interdisciplinary for those teachers headed for primary school or for the Hauptschule or Realschule (training for which originally took place in teacher-training colleges), while the studies of those teachers preparing for a teaching career in a Gymnasium or one of the vocational schools have focussed on the structure of the academic disciplines they specialized in.

During the sixties, the differences between these two types of first-phase teacher training were reduced to some extent. Teachers' colleges began to place more emphasis on disciplinary specialization, and the various courses of study were modified to bring them more into line with university study in the same fields. University training for prospective Gymnasium teachers, on the other hand, has turned somewhat in the other direction; here, there was a hesitant and comparatively slight increase in the emphasis placed on problems of teaching and child development alongside the still-dominant disciplinary orientation. In fact, university reform commissions in a number of Länder continue to focus their attention on effecting this professionalization of the hitherto heavily academic training of Gymnasium teachers.

By the late seventies, the process of integrating the teacher-training colleges into the universities—in the form of education departments—was more or less completed. This brings to an end, at least for the present, a long process of upgrading these institutions in terms both of the quality and of the range of education offered, a transformation process which reached its apogee in the sixties and early seventies. Perhaps one could even contend that by that time it was no longer necessary to dissolve the teacher-training colleges or reorganize them as university departments in order to establish or maintain them as professional schools, most of them had apparently already come close to this status prior to their integration into the universities, and would have been in a position to maintain and build upon it, had they remained independent institutions. In this light, the integration of teacher-training colleges into the universities would seem to have been a superficial measure, indeed no more than unnecessary name-changing.

Such an assessment fails, however, to take into account the difficulties that have always stood in the way of professionalizing the traditionally discipline-oriented first phase of the training of prospective Gymnasium teachers. Thus in the long run, the integration of teacher training into the universities may well be the means of bringing the education of Gymnasium teachers fully within the purview of efforts to professionalize such training. Nevertheless, one should not overlook the fact that there is some fear that, as integration is brought about, the tendency toward disciplinary specialization in the universities will continue to maintain such predominance as to threaten the measure of professionalization already achieved by the teacher-training colleges in the sixties and seventies.

CHAPTER 13

Going Back to School: Further Education

13.1. What is further education?

The range of educational possibilities and ways of learning sub-sumed under the rubric of further education is so wide that it is impossible to give a simple definition of this term. Further education is offered by labor unions and by occupational associations. Private firms and governmental agencies organize further education courses intended to teach their employees specialized knowledge needed for their work or to obtain advancement. Community-sponsored centers offer to a broad public a program extending from practical courses in crafts and in the arts, at one extreme, through travel reports, visits to museums, discussions of political and social questions, to courses enabling their participants to obtain one of the secondary school certificates. Commercial schools give language courses, courses in management skills or in subject matters specific to particular occupations. And finally, the universities, faced with the prospect of declining numbers of students in the 1990's for demographic reasons, are turning their attention to programs for further education (cf. Chapter 12).

When one considers the whole domain of educational activity in the Federal Republic, further education appears as a peripheral area of indefinite shape. However, its unclear demarcation works to its advantage, permitting a broad range of organizational forms that can accommodate quite diverse conceptions of the content and goals of further education. Perhaps the most important consequence of this flexible conception of further education is that the courses offered in its name are kept closely linked with the various spheres of life in which the participants in further education actually live, areas which are, on the whole, ignored by the educational system in the strict sense of the term.

In 1970, in its "Structural Plan for the Educational System," the German Education Council presented an overview of the educational system and its constituent parts. In this plan, further education was treated as a fourth sector of the educational system, on an equal footing with the preschool and primary sector (cf. Chapter 5), the secondary sector (cf. Chapters 7–10), and higher education. In so doing, the Council took into account widespread changes in attitude toward education which made it clear that for more and more persons education is not confined to their childhood and youth, but rather is continued in their later life.

In its plan the Education Council proposed a definition of further education that has since entered into general use. According to this definition, further education is the continuation or the resumption of formally organized learning after an initial phase of education varying in length. Further education is, then, all formally organized education that takes place after one has assumed a full-time work role, which is understood here to include working as a housewife. Further education may be either vocational or nonvocational in nature. Further education of the former kind includes both additional training in one's occupation and retraining for a new occupation. Nonvocational further education covers the whole range of general education, and is also understood to include the schooling which labor unions provide for shop stewards and other sponsors as well as similar educational programs offered by unions.

In comparison with the other three sectors of the educational system, the organizational structures of further education and the bodies responsible for it are extremely diverse. Programs for further education can be sponsored by the state (i.e., the federal and the Länder governments), the communities, the churches, privately owned firms, industrial, commercial, and craft chambers, various associations, political parties, or foundations established by any of these.

The goals of the participants in further education, as well as the contents of the courses and programs, are also very diverse. Those who follow the "second educational path" (cf. 9.3, 11.1, and 11.3) and obtain the Hauptschule certificate or the Abitur after they have left school might attend the appropriate courses at a Center for Adult Popular Education. Parents who want to inform themselves about educational questions at such a center have quite different intentions, as does also, say, a skilled worker who wants to advance to technician or master in his craft. How broad is the range of goals in further education can be suggested by listing a few of them: compensating for neglected opportunities during the initial phase of one's education, rising socially, adapting to changes in occupational requirements, occupational specialization, schooling in politics and labor union affairs, obtaining information about how conflicts can be resolved in the workplace and in the family, and broadening one's knowledge in areas that are of special personal interest (e.g., foreign countries, botany, the arts). There are also many people who want to give themselves an opportunity for reflection, perhaps to overcome a crisis, or simply in order to come to terms with their everyday experiences. Depending on the goals and the contents of further education programs, they attract participants who differ with respect to their previous education, their social situation, age and sex, and other socioeconomic characteristics.

13.2. History of further education in Germany

Further education in Germany has many historical roots. An important role in its evolution was played by various organizations which arouse out of a wide-spread concern for worker education in the 19th century. The churches as well as the workers' organizations and several associations that were created out of liberal or conservative political convictions supported activities aiming at a better education of the workers.

The workers' organizations emerging in the early 19th century engaged in educational activities as part of a much broader spectrum of functions. These extended from providing a social base for travelling journeymen and the rapidly growing numbers of the urban poor, to the attempt to develop a revolutionary program through a kind of grass-roots democracy within the organizations. Together with the often traditionalist attitudes of the workers, religious motives to a considerable extent entered into such efforts. Since associations founded for political purposes had been forbidden in Germany until 1848, and were again from 1854 on, these early organizations of the labor movement called themselves "Workingmen's Educational Associations." These associations entered into superregional federations, which were likewise prohibited for a time after the unsuccessful revolution of 1848. From these federations there later emerged, under the leadership of August Bebel and Wilhelm Liebknecht, the Social Democratic Workers' Party, one of the two predecessors of what is nowadays the Social Democratic Party of Germany.

On the one hand, workers' educational associations provided further vocational training to the workers and helped them acquire the basic education which the inadequate Volksschule had not given them. On the other hand, their educational programs were also supposed to meet their members' need to better understand the problems of the era. An example of such an educational program was the lectures and courses offered by the Educational Society for the Elevation of the Working Class, founded in Hamburg in 1845. They included lectures that were generally educational, courses in German, foreign languages, and history, but also in vocational subjects, above all in technical drawing. The political education of the members was accomplished through "exercises in oratory" that took place according to a regular schedule. These exercises dealt with philosophical, political, and social topics. In addition, the Educational Society had a library and a reading room where its members could find 17 different newspapers and periodicals, including the foremost radical journals of the period. The Workers' School, established in Berlin in 1891 by the Social Democratic Party, also offered a similarly diverse program. The workers showed the greatest interest, however, in basic subjects such as German and arithmetic, or in vocational courses, for example courses on bookkeeping and stenography.

The strong interest in vocational courses ran counter to the purpose for which this school had originally been established, namely, to educate workers to be active and effective participants in the labor movement. The persistent suspicion also emerged that an educational program as it was offered by this school led more to political conformism and to acceptance of the existing circumstances than to the workers' emancipation from the contradictions of bourgeois class society. This criticism was expressed ever more widely as educational activities in adult schools, as well as in the larger domain of popular education, came to be increasingly seen by the opponents of the labor movement as means which might be useful in turning workers aside from these goals and separating them from their political organizations.

In the last third of the 19th century, the complex of problems caused by the antagonistic relationship between the working class and the ruling social classes of Imperial Germany was one of the most pressing issues. During this time, various organizations for adult education were established, which, at least to a certain degree,

295

were also intended to counteract the efforts of the socialists. In this regard two movements were of great importance: the movement for the education of Catholic workers, and the Centers for Adult Popular Education. The latter movement was strongly influenced by the Society for the Propagation of Popular Education (later shortened to Society for Popular Education), which a few upper middle-class liberals established in 1871, the same year in which the German Reich was founded. The declaration made at the Society's founding stated:

> Now that legislators are to be elected for the first time by direct universal suffrage, the question of liberty has become a question of the education of the masses. Let us be honest with ourselves in this regard. Comparatively speaking, the number of the educated in our land might be large; nevertheless, in absolute terms it is quite small. Great masses of our population are still ignorant and mentally slothful. Incapable of judging for themselves and acting independently, they swim with the current, regardless whether the current leads to good or to evil. The success that a few unscrupulous men have had with their endeavors to advance the cause of socialism are clear proof of this . . . (Picht, 1950, pp. 43 ff)

These statements indicate the general political thrust of the various bourgeois educational organizations. However, one should not overlook the fact that liberal members of the movement to establish Centers for Adult Popular Education saw themselves as carrying on popular enlightenment in the tradition of the 18th century. At the same time they condemned, and sought to improve, the wretched living conditions and educational possibilities of the majority of the population.

As it was understood by those who carried it on, the educational work of the Society for the Propagation of Popular Education was completely nontendentious, i.e., politically neutral and not propounding any particular world view. They primarily wanted to spread what was traditionally understood as "culture" and thus open up to the socially disadvantaged strata of the population "the higher world of the spirit." Adult education as popular education, the dissemination among the masses of a common legacy of German culture, was intended to transcend all differences and antagonisms, whether political, social, or regional, and thus to help unify the German people. After these early initiatives, many associations for popular education were founded that had similar politically neutral goals, and that were oriented to the cultural values of humanism and German idealism. In 1910 there were about 7,500 such associations.

Prior to the First World War the first Centers for Adult Popular Education were established, following models in Great Britain and Denmark; among these were also residential centers, where the participants in courses or seminars could stay for their duration. The Society for the Propagation of Popular Education and other similar associations seem, however, to have reached more members of the petty bourgeoisie with their programs than they did workers.

The modest political success of these associations' educational efforts was all the more obvious in view of the rapid expansion at that time of Marxist workers' organizations. The associations' slight success, as well as the conception of education underlying their programs, soon found critics among the "popular educators" themselves. The criticism became more comprehensive and trenchant as popular education that was independent of the churches and the labor movement gradually became institutionalized beginning in the last decade of the 19th century; this accompanied the massive social and cultural changes in Imperial Germany.

After the traumatic disillusionment of the First World War and the transformation of at least the basic German political premises in the Weimar Period, a "new direction" in popular education succeeded in becoming the authoritative conception which guided the endeavors of individuals and organizations providing "independent" popular education. It is difficult to succinctly sketch the new direction's program, as both the motives for it and its many facets were quite diverse. The point of departure for the new direction in popular education was, first, the criticism of the often pragmatic character of previous educational activities, which had aimed merely at a simplifying popularization of the "higher" cultural traditions. Second, these essentially "humanist" traditions themselves were challenged as having turned hollow by industrialization, the emergence of a large working class and the World War. Instead, the advocates of the new popular education suggested a "holistic" educational ideal closely linked to an organicist conception of a national community ("Volksgemeinschaft"). With regard to the individual learner, the new direction in its educational theory and practice favored highly emotional ways of apprehending cultural and political contents rather than learning processes aiming at objectivity and cognitive distinctness, the latter being sometimes depreciated as unworthy forms of "rationalism."

Leaving aside the ideological romanticism of these views, they implied some new and quite fruitful approaches on the level of pedagogical methods for adult education. Thus, the proponents of the new popular education declared that it was intolerable, considering the developments in other countries, that in Germany the "common man" should continue to be the passive object of educational efforts by members of the higher social strata. They now hoped to achieve greater success by creating a new environment for learning. Personal contact and discussion among the participants in programs of popular education were to be intensified through "study groups" and through the use of residential centers modeled after those in Denmark.

However, the organizational forms proposed by the new conception of popular education, as well as its underlying cultural assumptions, revealed its limits. On the one hand, its contributions to a more individualized and democratic view of adult education are beyond doubt. Yet it had implications that were socially and politically questionable. For only a few were willing to and capable of participating in education through intensive discussion in courses and in study groups. In keeping with the tenets of the "new direction," educational efforts were concentrated on this small group. To the broad educational activities of the "old direction," which were intended to reach great numbers of workers, was now opposed an education in depth, intended to prepare a few mentally capable persons to lead the masses. Popular education, thus, in spite of its name and its ideology of an all-embracing national community, actually tended to isolate itself from the majority of the population and to miss the chance of serving democracy in a modern society riven by intense class conflicts.

The new direction in adult education was especially influential in shaping the movement for Centers for Adult Popular Education that began to flourish after the First World War. Before the war there had been 18 such centers, including those which could accomodate residential programs. By 1922 their number had grown to 853. The Centers for Adult Popular Education of the Weimar Period were organizationally and financially autonomous and were free to select the kinds of courses they offered. There was neither a central organization for administration and planning, nor was there institutionalized cooperation between the individual centers. Often, however, the centers were subsidized or directly sponsored by the community. In spite of basic positions that were generally shared, the unconditional resolve to safeguard not only the institutional autonomy of the individual centers, but also their freedom to offer whatever courses they chose, led to fierce quarrels within the movement. Only in 1927 were the centers finally loosely associated in the Reich Association of German Centers for Adult Popular Education. At this time, though, there were also isolated centers for adult education that abandoned the "new direction" and adhered more closely to the labor movement. Such centers were to be found in Leipzig and Jena, for example.

Nationalism and resentment against the modern era were features of the conception of popular education advanced by the new direction in adult education which gave it an affinity to the ideology of emerging National Socialism. However, once the National Socialist régime was in power, it began increasingly to subject most spheres of social activity, including adult education, to the centralized control of the Nazi party and the Nazi state, and thereby brushed aside the sacred principles of independent adult education, namely, its political neutrality, organizational autonomy, and ideological nonpartisanship.

After the Second World War adult education at first followed the model of the Centers for Adult Popular Education that had existed during the Weimar Period. The American and British military authorities encouraged and assisted the establishment of adult education programs in the interest of a democratic "reeducation" of the German population in their occupation zones. To the extent that the Centers for Adult Popular Education saw a threat to their independence in the activities of the military authorities, the relations between the two sides were not without conflicts. Nevertheless, the efforts of the American and British military authorities contributed greatly to the rapid increase in the numbers and the growth in importance of the Centers for Adult Popular Education after the war. In the autumn of 1947 there were 372 Centers for Adult Popular Education in the occupation zones of the Western Allies.

As during the time of the Weimar Republic, these centers were each independent, although often sponsored by the communities in which they were located. Alongside the centers, the churches and the labor unions also quickly developed their educational programs. Since 1951 the Federation of German Labor Unions and the Centers for Adult Popular Education have worked together nationally in a cooperative association, "Work and Life," a partnership that would have been unthinkable during the Weimar Republic.

13.3. *Sponsors, themes, and numbers of participants*

As mentioned above, the programs in further education are planned and carried out by many different sponsors and institutions. In comparison with other sectors of the educational system, this organizational diversity is a distinguishing characteristic of further education. The institutions providing it can be grouped according to whether their courses and activities are freely accessible to all or are accessible only to the members of the institution in question; in short, these institutions can be classified according to whether they provide "open" or "closed" further education.

With regard to open further education, its sponsors can be either governmental or nongovernmental bodies or agencies. The nongovernmental sponsors can be divided into two categories: nonprofit organizations intended to promote the common welfare, and commercial sponsors. The former usually refer to themselves as "independent sponsors" of further education. This designation has often given rise to misunderstanding of the character of these sponsors. As the preceding historical sketch showed, the term "independent popular education" does not necessarily mean that adult education is given solely for its own sake, and is free from the influence of particular political or economic interests or from a bias to a certain world view.

If one uses the criteria of the number of participants and the extent of the range of courses and other activities offered, then the most important vehicles of further education are the Centers for Adult Popular Education. At the present time these Centers are, for the most part, community-sponsored; the remainder take the legal form of officially registered associations. Such an association is regarded legally as a person, a status which frees its members from financial responsibility for the association's actions. Moreover, such associations can receive state assistance, and contributions to them are tax-deductible. Other governmental sponsors of further education are the Länder, which maintain the institutions of higher education and the schools along the "second educational path." The latter consist of Evening Realschulen, Evening Gymnasien, and Kollegs, special secondary schools which prepare adults for university study. The institutions of higher education also engage in further education, although to a lesser extent. Other important public sponsors of further education are the Catholic and the Lutheran Churches.

The Centers for Adult Popular Education offer a broad spectrum of general subjects and courses dealing with these themes. In contrast,

300

other sponsors, especially those whose primary purpose is the further education of their members, have in most cases a more limited range of offerings with a relatively small number of thematic subjects. *Table 13.1* shows the results of a study that attempted to obtain as complete data as possible on further education activities in West Berlin in 1979. Single lectures, tours, and similar activities were not taken into consideration. The general structures shown by the table are also typical of the other Länder.

When it is a matter of themes having to do with politics and society, the registered associations succeed in attracting by far the greatest number of participants in their courses, while in the more restricted sphere of occupationally relevant subject matters, such as management and business skills, or mathematics, natural sciences, and engineering, privately owned firms and occupational associations also have high numbers of registrants. Enterprises and occupational associations in the private sector of the economy have an extraordinarily strong position in further vocational education, the exact extent of which cannot be determined, however, since the pertinent figures are published only in a fragmentary fashion. On the other hand, the Centers for Adult Popular Education are in the forefront of general further education, especially in language courses and courses teaching manual skills and giving practical instruction in the arts.

With respect to language instruction, the Centers of Adult Popular Education, the programs of which are generally accessible, and the privately owned firms and governmental agencies which offer language courses only for their employees are in competition with the private language schools. The Berlitz Schools, the largest commercial language school in the Federal Republic, conducted a study of the market in language instruction. Using the number of hours of instruction given as the standard of measurement, this study found that private language schools dominated this market. Of the total number of language courses offered in the Federal Republic, 46 percent are given by private language schools, 32 percent by Centers for Adult Popular Education, and 14 and 8 percent by firms and language tours, respectively. If one considers the number of participants, however, then the Centers for Adult Popular Education clearly have the largest share of the market in language instruction.

The purpose of further education is to satisfy the educational needs and interests that arise for individuals in the later phases of their lives due to the dynamics of societal development. For this reason, it is important that institutions providing further education be able

Table 13.1: Registrations for Further Education in West Berlin According to Sponsor and Field of Study, 1979

Field of study	Participants in courses offered by							
	federal and Berlin government	Centers for Adult Popular Education	the Catholic and the Lutheran Churches	trade unions	private enterprises, professional organizations	foundations	various associations	other sponsors
Society, politics	2,832	6,047	2,140	2,624	186	4,183	20,080	1,845
Education	7,882	10,403	8,057	276	249	57	1,523	255
Arts	10	4,268	686	42	–	26	180	60
Mathematics, sciences	1,597	10,679	–	824	4,195	–	5,270	–
Administr., economics	10,726	14,581	–	881	3,447	–	6,252	–
Languages	926	74,167	–	20	265	–	3,020	2,702
Handicrafts, music	124	34,117	173	48	–	–	1,449	–
Home economics	8	8,287	–	–	–	–	–	–
Health	3,568	39,059	557	–	900	–	1,218	277
Other	1,382	2,431	–	57	116	–	467	416
Total	29,055	204,039	11,613	4,772	9,358	4,266	39,459	5,555

Source: Statistisches Landesamt Berlin: Berliner Statistik, No. 4, 1981.

to adapt their curricula to the new demands of their participants. The large number and the variety of sponsors for further education is thus useful, inasmuch as it serves to guarantee that further education will have the required flexibility and curricular diversity.

As a consequence of the heterogeneity of the sponsors of further education and of the forms in which further education is offered, data on the individual courses and activities are not collected together in a single set of statistics. It is therefore impossible to determine exactly how many persons in the Federal Republic participate each year in further education. However, on the basis of a poll of a representative sample of the population, it has been estimated that from 1974 to 1979 approximately 12.4 million persons ranging in age from 19 to 65 participated in further education. That is just slightly less than 40 percent of this age group. Their interests were concentrated to an equal extent on general education and, on the other hand, on vocational courses and political topics (cf. Figure 13.1).

Let us examine more closely two aspects of further education that can serve as examples: political further education and the resumption of secondary education to obtain one of the certificates conferred by the general educational system (the "second educational path"). Political education, particularly for adults, has been especially promoted in the Federal Republic, but it has also been considered especially suspect, not least of all because of the bad reputation of ideological indoctrination under the Third Reich. Political further education in the Federal Republic is provided by a large number of sponsors, and the range of offerings encompasses the entire spectrum of political viewpoints. Naturally, it is the political organizations in the narrower sense which are the most important sponsors of political education.

The political parties themselves and the foundations that are close to them, as well as the labor unions, succeed in reaching a significant number of their members and of the interested general public each year with their programs in political education. In 1980, the Friedrich Ebert Foundation, for example, which stands close to the Social Democratic Party, offered somewhat more than 1,200 seminars on themes such as "Energy and Improving the Quality of Life," "Terrorism," and "German Foreign Policy and Policy on National Security." These seminars were attended by about 32,000 participants. The program of political education of the Konrad Adenauer Foundation, associated with the Christian Democratic Union, ranges from the politics of the family to international relations. In 1980 approximately 40,000 persons took part in the courses and conferences

(in %)

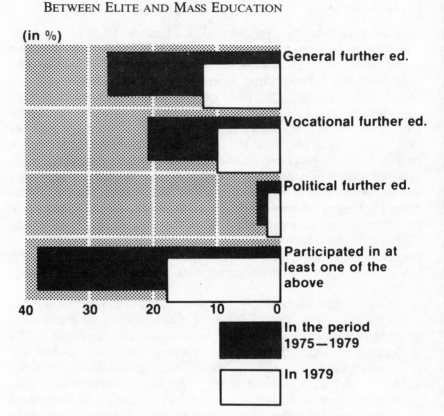

General further ed.

Vocational further ed.

Political further ed.

Participated in at least one of the above

40   30   20   10   0

In the period 1975—1979

In 1979

Figure 13.1. Participation Rate of 19- to 64-Year-Olds in Further Education, 1975-1979

organized by this foundation. As for the labor unions, it is estimated that the most important industrial union, the Metal Workers' Industrial Union, reaches 35,000-37,000 persons each year with its political education programs. Generally, the unions seem to reach between 1 and 5 percent of their members with these educational activities.

There is no doubt that the endeavors of political organizations are an important part of political education in the Federal Republic. Nevertheless, one should not overlook the fact that courses or lectures pertaining to political education are practically an obligatory part of the programs of almost all governmental or public sponsors of further education. Ultimately, these offerings reach many more people than the programs of the political organizations in the narrow sense of the term.

304

Although it might be surprising at first, the two dominant Christian churches in the Federal Republic, fulfilling what they consider to be their political responsibilities (cf. introduction to Chapter 3), also play an important role in providing further education in political matters. The educational organizations of the Lutheran Church reached more than 140,000 persons in 1980 with their courses and workshops on political topics. The number of those who attended the public lectures provided by these organizations exceeded 300,000. Corresponding figures for the Catholic Church's activities in the field of political further education are not available; however, the quantity of its offerings in further education and the number of the participants in its programs are, on the whole, considerably greater than those of the Lutheran Church.

After the churches, the most important sponsors of political further education are the Centers for Adult Popular Education. In 1979 some 183,000 people took advantage of their course offerings.

The statistics on further education usually contain only incomplete data on the resumption of secondary education. Nevertheless, it is clear that the number of those who have availed themselves of the "second educational path" has been continually increasing. At the beginning of the 1980's about 6 percent of first-semester students in institutions of higher education had obtained the Abitur via this route. The most important institutions for this kind of education are evening schools, Kollegs, and the Centers for Adult Popular Education. Since 1970, the Centers have developed a program consisting of several parts, each presupposing the completion of the preceding part. The certificates awarded for the completion of each phase of this program have been standardized throughout the Federal Republic, and it is now possible to obtain the Hauptschule or Realschule certificate or the Abitur, the general qualification for university study, with the help of the Centers' certification program. In spite of the expansion of the general school system since the end of the sixties, it is evident that, were it not for the second educational path, many people would not be able to obtain the level of education they want to achieve.

13.4. Financing and the legal bases for further education

The large number and variety of sponsors of further education makes it extraordinarily difficult to obtain an overview of the total amount of money spent on such education and its distribution. The funds for further education come in part from the fees paid by the participants, in part from the sponsors, and in part from the taxpayers. The best statistical information is available on the expenditures of the Centers for Adult Popular Education, on those of the Federal Employment Agency for further vocational education and for retraining, on the public funds spent to promote civic education, the public libraries, and the schools of the "second educational path." Figures are also available on the money spent by the labor unions for their educational programs. In contrast, neither the churches nor the private enterprises have made public the amounts of money they spend on further education.

The available data present the following picture of the financing of further education in the Federal Republic. In 1980, the Centers for Adult Popular Education had a budget of about 400 million DM at their disposal. Of this sum, approximately 40 percent was provided by the fees of the participants; the remaining 60 percent of the Centers' funds consisted of subsidies given by the Länder governments and the communities where the Centers are located. The Metal Workers Industrial Union, the largest single union in the Federation of German Labor Unions, spent some 28 million DM in 1980 for its educational activities, about 10 percent of its total expenditures in that year.

The federal and Länder governments and the communities have registered a continual rise in their expenditures for further education, which, all told, reached approximately 2 billion DM in 1979. This increase occurred in the context of an expanding total education budget. In 1970 the expenditures for further education constituted 2.1 percent of the total public budget for education in the Federal Republic; in 1979 they had risen to 2.8 percent. To this amount must be added the expenditures of the Federal Employment Agency for further vocational training and retraining, which were listed separately. In 1980 these last expenditures amounted to 2.4 billion DM. More than 60 percent of these funds were paid out as maintenance stipends to participants in programs of further vocational training.

To the degree that the public became convinced of the necessity for further education and aware of the forms in which it was available, further education became legally regulated. An important event in this process was the passage of the Employment Promotion Act in 1969. This law regulates the financial assistance given to a large part of further vocational education. Although the Federal Employment Agency had given financial aid to persons participating in programs of further vocational training since 1962, this aid was very limited and could not be given to all who requested it. Since 1970, many Länder have passed laws on adult education or further education which primarily regulate the public financing of institutions for further education and the cooperation between its various sponsors.

The Intra-Enterprise Labor-Management Relations Act, passed in 1972, marked a shift in further education policy. This law implied public acknowledgement that further education had to fulfill a task of political education in an extended sense of democratization in everyday life by providing opportunities of further education not only for persons pursuing vocational training, but also for members of the works councils elected to represent the workers in their plants. The laws on paid educational leaves of absence which have been passed in different Länder stipulate that employees should be given time off from their work for the purpose of political education. In framing these laws to encompass political education, the legislatures of the Länder followed the recommendation on paid educational leaves of absence made by the International Labor Conference in 1974.

13.5. Teachers and organizational forms

As a rule, further education usually takes the form of courses, lecture series, or other activities that the participants attend while continuing to work at their jobs, or of activities lasting only a short time. The specific form is determined by the subject matter to be treated. Thus, political topics and those belonging to the sphere of general education are often dealt with in a single educational event, for example, in a single lecture held in a Center for Adult Popular Education or in a weekend seminar organized by a labor union. On the other hand, foreign languages and certain technical information and skills can be learned better in a systematically organized course than in a loosely connected series of lectures or in conferences. By contrast, conferences are a good organizational form for learning about labor and social welfare laws, the worker's status in the Federal Republic, the role of the works council, and similar topics.

Further education activities are classified according to type, duration, and temporal organization. The different types are: the single lecture, the lecture series, courses, and conferences. These activities can take place either in the participants' leisure time or during their work time; and they can be spread out over a longer period of time

307

or they can be concentrated in a single block of time. The offerings of the Centers for Adult Popular Education are overwhelmingly courses, lecture series, and single activities that all take place in their participants' leisure time, usually in the evening. The vocational further education provided by firms or by industrial associations takes place mostly in the form of continuous courses during the participants' work time.

The decisions about the temporal organization, the duration, and the form of an offering in further education must take into consideration the population group for which the activity is intended. Such further education activities that take place in the free time of the target group presuppose a great deal of motivation on the part of their participants, and courses that continue over a long period of time presuppose that their participants are persistent and that their living conditions are stable and well ordered. The absence of these preconditions can prove to be obstacles to participation in further education that are difficult to overcome, even when interest in the themes of the courses or lectures is quite strong.

Another distinguishing characteristic of further education, in addition to the large number and diversity of its sponsors, is that most of its teachers engage in some other kind of work as their principal occupation, and some of them are not paid for their teaching. This makes sense, since a large portion of the courses, etc., offered as further education are closely related to practical problems or interests of the participants. But the teachers are therefore frequently faced with the task of incorporating the experiences of their students into their courses, showing the connections among them, and relating them to systematic bodies of knowledge. Thus it is understandable, not only in view of the subject matter, but also with regard to the didactic requirements of such courses, that their teachers should have first-hand practical knowledge of the subject matter in question.

However, these teachers, who are such only occasionally, or whose principal employment is in another occupation, often find it difficult to convey their knowledge and practical experience to their students in an effective manner. Instructional problems are also reported by the teachers of the Centers for Adult Popular Education, even though these are mostly professionally trained and have full-time positions at regular schools. Because of the expansion of further education, an attempt was made to improve the training of teachers employed in this sector and to better prepare them for the particular circumstances and difficulties they encounter in their work. Nevertheless, it is probably still true that, generally speaking, the way further education courses are taught does not take the backgrounds and the needs of their participants sufficiently into account.

13.6. Who goes back to school?

There is today hardly any occupation or sphere of life for which the initial phase of education still provides, once and for all, sufficient knowledge and an adequate range of possibilities for action. In addition, a number of laws provide remedies for the possible loss of income during participation in further education, so that such losses do not become excessive. In view of these circumstances, and since further education is offered in a wide range of areas and organizational forms, one would think that the different population groups would make use of the opportunities for further education to about the same extent. It turns out, though, that this assumption is wrong.

In further education the same social differences in participation manifest themselves that appear in the first phase of education. Unskilled workers, in particular, seldom take advantage of opportunities for further education. This is also true, relatively speaking, of women and of the inhabitants of rural areas. Workers in general hardly avail themselves of the offerings of the Centers for Adult Popular Education, which belong predominantly to the field of general education, but they also make relatively little use of opportunities for further vocational training. In the period from 1976 to 1978, 9.9 percent of all state officials, and 7.8 percent of all salaried employees, but only 3.3 percent of the workers participated in further vocational education (cf. Table 13.2).

In recent years a slight increase in participation by workers in further education has been registered. This can be attributed to the improvement since 1969 in governmental assistance to further vocational training, due to the Employment Promotion Act passed in that year. A higher percentage of the workers participates in the further educational activities of unions, which is in accordance with the large percentage of union members who are workers. Nevertheless, when one considers the proportion of workers to salaried employees in the unions, relative to the latter the former are underrepresented in union programs of further education.

The persons who participate most readily in further education are those who obtained one of the higher certificates in the initial phase of their education, that is, a Realschule certificate or the Abitur.

Table 13.2: Number of Employed, 1978, and of Participants in Vocational
Further Education According to Occupational Status, 1976–1978

| Occupational status | Employed 1978 | Participants in vocational further education, 1976–1978 | | | |
| | | total | | completed courses by April 1978 | |
	(in 1000)	number (in 1000)	percentage of employed	number (in 1000)	percentage of employed
	male				
Self-employed	1,809	65	3.6	60	3.3
Employed in family business	147	4	2.7	4	2.7
Officials	1,883	186	9.9	160	8.5
Salaried employees	4,539	445	9.8	396	8.7
Workers	7,948	306	3.9	249	3.1
	female				
Self-employed	482	15	3.1	14	2.9
Employed in family business	903	8	0.9	7	0.8
Officials	385	39	10.1	31	8.1
Salaried employees	4,857	288	5.9	239	4.9
Workers	3,068	54	1.8	40	1.3
	total				
Self-employed	2,291	81	3.5	74	3.2
Employed in family business	1,049	12	1.1	10	1.0
Officials	2,269	225	9.9	191	8.4
Salaried employees	9,396	734	7.8	635	6.8
Workers	11,016	360	3.3	289	2.6

Sources: Statistisches Bundesamt: Bildung im Zahlenspiegel 1981; Fachserie 1: Stand und
Entwicklung der Erwerbstätigkeit 1978.

Figure 13.2 breaks down the participants in further education according to age and school certificate obtained, on the basis of sample
data obtained in 1978/1979. This breakdown shows that, in all age
groups, holders of the Abitur have the highest rate of participation
in further education, and also that, although participation in further
education generally declines with increasing age, the higher the school

certificate obtained, the less is this decline. This holds true for all areas of further education. As a rule, those who attend the courses and lectures of the Centers for Adult Popular Education have at least the Realschule certificate. But holders of the higher school certificates are clearly overrepresented also in further vocational eduation.

Persons who have not completed initial vocational training appear to participate least of all in further education, as a closer look at former Hauptschule pupils shows. Among those who participate in further vocational education, the employed persons who have already completed an apprenticeship — these are, for the greatest part, former Hauptschule pupils — make up a percentage that roughly corresponds to their percentage of the entire employed population. Employed persons without vocational training, on the other hand, take advantage of opportunities for further vocational training and retraining to a much smaller extent. Unskilled workers are also underrepresented in the further education programs of unions. Clearly, the possibilities for further education have so far been of least benefit to those who are most seriously disadvantaged with regard to their life chances.

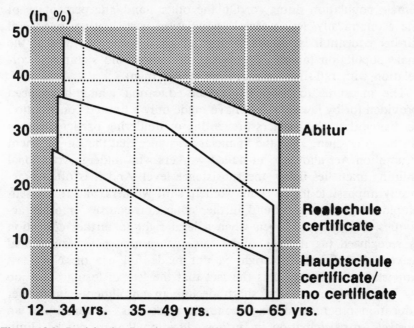

Figure 13.2. Participation Rate in Further Education According to Age and Secondary Education, 1979

The differential participation of the various population groups is also due to the regionally imbalanced distribution of opportunities for further education. In large cities and urban areas with a high population density, the offerings in further education are both greater in quantity and more varied, and also usually qualitatively better than in rural areas. In the cities there are more, and more diverse, sponsors for further education, as well as many more regular school teachers, among whom the teachers for further education programs can be recruited. The laws on further education enacted by the Länder are intended, among other things, to mitigate this imbalance by requiring coordination of the individual further education activities for the purpose of providing minimal programs throughout their territories. In the opinion of most experts, however, this goal has by no means been reached at the present time.

If one breaks down the participants in further education according to gender, then the data for the end of the seventies show the following picture. On the one hand, the part of the total male population participating in further vocational education — 14 percent — is somewhat more than twice as great as the part of the total female population doing so. On the other hand, the percentage of the economically active female population participating in general further education is on the average about the same as that of the male population (about 12 percent), and shows no significant correlation with full-time or part-time employment.

The measures to promote further education which have been provided for by law (cf. 13.4) have made only a limited contribution to dismantling the barriers preventing or hindering participation in further education. Thus the financial assistance that the Employment Promotion Act allows to unskilled workers who undergo vocational training often lies below the subsistence level. And it is often practically impossible for working women, shift workers, and many self-employed persons to attend further education courses or other activities. Furthermore, even when a legal right to further education is recognized (as in the Länder laws concerning paid educational leaves of absence), this right is not made full use of. Not least important in this regard is the fact that the fear of losing one's job — made evident in the sharp decline in enrollments in further education programs during economic recessions — constitutes an obstacle to participation in further education that cannot be eliminated under the current laws.

312

13.7. Recent developments

Since the 1960's, further education in the Federal Republic has taken an upturn. This is true both for general further education, offered primarily by the Centers for Adult Popular Education, and for further vocational education and obtaining school certificates via the "second educational path." The growth in the numbers of participants in the programs of the Centers for Adult Popular Education, shown in Table 13.3, clearly illustrates this growing interest in further education.

A very general explanation for this strong interest in further education lies in the marked political, social, and economic structural changes that have been taking place in the Federal Republic since about the middle of the fifties. The occupational changes show this process most clearly. In the period from 1955 to 1970, approximately one third of all employed males had to change their occupation at least once, and a quarter of all changes of occupation involved vocational training. More than the other members of the work force, those persons engaged in occupations requiring only a low level of qualification, or working in shrinking sectors of the economy, are forced to change occupations and undergo retraining in order to avoid falling to a lower level of income and prestige. As for those who remain in the occupation for which they were trained, they frequently find that the requirements of their occupations have been changed and broadened, and that they can meet these new require-

Table 13.3: Participation in Courses and Single Lectures Provided by Centers for Adult Popular Education, 1955–1980

Year	Courses		Lectures	
	number	enrollments	number	participants
1955	47,800	1,280,600	50,500	5,016,900
1965	77,800	1,695,700	66,000	5,086,700
1970	109,900	2,227,300	60,800	3,736,300
1975	195,500	3,761,000	64,800	3,748,000
1980	301,400[1]	4,633,000[1]	68,100	3,411,700

[1] Increase partly due to the change from a semester to a three-term system.

Sources: Deutscher Volkshochschulverband: 25 Jahre Deutscher Volkshochschulverband; Bundesministerium für Bildung und Wissenschaft: Grund- und Strukturdaten 1981/82.

ments only through further learning and by acquiring special skills. In Figure 13.3 the participation in the courses and programs offered by the Federal Employment Agency is used to show the development of further vocational education and retraining in the 1970's. The agency is one of the most important providers of such programs.

As various studies have shown, in some occupations the necessity of constantly scrutinizing, broadening, and revising the occupational qualifications that have been acquired is especially pronounced. This

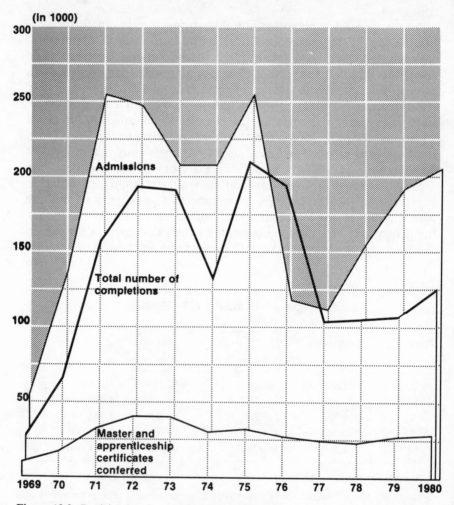

Figure 13.3. Participation in the Federal Employment Agency Further Vocational Education and Retraining, 1969-1980

is true of technical occupations in industry, of physicians and teachers, locomotive engineers, banking and insurance experts, certified public accountants and tax consultants. Consequently, many members of these occupational groups avail themselves of opportunities for further education. Organized further vocational education thus serves to safeguard employment by maintaining occupational qualifications at the required level and by adapting them to new requirements. It also serves the cause of occupational and social advancement. Firms often use their programs in further vocational education as an instrument of their personnel policies. Through their programs they select and train employees for management positions; but they also use these programs to instill loyalty into these employees and in general to channel their employees in their efforts to advance in the firm.

In other spheres of life changes have also taken place that very often engender interest in systematically acquiring additional knowledge. Thus the shift to the small nuclear family, women's employment, and their altered self-conception have also transformed the relations within the family, i.e., the relationships of the marriage partners to each other and to their children. The ways of doing things that people learned from their own families are no longer accepted without question. Instead, they look for alternatives, ask how something might be done better, and seek guidance in their quest from the further education offered by the churches, the Centers for Adult Popular Education, and other sponsoring organizations. Social relations in West German society have begun to change; they have lost much of their rigidity and their power to definitively shape individuals' values and life plans. As a result, the attitude of large portions of the population toward further education has changed. The old saw, "What Johnny doesn't learn, will never be learned by John" has suffered loss of credibility. People have more confidence in themselves, and take a more active stance toward the circumstances of their own lives. Organized, systematic further education now seems to many to be an effective way to acquire new knowledge and skills that will enable them to cope better in everyday life.

Bibliography

Recent English-Language Literature on the Educational System of the Federal Republic of Germany[1]

Access to Higher Education: Two Perspectives; A Comparative Study of the Federal Republic of Germany and the United States of America, Final Report. New York: International Council for Educational Development, German–U.S. Study Group, 1978.

Adamski, W. *Continuing Education in Western and Eastern European Societies: Ideology and Reality.* Paris: European Cultural Foundation, Institute of Education, 1978.

Andrews, J. S. (ed.). *Education in Germany: A Union List of Stock in Institute and School of Education Libraries:*3rd edition. Lancaster: University of Lancaster, 1979.

Baumert, J., and Goldschmidt, D. "Centralization and Decentralization as Determinants of Educational Policy in the Federal Republic of Germany (FRG)." 19 *Social Science Information* (1980), No. 6, pp. 1029–1070 (reprinted in 22 *Education* (1980): pp. 65–99).

Becker, W. *Barriers to Higher Education in the Federal Republic of Germany.* (Access to Higher Education, Vol. 2.) New York: International Council for Educational Development, 1977.

Bessoth, R., and Hopes, C. W. *Educational Administration in the Federal Republic of Germany.* Saarbrücken: Institut für Sozialforschung und Sozialwirtschaft, 1977.

Bildung und Wissenschaft: Education and Science in the Federal Republic of Germany. (Monthly in German, English and French.) 1972– .

Bodenman, P. S. *The Educational System of the Federal Republic of Germany.* Washington, D.C.: U.S. Department of Health, Education and Welfare, 1975.

---

1. Further literature, arranged by chapter topics and (with the exception of chapter 1) mainly in German, is given in the next section.

Bundesministerium für Bildung und Wissenschaft. Vocational Training Act (Berufsbildungsgesetz); Apprenticeship Promotion Act (Ausbildungsplatzförderungsgesetz). Bonn: 1979.

Bundesministerium für Forschung und Technologie. "Contributions by Science and Technology in the Federal Republic of Germany to the Solution of Socio-Economic Development Problems." National Paper Submitted by the Federal Republic of Germany for the United Nations Conference on Science and Technology for Development, Vienna, August 1979. Tübingen: 1979.

Carnegie Foundation for the Advancement of Teaching. *The Financial Status of the Professor in America and Germany*. New York: Arno Press, 1977.

Cerych, L., and Neave, G. *Structure, Promotion and Appointment of Academic Staff in Four Countries: Recent Developments*. Paris: European Cultural Foundation, Institute of Education, 1981.

Cobler, S. *Law, Order and Politics in West Germany*. Harmondsworth: Penguin, 1978.

Dahrendorf, R. "The Crisis in German Education," in Laqueur, W., and Mosse, G. L. (eds.). *Education and Social Structure in the Twentieth Century*, pp. 139–147. New York: Harper & Row, 1967.

Deutscher Volkshochschulverband. *The German Volkshochschule: Its Position and Function*. Bonn: 1979.

Dyson, K. H. F. "Anti-Communism in the Federal Republic of Germany: The Case of the 'Berufsverbot'." *Parliamentary Affairs*, 1974/1975, pp. 51–67.

Fomerand, J., Van De Graaff, J. H., and Wasser, H. *Higher Education in Western Europe and North America: A Selected and Annotated Bibliography*. New York: Council for European Studies, 1979.

Foster, C. R. (ed.). *Comparative Public Policy and Citizen Participation: Energy, Education, Health and Urban Issues in the U.S. and Germany*. New York: Pergamon Press, 1980.

Führ, Ch. "Review of Ten Years of Educational Reform in the Federal Republic of Germany, or Was There an Educational Catastrophe?" 6 *Western European Education* (1974/1975), No. 4, pp. 38–51.

Führ, Ch. *Education and Teaching in the Federal Republic of Germany*. Munich and Vienna: Hanser; Bonn-Bad Godesberg: Inter Nationes, 1979.

"Germany, Federal Republic," in Knowles, A. S. (ed.). *International Encyclopedia of Higher Education*, pp. 1840–1849. San Francisco: Jossey-Bass, 1977.

Goldschmidt, D. "Autonomy and Accountability of Higher Education in the Federal Republic of Germany," in Altbach, P. G. (ed.). *The University's Response to Societal Demands*, pp. 151–172. New York: International Council for Educational Development, 1975.

Goldschmidt, D. "Participatory Democracy in Schools and Higher Education: Emerging Problems in the Federal Republic of Germany and Sweden." 5 *Higher Education* (1976), No. 2, pp. 113–133.

Goldschmidt, D. "Power and Decision Making in Higher Education." 22 *Comparative Education Review* (1978), No. 2, pp. 212–241.

Goldschmidt, D., and Lehmann, H. "Bibliography: Publications in English on Education in Germany up to 1945, in the Federal Republic of Germany and in the German Democratic Republic." 19 *Social Science Information* (1980), No. 6, pp. 1071–1094.

Goldschmidt, D., and Schöfthaler, T. "The Establishment of Educational Sociology in the Federal Republic of Germany, 1945–1979." 20 *Education* (1979), pp. 7–25.

Gottstein, K. (ed.). *Brief Descriptions of Nongovernmental Institutions in the Federal Republic of Germany Co-operating with Developing Countries in Science and Technology.* Issued on the Occasion of the United Nations Conference on Science and Technology for Development, Vienna, August 21–30, 1979. Starnberg: Max-Planck-Institut zur Erforschung der Lebensbedingungen der wissenschaftlich-technischen Welt; Tübingen: Institut für wissenschaftliche Zusammenarbeit mit Entwicklungsländern, 1979.

Gottstein, K. (ed.). *Science and Technology for Development: Selected Papers.* Issued on the Occasion of the United Nations Conference on Science and Technology for Development, Vienna 1979. Starnberg: Max-Planck-Institut zur Erforschung der Lebensbedingungen der wissenschaftlich-technischen Welt; Tübingen: Institut für wissenschaftliche Zusammenarbeit mit Entwicklungsländern, 1979.

Habermas, J. *Towards a Rational Society: Student Protest, Science and Politics.* Boston: Beacon Press, 1970.

Haft, H. "In-Service Teacher Training in the Federal Republic of Germany: The General Situation, Contents, Needs of Participants and Relations to Curriculum Development," in Nissen, G., Teschner, W. P., Takala, S., and Haft, H. (eds.). *Curriculum Change through Qualification and Re-qualification of Teachers.* Lisse: Swets & Zeitlinger, 1981.

Hearnden, A. *Education in the Two Germanies.* Boulder, Colo.: Westview Press, 1974.

Hearnden, A. *Education, Culture and Politics in West Germany.* Oxford: Pergamon Press, 1976.

Hennis, W. "The Legislator and the German University." 15 *Minerva* (1977), No. 3/4, pp. 286–315.

Herbst, J. *The German Historical School in American Scholarship: A Study in the Transfer of Culture.* Ithaca, N.Y.: Cornell University Press, 1965.

"Higher Education Framework Law of January 26, 1976." 8 *Western European Education* (1976), No. 3, pp. 60–115.

Hochschuldienst: A Monthly Publication on German Academic Affairs. 1955– .

Hüfner, K., Köhler, H., and Naumann, J. *Higher Education and Manpower Planning in the Federal Republic of Germany.* Geneva and Bucharest: International Labour Office (ILO)/European Centre for Higher Education (CEPES), 1977.

Husén, T. (ed.). *International Study of Achievement in Mathematics: A Comparison of Twelve Countries.* 2 Vols. New York: Wiley, 1967.

Lempert, W. "Perspectives of Vocational Education in West Germany and Other Capitalist Countries," 2 *Economic and Industrial Democracy* (1981), No. 3, pp. 321–348.

Lewy, G. "The Persisting Heritage of the 1960s in West German Higher Education," 18 *Minerva* (1980), No. 1, pp. 1–28.

Littmann, U. *An Introduction to the Confusion of German Education*. Revised edition. Bonn-Bad Godesberg: Deutscher Akademischer Austauschdienst (DAAD), 1977.

Merelmann, R. M., and Foster, C. R. "Political Culture and Education in Advanced Industrial Societies: West Germany and the United States," 74 *International Review of Education* (1978), No. 4, pp. 443–465.

Merritt, A. J., and Merritt, R. L. (eds.). *Politics, Economics, and Society in the Two Germanies, 1945–1975: A Bibliography of English-Language Works*. Urbana, Ill.: University of Illinois Press, 1978.

Merritt, R. L. "The Courts, the Universities and the Right of Admission in the Federal German Republic," 17 *Minerva* (1979), No. 1, pp. 1–32.

Mitter, W. "Education in the Federal Republic of Germany; the Next Decade," 16 *Comparative Education* (1980): pp. 257–265.

Mohr, B. "Teacher Training in the Federal Republic of Germany," *Bildung und Wissenschaft*, 1977, No. 5, pp. 67–94.

Naumann, J., and Köhler, H. "The System of Education in the Federal Republic of Germany," *International Encyclopedia of Education: Research and Studies*. Oxford and New York: Pergamon Press (forthcoming).

Organization for Economic Cooperation & Development (OECD). *Reviews of National Policies for Education: Germany*. Paris: 1972.

OECD. *Reappraisal of Educational Planning; Country Report: Germany*. Paris: 1979.

Peisert, H., and Framhein, G. *Systems of Higher Education: Federal Republic of Germany*. New York: International Council for Educational Development, 1978.

Price, A. H. *The Federal Republic of Germany: A Selected Bibliography of English Language Publications*. 2nd revised edition. Washington, D.C.: Library of Congress, 1978.

Rist, R. C. *Guestworkers in Germany: The Prospect for Pluralism*. Part III: "The Education of the Guestworker Child," pp. 179–244. New York: Praeger, 1978.

Sandberger, J. U., and Lind, G. "The Outcomes of University Education: Some Empirical Findings on Aims and Expectation in the Federal Republic of Germany," 8 *Higher Education* (1979): pp. 179–203.

Schadt, A. L. *The Volkshochschule: A Comparative Study of Adult Education in the Federal Republic of Germany and the German Democratic Republic*. (Doctoral dissertation, Ohio State University, 1969.) Ann Arbor, Mich.: University Microfilms, 1973.

Schramm, J. "Development of Higher Education and Employment in the Federal Republic of Germany," 9 *Higher Education* (1980), No. 5, pp. 605–617.

Shils, E. "The Freedom of Teaching and Research," 11 *Minerva* (1973), pp. 433–441.

Siewert, P., and Köhler, H. "Federal Republic of Germany," in Noah, H. J., and Sherman, J. D. (eds.). *Educational Financing and Policy Goals for Primary Schools* (Country Reports, Vol. 1), pp. 109–168. Paris: Organization for Economic Cooperation and Development (OECD)/Centre for Educational Research and Innovation (CERI), 1979.

319

Spence, J. "Access to Higher Education in the Federal Republic of Germany: The Numerus Clausus Issue," 17 *Comparative Education* (1981), No. 3, pp. 285-292.

Ständige Konferenz der Kultusminister der Länder in der Bundesrepublik Deutschland (KMK). *Report on the Development of Education in the Länder of the Federal Republic of Germany 1973/74 and 1974/75 in Preparation for the 35th Session of the International Conference on Education to be Held in Geneva 1975.* Bonn: 1975.

——. *The Educational System in the Federal Republic of Germany.* New York: The College Board, 1979.

——. *Report on Educational Developments 1976-1978 in Preparation for the 37th Conference on Education 1979, on the Basis of the Guidelines of the International Bureau of Education/Geneva.* Bonn: 1979.

Stegmann, E. "The Educational System: Traditions, Reforms and a Student Surge," *Meet Germany*, pp. 100-123. 17th revised edition. Hamburg: Atlantik-Brücke, 1978.

Teather, D. C. B. (ed.). *Staff Development in Higher Education: An International Review and Bibliography.* New York: Nichols, 1979.

Teichler, U. "Higher Education and Employment in Western Germany: Trends and Changing Research Approaches from the Comparative Point of View," in Wasser, H. (ed.). *Proceedings of the Conference on Economics of Higher Education: A Comparative Perspective of Policy and Dilemma*, pp. 32-66. New York: City University Center for European Studies, 1978.

Teichler, U. "Higher Education and Work in the Federal Republic of Germany: Facts, Perceptions and Debates," in Hornsey, A. (ed.). *Education and Working Life. Report of an Anglo-German Conference Held at the University of London, Institute of Education*, April 20-22, 1978, pp. 59-75. London: 1978.

Van De Graaff, J. H., in cooperation with Clark, B. R., Furth, D., Goldschmidt, D., and Wheeler, D. F. *Academic Power: Patterns of Authority in Seven National Systems of Higher Education.* New York: Praeger, 1978.

Warren, R. L. *Education in Rebhausen, a German Village.* New York: Reinhart & Winston, 1967.

Wilhelmi, H. H. "The School Education System in the Federal Republic of Germany," *Bildung und Wissenschaft*, 1979, No. 12, pp. 155-170.

Williamson, W. "Patterns of Educational Inequality in West Germany," 13 *Comparative Education* (1977): pp. 29-44.

Woodhall, M. *Review of Student Support Schemes in Selected OECD Countries.* Paris: Organization for Economic Cooperation of Development, 1978.

Literature by Chapter Topics

Chapter 1: Transatlantic Influences[1]

Alexander, T., and Parker, B. *The New Education in the German Republic.* New York: John Day Co., 1929.

---

1. The titles listed here refer to basic selected works mainly in English. For further references cf. the notes to chapter 1.

Ben-David, J. *The Scientist's Role in Society: A Comparative Study.* Englewood Cliffs, N.J.: Prentice-Hall, 1971.

Böhme, K. (ed.). *Aufrufe und Reden deutscher Professoren im Ersten Weltkrieg.* Stuttgart: Reclam, 1975.

Boyers, R. (ed.). *The Legacy of the German Refugees Intellectuals.* New York: Schocken Books, 1972.

vom Brocke, B. "Der deutsch-amerikanische Professorenaustausch: Preussische Wissenschaftspolitik, internationale Wissenschaftsbeziehungen und die Anfänge einer deutschen auswärtigen Kulturpolitik vor dem Ersten Weltkrieg," in *Interne Faktoren auswärtiger Kulturpolitik im 19. und 20. Jahrhundert.* (Materialien zum Internationalen Kulturaustausch, Vol. 16.), pp. 128–182. Stuttgart: Institut für Auslandsbeziehungen, 1981.

Bungenstab, K.-E. *Umerziehung zur Demokratie? Re-education-Politik im Bildungswesen der US-Zone 1945–1949.* Düsseldorf: Bertelsmann, 1970.

Deutscher Akademischer Austauschdienst (ed.). *Der Deutsche Akademische Austauschdienst 1925–1975.* Bonn-Bad Godesberg, 1975.

Dewey, J. *German Philosophy and Politics.* First published 1915, enlarged edition: New York: Putnam's Sons, 1942.

Diehl, C. *Americans and German Scholarship 1770–1870.* New Haven and London: Yale University Press, 1978.

Düwell, K. *Deutschlands Auswärtige Kulturpolitik 1918–1932*: Grundlinien und Dokumente. Cologne: Böhlau-Verlag, 1976.

Fleming, D., and Bailyn, B. (eds.). *The Intellectual Migration: Europe and America, 1930–1960.* Cambridge, Mass.: Harvard University Press, 1969.

Flexner, A. *I Remember: The Autobiography of Abraham Flexner.* New York, N.Y.: Simon & Schuster, 1940. 2nd ed. 1960 under the title "An Autobiography."

Fraenkel, E., Galinsky, H., Gerhard, D., Brumm, U., and Lang, H.-J. *Jahrbuch für Amerikastudien.* Heidelberg: Winter, 1967.

Greffrath, M. (ed.). *Die Zerstörung einer Zukunft. Gespräche mit emigrierten Sozialwissenschaftlern.* (das neue buch, Vol. 123.) Reinbek bei Hamburg: Rowohlt, 1979.

Hartshorne, E. Y. *The German Universities and National Socialism.* Cambridge, Mass.: Harvard University Press, 1937.

Heinemann, M. (ed.). *Umerziehung und Wiederaufbau: Die Bildungspolitik der Besatzungsmächte in Deutschland und Österreich.* (Veröffentlichungen der Historischen Kommission der Deutschen Gesellschaft für Erziehungswissenschaft, Vol. 5.) Stuttgart: Klett, 1981.

Heintz, P. (ed.). *Soziologie der Schule.* (Kölner Zeitschrift für Soziologie und Sozialpsychologie, Sonderheft 4.) Cologne and Opladen: Westdeutscher Verlag, 1959.

Hylla, E. *Die Schule der Demokratie: Ein Aufriss des Bildungswesens der Vereinigten Staaten.* Berlin, Langensalza and Leipzig: *Beltz, 1928.*

Kandel, I. L. *Comparative Education. Boston, New York, Chicago, Dallas, Atlanta and San Francisco*: Houghton Mifflin Co., 1933.

Kandel, I. L. *The Making of Nazis.* New York: Teachers College, Columbia University, 1935.

Kerschensteiner, G. *Education for Citizenship.* (translated from German.) Chicago, Ill., London and New York: Rand McNally & Co., 1910.

321

Kerschensteiner, G. *A Comparison of Public Education in Germany and in the United States.* (United States Bureau of Education, Bulletin No. 24.) Washington, D.C.: Government Printing Office, 1913.

Laitenberger, V. *Akademischer Austausch und auswärtige Kulturpolitik 1923–1945: Der Deutsche Akademische Austauschdienst 1923–1945.* Göttingen, Frankfurt and Zürich: Musterschmidt, 1976.

Littmann, U. *German-American Exchanges: A Report on Facts and Developments.* Bonn: Commission for Educational Exchange between the USA and the Federal Republic of Germany (Fulbright Commission), May 1980.

Lundgreen, P. "Educational Expansion and Economic Growth in Nineteenth Century Germany: A Quantitative Study," in Stone, L. (ed.) *Schooling and Society: Studies in the History of Education,* pp. 20–66. Baltimore, Md.: Johns Hopkins University Press, 1976.

McClelland, Ch. E. *State, Society and University in Germany, 1700–1914.* Cambridge, Mass.: Cambridge University Press, 1980.

Metzger, W. P. "The German Contribution to the American Theory of Academic Freedom," 42 *American Association of University Professors Bulletin* No. 1, Spring 1956, pp. 214–230. Reprinted in: Metzger, W. P. (ed.). *The American Concept of Academic Freedom in Formation.* New York: Arno Press, 1977.

Müller-Shafer, S. *Postwar American Influence on the West German Volksschule.* (Comparative Education Dissertation Series, Vol. 3.) Ann Arbor, Mich.: University of Michigan, School of Education, 1964.

Münsterberg, H. *Aus Deutsch-Amerika.* Berlin: Mittler & Son, 1909.

Neumann, F. L., Peyre, H., Panofsky, E., Koehler, W., Tillich, P., and Crawford, W. R. *The Cultural Migration: The European Scholar in America.* University of Pennsylvania Press, 1953, reprint: New York: Arno Press, 1977.

Paulsen, F. *An Autobiography.* New York: Columbia University Press, 1938.

Radkau, J. *Die deutsche Emigration in den USA: Ihr Einfluss auf die amerikanische Europapolitik 1933–1945.* Düsseldorf: Bertelsmann, 1971.

Ringer, F. K. *The Decline of the German Mandarins: The German Academic Community, 1890–1933.* Cambridge, Mass.: Harvard University Press, 1969.

Ringer, F. K. *Education and Society in Modern Europe.* Part 1.2: The German System, pp. 32–112. Bloomington, Ill., and London: Indiana University Press, 1979.

Rossiter, M. W. *The Emergence of Agricultural Science: Justus Liebig and the Americans, 1840–1880.* New Haven, Conn.: Yale University Press, 1975.

Rust, V. D. *German Interest in Foreign Education since World War I.* (Comparative Education Dissertation Series, Vol. 13.) Ann Arbor, Mich.: University of Michigan, School of Education, 1965.

Schröder-Gudehus, B. "Deutsche Wissenschaft und Internationale Zusammenarbeit 1914–1928: Ein Beitrag zum Studium kultureller Beziehungen in politischen Krisenzeiten." (Dissertation, University of Geneva.) Geneva: 1966.

Stern, F. "Einstein's Germany," in Holton, G., and Elkana, Y. (eds.). *Albert Einstein—Historical and Cultural Perspectives: The Centennial Symposium*

BIBLIOGRAPHY

Thwing, Ch. F. *The American and the German University: One Hundred Years of History.* New York: Macmillan Co., 1928.

Veysey, L. R. *The Emergence of the American University.* Chicago: University of Chicago Press, 1965.

Zeitschrift für Kulturaustausch. Interne Faktoren auswärtiger Kulturpolitik im 19. und 20. Jahrhundert (2 parts). Stuttgart: Institut für Auslandsbeziehungen, 1981.

Zymek, B. *Das Ausland als Argument in der pädagogischen Reformdiskussion: Schulpolitische Selbstrechtfertigung, Ausländerpropaganda, internationale Verständigung und Ansätze zu einer Vergleichenden Erziehungswissenschaft in der internationalen Berichterstattung deutscher pädagogischer Zeitschriften, 1871–1952.* (Schriftenreihe zur Geschichte und politischen Bildung, Vol. 19.) Ratingen: Henn, 1975.

Chapter 2: Overall Educational Policies

"Bericht der Bundesregierung über die Lage der Jugend und über die Bestrebungen auf dem Gebiet der Jugendhilfe," in *Verhandlungen des Deutschen Bundestages*, 1967– .

Boli-Bennett, J., and Meyer, J. W. "The Ideology of Childhood and the State: Rules Distinguishing Children in National Constitutions, 1870–1979," 43 *American Sociological Review* (1978): pp. 797–812.

Bundesminister für Bildung und Wissenschaft. *Arbeiterkinder im Bildungssystem.* (Schriftenreihe Bildung und Wissenschaft, Vol. 19.) Bad Honnef: Bock, 1981.

Deutscher Bildungsrat. *Empfehlungen der Bildungskommission.* Stuttgart: Klett, 1967–1975.

Deutscher Bildungsrat. *Gutachten und Studien der Bildungskommission.* Stuttgart: Klett, 1967–1977.

Hüfner, K., and Naumann, J. *Konjunkturen der Bildungspolitik in der Bundesrepublik Deutschland.* Vol. 1: Der Aufschwung (1960–1967). Stuttgart: Klett, 1977; Vol. 2: Höhepunkt und Abschwung (forthcoming).

Inglehart, R. *The Silent Revolution: Changing Values and Political Styles among Western Publics.* Princeton, N.J.: Princeton University Press, 1977.

Jugend '81. Lebensentwürfe, Alltagskulturen, Zukunftsbilder. 3 Vols. Hamburg: Jugendwerk der Deutschen Shell, 1981.

Knoll, J. H. *Bildung und Wissenschaft in der Bundesrepublik Deutschland: Bildungspolitik, Schulen, Hochschulen, Erwachsenenbildung, Bildungsforschung: Ein Handbuch.* Munich: Hanser, 1977.

Köhler, H. "Amtliche Bildungsstatistik im Wandel," in Projektgruppe Bildungsbericht. *Bildung in der Bundesrepublik Deutschland: Daten und Analysen.* Vol. 2: Gegenwärtige Probleme, pp. 1215–1285. Stuttgart: Klett; Reinbek bei Hamburg: Rowohlt, 1980.

Leschinsky, A., and Roeder, P. M. *Schule im historischen Prozess. Zum Wechselverhältnis von institutioneller Erziehung und gesellschaftlicher Entwicklung.* Stuttgart: Klett, 1976.

323

BETWEEN ELITE AND MASS EDUCATION

Lundgreen, P. *Sozialgeschichte der deutschen Schule im Überblick.* Part I: 1770–1918; Part II: 1918–1980. Göttingen: Vandenhoeck & Ruprecht, 1980 and 1981.

Meyer, J. W., Ramirez, F. O., Rubinson, R., and Boli-Bennett, J. "The World Educational Revolution, 1950–1970," in Meyer, J. W., and Hannan, M. T. (eds.). *National Development and the World System: Educational, Economic, and Political Change, 1950–1970,* pp. 37–55. Chicago: University of Chicago Press, 1979.

Naumann, J. "Entwicklungstendenzen des Bildungswesens der Bundesrepublik Deutschland im Rahmen wirtschaftlicher und demographischer Veränderungen" in Projektgruppe Bildungsbericht. *Bildung in der Bundesrepublik Deutschland: Daten und Analysen.* Vol. 1: Entwicklungen seit 1950, pp. 21–102. Stuttgart: Klett; Reinbek bei Hamburg: Rowohlt, 1980.

Parsons, T. "Religion in Postindustrial America: The Problem of Secularization," in his *Action Theory and the Human Condition,* pp. 300–322. New York: Free Press, 1978.

Scheuerl, H. *Die Gliederung des deutschen Schulwesens: Analytische Darstellung und Gesichtspunkte zu seiner weiteren Entwicklung.* 2nd edition. (Gutachten und Studien der Bildungskommission, Vol. 2.) Stuttgart: Klett, 1970.

Trommer-Krug, L., and Krappmann, L. "Soziale Herkunft und Schulbesuch: Eine Zusammenstellung von Daten aus der amtlichen Statistik und aus empirischen Untersuchungen über die soziale Herkunft von Schülern an allgemeinbildenden Schulen," in Projektgruppe Bildungsbericht. *Bildung in der Bundesrepublik Deutschland: Daten und Analysen.* Vol. 1: Entwicklungen seit 1950, pp. 217–281. Stuttgart: Klett; Reinbek bei Hamburg: Rowohlt, 1980.

Zapf, W. (ed.). *Lebensbedingungen in der Bundesrepublik: Sozialer Wandel und Wohlfahrtsentwicklung.* (Sozialpolitisches Entscheidungs- und Indikatorensystem für die BRD (SPES), Project Vol. 10.) Frankfurt: Campus, 1977.

Chapter 3: The State as Trustee of Education

Baumert, J. "Aspekte der Schulorganisation und Schulverwaltung," in Projektgruppe Bildungsbericht. *Bildung in der Bundesrepublik Deutschland: Daten und Analysen.* Vol. 1: Entwicklungen seit 1950, pp. 589–748. Stuttgart: Klett; Reinbek bei Hamburg: Rowohlt, 1980.

Bericht der Bundesregierung über die strukturellen Probleme des föderativen Bildungssystems. Verhandlungen des Deutschen Bundestages, 1978.

Deutscher Juristentag (Kommission Schulrecht). *Schule im Rechtsstaat.* Vol. I: *Entwurf für ein Landesschulgesetz: Bericht der Kommission Schulrecht des Deutschen Juristentages.* Munich: Beck, 1981.

Goldschmidt, D., and Roeder, P. M. (eds.). *Alternative Schulen? Gestalt und Funktion nichtstaatlicher Schulen im Rahmen öffentlicher Bildungssysteme.* Stuttgart: Klett-Cotta, 1979.

Heckel, H., and Seipp, B. *Schulrechtskunde: Ein Informationsbuch für Lehrer, Schüler, Eltern und Schulverwaltung; Ein Studienbuch für die Lehrerbildung; Ein Handbuch für Wissenschaft und Rechtsprechung.* 5th edition. Berlin, Neuwied, and Darmstadt: Luchterhand, 1976.

Herrlitz, H.-G., Hopf, W., and Titze, H. *Deutsche Schulgeschichte von 1800 bis zur Gegenwart: Eine Einführung.* Königstein/Taunus: Athenaeum, 1981.

Hopf, Ch., Nevermann, K., and Richter, I. *Schulaufsicht und Schule: Eine empirische Analyse der administrativen Bedingungen schulischer Erziehung.* Stuttgart: Klett-Cotta, 1980.

Nevermann, K. *Der Schulleiter: Juristische und historische Aspekte zum Verhältnis von Bürokratie und Pädagogik.* Stuttgart: Klett-Cotta, 1982.

Nevermann, K., and Richter, I. (eds.). *Rechte der Lehrer, Rechte der Schüler, Rechte der Eltern.* (Erziehung in Wissenschaft und Praxis, Vol. 26.) Munich: Piper, 1977.

Niehues, N. *Schul- und Prüfungsrecht.* (Schriftenreihe der Neuen Juristischen Wochenschrift, Vol. 27.) Munich: Beck, 1976.

Oppermann, T. *Nach welchen rechtlichen Grundsätzen sind das öffentliche Schulwesen und die Stellung der an ihm Beteiligten zu ordnen?* Gutachten C für den Deutschen Juristentag. (Verhandlungen des Deutschen Juristentages, 51, 1, C.) Munich: Beck, 1976.

Raschert, J. "Bildungspolitik im kooperativen Föderalismus: Die Entwicklung der länderübergreifenden Planung und Koordination des Bildungswesens der Bundesrepublik Deutschland," in Projektgruppe Bildungsbericht. *Bildung in der Bundesrepublik Deutschland: Daten und Analysen.* Vol 1: Entwicklungen seit 1950, pp. 103–215. Stuttgart: Klett; Reinbek bei Hamburg: Rowohlt, 1980.

Richter, I. *Bildungsverfassungsrecht: Studien zum Verfassungswandel im Bildungswesen.* (Texte und Dokumente zur Bildungsforschung, Vol. 25.) Stuttgart: Klett, 1973.

Chapter 4: Modernizing the School System

Baumert, J. "Aspekte der Schulorganisation und Schulverwaltung," in Projektgruppe Bildungsbericht. *Bildung in der Bundesrepublik Deutschland: Daten und Analysen.* Vol. 1: Entwicklungen seit 1950, pp. 589–748. Stuttgart: Klett; Reinbek bei Hamburg: Rowohlt, 1980.

Baumert, J., and Raschert, J., in cooperation with Hopf, D., Naumann, J., and Thomas, H. *Vom Experiment zur Regelschule: Schulplanung, Curriculumentwicklung und Lehrerfortbildung in Zusammenarbeit von Lehrern und Verwaltung bei der Expansion der Berliner Gesamtschule.* (Veröffentlichungen des Max-Planck-Instituts für Bildungsforschung.) Stuttgart: Klett-Cotta, 1978.

Deutscher Bildungsrat. *Strukturplan für das Bildungswesen.* (Empfehlungen der Bildungskommission.) Stuttgart: Klett, 1970.

Deutscher Bildungsrat. Bericht '75: *Entwicklungen im Bildungswesen.* (Empfehlungen der Bildungskommission.) Stuttgart: Klett, 1975.

Flitner, A. *Missratener Fortschritt: Anmerkungen zur Bildungspolitik.* (Serie Piper, Vol. 166.) Munich: Piper, 1977.

Goldschmidt, D., and Roeder, P. M. (eds.). *Alternative Schulen? Gestalt und Funktion nichtstaatlicher Schulen im Rahmen öffentlicher Bildungssysteme.* Stuttgart: Klett-Cotta, 1979.

Leschinsky, A., and Roeder, P. M. "Didaktik und Unterricht in der Sekundarstufe I seit 1950: Entwicklung der Rahmenbedingungen," in Projektgruppe Bildungsbericht. *Bildung in der Bundesrepublik Deutschland:*

BETWEEN ELITE AND MASS EDUCATION

Daten und Analysen. Vol. 1: Entwicklungen seit 1950, pp. 283–391. Stuttgart: Klett; Reinbek bei Hamburg: Rowohlt, 1980.

Roeder, P. M. "Bildungsreform und Bildungsforschung," *Zeitschrift für Pädagogik* (forthcoming).

Rolff, H.-G., Hansen, G., Klemm, K., and Tillman, K.-J. (eds.). *Jahrbuch der Schulentwicklung: Daten, Beispiele und Perspektiven.* Vols. 1 and 2, Weinheim and Basle: Beltz, 1980 and 1981.

27 *Zeitschrift für Pädagogik* (1981), No. 4.

Chapter 5: Preschool and Primary School

Barnitzky, H., and Christiani, R. (eds.). *Handbuch der Grundschulpraxis und Grundschuldidaktik.* Stuttgart: Kohlhammer, 1981.

Baumgartner, A., and Geulen, D. (eds.). *Vorschulische Erziehung.* 2 Vols. (Beltz-Studienbuch, Vols. 82 and 83.) Weinheim: Beltz, 1975.

Bolscho, D., Burk, K., and Haarmann, D. (eds.). *Grundschule ohne Noten: Neue Zeugnisse in der Diskussion.* (Beiträge zur Reform der Grundschule, Vols. 38 and 39.) Frankfurt am Main: Arbeitskreis Grundschule, 1979.

Garlichs, A. "Die Grundschule am Ausgang der Bildungsreform," 71 *Die Deutsche Schule* (1979), pp. 221–228.

Haarmann, D., Horn, H. A., and Warwel, K. (eds.). *Lernen und Lehren in der Grundschule: Studienbuch für den Unterricht der Primarstufe.* Brunswick: Westermann, 1977.

Hild, P. *Probleme der Grundschule.* Munich: List, 1979.

Schwartz, E. *Die Grundschule: Funktion und Reform.* Brunswick: Westermann, 1969.

Zimmer, J. (ed.). *Curriculumentwicklung im Vorschulbereich.* 2 Vols. Munich: Juventa, 1974.

Chapter 6: Children in Need of Special Attention

Deutscher Bildungsrat. *Zur pädagogischen Förderung behinderter und von Behinderung bedrohter Kinder und Jugendlicher.* (Empfehlungen der Bildungskommission.) Stuttgart: Klett, 1973.

Kniel, A. *Die Schule für Lernbehinderte und ihre Alternativen: Eine Analyse empirischer Untersuchungen.* (Schriftenreihe Schulische und soziale Integration Behinderter, Vol. 2.) Rheinstetten: Schindele, 1979.

Mehrländer, U. *Situation der ausländischen Arbeitnehmer und ihrer Familienangehörigen in der Bundesrepublik Deutschland: Repräsentativuntersuchung '80.* Bonn: Friedrich-Ebert-Stiftung, 1981.

Muth, J. (ed.). *Sonderpädagogik.* 7 Vols. (Gutachten und Studien der Bildungskommission, Vols. 25, 30, 34, 35, 37, 52, 53.) Stuttgart: Klett, 1973–1975.

Rist, R. C. *Guestworkers in Germany: The Prospects of Pluralism.* New York: Praeger, 1978.

Schindele, R. (ed.). *Unterricht und Erziehung Behinderter in Regelschulen.* (Schriftenreihe Schulische und soziale Integration Behinderter, Vol. 1.) Rheinstetten: Schindele, 1977.

326

Schrader, A., Nikles, B. W., and Griese, H. M. *Die zweite Generation: Sozialisation und Akkulturation ausländischer Kinder in der Bundesrepublik.* Kronberg/Taunus: Athenaeum, 1976.

Siewert, P. "Zur Entwicklung der Gastarbeiterpolitik und der schulpolitischen Abstimmung der Kultusministerkonferenz," in Projektgruppe Bildungsbericht. *Bildung in der Bundesrepublik Deutschland: Daten und Analysen.* Vol. 2: Gegenwärtige Probleme, pp. 1053–1112. Stuttgart: Klett; Reinbek bei Hamburg: Rowohlt, 1980.

Ständige Konferenz der Kultusminister der Länder in der Bundesrepublik Deutschland (KMK). *Empfehlung zur Ordnung des Sonderschulwesens.* Bonn: 1972.

KMK. *Neufassung der Vereinbarung* "Unterricht für Kinder ausländischer Arbeitnehmer." Bonn: 1976.

Chapter 7: The Hauptschule

Beckmann, H.-K., Jens, G., and Sawallisch, H.-J. (eds.). *Hauptschule in der Diskussion.* Brunswick: Westermann, 1977.

Brinkmann, G. (ed.). *Praxis Hauptschule: Anregungen für die Gestaltung des Unterrichts.* Kronberg/Taunus: Scriptor, 1977.

Dietrich, T., Klink, J.-G., and Scheibe, W. (eds.). *Zur Geschichte der Volksschule.* 2 Vols. (Klinkhardts pädagogische Quellentexte.) Bad Heilbrunn: Klinkhardt, 1974.

Franz, U., and Hoffmann, M. (eds.). *Hauptschule: Erfahrungen, Prozesse, Bilanz.* Kronberg/Taunus: Scriptor, 1975.

"Hauptschule Nebensache," in 34 *Westermanns Pädagogische Beiträge* (1982), No. 2 (Themenheft).

Leschinsky, A., and Roeder, P. M. "Didaktik und Unterricht in der Sekundarstufe I seit 1950: Entwicklung der Rahmenbedingungen," in Projektgruppe Bildungsbericht. *Bildung in der Bundesrepublik Deutschland: Daten und Analysen.* Vol. 1: Entwicklungen seit 1950, pp. 283–391. Stuttgart: Klett; Reinbek bei Hamburg: Rowohlt, 1980.

Lorenz, U. *Handwerk und Hauptschüler: Qualifikationen von Hauptschulabsolventen im Blick des Beschäftigungssystems; Empirische Untersuchung und Überlegungen zur Reform der Hauptschule.* Munich: Ehrenwirth, 1980.

Roeder, P. M. "Alternativen für die Hauptschule?" in Bohnsack, F. (ed.). *Kooperative Schule,* pp. 57–71. Weinheim: Beltz, 1978.

Scholz, G. (ed.). *Hauptschule.* (Beltz Bibliothek, betrifft:erziehung tabu, Vol. 56.) Weinheim: Beltz, 1977.

Wilhelm, T. *Theorie der Schule: Hauptschule und Gymnasium im Zeitalter der Wissenschaften.* 2nd edition. Stuttgart: Metzler, 1969.

Wollenweber, H. (ed.). *Das gegliederte Schulwesen in der Bundesrepublik Deutschland.* Paderborn et al.: Schoeningh, 1980.

Chapter 8: The Realschule

Derbolav, J. (ed.). *Wesen und Werden der Realschule: Beiträge zur Theorie und Geschichte unseres Bildungswesens.* Bonn: Bouvier, 1960.

Derbolav, J. *Probleme des mittleren Bildungswesens: Die Realschullehrerbildung in der BRD, Ein Beitrag zur Diskussion um die Sekundarstufe.* Hanover: Schroedel, 1970.

Hegelheimer, A. *Die Realschule im Bildungs- und Beschäftigungssystem.* Paderborn et al.: Schoeningh, 1980.

Maskus, R. (ed.). *Zur Geschichte der Mittel- und Realschule.* (Klinkhardts pädagogische Quellentexte.) Bad Heilbrunn: Klinkhardt, 1966.

Peege, J., and Böhmer, M. "Individualisierung des Unterrichts durch Wahlpflichtdifferenzierung in der Realschule," 85 *Die Realschule* (1977), No. 5/6, pp. 292–385.

Wollenweber, H. (ed.). *Die Realschule.* Vol. 1: *Begründung und Gestaltung;* Vol. 2: *Unterricht und Bildungsgänge.* Paderborn et al.: Schoeningh, 1979.

Chapter 9: The New Gymnasium

Blankertz, H. "Die Verbindung von Abitur und Berufsausbildung: Konzept und Modellversuche zur Fortsetzung expansiver Bildungspolitik," 23 *Zeitschrift für Pädagogik* (1977): pp. 329–343.

Blättner, F. *Das Gymnasium: Aufgaben der höheren Schule in Geschichte und Gegenwart.* Heidelberg: Quelle & Meyer, 1960.

Flitner, A., and Lenzen, D. (eds.). *Abiturnormen gefährden die Schule.* Munich: Piper, 1977.

Flitner, W. *Hochschulreife und Gymnasium: Vom Sinn wissenschaftlicher Studien und von der Aufgabe der gymnasialen Oberstufe.* 2nd edition. (Anthropologie und Erziehung, Vol. 1). Heidelberg: Quelle & Meyer, 1960.

Furck, C.-L. *Das unzeitgemässe Gymnasium: Studien zur Gymnasialpädagogik.* Weinheim: Beltz, 1965.

Heck, G., Edlich, G., and Ballauff, T. (eds.). *Die Sekundarstufe II: Grundlagen, Modelle, Entwürfe.* (Wege der Forschung, Vol. 456.) Darmstadt: Wissenschaftliche Buchgesellschaft, 1978.

von Hentig, H. *Die Krise des Abiturs und eine Alternative.* Stuttgart: Klett-Cotta, 1980.

Paulsen, F. *Geschichte des gelehrten Unterrichts auf den deutschen Schulen und Universitäten vom Ausgang des Mittelalters bis zur Gegenwart: Mit besonderer Rücksicht auf den klassischen Unterricht.* Leipzig: Veit, 1919–1921.

Romberg, H. *Staat und Höhere Schule: Ein Beitrag zur deutschen Bildungsverfassung vom Anfang des 19. Jahrhunderts bis zum Ersten Weltkrieg.* (Studien und Dokumentationen zur deutschen Bildungsgeschichte, Vol. 11.) Weinheim and Basle: Beltz, 1979.

Wilhelm, T. *Theorie der Schule: Hauptschule und Gymnasium im Zeitalter der Wissenschaften.* 2nd edition. Stuttgart: Metzler, 1969.

16 *Zeitschrift für Pädagogik* (1969), No. 1; Vol. 26 (1980), No. 2; Vol. 28 (1982), No. 1.

Chapter 10: The Comprehensive School

Deutscher Bildungsrat. *Einrichtung von Schulversuchen mit Gesamtschulen.* (Empfehlungen der Bildungskommission.) Stuttgart: Klett, 1969.

Diederich, J., and Wulf, Ch. *Gesamtschulalltag: Die Fallstudie Kierspe; Lehr-, Lern- und Sozialverhalten an nordrhein-westfälischen Gesamtschulen.* Paderborn et al.: Schoeningh, 1979.

Fend, H. *Gesamtschule im Vergleich.* Weinheim: Beltz, 1982.

Haenisch, H., and Lukesch, H. *Ist die Gesamtschule besser? Gesamtschulen und Schulen des gegliederten Schulsystems im Leistungsvergleich.* Munich et al.: Urban & Schwarzenberg, 1980.

Ludwig, H. (ed.). *Gesamtschule in der Diskussion.* (Klinkhardts pädagogische Quellentexte.) Bad Heilbrunn: Klinkhardt, 1981.

Pädagogisches Zentrum Berlin, Informationsstelle Gesamtschule. *Gesamtschulinformationen: Nachrichten, Berichte, Bibliographien, Dokumente.* Berlin: Pädagogisches Zentrum, 1968- .

Raschert, J. *Gesamtschule: Ein gesellschaftliches Experiment; Möglichkeiten einer rationalen Begründung bildungspolitischer Entscheidungen durch Schulversuche.* (Veröffentlichungen des Max-Planck-Instituts für Bildungsforschung.) Stuttgart: Klett, 1974.

Rolff, H.-G. *Brennpunkt Gesamtschule: Perspektiven der Schultheorie und Bildungspolitik.* Munich: Juventa, 1979.

Tillmann, K.-J., in cooperation with Bussigel, M., Philipp, E., and Roesner, E. *Kooperative Gesamtschule: Modell und Realität; Eine Analyse schulischer Innovationsprozesse.* Weinheim: Beltz, 1979.

Wottawa, H. *Gesamtschule: Was sie uns wirklich bringt; Eine methodenkritische Darstellung der Schulvergleiche in Hessen, Nordrhein-Westfalen und Niedersachsen.* Düsseldorf: Pädagogischer Verlag Schwann, 1982.

Chapter 11: Vocational Education

Böhnert, M., Crusius, R., Haug, H.-J., Haug-Gassner, G., Hoppe, D., Kahl, G., Müller, S., Rehlich, K., Vollmer, G., Voss, J., Wichmann, A., and Wilke, M. (eds.). *Lehrlingshandbuch: Alles über Lehre, Berufswahl, Arbeitswelt für Lehrlinge, Schüler, Eltern, Ausbilder, Lehrer.* 2nd edition. Reinbek bei Hamburg: Rowohlt, 1979.

Bundesminister für Bildung und Wissenschaft. *Berufsbildungsbericht.* (Schriftenreihe Berufliche Bildung, Vols. 4, 9, 10, 11, 13 ff.) Bonn: 1977-

Dauenhauer, E. *Berufsbildungspolitik.* Berlin et al.: Springer, 1981.

Deutscher Bildungsrat. *Zur Neuordnung der Sekundarstufe II: Konzept für eine Verbindung von allgemeinem und beruflichem Lernen.* (Empfehlungen der Bildungskommission.) Stuttgart: Klett, 1974.

Franzke, R. *Berufsausbildung und Arbeitsmarkt: Funktionen und Probleme des "dualen Systems".* (Studien und Berichte, Vol. 39.) Berlin: Max-Planck-Institut für Bildungsforschung, 1978.

Hegelheimer, B. *Berufsqualifikation und Berufschancen von Frauen in der Bundesrepublik Deutschland.* (Materialien aus der Bildungsforschung, Vol. 11.) Berlin: Max-Planck-Institut für Bildungsforschung, 1977.

Lempert, W., and Franzke, R. *Die Berufserziehung.* (Grundfragen der Erziehungswissenschaft, Vol. 12.) Munich: Juventa, 1976.

Münch, J. *Das duale System: Lehrlingsausbildung in der Bundesrepublik Deutschland.* (Schriftenreihe des Deutschen Industrie- und Handelstages, Vol. 177.) Bonn: Deutscher Industrie- und Handelstag, 1979.

Sachverständigenkommission Kosten und Finanzierung der Beruflichen Bildung. *Kosten und Finanzierung der ausserschulischen beruflichen Bildung.* Bielefeld: Bertelsmann, 1974.

Winterhager, W. D. "Berufsbildung und Jugendarbeitslosigkeit: Einschätzung der Situation," in Projektgruppe Bildungsbericht. *Bildung in der Bundesrepublik Deutschland: Daten und Analysen.* Vol. 2: Gegenwärtige Probleme, pp. 981–1002. Stuttgart: Klett; Reinbek bei Hamburg: Rowohlt, 1980.

Chapter 12: University Expansion

Bundesministerium für Forschung und Technologie. *Bundesbericht Forschung.* Vol. VI. (Berichte und Dokumentationen, Vol. 4.) Bonn: 1979.

Kath, G. (ed.). *Das soziale Bild der Studentenschaft in der Bundesrepublik Deutschland: Ergebnisse der 9.* Sozialerhebung des Deutschen Studentenwerks. Bonn: Der Bundesminister für Bildung und Wissenschaft, 1980.

Kühlewind, G. "Rückblick auf Arbeitsmarktprojektionen für die siebziger Jahre in der Bundesrepublik Deutschland," 13 *Mitteilungen aus der Arbeitsmarkt- und Berufsforschung* (1980), No. 3, pp. 322–359.

Parsons, T., and Platt, G. *The American University.* Cambridge, Mass.: Harvard University Press, 1973.

Peisert, H., and Framhein, G. *Das Hochschulsystem in der Bundesrepublik Deutschland: Funktionsweise und Leistungsfähigkeit.* 2nd edition. Stuttgart: Klett-Cotta, 1980.

Schelsky, H. *Abschied von der Hochschulpolitik: Oder die Universität im Fadenkreuz des Versagens.* Bielefeld: Bertelsmann, 1969.

Schelsky, H. *Einsamkeit und Freiheit: Idee und Gestalt der deutschen Universität und ihrer Reformen.* 2nd edition, with "Nachtrag 1970". (Wissenschaftstheorie, Wissenschaftspolitik, Wissenschaftsplanung, Vol. 20.) Düsseldorf: Bertelsmann, 1971.

Schlicht, U. *Vom Burschenschafter bis zum Sponti: Studentische Opposition gestern und heute.* Berlin: Colloquium, 1980.

Tessaring, M. "Evaluation von Bildungs- und Qualifikationsprognosen, insbesondere für hochqualifizierte Arbeitskräfte," 13 *Mitteilungen aus der Arbeitsmarkt- und Berufsforschung* (1980), No. 3, pp. 374–397.

Wissenschaftsrat. *Empfehlungen und Stellungnahmen des Wissenschaftsrates.* Bonn: 1972– .

Chapter 13: Further Education

Dahm, G., Gerhard, R., Graessner, G., Kommer, A., and Preuss, V. (eds.). *Wörterbuch der Weiterbildung.* Munich: Kösel, 1980.

Faulstich, P. *Erwachsenenbildung und Hochschule: Bestandsaufnahme, Modelle, Perspektiven.* Munich et al.: Urban and Schwarzenberg, 1982.

Görs, D. (ed.). *Gewerkschaftliche Bildungsarbeit: Kontroversen und Konzepte.* Munich et al.: Urban and Schwarzenberg, 1982.

Hofbauer, H. "Wirksamkeit der beruflichen Erwachsenenbildung." 12 *Mitteilungen aus der Arbeitsmarkt- und Berufsforschung* (1979), No. 1, pp. 42–50.

Keim, H., and Urbach, D. *Volksbildung in Deutschland, 1933–1945.* Brunswick: Westermann, 1976.

Picht, W. *Das Schicksal der Volksbildung in Deutschland.* Brunswick, Berlin, and Hamburg: Westermann, 1950.

Pöggeler, F. *Handbuch der Erwachsenenbildung.* Vol. 1 ff. Stuttgart: Kohlhammer, 1964 ff.

Schulenberg, W., Loeber, H.-D., Loeber-Pautsch, U., and Pühler, S., in cooperation with Driesen, H., and Scharf, W. *Soziale Faktoren der Bildungsbereitschaft Erwachsener: Eine empirische Untersuchung.* Stuttgart: Klett-Cotta, 1978.

Strzelewicz, W., Raapke, H., and Schulenberg, W. *Bildung und gesellschaftliches Bewusstsein.* (Göttinger Abhandlungen zur Soziologie, Vol. 10.) Stuttgart: Enke, 1966.

Tietgens, H. *Erwachsenenbildung.* (Grundfragen der Erziehungswissenschaft, Vol. 14.) Munich: Juventa, 1981.

Ulich, M. E. *Patterns of Adult Education: A Comparative Study.* New York: Pageant Press, 1965.

Weymann, A. *Handbuch für die Soziologie der Weiterbildung.* Darmstadt and Neuwied: Luchterhand, 1980.

Wittwer, W. *Weiterbildung im Betrieb: Darstellung und Analyse.* Munich et al.: Urban and Schwarzenberg, 1982.

About the Authors

The Max Planck Institute for Human Development and Education (MPI) was founded in 1963. It is one of the approximately 50 institutes under the aegis of the Max Planck Society for the Advancement of Science, an independent research-sponsoring agency financed by the West German federal and Länder governments. At present, the Institute has some 45 professional and about 100 technical staff members. The main areas of research are: development and socialization; education, work and social change; psychology and human development; and school systems and instruction.

Jürgen Baumert (b. 1941), Dr. phil. in classical languages and philosophy; also studied psychology and education; Habilitation in education at the Free University, Berlin. Research associate at MPI. Research and publications on: sociology of education; school administration; in-service teacher training; curriculum development.

Reinhard Franzke (b. 1945), Dr. rer. pol. in sociology. Teaches at the Institute für Berufspädagogik of the University of Hannover. From 1971 to 1976 research associate at MPI. Research and publications on: vocational and business education; the politics of vocational training; the relationship between the educational system and the structure of employment.

Dietrich Goldschmidt (b. 1914), Dr. rer. pol. in sociology; adjunct professor of sociology at the Free University, Berlin, member of the board of directors of MPI since 1963; 1973/1974 visiting professor at the Institute for Social and Policy Studies and the Department of Sociology at Yale University. Research and publications on: sociology of higher education; educational and cultural policies of developing countries.

Adriane Heinrichs-Goodwin (b. 1938), graduated in Political Science and English at the Free University, Berlin, after studying at San José State College, and Stanford University. Teaches at Werner von Siemens Gymnasium, Berlin.

Diether Hopf (b. 1933), Dr. phil. in education; also studied classical languages and psychology; Habilitation in education at the Free University, Berlin. Since 1971 research associate at MPI. Research and publications on: grouping; teaching and learning; educational measurement.

332

ABOUT THE AUTHORS

Achim Leschinsky (b. 1944), Dr. phil. in education; Habilitation in education at the Free University, Berlin. Since 1973 research associate at MPI. Research and publications on: the history of German schools; sociology of the educational system; the evolution of the Hauptschule.

Helmut Köhler (b. 1940), Dr. phil. in economics. Since 1971 research associate at MPI. Research and publications on: statistical-quantitative analyses of the development of the demand for and the supply of teachers; changes in age-specific attendance of secondary schools and tertiary level institutions; foreigners in the Federal Republic of Germany.

Beate Krais (b. 1944), Dr. rer. pol. in sociology. Research associate at MPI. Research and publications on: vocational training; the labor market; development of occupational qualifications; the educational system and social structure; education and economics.

Lothar Krappmann (b. 1936), Dr. phil. in sociology. Senior research associate at MPI. Teaches at the Free University, Berlin. Research and publications on: socialization processes in the family and school; theories of social and personal identity.

Raymond Meyer (b. 1943), Ph. D. in German studies. Among other things, free-lance translator.

Jens Naumann (b. 1943), M.A. in economics (Stanford University); Dr. rer. pol. in economics. Since 1966 research associate at MPI. Current research centers on: educational policies and planning in Germany and developing African countries; the development and role of international organizations.

Knut Nevermann (b. 1944), Dr. jur. From 1970 to 1973 technical assistant to the German Education Council. Research associate at MPI since 1974. Research and publications on: educational law; educational administration.

Gottfried Pfeffer (b. 1934), Dr. phil. in French literature. Research associate and editor at MPI. Publications on educational policy.

Peter Siewert (b. 1941), Dr. phil. in economics. Research associate at MPI. Currently on leave of absence to direct project for the government of West Berlin on the reformed secondary school system. Participated in projects of CERI/OECD on educational financing and education for special populations. Publications on: educational planning, financing, and administration; and minorities.

Jürgen Raschert (b. 1937), Dr. rer. pol. in sociology. Professor of educational politics and educational planning at the Free University, Berlin. Until 1976 research associate at MPI. Research and publications on: educational politics; educational planning; the development of the comprehensive school in the Federal Republic of Germany.

Ingo Richter (b. 1938), Dr. jur.; Docteur de l'Université. Research associate at MPI from 1967 to 1975. Currently professor of public law at the University of Hamburg. Research and publications on: German governmental and administrative law; educational law; educational administration.

Luitgard Trommer (b. 1941), Diplom in business administration. Employed as statistical specialist by Statistisches Landesamt of Berlin. Research associate at MPI since 1976. Research centers on: statistical analyses and evaluation of statistics.

Anglo-German List of Selected Terminology

Basic Law (BL)	Grundgesetz (GG)
Centers for Adult Popular Education	Volkshochschulen
Comprehensive school	Gesamtschule
Conference of West German University Rectors	Westdeutsche Rektorenkonferenz (WRK)
Employment Promotion Act	Arbeitsförderungsgesetz (1969)
Federal Education and Training Promotion Act	Bundesausbildungsförderungsgesetz (BAFÖG)
Federal Employment Agency	Bundesanstalt für Arbeit (BfA)
Federal Framework Law for Higher Education	Hochschulrahmengesetz (1976)
Federal Institute for Vocational Training	Bundesinstitut für Berufsbildung (BIBB)
Federal Minister for Education and Science	Bundesminister für Bildung und Wissenschaft
General Education Plan	Bildungsgesamtplan
German Academic Exchange Service	Deutscher Akademischer Austauschdienst (DAAD)

Current German abbreviations are added. For German terms which have not been translated in this book, e.g. Abitur, Gymnasium, see Subject Index.

German Committee for Education	Deutscher Ausschuss für das Erziehungs- und Bildungswesen
German Education Council	Deutscher Bildungsrat
German Research Society	Deutsche Forschungsgemeinschaft (DFG)
Joint Commission of the Federal and Länder Governments for Educational Planning and Advancement of Research	Bund-Länder-Kommission für Bildungsplanung und Forschungsförderung (BLK)
Max Planck Society for the Advancement of Science	Max-Planck-Gesellschaft zur Förderung der Wissenschaften (MPG)
Nursery school	Kindergarten
Orientation level	Orientierungsstufe
Part-time vocational school	Berufsschule
Permanent Conference of the Länder Ministers of Culture	Ständige Konferenz der Kultusminister der Länder in der Bundesrepublik Deutschland, *or* Kultusministerkonferenz (KMK)
Polytechnic colleges	Fachhochschulen
Primary school	Grundschule
Science Council	Wissenschaftsrat
Specialized technical school	Fachschule
Specialized technical secondary school	Fachoberschule
Special school	Sonderschule
Structural Plan for the Educational System	Strukturplan für das Bildungswesen (1970)
Teacher Training College	Pädagogische Hochschule
Vocational extension school	Berufsaufbauschule
Vocational Training Act	Berufsbildungsgesetz (1969)
Year of basic vocational training	Berufsgrundbildungsjahr (BGJ)

Name Index

336

Subject Index

Ability grouping, 169, 218–19, 223, 229
Abitur, 101, 108, 207–08; age, 264; certificate, 108, 198, 208, 305; examination, 207; graduates, 212–13; requirements, 205–07; via 2nd educational path, 201–03; standards, 207, 210, 265; and university admission, 101, 198, 203, 210–13
Academic: disciplines, 141, 197–203, 208–213; freedom, 99–101, 264–65; of university teachers, 99, 106, 266–68, 270–73; of students, 99–100, 104, 264; vs. vocationally oriented programs, 191–93, 212–13, 216, 236–39. *See also* Autonomy of the university
Access: to higher education, 108, 164, 184, 189, 198, 203, 210–13, 215–16, 237; to jobs and careers, 111, 177–78, 187–89, 236–39, 244–47; to public service, 187–188
Adult education. *See* Further education
Advanced and basic courses, 140–41, 169–70, 204–10
Age-group class: and differentiated courses, 128–29, 169–73, 204–10, 218–19, 222–25, 229–31; vs. undifferentiated schools, 125, 170–73; and pupils' social relationships, 209–10, 229–32
Akademie der Arbeit (Academy of Labor), Frankfort, 43
All-day-school, 133, 210, 219, 225–26, 230

Allied occupying powers, 46–47, 71–73, 107, 196–97
American: attitudes towards Germany, 3, 4–5, 13, 16–18, 31–32, 37, 46–49; influences on German educational system, 9–11, 13–15, 28–31, 46–47, 56n.42, 71–73, 130, 196–97, 210; interest in German education and science, 2, 4–5, 11, 25–26, 31, 34, 38–39; teachers of German origin, 13, 45
Anti-semitism, 17, 23, 39–41
Apprentice, 242–43, 247–49, 253
Apprenticeship, 236–48, 253–55, 258–59. *See also* Dual system
Apprenticeship Promotion Act, 255
Art, 190–93, 197, 199, 202, 205–06, 222, 301–02
Aufbaugymnasium, 201

Basic education, standard, 189, 194, 218, 221
Basic Law of the Federal Republic of Germany, 87–90, 93–94, 99, 101, 103–04, 106, 266, 270, 276
Basic Rights, 87, 103
Behavioral problems, 145, 150–54, 173, 180–81, 227
Bekenntnisschulen, 85–86, 125–26, 170–72
"Berufsverbot", 275
Bureau of Social Research, Princeton, 43
Büro für Sozialpolitik (Academy for Social Policy), Berlin, 43

340

Carnegie Institute, 14
Catholicism, 19, 27, 74, 85. *See also*
Churches, Roman Catholic
Centers for Adult Popular Education:
course structure, 308; enrollments in,
300, 302, 313; expenditures of, 306;
history of, 296–99; programmes,
300–02, 305; teaching staff at, 308
Central Institute for Education, 27,
28–29, 30, 38
Centralism in education, 67, 83, 86, 88,
221, 231. *See also* Länder and
centralization of education
Certificates, 111; academic, 101, 111,
272–73; Hauptschule, 109, 126–27,
172, 174, 178, 232, 251, 305;
intermediate, 108, 183, 187–88, 197,
212; occupational, 237, 243–47,
251–52; Realschule, 109, 126–27, 166,
183–84, 188–89, 194, 212, 232, 251,
305. *See also* Abitur; Degrees,
academic
Chambers of Industry and Commerce,
241–43, 257, 293
Choice of course. *See* Elective courses
Christian Democratic Union, 66, 75,
122–23, 289, 303
Churches, 76, 294, 305, 315; Lutheran
Protestant, 76, 84–86, 300, 302, 305;
Roman Catholic, 76, 84–86, 300, 302,
305. *See also* Bekenntnisschulen
Citizens' Rights, 87–88. *See also* Basic
Law
Civil servants. *See* State officials
Codetermination rights: of parents,
87–88, 105; of pupils or students,
87–88, 105; of teachers, 86–88,
97–98, 106, 221, 231; of workers,
243, 307
Commission of Experts on the Costs
and Financing of Vocational
Training, 254
Communities. *See* Local communities
Comparative research in education. *See*
International comparison
Comprehensive school, 217–35;
attendance at, 226–27, 232–33; British
and Swedish, 218, 222; certificates,
218, 225, 232; cooperative form of,
123, 194–95, 219–20, 223, 232–35;
curricula, 221, 231; enrollment, 113,
117, 124, 220, 228; experimental
program, 114, 123–24, 218–22,
227–28, 232–34; and Gymnasium,
226, 227, 231; and Hauptschule or
Realschule, 194–195, 227, 229,

232–35; intended goals, 218, 227–28;
integrated form of, 123–24, 219–35;
internal problems, 228–32; and
Länder policies, 124, 218–22, 227–28,
234–35; as a political issue, 70, 73,
114, 123–24, 217–20, 227–28, 234–35;
precursor role of, 228–32; pupils,
229–31, 232–33; and tripartite school
system, 123–24, 194–95, 217–22,
227–28, 229, 234–35. *See also*
Einheitsschule
Compulsory education, 68, 84, 138;
full-time, 108, 114–15, 126–27,
165–66, 174; part-time, 108, 236,
240–41
Conference of West German University
Rectors, 272
Constitutional law, 86–88
Constitution, German, 19, 27, 59n.57,
86–87. *See also* Basic Law of the
Federal Republic of Germany
Contents. *See* Curricula; Subjects
Course: guidelines, 94–96, 109, 128,
130–31, 140–41, 220–21, 231, 249;
schedules, 94–96, 168, 197, 201, 202,
211–12, 220–21, 249; structure,
differentiated. *See* Advanced and
basic courses; Grouping of pupils
Court decisions, 103–105, 268
Crafts, 239–40, 242–43, 246, 248,
258–59
Crisis, economic, 66, 78–79, 256–61,
279–80
Curricula, 96, 109, 111, 127–28; in
secondary level I, 129–32; reform of,
96, 114, 129–32, 221, 231; as a
political issue, 130–31

Decision-making, political and
administrative: in the federal system,
88–93, 103–05; in the Länder,
93–100; at the school level, 96–98,
106, 121, 131; in university and
research policy, 98–101, 266–68,
270–74, 275–76
Degrees: academic, 100–01, 265,
272–73; doctoral, 100
Democratization, 87–88, 103–05, 197,
218, 274–75
Demographic trends, 115–19; and
comprehensive school, 225, 235; and
Hauptschule, 116, 175; and higher
education, 277–81; and the primary
level, 134–38; and secondary level I,
115–19, 195

341

SUBJECT INDEX

secondary level II, 183–84, 189, 193, 201–03, 224–25
Tutzing Abitur Catalogue, 210

Undergraduate education, 208, 264
Unemployment, 178, 256–60, 279–80
United States and Germany: educational systems, 11, 28–31, 33–35, 44, 55–56n.42, 71–73, 67, 264; exchanges, general cultural, 2–3, 7–9, 13, 16, 21–22, 36; immigrants in the United States, 6, 11, 13, 39–46, 61–65n.66–75; mutual influence in science and higher education, 5, 8–11, 12–13 23–26, 40–46; philosophy of education, influence on, 5, 7, 12–15, 34–35, 45–46; relations, political and general, 3, 10, 16, 21–23, 36, 37, 46–49; university exchanges, 4–18, 14, 21–25, 36, 47–48
Universities
  American: California, 7, 52, 62, 64; Chicago, 5, 43, 44, 52, 61, 65; Clark, 5, 12; Columbia, 7, 23, 43, 44, 50, 56, 60–61; International Institute of Teachers College, 29, 30, 31, 59; Teachers College, 32, 38; Cornell, 7, 9, 56, 64; Harvard, 4, 5, 7, 24–25, 37, 60, 64, 65; Iowa, 64; Johns Hopkins, 5; Michigan, 7; Minnesota, 64; Wisconsin, 53; Yale, 4, 9
  German: Aachen (Technical), 9; Berlin, 4, 7, 8, 25, 52, 269; (Free) 269; (Technical) 9, 52; Bonn, 30; Cologne, 30; Frankfort, 7, 43; Göttingen, 4, 25; Hamburg, 8, 30, 38, 65; Heidelberg, 25; Leipzig, 25; Munich, 25, 30, 65
University: autonomy, 99–101, 265, 266–68; 270–73; constitution of, 266, 274; decision-making for, 99–101, 266–68, 270–74, 275–76; degrees, 100, 272–73; enrollments, 277–83; entrance, 101, 105, 265; examinations, 100–01; finance, 265, 266, 276; legislation on, 90, 104–06, 266, 268, 270–71, 274; policy, 268–75; political conflict at, 273–75; as professional school, 262–63; reform of, 274–75, 284–85; and research, 99–101, 263, 265–67, 272; staff,

99–100, 268, 270–73; standards, 100–01, 265; and the state, 98–101, 266–68; traditional German, 4–7, 263–73; and United States' higher education system, 4–11, 21–26, 48, 67, 264–65
Unskilled workers, 236, 262, 309, 311
Upper level reform of Gymnasium, 128–29, 203–10, 216

Vertical vs. horizontal structure of school system. See Educational system, tripartite secondary
Vocational education and training: and access to higher education, 237, 252; and employment, 244–47, 256–60; further, 301, 304, 306, 313–15; and general education, 115, 213, 237–40; initial, 236–62; legislation on, 90, 241, 243, 255; occupational character of, 245–47; reform of, 254–56; schools, 236–37, 248–52; regulations of, 102–03, 241, 243, 244–46; responsibility for, 102–03, 241–44; theory of, 14–15, 237–41
Vocational extension schools, 251–52
Vocational orientation, 173–75, 186–87, 191–93, 222, 224
Vocational Training Promotion Act, 255
Volksschule, 26, 55n.41, 108, 124–26, 166–73, 189, 239. See also Hauptschule; Primary school

Weimar, Republic of, 18–20, 27, 85–86, 138, 298
Women in further and higher education, 281–82, 312. See also Disadvantaged groups by gender
Women's liberation movement, 75
Working class: children, 112, 177–78, 188, 213–15, 232–33, 239; and further education, 294–96, 309–11; and university education, 281–84
World economic crisis. See Crisis, economic
World educational revolution, 70
World Wars: I, 11, 15–19, 297; II, 46, 71, 268, 299

Year of basic vocational training, 147, 149–51, 258

348